Assessment of Young Children with Special Needs

Susan Benner

THOMSON

DELMAR LEARNING

Australia Canada Mexico Singapore Spain United Kingdom United States

THOMSON

DELMAR LEARNING

Assessment of Young Children with Special Needs
A Context-Based Approach
Susan M. Benner, Ed. D.

Strategic Business Unit Director:
Susan L. Simpfenderfer

Executive Production Manager:
Wendy A. Troeger

Executive Marketing Manager:
Donna J. Lewis

Acquisitions Editor:
Erin O'Connor Traylor

Production Editor:
J.P. Henkel

Channel Manager:
Nigar Hale

Editorial Assistant:
Ivy Ip

Technology Project Manager:
Joe Saba

Cover Design:
TDB

Library of Congress Cataloging-in-Publication Data
Benner, Susan M.
  Assessment of young children with special needs : a context-based approach / Susan M. Benner.
    p. cm.
  Includes bibliographical references and index.
    ISBN 1-40182-527-3
    1. Developmentally disabled children.
  2. Medical care–Needs assessment.
  3. Children with disabilities–Education.
  4. Developmental disabilities. I. Title
RJ135 .B466 2003
    618.92'0075–dc21   2002035045

Contents

Acknowledgements

I am grateful to the families and children in the East Tennessee area that have shared their experiences with me regarding the assessment of their young children. Some of these experiences have come straight from the families. Others have come indirectly through the field-based experiences of my students at The University of Tennessee. The parental perspective offers much for educators to consider as we go about the task of providing the best possible services and assessments for young children.

Many people contributed over the past six years to the development of *Assessment of Young Children With Special Needs: A Context-Based Approach*. I wish to thank the initial editor for the project, Vicki Knight, who was with Brookes/Cole at the original signing of the project. She encouraged me through the development of a prospectus and reviews of my prior work on this same topic. After a number of years that involved a promotion for Vicki, mergers for Brookes/Cole and other imprints, and reorganizations within the International Thompson Publishing, the project eventually became a Delmar publication. I am grateful to editor Erin O'Connor and her assistant Ivy Ip, J.P. Henkel, and all the other Delmar staff who have done a great job picking up the project and seeing it to completion. I also wish to thank Bridget Lulay, project editor with Carlisle Publishers Services and Sharon O'Donnell who provided copyediting.

I am grateful to the thoughtful reviewers who provided constructive feedback and suggestions on earlier versions of the text:

Alice Beyrent
Hesser College
Manchester, NH

Marie Brand
State University of New York at New Paltz
New Paltz, NY

Sylvia Brooks, Ed.D.
University of Delaware
Newark, DE

Mark Brown, Ph.D.
Eastern Illinois University
Charleston, IL

Paddy Favazza, Ed.D.
University of Memphis
Memphis, TN

Dedication

This book is dedicated to my husband, David, who always supports and encourages my writing.

CHAPTER 1

Assessment in Context: Principles for Practice

Key Terms and Concepts

Individuals with Disabilities Education Act (IDEA)
Part C
Developmental delay
Risk
- Established risk
- Biological risk
- Environmental risk

Ecological psychology
- Micro-system
- Meso-system
- Exo-system
- Macro-system

Family systems theory
Constructivism
Developmentally appropriate practices
Zone of proximal development

Chapter Objectives

After reading this chapter, you should be able to:

1. Identify critical legislation defining the rights of all children to a public education.
2. Define *developmental delay* and other diagnostic categories.
3. Discuss the meaning and impact of risk factors in the lives of young children.
4. Describe ecological perspectives, family systems theories, and constructivist principles.
5. Explain the rationale for a contextual perspective toward assessment of young children.

Chapter Overview

Typically, infants, toddlers, and preschool children with developmental delays, specific disabilities, and those considered at risk to experience developmental difficulties participate in various individual assessments prior to and during early intervention. These assessments are generally designed to determine the extent of delays, current levels of development, and suitable instructional content and strategies. In order for such assessments to be interpreted correctly they need to incorporate the past, present, and anticipated future "context" of the child. If we proceed with assessments without considering a child's family and community circumstances, our results may well be incomplete, incorrect, or unfair to the child. Isolating a child from his context for purposes of assessment removes from the discussion critical influences to the child's development, such as the language environment in which the child has been living and developing, physical and emotional expectations placed on the child, and the cultural meaning of disability to his family and community.

Ultimately, the information gained from assessments that incorporate contextual information about a child can be integrated to form a more complete picture of a child, guiding parents and professionals in their design of the best possible interventions. The context-based perspective of assessment fundamentally requires the consideration of a child's total environment, including his family and community life in every aspect of the assessment process.

This chapter begins with a brief review of the current federal legislation that influences and guides the practices used in the assessment of young children with disabilities, and an overview of disability terms and definitions used in early childhood special education. The next section of the chapter covers the theoretical basis for context-based assessment, including brief reviews of ecological psychology, family systems theory, and constructivism. The final portion of the chapter provides the rationale for adopting a context-based perspective in the assessment of infants and young children.

Federal Legislation

Federal legislation has played a critical role in the provision of services to children of all ages who have disabilities. Since 1975 the federal law, now known as the **Individuals with Disabilities Education Act (IDEA),** has mandated that states receiving any federal funds to support their educational programs exclude no children from educational opportunities based on the presence of a disability. Over the last quarter of a century, this law legislating special education and related services has been amended numerous times. These amendments have resulted in an increase in the number of eligible children included in the law through extensions of the mandated age range both downward and upward, and the addition of new disability categories. The federal law sets the guiding standards with which all states must comply. All states must provide children with disabilities the needed special education and related services, beginning with their third birthday. Related

services include transportation, physical therapy, occupational therapy, adapted physical education, and psychological assessments necessary for the child to gain the benefits of an education. Although all must comply with federal law, states do vary in the particulars of how they determine eligibility for services, the nature of service delivery systems, and some categorical definitions. Figure 1–1 lists the basic elements found in IDEA.

Part C of IDEA provides legislation supporting and regulating early intervention services to infants and toddlers with disabilities and their families. It specifies the requirements of programs that receive funds to provide service coordination and direct services for children and families prior to the child's third birthday. In Part C the emphasis is on a system that provides family-directed assessment and intervention, recognizing the critical role of the family and parents in these children's lives. Although it is not mandatory that states participate in Part C of IDEA, every state has chosen to do so. Figure 1–2 describes the components of Part C programs.

FIGURE 1–1 The Basic Elements of IDEA

1. Free appropriate education in the least restrictive environment for all children from their third birthday to their twenty-second birthday, regardless of the severity of their disability;
2. Provision of related services as needed to enable a child to profit from an education;
3. Development of an Individualized Education Program (IEP), including
   a. The child's present levels of educational performance,
   b. How the disability affects the child's involvement in the general curriculum or participation in age-appropriate activities for preschoolers,
   c. Measurable annual goals of the child's educational program with benchmarks or short-term objectives and a plan for evaluating the progress made toward them,
   d. Involvement of the child in the regular education program,
   e. Special education and related services and supplemental aids, and
   f. The extent to which the child will participate in any state educational testing;
4. Educational decision making by an IEP team, including regular and special education teachers, administrators, other appropriate professionals (e.g., psychologists, physical therapists, or speech and language therapists) and parents; and
5. Due process for parents or schools when agreements regarding educational placements and related services cannot be reached through the IEP team process.

FIGURE 1–2 Part C Requirements

1. Development and implementation of a statewide, comprehensive, coordinated, multidisciplinary, interagency program of service coordination and early intervention services for infants and toddlers with disabilities and their families;
2. Coordination of the payment for early intervention services from Federal, State, local, and private sources (including public and private insurance coverage);
3. Enhancement of the capacity to provide quality early intervention services and expansion and improvement of existing early intervention services being provided to infants and toddlers with disabilities and their families;
4. Establishment of a definition of developmental delay and eligibility criteria for Part C services;
5. Facilitation of interagency collaboration;
6. Development of Individualized Family Service Plan (IFSP) procedures, service coordination systems, multidisciplinary assessment standards and systems;
7. Establishment of timely reimbursement policies;
8. Provision of assurances of qualified personnel as providers of early intervention; and
9. Establishment of public awareness of the program, and sponsorship of child find activities.

Early intervention as defined by Part C includes a wide array of services that are provided under public supervision and designed to meet the developmental needs of an infant or toddler. These developmental needs can appear in one or more of the following areas: physical development; cognitive development; communication development; social or emotional development; or adaptive development. The specific types of services appropriate under Part C are listed in Figure 1–3.

Professional collaboration with the family in early intervention became a prominent feature of federal legislation in the amendments of 1986. That emphasis is based on the evidence that far more developmental progress can be seen when professionals work collaboratively with families. Family collaboration had to

FIGURE 1–3 Types of Services Provided through Part C

Through Part C, eligible children and their families can receive the following:

- family training
- counseling, and home visits
- special instruction
- speech-language pathology and audiology services
- occupational therapy
- physical therapy
- psychological services
- service coordination services

- medical services only for diagnostic or evaluation purposes
- early identification, screening, and assessment services
- health services necessary to enable the child to benefit from the other early intervention services
- social work services
- vision services
- assistive technology devices and assistive technology services
- transportation and related costs

be mandated in the legislation because many early intervention programs had adopted traditional child-centered diagnostic/prescriptive approaches extended downward from service models for older children.

Many assessment instruments in use today with infants and young children with special needs have origins in some of the earliest federally funded early intervention programs, known as First Chance Projects and Handicapped Children's Early Education Programs, which emerged throughout the latter part of the 1970s. The federal legislation authorizing expenditure of funds for early intervention required that programs document their efficacy through the demonstrated progress of the participating children. Since no existing developmental checklists offered sufficient breakdown of developmental milestones, these programs typically developed their own curriculum-based assessments. These instruments were usually linked directly to objectives and activities for children.

During the past thirty years over three hundred assessment instruments for young children with special needs have been described in the literature. Many such instruments were never put on the market for commercial distribution or updated after their initial version. Others have been updated, expanded, and revised as "best practices" have evolved. These now emphasize the importance of family collaboration in the assessment as well as the use of developmentally appropriate and play-based interventions. One such instrument that grew out of an initial federal early intervention project that has been revised and updated over the years is the *Hawaii Early Learning Profile, or HELP* (VORT Corporation, 1995, 1997).

Defining the Population

Categories of disabilities associated with school-age special education programs (K–12) are specifically delineated. Early intervention and preschool programs can employ the broad concepts of **developmental risk** and **developmental delay.** In some instances developmental delay can continue to be used through the primary grades. Young children who are "at-risk" for becoming disabled or who do have a disability present are a diverse group. Infants, toddlers, and preschool-age children with genetic disorders present at birth, with delays in speech and language development, with visual and hearing loss, with emotional and behavioral problems, with medical and physical problems resulting from a premature birth all belong within the umbrella of developmental delay.

For some, the nature of their conditions can be quickly identified and diagnosed, whereas others may go for years without a clear diagnosis or explanation as to the underlying reason for developmental delays. The diagnosis of Down syndrome is based upon specific cell distributions evident in a child's genetic makeup. In contrast, when a child is diagnosed as having autism, no clear link can be made to the cause because current medical understanding of this condition remains speculative and somewhat theoretical.

A specific diagnosis does often provide family members a path to take in seeking services for their child. However, establishing a specific diagnosis for some infants and toddlers is not always appropriate or even possible. In such cases, the emphasis can shift from diagnostic assessment to functional assessment.

TABLE 1–1 Federal Definitions of Noncategorical Terms

Term	Meaning
Infant or toddler with a disability	(A) an individual under 3 years of age who needs early intervention services because the individual— (i) is experiencing developmental delays, as measured by appropriate diagnostic instruments and procedures in one or more of the areas of cognitive development, physical development, communication development, social or emotional development, and adaptive development; or (ii) has a diagnosed physical or mental condition which has a high probability of resulting in developmental delay; and (B) may also include, at a State's discretion, at-risk infants and toddlers
At-risk infant or toddler	an individual under 3 years of age who would be at risk of experiencing substantial developmental delay if early intervention services were not provided to the individual.
Child with a disability	a child— (i) with mental retardation, hearing impairments (including deafness), speech or language impairments, visual impairments (including blindness), serious emotional disturbance (hereinafter referred to as 'emotional disturbance'), orthopedic impairments, autism, traumatic brain injury, other health impairments, or specific learning disabilities; and (ii) who, by reason thereof, needs special education and related services. The term 'child with a disability' for a child aged 3 through 9 may, at the discretion of the State and the local educational agency, include a child— (i) experiencing developmental delays, as defined by the State and as measured by appropriate diagnostic instruments and procedures, in one or more of the following areas: physical development, cognitive development, communication development, social or emotional development, or adaptive development; and (ii) who, by reason thereof, needs special education and related services

Source: IDEA (Authority: 20 U.S.C. 1432(5) Sec. 303.16 and 20 U.S.C. 1401 (3)(A) and (B); 1401(26) Sec. 300.7).

The use of the noncategorical term *developmental delay* allows these children to receive services even though they have no clinical diagnosis. The definitions used to determine eligibility for federally supported programs through Part C of IDEA permit the use of both specific diagnoses and developmental delay. The noncategorical federal definitions used in early intervention for infants and toddlers and special education for children from three to nine years of age are presented in Table 1–1.

Using the federal definitions as guides, each state has developed its own definitions and eligibility criteria for early intervention and preschool special education services. There are drawbacks to the use of eligibility criteria for access to services. The presence of eligibility criteria for program participation can work against efforts to establish programs intended to be preventive in nature (Simeonsson, 1994). Many biological and environmental risk factors present in the lives of infants, toddlers, and preschool children can result in developmental delays. As children mature, the nature of these observable delays may become more apparent, resulting in a specific diagnosis or a better understanding of the long-term capabilities of the child. Under Part C it is permissible to provide services to infants and toddlers who are considered to be at-risk. However, budgetary restraints typically make states avoid the inclusion of the at-risk population. The following sections elaborate further on the meanings of and uses for the concepts of developmental risk, developmental delay, and categorical disabilities.

Developmental Risk

Developmental risk relates to the risk factors, vulnerability, resilience, and protective factors present in the lives of infants, toddlers, and young children. Professionals from different fields assign various meanings to the terms *developmental risk, high-risk,* and *at-risk.* Kopp (1987) uses the term *developmental risk* to indicate that the "well-being of children is in jeopardy" (p. 881). Risk incorporates several subcategories of infants and children whose chances of experiencing normal development are in danger. Medical personnel tend to use the term *high-risk* for neonates whose ability to survive is in question (Rossetti, 1986). Other professionals who become involved with the infants once their survival is established are concerned with risks that might result in developmental delays. Educators use the term *at-risk* in reference to the child's future school achievement being jeopardized. High-risk neonates who survive may retain their at-risk status for several years, until they demonstrate an ability to achieve in school through the elementary years.

Risk Factors

A multitude of circumstances can contribute to the risk an infant faces as she begins her life. In the United States, every thirty seconds a child is born into poverty and every fifty-nine seconds a baby is born to a teen mother (Children's Defense Fund, 1994). Although neither of these two conditions guarantees that a child will experience developmental delays, each seems to place the child in jeopardy. Since these conditions often occur together, the risk factors interact with one another, multiplying their potential effects. Poverty may reduce a family's access to health care and proper nutrition. In turn, poor health care and inadequate nutrition increase the risk of a child having developmental delays and medically related impairments. The ability of a teen to meet the demands of motherhood in a manner that fosters healthy psychological development, when she is still struggling with the challenge of maturing into adulthood herself, can place her child at-risk as well. The confounding nature of the at-risk category becomes further apparent when we consider the relationships between biological risk factors, such as prematurity, and environmental risk factors, such as poverty or maternal use of drugs during pregnancy.

Risk factors can appear before, during, or after a child's birth. Prenatal risk factors include radiation, genetic disorders, malnutrition, maternal infection,

metabolic disorders, and exposure to harmful drugs. At the time of birth, labor and delivery complications, neonatal medications, prematurity, cardiopulmonary problems, congenital malformations, metabolic disorders, and infections can pose dangers. Postnatal risks include acute illness, chronic disease, accidents and poisoning, malnutrition, poverty, the onset of genetic disorders during early childhood, family dysfunction, and sociocultural disadvantages (Ramey, Trohanis, & Hostler, 1982).

Tjossem (1976) defined three categories of risk factors—**established risk, biological risk,** and **environmental risk** that can provide guidance for us in understanding the nature of risk. The definitions of these categories and examples of each are shown in Table 1–2.

An overlapping relationship exists between these three risk categories. For example, children who are facing environmental risk will be more likely to experience biological risk as well. Mothers might be unable to obtain adequate prenatal care for themselves, unaware of the nutritional needs of infants and small children, and/or unable to meet the emotional needs of their young children. The interrelatedness of these at-risk categories will be evident for most children who experience any one of them. Sameroff and Chandler (1975) emphasize this transactional relationship between biological and environmental factors and the extent to which an infant is at-risk. In their model of development, the child's physical characteristics and his experiences with the environment and the quality of his care become inseparable as the child matures.

The interplay among multiple factors that may contribute to an infant's risk makes the identification of who is at-risk a complicated matter. Evidence of a child's individual resilience and the protective factors within his world (e.g., genetic predisposition, nurturance by an extended family member) further complicate the identification of children who are at-risk (Werner, 1990). Simeonsson (1994) proposes that we take an epidemiological approach to the problem, seeking "to identify the distribution of a defined condition in the populations and identify risk factors" (p. 16). The approach incorporates the frequency with which we see specific conditions and the intensity of the nature of the condition, as illustrated in Figure 1–4.

The opportunity to target children who are at-risk, but who might be able to avoid the damaging effects of that risk, is one of the greatest challenges to our current intervention models. When does a home environment constitute such a grave danger to the

TABLE 1–2 Categories of Risk Factors

Category	Definition	Example
Established risk	Children who have genetic conditions or other medically diagnosed disorders known to cause developmental disabilities.	Children with a birth defect such as myelomeningocele (neural tube defect resulting in an open spine) inevitably face disabilities related to movement and control of lower parts of the body. The child might also experience cognitive disabilities, depending on the extent of the neurological damage associated with complications of the condition. These children also appear to be at-risk to experience social difficulties.
Biological risk	Children with biological histories or conditions that are associated with a high probability for developmental delays.	Birth trauma, prematurity, infections such as encephalitis, maternal difficulties, or complications during pregnancy all put a child at biological risk. The ability of medical personnel to save very low birth weight infants and infants born prematurely has increased substantially over the past few years (Als, 1997). These babies are at far greater risk to experience developmental delays and/or medical complications than a full-term baby born within normal weight expectations.
Environmental risk	When caregivers are unable to provide an adequate environment to meet a child's multitude of needs, ranging from proper nutrition, warmth, and clothing to emotional and psychological security, the child is placed at-risk for developing disabilities. Children living in inadequate environments may experience mental, emotional, and/or physical disabilities.	Such environments can be characterized as neglectful, harmful, or both. Children who are raised in such environments may have parents who experienced poor care-taking by their parents, have limited education, are teenagers, have no support systems available, suffer from emotional problems or developmental disabilities, and/or have inadequate economic resources (Ensher & Clark, 1986).

Source: Adapted from Tjossem, T. D. (1976). Early intervention: Issues and approaches. In T. D. Tjossem (Ed.), *Intervention Strategies for High Risk Infants and Young Children.* Baltimore: University Park Press.

child that he should be removed from it? How much risk or deprivation can a particular child tolerate? At what point is the medical status of a premature infant so tenuous that the value of survival is questioned? These questions raise some of the most challenging dilemmas and ethical considerations for professionals working with this population.

Developmental Delay

The education community has no universally agreed upon definition of *developmental delay*. Typically, it is used in reference to young children who are below expectations in one or more areas of development. Determining to what extent a child is developmentally delayed is not simple. Special educators hear

FIGURE 1–4 Representative Childhood Conditions and Problems as a Function of Intensity and Frequency

		Frequency	
		Higher	Lower
Intensity	**Higher**		Visual Impairment Autism Hearing Impairment Genetic Disorders Chronic Illness Mental Retardation
	Lower	Learning Problems Conduct Disorders Childhood Obesity School Failure Teenage Pregnancy Drug Abuse	

Source: Adapted from "Toward an Epidemiology of Developmental, Educational, and Social Problems in Childhood," by R. J. Simeonsson, in *Risk Resilience and Prevention: Promoting the Well-Being of All Children,* pp. 13–31, by R. J. Simeonsson, (Ed.), 1994, Baltimore: Paul H. Brookes.

tales from frustrated parents who were reassured incorrectly for years by their pediatricians that the child would outgrow his problems. After years of frustration, these parents and their doctors eventually had to face the reality of the child's delay. At the other extreme are parents who reported that the negative predictions made by professionals about their child's performance proved to be gross underestimates of their child's ability. The goal, then, is to be able to identify and distinguish between a child experiencing a delay requiring early intervention and a child experiencing normal fluctuations and ranges of child development.

Generally, definitions of developmental delay associated with eligibility for federally funded programs at the infant through preschool level stipulate a specific percentage of delay across one or more major developmental domains. These domains include cognition, language and communication, gross and fine motor development, and social-emotional development. Typical minimum eligibility criteria applied to infants through preschool children target a 40 percent or greater delay in one developmental domain or a 25 percent or greater delay in two or more developmental domains. The particular percentages used vary from state to state, but the general approach to defining de-

velopmental delay is consistent. Alterations in these eligibility cutoffs as well as the variance seen in assessment instruments directly influence the number of eligible children.

Disability Categories

In some instances the diagnosis of a specific condition is critical to planning appropriate intervention. For example, Terrance, a four-year-old child who is not speaking due to a hearing loss needs specific medical and therapeutic interventions different from Maria, who is delayed in speaking due to the immigration of her family to a new country. Diagnostic categories can be used in conjunction with developmental delay as needed to get the best possible services for the child. The most widely used list of categories of disabilities for educational purposes is in IDEA. The IDEA regulations stipulate that children with a variety of specific conditions are disabled, and may be eligible for special education. Table 1–3 lists the diagnostic categories and their definitions.

Although it is not included on the federal list of disabilities, the diagnosis of Attention Deficit/Hyperactivity Disorder (ADHD) is common among

TABLE 1–3 Federal Definitions of Categorical Disabilities

Autism	A developmental disability significantly affecting verbal and nonverbal communication and social interaction, generally evident before age 3, that adversely affects educational performance. Other characteristics often associated with autism are engagement in repetitive activities and stereotyped movements, resistance to environmental change or changes in daily routines, and unusual responses to sensory experiences. The term does not apply if a child's educational performance is adversely affected primarily because the child has a serious emotional disturbance.
Hearing impairment (including deafness)	Deafness: Hearing impairment that is so severe that the child is impaired in processing linguistic information through hearing, with or without amplification, that adversely affects a child's educational performance. Hearing Impairment: An impairment in hearing, whether permanent or fluctuating, that adversely affects a child's educational performance but which is not included under the definition of deafness.
Mental retardation	Significantly subaverage general intellectual functioning existing concurrently with deficits in adaptive behavior and manifested during the developmental period that adversely affects a child's educational performance.
Orthopedic impairments	Severe orthopedic impairment which adversely affects a child's educational performance. The term includes impairments caused by congenital anomaly, impairments caused by disease, and impairments from other causes.
Other health impairments	Limited strength, vitality or alertness, due to chronic or acute health problems, which adversely affects a child's educational performance.
Serious emotional disturbance (referred to as emotional disturbance)	The term means a condition exhibiting one or more of the following characteristics over a long period of time and to a marked degree, which adversely affects educational performance: • An inability to learn which cannot be explained by intellectual, sensory, or health factors; • An inability to build or maintain satisfactory interpersonal relationships with peers and teachers; • Inappropriate types of behavior or feelings under normal circumstances; • A general pervasive mood of unhappiness or depression; or • A tendency to develop physical symptoms or fears associated with personal or school problems.
Specific learning disability	A disorder in one or more of the basic psychological processes involved in understanding or in using language, spoken or written, which disorder may manifest itself in imperfect ability to listen, think, speak, read, write, spell, or do mathematical calculations. The term includes such conditions as perceptual disabilities, brain injury, minimal brain dysfunction, dyslexia, and developmental aphasia. It does not include a learning problem that is primarily the result of visual, hearing, or motor disabilities, of mental retardation, of emotional disturbance, or of environmental, cultural, or economic disadvantage.
Speech or language impairments	A communication disorder, such as stuttering, impaired articulation, a language impairment, or a voice impairment, which adversely affects a child's educational performance.
Traumatic brain injury	An acquired injury to the brain caused by an external force, resulting in total or partial functional disability or psychosocial impairment, or both, that adversely affects a child's educational performance. The term applies to closed head injuries resulting in impairments in 1 or more areas, such as cognition; language; memory; attention; reasoning; abstract thinking; behavior; physical functions; information processing; and speech. The term does not apply to brain injuries that are congenital or degenerative, or brain injuries induced by birth trauma.
Visual impairments (including blindness)	A visual impairment, which even with correction, adversely affects a child's educational performance.

Source: IDEA (Authority: 20 U.S.C. 1401 (3)(A) and (B); 1401 (26) Sec. 300.7).

Finding A Better Way

Sometimes, the presence of a disability can influence a child's performance in all domains, particularly when standardized testing procedures are used. Vicki, a three-year-old with visual impairments, has delays in her gross and fine motor development. These motor delays mean that her ability to demonstrate normal cognitive development through required motor responses is compromised. Although she performs poorly on the required tasks, she may be above average in her cognitive potential. Developmental delay offers a "category" that emphasizes current functioning of a child, rather than diagnosis. The use of developmental delay as her eligibility category puts the emphasis on her current functioning, and allows us to avoid premature or inaccurate predictions of future functioning. Vicki can receive early intervention to address her developmental delays and reduce the risk of further delays without the necessity of an inaccurate label.

school-age children. Many children with this diagnosis receive special education services because they exhibit the diagnostic characteristics associated with learning disabilities or severe emotional disturbance. Others are eligible for some disability-related accommodations through Section 504 of the Vocational and Rehabilitation Act. The *Diagnostic and Statistical Manual of Mental Disorders,* fourth edition or DSM–IV (American Psychiatric Association, 1994), published by the American Psychiatric Association (APA) in 1994, stipulates that in order to be diagnosed as having ADHD a child must have symptoms that are (1) severe (more frequent and severe than typically developing children); (2) early onset (beginning prior to the age of seven); and (3) enduring (persisting for at least six months prior to the diagnosis). Symptoms of the disorder as outlined in the DSM–IV are presented in Figure 1–5. Children who receive this medical diagnosis may meet eligibility standards for special education by concurrently meeting the diagnostic criteria for one of the categories included in IDEA or through the Other Health Impairments category. This diagnosis is not frequently applied to preschool and younger children,

but is mentioned here because of the frequency with which it is applied to children starting in the primary grades.

Theoretical Basis for a Contextual Perspective

The theoretical understanding of and basis for assessment of young children with special needs influence the approaches we take. Our beliefs about the effects of family and environment on child development should guide the assessment techniques we select as well as how we approach the task of analyzing and interpreting assessment results. The wide array of assessment tools available for use with young children can be overwhelming. The quality and depth of these assessment tools varies widely, as do the principles upon which they are based. Commercial assessment instruments frequently fail to live up to the claims made regarding their theoretical foundations. Our goals should be to adhere to assessment practices that benefit the children with whom we work and avoid those designed to market well or to offer oversimplified administrative solutions to the complex needs of children.

Ecological psychology, family systems theory, and **constructivism** form the theoretical foundation for context-based assessments. Each of these fundamental perspectives can provide us with practical guidance for assessment practices as illustrated in Figure 1–6.

Ecological Psychology

Ecological psychology is the study of the interdependent relationships between the goal-directed actions of individuals and the behavior settings in which these actions occur. A young child will relax and enjoy playing when a trusted caretaker sits nearby on a park bench. That same child might become agitated, clinging to the adult, while waiting in the doctor's office. The toys, distance between adult and child, others present—all might be very similar, while the behaviors seen are quite different.

Ecological psychologists seek to understand the sequences of interactions that link the perceptions, decisions, and actions of people with events that occur in settings. Figure 1–7 presents three basic assumptions held by both biological and human ecologists.

FIGURE 1–5 Attention Deficit/Hyperactivity Disorder

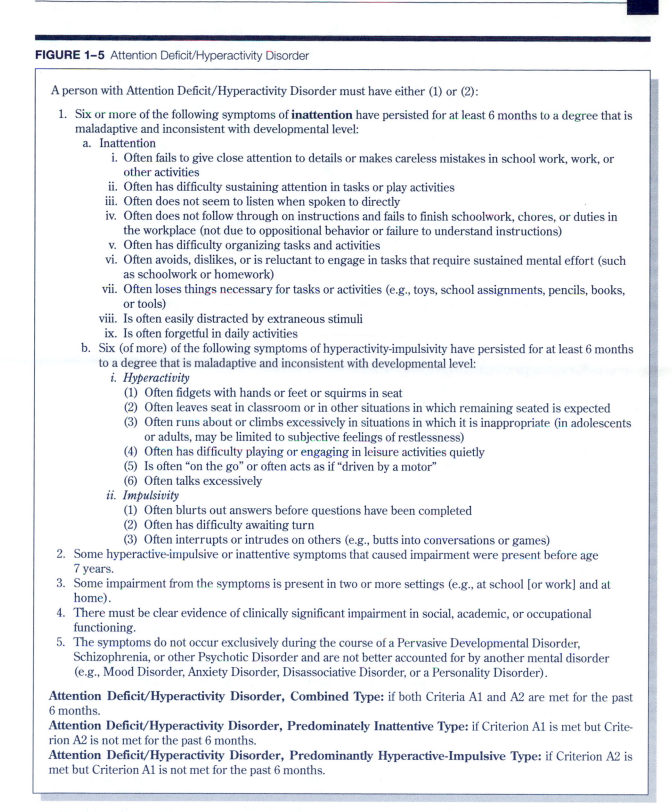

A person with Attention Deficit/Hyperactivity Disorder must have either (1) or (2):

1. Six or more of the following symptoms of **inattention** have persisted for at least 6 months to a degree that is maladaptive and inconsistent with developmental level:
   a. Inattention
      i. Often fails to give close attention to details or makes careless mistakes in school work, work, or other activities
      ii. Often has difficulty sustaining attention in tasks or play activities
      iii. Often does not seem to listen when spoken to directly
      iv. Often does not follow through on instructions and fails to finish schoolwork, chores, or duties in the workplace (not due to oppositional behavior or failure to understand instructions)
      v. Often has difficulty organizing tasks and activities
      vi. Often avoids, dislikes, or is reluctant to engage in tasks that require sustained mental effort (such as schoolwork or homework)
      vii. Often loses things necessary for tasks or activities (e.g., toys, school assignments, pencils, books, or tools)
      viii. Is often easily distracted by extraneous stimuli
      ix. Is often forgetful in daily activities
   b. Six (of more) of the following symptoms of hyperactivity-impulsivity have persisted for at least 6 months to a degree that is maladaptive and inconsistent with developmental level:
      i. *Hyperactivity*
         (1) Often fidgets with hands or feet or squirms in seat
         (2) Often leaves seat in classroom or in other situations in which remaining seated is expected
         (3) Often runs about or climbs excessively in situations in which it is inappropriate (in adolescents or adults, may be limited to subjective feelings of restlessness)
         (4) Often has difficulty playing or engaging in leisure activities quietly
         (5) Is often "on the go" or often acts as if "driven by a motor"
         (6) Often talks excessively
      ii. *Impulsivity*
         (1) Often blurts out answers before questions have been completed
         (2) Often has difficulty awaiting turn
         (3) Often interrupts or intrudes on others (e.g., butts into conversations or games)
2. Some hyperactive-impulsive or inattentive symptoms that caused impairment were present before age 7 years.
3. Some impairment from the symptoms is present in two or more settings (e.g., at school [or work] and at home).
4. There must be clear evidence of clinically significant impairment in social, academic, or occupational functioning.
5. The symptoms do not occur exclusively during the course of a Pervasive Developmental Disorder, Schizophrenia, or other Psychotic Disorder and are not better accounted for by another mental disorder (e.g., Mood Disorder, Anxiety Disorder, Disassociative Disorder, or a Personality Disorder).

Attention Deficit/Hyperactivity Disorder, Combined Type: if both Criteria A1 and A2 are met for the past 6 months.
Attention Deficit/Hyperactivity Disorder, Predominately Inattentive Type: if Criterion A1 is met but Criterion A2 is not met for the past 6 months.
Attention Deficit/Hyperactivity Disorder, Predominantly Hyperactive-Impulsive Type: if Criterion A2 is met but Criterion A1 is not met for the past 6 months.

Source: From *Diagnostic and Statistical Manual of Mental Disorders* (4th ed., pp. 83–85), by the American Psychiatric Association, 1994, Washington, DC: Author.

FIGURE 1–6 Theoretical Foundations for Context-Based Assessment

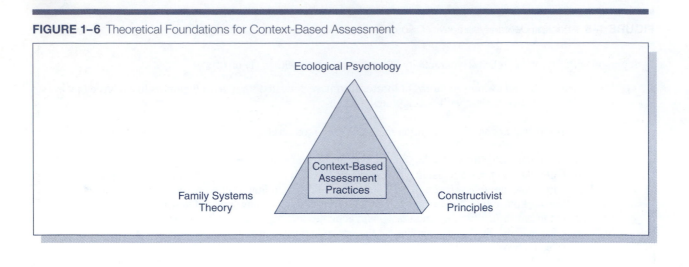

Ecological Psychology

Context-Based Assessment Practices

Family Systems Theory

Constructivist Principles

FIGURE 1–7 Basic Assumptions of Biological and Human Ecologists

1. Organisms (plants and animals, including humans) cannot be considered to exist or act in isolation. Every organism, whether it's a lodgepole pine or a human being, is linked with other organisms in a complex network of relationships.
2. All organisms are affected by forces inside themselves, such as hunger pangs or genetic programs that incline their roots downward, as well as by external forces, such as the prevailing winds or behaviors of other members of the species.

3. Living organisms adapt—that is, they act in such a way as to achieve a harmonious working relationship with their environment. They act selectively toward their environment, distinguishing between features that are appropriate for their needs and those that are not. Green plants grow in the direction of sunlight, which they need for photosynthesis. Large carnivorous animals, like lions, stalk only larger mammals; to hunt and eat mice would require more energy and would not satisfy their appetite.

Source: Adapted from Wicker, A. W. (1979). *An Introduction to Ecological Psychology.* Montery, CA: Brooks-Cole.

Behavior settings are active, organized, self-regulating systems, not simply backdrops where we live our lives. Behavior settings can restrict or promote certain actions, encourage or discourage behaviors, and prohibit or demand human behavior. Cantrell and Cantrell (1985), using the ideas of Moos, have concluded that (1) substantial proportions of the variance in individual behaviors can be accounted for by characteristics of settings and interactions between persons and settings; (2) the accuracy of our prediction of behavior is greatly limited if we fail to include environmental and setting variables; (3) community settings in which persons must function after treatment critically affect their behavior and outcome; and (4) tremendous differences in personality development may be made by the selection of environments.

Bronfenbrenner (1976, 1986) proposed that an ecological perspective be used in educational experimentation, as contrasted with contrived, or laboratory, experimentation. For educators, this recommendation meant a shift from laboratory-based research to classroom-based research on topics such as behavior management and effective methods of instruction. Bronfenbrenner (1979) argued that an understanding of development requires using an ecological structure reflecting the natural environment, including micro-systems, meso-systems, exo-systems, and macro-systems. These nested, yet expanding levels of systems equally influence the behaviors of children and

FIGURE 1–8 Concentric Circles Representing Bronfenbrenner's Ecological Psychology

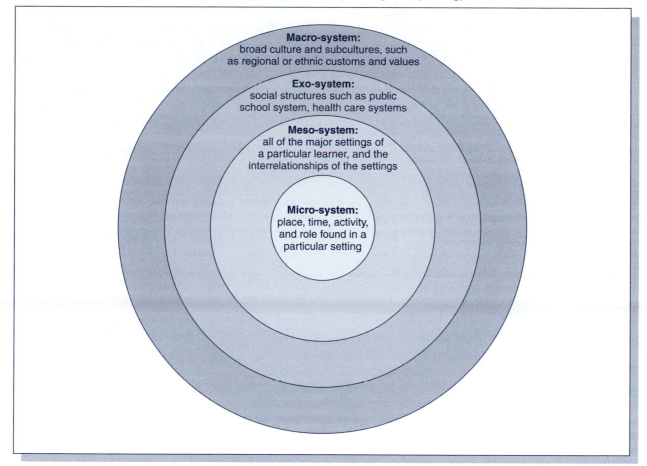

the meaning we attribute to our observations of children. A series of concentric circles illustrate these levels, with the child within the center circle. This representation is shown in Figure 1–8.

The child whose home and child care settings offer safety, security, appropriate stimulation, proper nutrition, nurturance, structure, organization, and so forth will grow and develop within that context. Who that child would have become in a micro-system, characterized by chaos, inconsistent nutrition, violence, and no positive models for language development, is unknown. However, most likely she would have become someone different.

Assessments that isolate the child from such influential variables are simply insufficient. Test scores might give us information about how a child is able to perform on a particular set of tasks at a given moment, but should only be interpreted within the historical and current context of the child before we put meaning to them. Such a perspective is in contrast to the traditional practice associated with standardized testing to value the testing results without consideration given to these contextual factors.

Know The Facts

When the Oregon lumber industry developed unemployment rates in the double digits, a 46 percent increase in child maltreatment was reported (Birch, as cited in Garbarino, 1990). The context and events around us do influence our behaviors, even in the most private of settings—our own homes.

The importance of systems to the developing child is directly related to what materials his family considers necessities and how his parents choose to use their monetary resources as well as their time and energy. Garbarino uses disposable diapers to illustrate this point. Even families well below the poverty line consider disposable diapers a necessity—and they might be if no laundry facilities are readily accessible. Globally, we can see the impact of government structures, economic resources, and job opportunities on the degree of health care provided to and custodial management of abandoned children.

American children grow up accustomed to accessing telephone service whenever and wherever they want it, whereas telephones have only recently been introduced in some remote areas of Africa, where a single telephone is available for an entire village. Were we to measure cognitive competence through a child's familiarity with and knowledge of telephone parts, one group would likely be brilliant whereas the other would appear quite delayed. Wireless services add a whole new dimension to this example, as familiarity with sophisticated devices is common for some children but completely foreign to others.

Bronfenbrenner (1976, 1999) has advanced a bioecological model of development that incorporates both the environment and the processes that occur within the environment. The model has two primary propositions that show the interconnected nature of human development: environments and processes, shown in Table 1–4. Just as Bronfenbrenner urges that educational researchers increase the validity of their findings by using real-life or natural settings instead of laboratory or contrived experimentation, assessments built upon context-based principles offer more meaningful findings than can isolated clinical assessments.

Family Systems Theory

Family systems theory grew from general systems theory developed by Ludwig von Bertalanffy (1968). As a biologist, he explored the interacting systems within the natural sciences. Professionals from the social sciences, including psychology and sociology, then adapted these principles to the interactions occurring within families. Family systems theories derive from a variety of different models, including that of Satir (1983, 1988), Bowen (1985), and Minuchin (1974).

The Process Model, developed by Satir, is based on a positive belief in human potential and the individual's ability to transform his own life. She proposed that there are two views of the world. One is characterized as a threat and reward model, dominated by a hierarchical nature. In this view, people are seen as inherently bad and weak by nature, and a controlling hierarchy is necessary to determine and maintain standards of behavior. Those in control believe that they are acting for the good of all and use one's degree of conformity as a standard benchmark. Lambie and Daniels-Mohring (1993) note, "For those at the lower end of the hierarchy, the consequences of these ways of defining people and their relationships include stagnation, fear, despair, hopelessness, and rebellion. Those at the top may appear happier with their jobs" (p. 254). For persons holding such a view, change is generally not welcome because it is a threat to the status quo. Dictatorial parents who rely heavily on guilt and blame in managing their family characterize families operating under this view. They operate under a closed system with the rigid application of rules regardless of their appropriateness. Satir described such a family as "dominated by power, obedience, deprivation, conformity, and guilt. It cannot allow any changes, for changes will upset the balance" (Satir & Baldwin, 1983, p. 192).

Satir prefers the alternate worldview, which she describes as the organic or seed model. In this case, people are seen as having an innate potential for goodness and wholeness. Uniqueness and individuality are cause for celebration and support rather than concern. From such a perspective, relationships are based on the mutual appreciation of the uniqueness of oneself and others, and are democratic in nature. Change is considered a positive by-product of relationships and a growth orientation is the outcome. The seed model is systemic, with recognized relationships among all components. Events are seen as the result of complex, interrelated variables in contrast to a linear cause-and-effect interpretation. Families operating under such views are open to change with changing contexts, and accept all expression and feelings, including hope, love, anger, frustration, sadness, joy, and compassion.

Satir recognized the systems perspective of homeostasis, referring to the innate tendency people have to establish a dynamic balance amidst changing conditions and relationships. She notes that we establish predictable patterns of communication within families

TABLE 1–4 Bronfenbrenner's Bioecological Propositions

Proposition	Description
Proposition 1	Especially in its early phases, and to a great extent throughout the life course, human development takes place through processes of progressively more complex reciprocal interaction between an active, evolving biopsychological human organism and the persons, objects, and symbols in its immediate external environment. To be effective, the interaction must occur on a fairly regular basis over extended periods of *time*. Such enduring forms of interaction in the immediate environment are referred to as *proximal processes*. Examples of enduring patterns of proximal process are found in parent-child and child-child activities, group or solitary play, reading, learning new skills, studying, athletic activities, and performing complex tasks.
Proposition 2	The form, power, content, and direction of the proximal processes affecting development vary systematically as a joint function of the characteristics of the *developing person,* the *environment*—both immediate and more remote—in which the processes are taking place, the nature of the *developmental outcomes* under consideration, and the social continuities and changes occurring over time during the historical period through which the person has lived.

Source: From "Environments in Developmental Perspective: Theoretical and Operational Models," by U. Bronfenbrenner, in *Measuring Environment Across the Life Span: Emerging Methods and Concepts* (pp. 3–28), by S. L. Friedman and T. D. Wachs (Eds.), 1999, Washington, DC: American Psychological Association.

and that family members operate to maintain the survival of the family and achieve balance within the family system. Another concept included in the model is the development of self-identity and personhood through mother-father-child triads. Through these triangular relationships children develop a sense of their self-worth or lack thereof. Low self-worth leads people to be anxious and unsure of themselves, hypersensitive to how others see them, and likely to oppose change, preferring the safety of conformity.

Bowen (1985) places an emphasis on biological processes that account for desires for individuality and togetherness. The person controlled primarily by biological processes is likely to be emotionally reactive, whereas the person who maintains greater neutrality and tolerates individual choice is relying on cognitive and feeling resources. These individual differences in functioning emerge through learning. All human relationships are characterized by our seeking equilibrium between the drives for autonomy and connection. Similarly, we seek to balance the functions of intellect and emotion.

Bowen espouses the notion of a solid-self and a pseudo-self. The solid-self is able to maintain a healthy balance between the forces of togetherness-separateness, embodying "an individual's beliefs, principles, attitudes, and opinions that are nonnegotiable under any circumstances" (Lambie & Daniels-Mohring, 1993, p. 264). The pseudo-self appears when there is an unhealthy fusion between one's emotional and intellectual systems, typically resulting from anxiety and stress. It is a "pretend" self that takes on the beliefs and principles of another, often aimed at increasing the person's sense of belonging and sense of togetherness. However, the pseudo-self can also work in an opposite fashion, resulting in increased separation in a relationship. Over time and life events the levels of solid-self and pseudo-self will ebb and flow. The birth of a child with a disability offers an example of a stressful event that could trigger functioning of parents at a pseudo-self level as a means of adapting to the change in their lives.

Bowen's theory entails numerous other concepts such as triangles as the building blocks of relationships, the nuclear family emotional system, the family projection process, emotional cutoff, sibling position, the multigenerational transmission process, and societal regression. Each of these concepts can play a role in families, influencing the developmental outcomes of children and the emotional health of all. In the family projection process a father may be anxious about some aspect of his child's development. He unintentionally conveys this anxiety to the child. The child then becomes anxious. When the father sees that his worries about his child are valid, he becomes less anxious. The child also relaxes. The child has internalized the father's perceptions and became the child about whom he was anxious.

Effective family functioning is associated with the characteristics of openness, flexibility, and organization as noted in the theoretical model for structural family therapy developed by Minuchin (1974). Structural family therapy relies on the assumption that family members interact with one another in a predictable set of observable patterns repeated over time. Minuchin targeted changing these patterns through changing the organization or structure of the family. As a family's structure changes, the behavior of its members should change as well. The family unit, while maintaining stability, must be able to respond to changing circumstances with some degree of flexibility. Stress upon the family can overload the general functioning of the family system. A family without the ability to respond to the demands of changing roles is likely to experience conflict with resulting dysfunctional behavior.

From a systems perspective, the two-parent nuclear family is composed of four major subsystems: marital, parental, sibling, and extrafamilial. Each of these subsystems operates with its own interaction patterns and functions. Boundaries are established that set the rules governing who functions within a subsystem and how each person carries out his function. These boundaries need to be defined, yet flexible. Professionals preparing to assess young children with special needs become members of the extrafamilial subsystem of the child's family. Although they may interact directly with only one or two members of a family, these interactions will likely be felt throughout the entire family system and its various subsystems.

Constructivism

The constructivist perspective of child development is built upon the theoretical understanding that children directly contribute to their own learning through interactive experiences with the world around them (Dewey, 1916; Piaget, 1952; Vygotsky, 1993; & Gardner, 1991). Beginning with the simplest of tasks, children rely on their own interactions with the world to gain competence and understanding. Constructivism is predicated upon the belief that

> children need to form their own hypotheses and keep trying them out through social interaction, physical manipulation, and their own thought processes—observing what happens, reflecting on their findings, asking questions, and formulating answers. When objects, events, and other people challenge the working model that the child has mentally constructed, the child is forced to adjust the model or alter the mental structures to account for the new information. (Bredekamp & Copple, 1997, p. 13)

Vygotsky (1993) focused on the concepts of **actual** developmental level and the level of **potential** development. Actual developmental level is that which is typically measured in assessments. It consists of those things a child can do independently. However, children may have many skills that are in the process of developing. The child cannot accomplish the task or understand the thought independently, but with some prompting or assistance, she can complete or partially complete the task or give meaning to an idea.

Vygotsky refers to the distance between a child's actual developmental level and her potential development as the **zone of proximal development.** Vygotsky makes an analogy to a garden to clarify this concept. If a garden's productivity at midseason were measured by only those fruits or vegetables that had reached full maturation, a very incomplete picture would result. By harvest's end we would have seen all the food in the garden come to maturation. Routine assessments of children are conducted in a parallel fashion. Unless the child can complete a task independently, free from practice, prompts, modeling, or other clues, we typically give the child no credit. Vygotsky's view is that learning precedes development, creating the zone of proximal development. This perspective opens the door to dynamic approaches to assessment that include teaching and modeling problem solving as part of the "testing."

The application of constructivist principles to the assessment process can enable practitioners to honor these ideas. The National Association for the Education of Young Children (NAEYC) has developed a set of eighteen such principles to guide the assessment of young children (Bredekamp & Rosegrant, 1992).

FIGURE 1-9 Selected Principles to Guide Assessment Procedures for Young Children

- Curriculum and assessment are integrated throughout the program; assessment is congruent with and relevant to the goals, objectives, and content of the program.
- Assessment results in benefits to the child, such as needed adjustments in the curriculum or more individualized instruction and improvements in the program.
- Assessment involves regular and periodic observation of the child in a wide variety of circumstances that are representative of the child's behavior in the program over time.
- Assessment relies primarily on procedures that reflect the ongoing life of the classroom and typical activities of the children. Assessment avoids approaches that place children in artificial situations, impede the usual learning and developmental experiences in the classroom, or divert children from their natural learning processes.
- Assessment relies on demonstrated performance during real, not contrived, activities.
- Assessment supports children's development and learning; it does *not* threaten children's psychological safety or feelings of self-esteem.
- Assessment supports parents' relationships with their children and does not undermine parents'

confidence in their children's or their own ability, nor does it devalue the language and culture of the family.
- Assessment demonstrates children's overall strengths and progress, what children *can* do, not just their wrong answers and what they cannot do or do not know.
- Assessment addresses what children can do independently and what they can demonstrate with assistance since the latter show the direction of their growth.
- Information about each child's growth, development, and learning is systematically collected and recorded at regular intervals. Information such as samples of children's work, descriptions of their performance, and anecdotal records is used for planning instruction and communicating with parents.
- A regular process exists for periodic information sharing between teachers and parents about children's growth and development and performance. The method of reporting to parents does not rely on letter or numerical grades but rather provides more meaningful, descriptive information in narrative form.

Source: Adapted from *Reaching Potentials: Appropriate Curriculum and Assessment for Young Children* (Vol. 1), by S. Bredekamp, and T. Rosegrant (Eds.), (1992). Washington, DC: National Association for the Education of Young Children.

Although they are not designed specifically for children with special needs, these principles offer appropriate guidance to special educators seeking to apply constructivist concepts to their assessment practices. Selected examples of these principles are presented in Figure 1-9.

Principles of Context-Based Assessment

The integration of these foundations for context-based assessment requires that we keep many things in mind during the planning and completion of child assessments. At the same time, the assessment process naturally requires that we view children and their behaviors in manageable parts. Thus, we need to start by gathering as much contextual information about the

child as possible, move to careful observation and analysis of the child's specific behaviors, and finally integrate the specific and the global information we have about the child into a complete picture of the child. The following nine elements provide a foundation for this effort.

The first element, **ecological validity,** requires that all aspects of a setting including place, time, roles, and activities accurately reflect reality. The point for assessment is that it should be conducted in a context that is realistic. The effectiveness of a behavior management system for a particular child within a preschool program could not be validated through clinical experimentation using a 1:1 teacher-to-child ratio in a laboratory setting. A child is not likely to perform in "typical" fashion when set apart from his routines into a "testing" environment. On occasion, it might be necessary to perform clinical assessments, but they should not then be interpreted as representing typical behavior unless other sources also verify that they are indeed typical of the child (e.g., parent report). Expressive language, persistence in completing tasks, and cooperativeness are just three examples of child behaviors that can be dramatically altered between natural and clinical settings.

Participant understanding of and perspectives toward a setting also need to be considered. For example, the interventionist who feels that a proposed behavior management system "simply will not work in her situation" is biased from the outset, and will likely influence the effectiveness of the system. Such biases regarding the abilities of a young child alter the perceived outcomes of assessments if we do not take precautions to avoid their harmful effects.

Setting analysis is the second element of context-based assessment. We must study the properties of physical settings and social structures in addition to child behaviors. An assessment focused on child behaviors, exclusive of the physical and social settings in which they occur, offers very limited applicable information for classroom teachers. An environment that is cluttered with disorganized broken toys, has a poor adult-to-child ratio, and offers no structure for preschool children is likely to produce children who are "behavior problems." However, it is quite possible that the "problems" would be more appropriately identified with the setting than with the children. Setting analysis can include a multitude of features within the environment, including physical layout, persons present and the roles they are playing, structure, occurring events, the timing of activities, and so forth.

The third element, **reciprocity,** conveys the idea that reactions and behaviors of one person will be related to and influence the reactions and behaviors of others. Social systems are not unidirectional; rather, they are reciprocal in nature. An analysis of the effects of teacher behavior on child performance cannot ignore the influence child behavior has on teacher performance. Children do not simply react, they act, react, and are reacted to. Each interaction has an influence on the next one, thus the reciprocal nature of real social systems.

During the assessment process, the reciprocity of relationships equally must be considered. Both immediate reciprocity issues and historical reciprocity issues should be acknowledged. For example, a child might have a positive relationship with a parent who accompanies a child to an assessment. The parent reassures the child, and soothes his anxieties. Soon he may be playing comfortably with the examiner. Change any variable in this mix, and the behaviors of the parents, child, and examiner are likely to change reciprocally.

As well as these direct elements, there may be **indirect factors** affecting behavior, such as the presence of another person in the room. The expansion of this idea can be continued to include a multitude of possible relationships and interactions. The natural environment of a preschool setting includes any number of children (depending upon the size of the preschool) and several adults, who may be parents, teaching assistants, teachers, the program director, volunteers, program monitors, or other visitors. As they interact, they influence and are influenced by each other. A child is disappointed that her "best friend" is absent, but the teacher is relieved to have a day free from running interference between these two children and the remainder of the group. The child spends a greater than usual amount of time in isolated play, and is rarely approached by other children during free play. After all, they have learned over time that this child prefers to play with the absent friend. The teacher makes little if any effort to encourage peer interactions between this child and the others during the free play. Taken out of context, the child's isolate behavior could be misinterpreted as indicative of poor social development and the teacher's behavior as insensitive to the child's social development. Neither would be accurate.

Influences of the **physical and temporal environment** can become particularly significant when assessing a child's competence in performing a specific task. If the light switch is four feet off the floor and the child can only reach three and one-half feet, she is incompetent to perform the task of turning on and off the light. Bringing a short stool into the setting will change the environment sufficiently, so the child is now competent to perform the task. Nothing about the child changed, but she went from being incompetent to competent through a simple manipulation of the environment.

The next element addresses the conceptualization and analysis of **the setting as a system.** Any behavior setting can be viewed as a system. For example, a preschool setting includes components such as employment policies, daily scheduling, and philosophical and theoretical bases for program development. Components of the setting can exert significant influence on the outcomes of child assessment. An excellent preschool teacher might be limited by a mandatory curriculum that eliminates her opportunities for creativity, and results in her developing a poor attitude. The teacher's poor attitude influences the atmosphere within the preschool, souring the teaching assistant and the children toward the required curriculum. If we attempted to assess any of these children with materials and content similar to the disliked curriculum, we would likely get poor results.

Reciprocity between individuals expands to **reciprocal interactions between settings.** Results of a hypothetical study on the effectiveness of a behavior management system within a preschool setting would be influenced by recent events in other settings, including the homes of all the children, teachers and assistants, the busses used to transport children to the center, and even the home of the bus driver. Each of these persons enters the environment with varying circumstances and experiences, attitudes and beliefs, and priorities for the day. As they interact with one another, their own life circumstances begin to influence the others. At the end of the day, the cumulative effects for each child and adult again trigger interactions across systems. The child who has enjoyed her day of playing, learning, and growing at preschool with other children and teachers, comes home excited about her day, ready to interact positively with siblings, friends, and adults. The mother who may have faced multiple stressing events that day might not have been able to cope with a hostile, angry child appearing on her doorstep, but finds herself starting to relax in light of her child's mood. The reciprocity across settings has begun.

Assessing children across a variety of settings in which they are expected to function is important, but further analysis of how **settings influence behavior in other settings** must also be addressed. When the systems perspective is incorporated with ecological psychology, features of the community and surrounding environment take on acknowledged roles in the behavior and development of young children.

The importance of **macro-system influences** is demonstrated through the observable differences in child development seen in cross-cultural studies. For example, two-year-olds in China are able to sit quietly for extended periods of time, whereas in America we refer to this age as the "terrible two's." We might fantasize about a two-year-old sitting still for extended periods of time. However, if a child actually did so, Americans would likely express concern about the normalcy of the child's development, rather than be pleased with the behavior.

Closing Thoughts

Assessment carries with it social meaning and social consequences. It is often not the neutral activity we would like to think of it as being. Although we can generate any number of test scores, those scores in isolation do not produce pure facts about a child's abilities and inabilities. Results can be influenced or even altered by the people doing the assessment, by those being assessed, and by the social context in which assessments occur. The testing industry itself can and does yield influence over our assessment practices. Political decisions, not just educational decisions, influence the testing industry. For example, legislative eligibility criteria and disability categories have driven the market to produce many of the instruments available to us today. As the federal government moves toward the establishment of national standards for school progression, the testing industry is ready to market the needed instruments.

Authors and publishers of testing materials are sensitive to the marketplace. They hope to produce tests that will be bought and used. Since standardized tests carry great weight in American culture and are used as measures of teacher effectiveness, teachers, their supervisors, and school boards will adjust curricula accordingly. "In other words, teachers are very likely to shape their instruction to match a test's specific focus" (Meisels, 1989b, p. 17). The testing industry influences curricula, thereby influencing educational goals and values throughout our educational system from preschool through higher education. The effects are felt equally in the assessment and education of infants, toddlers, and preschool children with disabilities. Program directors have a responsibility to parents and funding agencies to document the efficacy of their programs. To do so they must monitor child progress through assessments that should match the goals and curriculum presented to the children. However, the link between curriculum and assessment can become a well-intentioned trap. Meisels notes that we have transformed "testing programs, ideally servants of educational programs, into masters of the educational process" (Meisels, 1989b, p. 17).

When instruction is "measurement-driven" (Madaus, 1988), then educational objectives, teaching strategies and placement will all be affected by our assessment practices. For example, young children may have deficits in adaptive and socioemotional behavior, hence educational objectives for these children would appropriately include objectives directed toward improving adaptive behavior. However, the construct of adaptive behavior does not lend itself to mass assessment techniques. It is possible that an adaptive behavior component of a child's program could receive short shrift in a curriculum or no attention at all simply because such items did not appear on the adopted assessment tool, although it should have been the most significant part of a child's program.

Ideally, teaching content and intervention strategies are influenced by the individual needs of children. In special education, there is an underlying assumption that educators will attempt to adapt interventions for each child. However, if we are constrained in our decision making regarding interventions because assessment policies require that children be able to demonstrate their knowledge in one specific way (i.e., on a standardized test), there is a danger that we will allow assessment to drive our practices rather than the needs of the child.

Careful evaluation of the child in isolation might produce very accurate and informative details about the child's current functioning under specific conditions, in a particular setting. It may not reveal *why* a child is not able to perform certain tasks or whether he can perform similar tasks in different settings. Confusion and misinterpretations can result from missing information and divergent priorities, and conflicting value systems between professionals and families. For instance, the child may be asked to cut with a pair of scissors. She refuses even to hold the scissors, despite assurances and support by the examiner, pulling away and resisting the examiner's approach. What might appear on the record sheet after such child-focused assessment is, "Child cannot cut, refuses even to hold scissors; uncooperative during the activity." The missing information might be that last week the child got into her mother's sewing basket and was playing with the scissors.

Upon discovering this situation, the mother spoke sharply to the child, thus startling her, causing the scissors to drop onto the child's leg and resulting in a painful stab. The mother, while dressing the wound, continued to berate the child for playing with the scissors and made her promise never to do such a thing again. The child's behavior during the assessment, in fact, might demonstrate an obedience to her mother and avoidance of pain more than a lack of cooperation with the examiner or inability to perform the task. Awareness of the child's recent experience with scissors and her present construction of knowledge about their use would give the examiner a new interpretation of her refusal to engage in the requested task.

Recommendations based on isolated clinical assessments can be directly counter to the family's wishes for the child. For example, developmental specialists may believe a child is ready to be toilet trained, but the mother has no interest in such a project. Previous attempts have failed, and the father was harsh with the child when accidents occurred. Another child in the home is still in diapers, so the mother has decided that working with them together in about six months is the best approach. The professional who is unaware of her view can easily judge the mother as lazy or uninterested in her child's development. The toilet-training readiness for the child holds meaning only within the context of her family priorities and circumstances.

Cultural mores may dictate that certain speech and language patterns are preferred over Standard English. The parents and community may not want a child to speak in the manner the examiner thinks the child ought to speak. Respect for and appreciation of the family beliefs are crucial for successful communication with parents. Conflicts of this nature can involve racial and ethnic issues of Americans who come from minority cultures, immigrants, as well as cultural values of the deaf population. If the ultimate goal of assessing young children is to improve their lives and help them to reach the highest quality of life possible, professionals must be willing to go beyond the standard practice that limits itself to the simple, the straightforward, the traditional clinical approach to assessment. Professionals may have to acknowledge that their values and beliefs about the best quality of life for a child may not match those of the family.

The process of assessing infants and young children must be undertaken with great caution and respect for that child and his family. Our sensitivity to the child and family requires not only a comprehensive understanding of appropriate assessment procedures, but also an appreciation and valuing of the context in which the child and family exist. The significance and meaning of disability can vary across cultures and subcultures, religious faiths, socioeconomic strata, and innumerable other variables. The willingness to seek help from outsiders, the importance of physical strength, the need for independent mobility and access to automobiles are just a few other illustrative examples of cultural and subcultural values or characteristics that take on heightened significance for families that include a child with disabilities. When the focus in the assessment process is on achieving the best possible outcomes for the child and family, not merely the completion of required documentation, the emphasis in the assessment process shifts to incorporate the child's context. It becomes as important to avoid causing unnecessary pain or confusion for child and family members as it is to complete an assessment and have it in the child's folder.

▦ For Your Consideration

1. What is meant by context-based assessment and how does it differ from traditional assessment used in special education?

2. What are the advantages and disadvantages of using a noncategorical diagnosis, such as developmental delay, for young children?

3. According to ecological psychologists, how does the setting in which we assess a child impact the outcome of our assessment?

4. Can we integrate family systems perspectives into the assessment process without going beyond the professional boundaries appropriate for early interventionists?

CYBERSOURCES

Check out the following Web sites for more information related to the ideas presented in this chapter.

Office of Special Education Programs

http://www.ed.gov/offices/OSERS/OSEP/

Federal Resource Center for Special Education

http://www.dssc.org/frc/

Council for Exceptional Children

http://www.cec.sped.org/

IDEA Practices: partnership between organizations and government to consolidate IDEA resources

http://www.ideapractices.org/

National Information Center for Children and Youth with Disabilities

http://www.nichcy.org/

Office of Special Education Programs Technical Assistance and Dissemination Network

http://www.dssc.org/frc/oseptad.htm

American Academy of Pediatrics, Diagnosis and Evaluation of the Child with Attention-Deficit/Hyperactivity Disorder

http://www.aap.org/policy/ac0002.html

Eligibility information from National Early Childhood Technical Assistance Center

http://www.nectac.org/topics/earlyid/earlyid.asp

 For additional resources on assessment, visit us on-line at www.earlychilded.delmar.com

CHAPTER 2

Purposes of Assessment

Key Terms and Concepts

High-stakes testing
Case-finding
Screening and monitoring
Diagnosis
Child Find

Apgar
False positive
False negative

Chapter Objectives

After reading this chapter, you should be able to:

1. Describe and define the purposes of assessment.

2. Start the planning process to conduct context-based individual assessments.

3. Use an assessment model that gives high priority to the concerns of the family.

4. Understand the importance of matching intended outcomes of assessment with assessment strategies.

Chapter Overview

Before we conduct or request assessments, we must be clear why they are being done. The information we seek and how we intend to use that information should form the foundation of a thoughtful and beneficial assessment plan. Often initial assessments involve determining if a disability is present and why. In many instances this diagnostic process is critical to the successful development of intervention plans. For example, we see the hyperactive, aggressive nonverbal four-year-old in a different light when we learn that she has a significant hearing loss. Treatment would be far different for this child if it were assumed the behaviors were associated with emotional problems rather than a sensory loss. Even though the diagnostic information clarifies the nature of the child's difficulties, it still does not give a teacher sufficient information to begin intervention. She would still need information about the existing abilities of the child and how she communicates with her family, her likes and dislikes, the resources available to her family, and so forth to develop an appropriate program.

Assessment of infants, toddlers, and preschool children with special needs as a context-based process encompasses numerous data-gathering techniques, including direct observations, interviews, work samples, developmental checklists, informal observations, and tests. We can determine which of these techniques should be applied and how by understanding the purpose(s) of an assessment and knowing who is the target of the assessment. The general purposes of assessment fall into three broad categories: (1) identification and diagnosis, (2) program planning, and (3) program evaluation. We may need to address more than one purpose simultaneously, such as diagnosis and program planning. It is possible to combine portions of such assessments through intentional planning; however, one does not substitute for the other.

We must avoid using assessment techniques and standardized instruments unsuited to our intended outcomes. For example, screening tools are inadequate to provide a diagnosis or to establish a foundation for program planning. Likewise, screening instruments cannot be used to gather meaningful data to monitor child progress or to determine program effectiveness. Well-designed screening instruments do offer a useful means of identifying the proper subgroup of children for diagnostic follow-up. Although test developers might claim that their instruments can serve multiple purposes, it is our obligation to verify that the information we gather is accurate, meaningful, and useful to the child and her family and the professionals providing intervention services to them.

Assessments vary as to the social consequences they can hold for a child and his family. For example, an informal assessment to determine a child's preference for one activity over another would carry "low stakes," whereas assessments that determine a child's eligibility for early intervention would have "high stakes." When the stakes are high for the child and family, professionals have an obligation to take the time to ensure that they have an adequate depth of information based upon low-inference measures. Little inference is required when we rely on numerous observations of children in their natural environments, play-based assessments, and other performance-based techniques. However, these are likely to require far greater time and effort than do traditional clinical assessments with standardized tests.

Identification and Diagnosis

Infants, toddlers, and preschool children proceed through some portions of **case-finding, screening and monitoring,** and the **diagnostic assessment** on their way to receiving early intervention. For some, in-depth investigations as to the causes of disabilities or developmental delays are needed. Genetic testing to verify the presence of a particular disorder and its inheritance pattern is an example of such in-depth diagnostic assessment. In practice, the processes involved in case-finding, screening and monitoring, and diagnostic assessment can overlap and are not always distinct from one another, and can vary in their timing for individual children and families. For a family with a preschool child whose disability was diagnosed shortly after birth, leading to the immediate provision of early intervention services, the case-finding and screening and monitoring processes happened without delay. For others, these two phases in the assessment process are clearly separate steps toward their awareness of their child's disability and his need for early intervention services.

The process of identification and diagnosis generally begins with a means of sorting children into risk categories and following up with varying degrees of intensity of diagnostic assessment. For example, most infants born in the United States today receive a blood test to determine their risk of having phenylketonuria (PKU). The target population to be screened is all newborns. Only a small number of infants will then be identified for follow-up testing. Even fewer will actually be diagnosed with this genetic disorder. Family members of these few children will then have the opportunity to undergo the genetic testing needed to determine the pattern of inheritance and risk to other offspring and the offspring of extended family members. There is no need for the parents of newborns without the indicators of PKU to undergo such genetic testing. Figure 2–1 provides a schematic flowchart depicting this narrowing of the identification and diagnostic process.

FIGURE 2–1 Schematic Depiction of Identification and Diagnostic Process

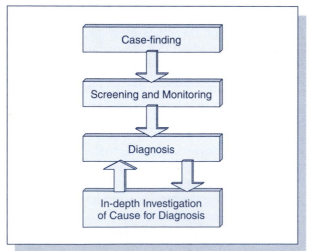

Case-Finding and Child Find

Case-finding involves a comprehensive search for children to be screened within a select geographic area. For example, a county might decide to screen all three-year-olds for hearing and visual acuity. In this instance, case-finding would involve contacting all families that include three-year-olds within the target geographic region. The actual screening might take place at a public health department over a two-week period for children not screened in their doctor's office. Public service announcements on the television and radio, postings on community bulletin boards and in pediatricians' offices, and announcements through churches and child care programs, would be used to spread the word throughout the community about the screening. Parents would be asked to bring their three-year-olds to the health department to have their vision and hearing checked. Children who failed the screening would be referred for diagnostic testing. School systems routinely conduct such vision and hearing screenings of primary-grade children at the schools. The success of the case-finding could be measured by determining how many three-year-olds living in the county had their vision and hearing checked.

Case-finding generally requires that the target population be defined according to geographic, economic, or disability type restrictions linked to follow-up services. The age range of eligible children must also be clearly delineated along with the goal of the case-finding. To target specific characteristics it is possible to include in a case-finding all children meeting geographic and age criteria, only those children within the population who have demonstrated certain characteristics, or those children who are at high risk. In the above example, the population for the screening was limited to three-year-olds living within a specific county. Those outside the county, or younger or older than three would not be included. The case-finding could have been further limited by including only those children whose child care teachers or parents noted to have poor speech development or symptoms related to visual problems.

A variety of approaches can be used in the case-finding process. The groundwork typically involves the process of building community awareness through public service announcements, presentations to community groups, and the formation of advocacy groups designed to increase visibility and local support for case-finding efforts. Positive public relations are vital to any case-finding activity because community attitudes will directly influence the outcomes. Persons responsible for case-finding need to maintain ongoing communication with key community leaders and cooperating agencies year after year. Reports summarizing the results of case-finding efforts from the previous year should be disseminated to all referral sources as well as to the public within the community.

Child Find is a mandated component of IDEA that involves case-finding of both infants and toddlers and preschool children who might be experiencing developmental delays. Both special educators serving preschool children and early interventionists providing services through Part C are required to serve all eligible children, not just those who happen to ask for services. States and local education agencies must have comprehensive Child Find plans designed to make all eligible children and families aware of services available. Local education agencies generally provide screening and assessment services for the preschool and older population, whereas families with infants and toddlers receive these services through a variety of Part C systems. Although the structural characteristics of Part C systems vary across the states, the obligation to engage in Child Find activities and to provide screening services is a federal requirement.

Professionals working through these systems might perform assessments through the coordination of community screenings or "round-ups," the conduction of individual screenings at a referred child's home, or through contracting for the screening of a child by a service provider or team of professionals. For example, a child might be referred to a speech and language therapist for a screening if that child is suspected of having delays in language development. If the results of the screening are consistent with these suspicions, the therapist would then follow up with diagnostic assessments.

Well-baby checkups also function as a means of targeting children for Child Find. Parents might complete a developmental screening questionnaire, such as the Denver Developmental Screening Test-II (Frankenburg & Dodds, 1990), as a routine part of these exams. If potential developmental delays seem evident, physicians or health department personnel would then refer parents to Part C system providers (birth to age three) or to local education agencies (three and older) for further assessments. Physicians vary as to their quickness to make such referrals based upon the assessment results that they consider

sufficient to take such action, their familiarity with early intervention services that are available within their communities, and their confidence in pediatric screening tools (Dworkin, 1992; Meisels, 1989a).

Local education agencies must assume responsibility for Child Find services for preschool and older children. Community agencies such as health clinics, social service offices, local preschool and child care programs, rehabilitation agencies serving children with disabilities, and private practitioners often assist the school system in publicizing Child Find activities. Since school systems are obligated to begin services at the point of a child's third birthday, Child Find activities occur throughout the year. These activities typically encompass the public awareness activities mentioned previously and developmental screenings. For example, school personnel might offer on-site developmental screenings at child care centers. Children whose performance on such developmental screenings indicates possible developmental delays could be monitored over a brief period and referred for a comprehensive diagnostic assessment if necessary.

Screening and Monitoring

Screening is an assessment technique that allows us to distinguish between children who need follow-up diagnostic assessments and/or careful monitoring from those who do not have significant indications of developmental problems or other targeted conditions. Screening can be a part of the Child Find process or separate from it. Toward the end of the school year, kindergarten teachers typically perform screening tests to determine the readiness of children for first-grade work. Screening instruments can be designed for individual administration, such as the Brigance series of screening instruments, including the Brigance Early Preschool Screen (Brigance, 1998a); Brigance Preschool Screen (Brigance, 1998b); and the Brigance K & 1 Screen-Revised (Brigance, 1997). Screening instruments designed for group administration are also available, such as the Developmental Indicators for the Assessment of Learning-Revised (DIAL-3, Mardell-Czudnowski & Goldenberg, 1998). They can be targeted toward specific personal characteristics (e.g., genetic traits, hearing or vision), specific areas of development (e.g., social competence, readiness for reading), offer a quick look across multiple developmental domains, or serve as an ongoing monitoring system as seen in the Ages and Stages Questionnaire (Bricker, Squires, & Mounts, 1995).

Physicians screen newborn babies even before they leave the delivery room using the Apgar scoring system (Apgar, 1953). Infants born in hospitals typically receive this first assessment one minute and five minutes after birth. The physician rates the infant on a scale of zero to two on five signs shown in Table 2–1. Infants who receive very low Apgar scores are considered to be at high risk for future complications. Although the predictive validity of the Apgar rating shows a strong relationship between low ratings and infant mortality, predictions of later developmental progress are inconsistent (Francis, Self, & Horowitz, 1987). Nevertheless, the scoring system offers physicians a simple means of recognizing those neonates who need immediate special attention. Other neonate screening tools also available for use with infants during the first few weeks of life are presented in Table 2–2.

Parents can also play an important role in the screening process while reducing the costs of screening. Professionals then have the benefit of the parents' perspective of child functioning across multiple times and settings (Diamond & Squires, 1993). The Ages and Stages Questionnaire, or ASQ (Bricker et al., 1995) provides a means for parents to observe systematically the developmental progress of their infants (Squires, 1996). The instrument can be used effectively with a number of strategies for data gathering, including mail-outs, home visits, and center-based parent interviews. Such a tool can enable parents to know better when they should seek early intervention for their child without the high costs that would be associated with frequent professional assessments. The ASQ consists of questionnaires that can identify infants and toddlers between the ages of four and forty-eight months who display potential developmental problems. Each questionnaire contains 30 developmental items divided into five areas: communication, gross motor, fine motor, problem solving, and personal-social. Another section addresses general concerns of the parents. Parents respond to each developmental item with a yes, sometimes, or not yet based on the functioning of their child at frequent intervals. These responses are then converted into point values that can be compared to established cutoff points for further diagnostic follow-up. The ASQ includes extensive documentation of its reliability and validity as an effective screening device. Sample questions from these questionnaires are displayed in Figure 2–2.

Another effective option involves the teaming of professionals for special developmental screenings within the community. Successful community-based screenings can involve collaboration between child development specialists and pediatricians (Solomon, Clougherty, Shaffer, Hofkosh, & Edwards, 1994). In this model, a child development specialist performs screenings and assessments at pediatric clinics and provides information about early intervention services to medical personnel. She communicates immediately with family members regarding the assessments and follows up with the referring pediatrician. The model can be cost-effective (by lowering the number of children who would have received a more expensive assessment had the screening not been conducted), and satisfying for families and pediatricians.

TABLE 2–1 Apgar Rating Scale for Newborns

Sign	0	1	2
Pulse	Absent	Below 100 bpm*	100–140 bpm
Respiration	Absent	Slow, irregular	Good, crying
Grimace (reflex irritability)	No response	Grimace	Sneeze, cough, pulls away
Activity (muscle tone)	Absent	Arms and legs flexed	Active movement
Appearance (skin color)	Blue-gray, pale all over	Normal, except extremities	Normal all over

Bpm stands for beats per minute.
Source: Adapted from Apgar, V. (1953). A proposal for a new method of evaluation of the newborn infant. *Current Researchers in Anesthesia and Analgesia, 32,* p. 260–267.

TABLE 2-2 Assessment Tools for Newborns

Name of Instrument	Authors	Description
First-Week Evaluation Scale	Cohen, et al., 1972	Global rating of the newborn's constitution. Two raters review an infant's medical records and, using a scale from 1 to 5, score the infant on the following: • health • physiological adaptation • calmness • vigor • attention • neurological status
Graham / Rosenblith Scales	Rosenblith; 1975	Requires direct observation of the infant, and provides opportunities for examiners to interact with the infant in an effort to elicit behaviors. Contains the following: • motor scale (e.g., head reaction in prone position) • tactile-adaptive scale (e.g., responses to cotton over the nose) • visual responsiveness (e.g., fixation/degree of horizontal and vertical pursuit of object) • auditory responsiveness (e.g., responses to rattle and bell) • muscle tonus (e.g., nature [flexed or extended] of spontaneous lower limb position) • irritability rating (based on behavior throughout the entire examination)
Brazelton Neonatal Behavioral Assessment Scale	Brazelton; 1973, 1984	Measures both reflexive/elicited and behavioral characteristics of the neonate. Reflexive/elicited behaviors observed include: • plantar grasp • standing • automatic walking • nystagmus • tonic neck reflex • rooting and sucking Behavioral items on the scale include observation of infant behaviors such as: • response decrement to light, rattle, bell, and pinprick • degree of alertness, cuddliness consolability with intervention • amount of startle • hand-to-mouth facility
Neonatal Behavioral Assessment Scale-K	Horowitz; Sullivan, and Linn, 1978	Five additional behavioral items added to Brazleton Neonatal Behavioral Assessment Scale. • Infant's overall responsiveness • Examiner persistence required to test infant • Infant's overall irritability • Degree infant is reinforcing to the examiner • Infant's typical behavior (not just best behavior)
Neurological Assessment of the Preterm and Full-Term Newborn Infant	Dubowitz and Dubowitz, 1981	Instrument that can be administered by staff untrained in neonatal neurology, can be used on preterm neonates, and requires no more than, 10–15 minutes to complete and record; uses a five-point rating scale based on brief descriptions and/or illustrations of specific motoric responses. Covers the following: • habituation (state of the infant) • movement and tone • reflexes • neurobehavioral items (e.g., auditory orientation, alertness)

FIGURE 2–2 Examples of Questions from Ages and Stages Questionnaires

6-Month Questionnaire

Communication
- Does your baby make high-pitched squeals?
- When a loud noise occurs, does your baby turn to see where the sound came from?

Gross Motor
- When she is on her tummy, does your baby straighten both arms and push her whole chest off the bed or floor?
- If you hold both hands just to balance him, does your baby support his own weight while standing?

30-Month Questionnaire

Fine Motor
- Does your child use a turning motion with her hand while trying to turn doorknobs, wind up toys, twist tops, or screw lids on and off jars?
- Does your child thread a shoelace through either a bead or eyelet of a shoe?

Problem Solving
- If your child wants something he cannot reach, does he find a chair or box to stand on to reach it?
- After she draws a "picture," even a simple scribble, does your child tell you what she drew? You may say, "Tell me about your picture," or ask, "What is this?" to prompt her.

Source: Adapted from Bricker, D., Squires, J., & Mounts, L. (1995). *Ages and Stages Questionnaires: A Parent-Completed, Child-Monitoring System.* Baltimore: Paul H. Brookes.

There are two types of errors that we must try to control for when implementing a screening procedure. They are described, along with their possible consequences, in Table 2–3. Errors in screening can have serious consequences. A screening system that includes some form of ongoing monitoring of child performance can diminish some of the risks of errors.

The ability of a screening instrument to select children with a minimum of false positives or false negatives is determined by the test's **detection accuracy, base rate,** and **hit rate** (McCall, 1982). Table 2–4 summarizes what each of these factors represents. The hit rate will rise as the percentage of children with the condition present in the population to be screened increases. Therefore, prescreening by pediatricians, referrals for screening from nurses, and other selective case-finding procedures can reduce errors. Many children without the condition will have already been removed from the population being screened.

Some screening procedures require specially trained professionals and expensive equipment. Others can be conducted by volunteers or parents after brief training sessions. Expense versus benefit is always a consideration. Additionally, the dangers of

Know The Facts

An infant is screened as not having a high blood phenylalanine level when, in fact, she does. Permanent brain damage is the result. The parents fed the baby a normal diet, resulting in serious damage to the infant because she actually has PKU. Holtzman, Morales, Cunningham, and Wells (1975), in summarizing research on the critical age at which to begin the diet, reached the conclusion that treatment must begin within the first month of life, before the critical age of three to four weeks, to avoid mental retardation. Had the screening for a high blood phenylalanine level provided accurate results, the parents would have been instructed to follow up to verify that the baby had PKU, and provided information and supplies for an adjusted diet. With the adjusted diet, she could have grown into a normal, healthy child and adult, with no loss of functioning. A false negative result at the screening cost this child her normal mental ability.

TABLE 2–3 Errors in Screening

Error Type	Description	Consequences
False negative	Children with disabilities pass through a screening process undetected	■ Child's condition goes undetected ■ Opportunity to provide needed intervention services is lost or delayed ■ Parents and professionals presume that the child is progressing within normal limits or is free from whatever condition is being screened ■ Concern may be falsely reduced or eliminated
False positive	Identification of children as needing diagnostic follow-up without any real cause	■ Unnecessary anxiety, time, and expense caused for the parents as they pursue diagnostic follow-up ■ Ongoing anxiety about the child's development ■ Inaccurate results might become part of the child's permanent record

TABLE 2–4 Accuracy of Screening Instruments

Detection accuracy	The percentage of children with the condition being screened that were detected, as well as the percentage of children incorrectly identified as needing diagnostic follow-up
Base rate	The real (although unknown) percentage of children with the condition present in the population to be screened
Hit rate	The percentage of these children who are correctly identified by the screening instrument

overidentification and underidentification can be so serious that no screening program might be preferable to one with a high error rate. For infants and toddlers, routine medical screenings play a crucial role in the early detection of conditions warranting further investigation and possible intervention. The well-child model, developed by the American Academy of Pediatrics (2000), includes screening for factors listed in Figure 2–3.

When a child is known to be at a high risk for developing special health conditions due to a disability, the well-child model is expanded to a pathophysiologic/medical model. This model includes additional areas for possible assessment and intervention: therapy and special care routines, medications, prevention of complications or secondary handicaps, special equipment,

and safety (Zelle & Coyner, 1983). However, many pediatricians opt not to offer developmental screenings beyond the basic well-child checkup due to the time-consuming nature of such screening coupled with the fact that screening as well as prescreening instruments "are inaccurate with poor levels of test sensitivity" (Solomon et al., 1994, p. 68). Physicians may find the newer monitoring systems that involve parent reporting to be more cost effective and accurate than the single administration of a screening test.

Diagnosis

Diagnosis involves an in-depth look at the individual child to determine if a disability or developmental delay exists, the nature of the condition, and the

FIGURE 2–3 Factors Monitored in Well-Child Medical Guidelines

- Adequate nutrition
- Adequate patterns of physical and emotional health
- Achievement of milestones in
  - motor development
  - communication development
  - social development
  - cognitive development
- Sensory screening
- Protection against preventable disease and injury
- Absence of illness
- Correction of correctable abnormality

causes of the condition. A child targeted during a screening as having a hearing loss needs to undergo a diagnostic evaluation to determine the cause of the hearing loss to begin the process of planning possible interventions. After a thorough examination of the child, an apparent hearing loss could be attributed to emotional problems that have no biological cause whatsoever, or a temporary hearing loss due to a middle ear infection. It could be a conductive hearing loss, the impact of which could be reduced through the use of amplification. The hearing loss might be the result of neurological impairment, in which case amplification might not be of any value. The child might be a good candidate for a cochlear implant, or may not benefit from such technology. A comprehensive diagnosis reveals such vital information. It serves as a follow-up to screening, providing useful information as to the appropriate nature of intervention. However, diagnosis does not include the detailed specificity of skill development for teachers to plan and develop intervention goals and strategies. Nor does it settle the debate between advocates for conflicting approaches to interventions for children with hearing impairments.

Context-based diagnostic assessments involve data gathering from multiple sources across time, not isolated clinical assessments conducted by strangers in a single day. Information from parents and/or primary caregivers, and former and/or current teachers or child care workers can be synthesized with data gathered from observations in natural environments along with child performance on standardized tests. How thorough a diagnostic analysis is needed will

vary from child to child. In the illustration cited above about a child with a hearing loss, a determination that the perceived hearing loss was actually the manifestation of an emotional problem would require the most comprehensive diagnostic workup, in which all biological causes would have to be investigated and ruled out. The middle ear infection could be detected through a clinical examination of the ear canal. If treatment of the infection eliminated the functional hearing loss, further diagnostic work would not be required unless the condition became chronic.

It is possible to conduct a comprehensive diagnostic assessment and still fail to determine the exact cause of a child's condition. Such a failure can be most frustrating to diagnosticians, parents, teachers, and the children involved. Nevertheless, there will come a point in the assessment process where it is more productive to move on to assessment for program planning than it is to continue seeking the answer to an illusive question. The results of context-based child assessments, thorough environmental assessments, and the identification of family resources, priorities, and concerns should provide guidance in the development of goals for intervention even when the causes of a child's condition remain unknown. Currently, autism offers a puzzling example of such frustration in the pursuit of causes. Although the medical community continues to investigate a variety of plausible causes of autism, including genetic factors and viruses, educators, therapists, and parents are obligated to develop and seek the most effective interventions possible for their children. Since nothing is absolute, conflicting theories abound. The intensity of the debates over the causes of autism and the best interventions for children with autism simply reflect the state-of-the-art and our limited understanding of this condition.

Program Planning

Program planning includes identification of family resources priorities and concerns; environmental assessment; and assessment of the child's functioning. The process involves the use of criterion-referenced developmental assessments, play-based assessments, observations, parent interviews, family surveys, environmental assessments, assistive technology assessments, and standardized developmental checklists. It can also include broader contextual elements, such as the identification of community values and beliefs, or formal and informal networks of support available to the family. Information about changing patterns of child behavior, such as motivation to master new tasks, favorite activities, preferred peers, and self-initiated play behaviors, also aid in program planning.

Historically, the primary source of information associated with program planning involved the determination of a child's ability or inability to perform certain developmental skills. Although the child's functioning is still the cornerstone of assessment for program planning, we no longer view it in isolation. The emphasis for program planning assessment is on gathering the most descriptive information possible about the child's current behaviors, not just acquired skills. These behaviors are studied across a variety of environments in order to determine the most suitable goals of early intervention for the individual child. Beyond the task of gathering information about what developmental skills a child has accomplished, assessment for program planning includes consideration of needed adaptations to equipment and environments. For example, the use of adapted toys that are controlled by electronic switches with a one-year-old who has extreme physical limitations can give her a new understanding of cause and effect, and give us a new ways to support her development.

As we plan assessments for program planning there are a number of principles that can increase the quality and long-term benefits of our efforts. The priorities of the parents do matter. Settings in which the child functions do matter. The availability of assistive technology can radically alter a child's competence level. Recognizing and using child preferences can substantially influence the effectiveness of our efforts. Through the process, we have the obligation to find out what the child can do currently, how he can best move forward to gain new skills, and to monitor the effectiveness of our efforts toward these ends.

Family Resources, Priorities, and Concerns

The establishment of goals of early intervention for a young child with special needs is most effectively done within the context of the family system. Information obtained from the family should lead to the identification of family priorities for intervention, be reflective of the types of services that parents prefer for their child, and target what resources are available within the community to help the family reach their priority goals. The parents, along with professionals working with their child, can form a powerful alliance to plan a program of early intervention to enhance the child's development. A program plan that does not incorporate the family perspective is unlikely to have the equivalent impact on the child's development as one that does.

It is possible that through the data gathering process, parents and professionals will discover differing views of what are the most important goals for a child or the most desirable means of achieving those goals. These differences can center around three components of services, as presented in Table 2–5.

These differences become apparent when identification of family resources, priorities, and concerns occurs. Professional educators should acknowledge any such differences of opinion and have open conversation about the reasons for their views with the parents. However, they must also acknowledge that parents of young children live with their children twenty-four hours a day, see their children across many different settings with many different people, and are the primary decision-makers in their children's lives. Professionals must balance expression of their professional beliefs regarding the best intervention services for a child with sensitivity to the positions held by the parents.

Environmental Assessment

It is impossible to determine accurately a child's ability to perform any task or developmental skill apart from the setting in which it occurs. Perhaps a child can focus and attend well to tasks such as putting puzzles together in a relatively structured environment free from high levels and noise and visual distractions. When the noise level accelerates, the distractibility for this child might increase and his ability to put a puzzle together correctly diminishes. When talking to peers, a child is able to speak and be understood, but when that same child speaks to an adult, his speaking becomes garbled and difficult to understand. The factors influencing the competence of the child to demonstrate a skill are external to the child, but interact with the child to influence his performance. An environmental assessment of the child's settings should include not only evaluation of the child's surroundings, but also analysis of conditions that seem to increase the child's competence.

Characteristics of the settings in which the child spends time can provide guidance for program planning. For example, a child's preschool has one hour per day of free-choice time, during which the child consistently wanders aimlessly about the room. It

TABLE 2–5 Components of Services

Component	Examples
Location of services	• Inclusive early education settings • Home settings • Therapeutic clinics • Schools
Nature of services	• Play-based • One-on-one teacher-directed • Discrete trials • Discipline-specific • Transdisciplinary
Goals of services	• Emphasis on performance, such as walking or speaking • Emphasis on function, such as movement using a wheelchair or expressive communication via an augmentative communication device

Finding A Better Way

An observer takes language samples for Eddie, a four-year-old. The sample taken in a clinical setting during structured lessons had no child-initiated speech, one- and two-word responses, and imitation as requested by the adult. During another ten-minute sample taken outside during free play in a preschool setting, Eddie initiated speech to peers or adults four times, used vocalizations during play, and sang as part of a group game. The sample taken during the family-style lunch at the preschool had even more spontaneous speech, demonstrating Eddie's ability to use speech to communicate his needs during the meal. The final sample taken at home with only family members present showed Eddie taking turns in conversation with his mother as they played a simple game. How does having four language samples change our assessment of Eddie's verbal skills?

ing, or any number of other possible explanations. Assessment for program planning and monitoring can center on introducing a number of schemes aimed at increasing her engagement in playing with materials and/or peers during this hour. Such schemes could include the use of a buddy system where assigned peer partners play together in the same centers for a portion of the time, reducing the choices and distractions within the settings, or embedding one play activity with an attractive element likely to increase the child's interest in playing (e.g., place favorite adult in one center).

Developmental Assessment

There should be a clear linkage between the information gathered and the program planned for an infant or young child (Bagnato, Neisworth, & Munson, 1997). For school-age children we use testing across academic skill areas, such as reading and mathematics, to measure current abilities and match them to educational curriculum. Infants and toddlers clearly are not ready for any such academic testing. Rather, we would look at their mastery of developmental tasks, such as independent feeding skills, walking up and down stairs, speaking and responding to language, and so forth. At the preschool level, we do begin looking at the readiness skills of preschool children, including concept development, shape number and letter recognition, and eye-hand coordination. As young children enter kindergarten and the primary

appears that given the existing conditions, she is unable to choose where she wants to play, with whom she wants to play, or with what materials she wants to play. She might be overwhelmed by the choices, fear social rejection by her peers already playing with her preferred toys, be uncertain about how to begin play-

grades we begin measuring their early academic skills. Developmental assessment covers this broad range of developmental and educational skills that we expect to emerge between infancy and eight years of age. Assessment of play skills, emotional maturity, and social skills are also included.

Developmental assessment covers current skill levels and can also provide a means of continual monitoring of a child's developmental and/or educational progress. Domains that are typically covered in a developmental assessment are listed in Figure 2–4.

If screening and/or diagnostic examination of a child reveals the need for intervention in only one or two domains, we might focus additional assessments on these specific domains. However, early interventionists need information about child functioning across all developmental domains, since functioning in one domain directly and indirectly influences functioning in all others. For example, a two-year-old with cerebral palsy will likely exhibit some physical limitations or delays that impede her ability to play with blocks, work with puzzles, manipulate knobs and lids, and so forth. We must not allow her physical limitations to be automatically seen as indicators of cognitive delays. A four-year-old from a Spanish-speaking family who is being exposed to English for the first time in his Head Start program could be expected to function below age level in communication skills. Since many problem-solving skills and measures of cognitive development of four-year-olds rely on communication skills, we could misinterpret a low performance on English-based cognitive assessments to indicate a delay there as well. In fact, we would need to find alternative means to assess his cognitive development and problem-solving skills that were not compromised by his linguistic background. Likely, that would involve using play-based assessments and observation of the child in natural settings instead of developmental checklists or standardized instruments with associated age norms. Even reliance on a Spanish edition of a cognitive assessment could be misleading if the child has already begun learning new concepts in English and/or has experienced multiple cultures in his short life.

Ongoing assessment of a child's competence is a frequent and routine component of a well-designed intervention program. As we monitor child progress, we can determine the effectiveness of the present intervention. Analysis of child progress across and within developmental domains can identify areas of uneven gains made by the child, areas of most rapid

FIGURE 2–4 Domains Included in Comprehensive Developmental Assessment

- Cognitive development and problem-solving skills
- Communication and language development (production and comprehension)
- Gross motor development
- Fine motor development
- Social and emotional development
- Self-care and adaptive behaviors
- Play behaviors and motivation
- Auditory and visual functioning

gains, and those areas in which little or no progress is being made. Performance monitoring can provide a continuous record of the child's status in regard to achieving stated goals and objectives in an individualized program. Evaluation of the effectiveness of specific teaching techniques can also be achieved through the use of performance monitoring.

Performance monitoring needs to be based upon simple data collection procedures that can easily be integrated into intervention programs. We should begin with an accurate picture of the child's current abilities for each instructional objective or outcome statement that appears on an individualized family service plan (IFSP) or an individualized education program (IEP). From this initial point, we should be able to develop data collection procedures that provide a straightforward means to monitor the child's progress. The frequency of our data collection might depend on the nature of the task, the frequency of intervention, and the availability of personnel to assist in the data collection procedures. A sample data collection procedure for an expressive language objective is depicted in Figure 2–5.

Multiple sources of information are needed in ongoing performance monitoring. On a frequent, if not daily basis, recording of child performance on specific skills and collection of anecdotal records are most helpful. To give the data contextual meaning, we should note factors associated with peak performance and those associated with poor performance. For example, a program that provides home-based, center-based, and inclusion-based intervention for the same child should monitor in which placements the child demonstrates the greatest development. It is possible that the child demonstrates greater skill performance

FIGURE 2–5 Sample Performance Monitoring Data Collection System

Objective: Amos will speak using 2-word combinations across settings and people
Present skill level: consistent use of 1-word expressions, little or no use of 2-word expressions

Setting for Assessment	Weekly Expressive Language Samples					
	Expression	Target of Expression				
Persons Present		1st	2nd	3rd	4th	5th
Free play in household center	Gestures			Glenn		
	Sounds	Sharon				
	1-word		Sharon			Clint
TA: Sharon	2-word				Sharon	
Peers: Glenn Clint	3-word					
	4-word					
Free play in blocks center	Gestures	Wendy				
	Sounds		Wendy			
	1-word			Wendy Tom		
TA: Larry	2-word				Larry	Wendy
Peers: Wendy Tom	3-word					
	4-word					
Snacks and Lunch	Gestures	Wendy				
	Sounds	Marian				
	1-word		Glenn	Marian	Wendy Glenn	
Teacher: Marian	2-word					Marian
Peers: Glenn, Clint, Wendy, Tom, Beth	3-word					
	4-word					
Teacher-directed group time	Gestures	Sharon				
	Sounds		Marian			
Teacher: Marian	1-word					Glenn
TA: Sharon Larry	2-word			Marian	Wendy	
Peers: Glenn, Clint, Wendy, Tom, Beth	3-word					
	4-word					

Comments:
Amos needed time to adjust to new activities before using words; interacted with 3 different adults across multiple settings; talked to Wendy and Glenn more than other peers; relies on Wendy to help him get toys and snack items; imitated 2-word phrases by Sharon in household play center.

at one setting in one domain and achieves greater development in a different setting in a different domain. Such data could corroborate the value of multiple places for intervention services for an individual child. Time of day, other children present in a group, persons teaching, materials used, adult-to-child ratios, and methods of intervention are examples of other factors that we should consider when analyzing child progress. Interventionists can make rapid adjustments to curricula and approaches used when data collected about child performance reveals such a need. Developmental checklists and behavior rating scales can be used for performance monitoring on a monthly or quarterly basis, providing a mechanism for monitoring the child's progress against a background of typical developmental sequences and age expectations. However, for monitoring on a daily basis for specific objectives, we need to develop individualized data collection systems such as the one presented in Figure 2–5. With the move toward activity-based and play-based intervention models, such monitoring can guide teachers and parents in their evaluations of the effects of their efforts.

One of the most powerful determinants of a child's potential to learn new skills is her motivation to master new skills (Brockman, Morgan, & Harmon, 1988). The infant who has the motivation to learn to stand can easily tolerate the failure that is inevitable as she attempts to pull herself up to standing only to find herself suddenly back on the floor, falling down over and over again. A child who is following a typical developmental sequence in a nurturing environment will experience a balance of successes and failures. This balance can help her maintain a level of motivation needed to continue trying to develop new skills. The child who is physically or mentally unable to achieve a balance of successes to offset the many failures may lose her motivation to master tasks. Loss of the motivation to learn new skills can be as detrimental as the initial disability. Such a child may actually have potential that can be lost as a result of the lost motivation to achieve. Assessment for program planning should include a component to determine a child's willingness to persist on a new task.

Program Evaluation

Assessment designed for program evaluation should provide information about the benefits of early inter-

vention for individual children as well as the overall effectiveness of programs for groups of children. Program evaluation models today must be flexible enough to address a wide variety of service delivery models, including home-based services, segregated center-based services, individual placements in inclusive child care settings, integrated comprehensive and special education programs (e. g., Head Start and Title One programs serving children with disabilities), and integrated center-based programs. Program evaluation is most often thought of in terms of program outcomes for the children receiving services.

Although factors such as parent satisfaction and professional perceptions may be included elements of an evaluation, they are not usually sufficient measures of performance. For example, a program might have satisfied parents without being able to demonstrate that the children are making reasonable progress toward any specific goals. If parent satisfaction is the primary goal of the program, perhaps the director could claim to be offering an effective program. However, parent satisfaction without documented developmental progression of the children would be a very low standard of success. On the other hand, documented child progress coupled with a high degree of parent dissatisfaction would be an equally troubling outcome of a program evaluation.

Much has been written regarding the effectiveness of early intervention programs (see Guralnick, 1997 for a comprehensive resource on efficacy studies). The data have been difficult to analyze and interpret for a number of reasons. Populations used in efficacy studies have been inadequately described, or described using ambiguous terms. The most effective age to initiate intervention across disabilities is still being debated as are the most effective intervention techniques. The debates on age of intervention even go down to the first days of life, as is the case with the research regarding the earliest intervention for preterm infants (Als, 1997).

These debates will most likely never end since the questions surrounding the most effective intervention age and techniques have individual answers, requiring a context-based decision rather than mass programming. When we find that one child with Down syndrome has a successful experience in an inclusive preschool, we do not then close down all other options for service delivery to preschool children with Down syndrome and assume that we have found the answer for all three-year-olds with Down syndrome. However, we are obligated to determine the effectiveness of early intervention programs for the children and families being served by them and attempt to identify and follow those practices associated with the best results.

Outcomes used to measure whether a program has been effective often reflect back to the stated goals of the program. For example, determining the effectiveness of a program that has as a goal to enhance a child's social skills and ability to interact positively with other children would not be well served by determining effectiveness through pre- and posttest standardized assessments of cognitive development. Determining a reasonable expectation of developmental gain for young children with wide-ranging disabilities can be challenging for the interventionist. How much progress is reasonable to expect in a three-year-old with a developmental age of nine months? How can a determination that a program has been "effective" be reached for such a child?

Often interventionists rely on goal attainment, assuming that the goals were a reasonable estimate of what the child should be able to accomplish within a given period. At some point the stated goals must also be evaluated to determine how reasonable they actually were. It is possible that a teacher may determine that his program has not been effective for a child, when the stated goals were never realistically within the child's developmental ability. On the other hand, a teacher who writes goals for a child that fall short of the child's true potential might erroneously appear to have offered a very effective program. The use of multiple sources of data, such as a change in rate of development index, curriculum-based assessments, play-based assessments, portfolio assessment, and parent satisfaction surveys can eliminate some of the pitfalls associated with program evaluation based on single criteria.

Closing Thoughts

This chapter covered the various purposes of assessment and the stages of a context-based approach to assessment. The purposes include three broad categories: identification and diagnosis, program planning, and program evaluation. Identification and diagnosis includes case-finding, screening and monitoring, and the diagnostic process. Program planning includes three key components: identification of family resources, priorities, and concerns; environmental assessment; and developmental assessment. Devel-

opmental assessment covers a broad range of developmental and academic skills appropriate for the chronological age of the child. The third category of assessment—program evaluation—includes reviewing child progress on various outcomes, determining parent satisfaction with programs, and monitoring long-term measures, such as future educational placements and progress made by program participants. Program evaluation should be linked with the effectiveness with which a program met each individual child's needs as well as its overall effectiveness. The linkage between program planning and program evaluation should always be strong. Results of developmental assessments can easily be incorporated into program evaluation designs.

For Your Consideration

1. Why do we conduct assessments of young children?

2. What types of information can we obtain best from a screening instrument?

3. Who is responsible for conducting Child Find activities and why was Child Find included in federal special education law?

4. How can we make sure that assessments are planned with family perspectives in mind?

5. What should be included when planning an assessment that is intended to provide program planning for a preschool teacher?

6. What is the relationship between child assessment and program evaluation?

CYBERSOURCES

Check out the following Web sites for more information related to the ideas presented in this chapter.

North Central Regional Educational Laboratory

http://www.ncrel.org/sdrs/areas/as0cont.htm

National Early Childhood Technical Assistance Center

http://www.nectac.org/default.asp

For additional resources on assessment, visit us on-line at www.earlychilded.delmar.com

CHAPTER 3

Developing a Framework for Context-Based Assessments

Key Terms and Concepts

Stages of assessment
- Planning
- Assessing
- Interpreting
- Evaluating

Context-based model of assessment

Critical events

Personal interactions

Developmental functioning

Environmental analysis

Vision to guide assessment of infants, toddlers, and preschool children

Strengths-based assessment

Chapter Objectives

After reading this chapter, you should be able to:

1. Describe the stages and processes involved in planning and implementing an assessment.
2. Discuss the meaning of the guiding practices for context-based assessment.
3. Begin the assessment process by discussing with the parents and others working with the child critical questions that can guide the remainder of the process.
4. Develop the ability to target key components to include in an assessment.
5. Avoid inappropriate assessment practices and adopt appropriate ones for infants, toddlers, and preschool children.

Chapter Overview

In this chapter a context-based structure to approach assessment is presented along with special considerations for the assessment of infants, toddlers, and young children. The structure serves as a framework for planning and implementing assessments of infants and young children with special needs that helps keep the whole child and family context in perspective. It is intended for individual assessments, giving prominence to the questions to which we are seeking answers. The emphasis is placed on the information we need to have rather than which test instruments will be given to the child.

Regardless of the intended purpose of an assessment, a well-designed process incorporates four fluid stages: planning, assessing, interpreting, and evaluating. A context-based assessment approach incorporates specific components during each of these stages of assessment. Figure 3–1 provides a schematic illustration of these fluid stages and components.

FIGURE 3–1 Fluid Stages of the Context-Based Approach to Assessment

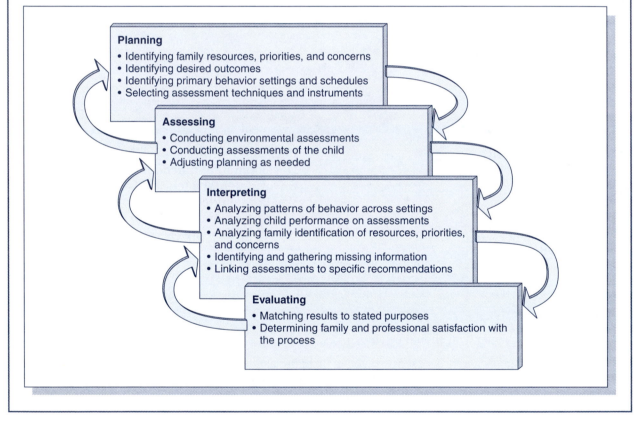

It is a challenge to anyone conducting assessments of young children with special needs to do so without losing sight of the whole child and the context in which that child is developing. The emphasis taken throughout this text is that the child must be viewed within his context, seen as a complex individual set within multiple systems and subsystems. This context-based emphasis has to be integrated into the existing analytical, domain-specific approach often used in child assessment. Although the child's context must remain in our thoughts throughout the assessment process, current practices within the field remain dominated by domain-specific perspectives. After all, it is necessary at some point to break down the task of gathering information into manageable parts. The most critical distinction of the context-based approach to assessment is the emphasis placed at the planning and interpreting stages of the process on contextual factors. During the assessment stage many of the approaches to data gathering might be indistinguishable from traditional child-focused, domain-specific assessment practices. However, in the process of interpreting the meaning of these data we resume a context-based perspective. Indeed, the traditional practice in standardized testing of decontextualizing the individual and the setting run counter to the guiding practices of context-based assessment, which are presented in Table 3–1.

The amount of information that can be gathered about any one child, his family, and the environments in which he functions requires that the task be broken down into manageable parts. Typically, this division is accomplished through the assessment of child functioning by developmental domains. Such divisions can provide teachers with a useful profile of a child's functioning across multiple domains. It also enables them to target specific areas of concern for in-depth study, when a child's difficulties appear to be isolated in one domain. However, such division can falsely imply that the development in each domain occurs in isolation from the others. In reality, impaired functioning often has an interactive effect on a child's ability to develop across domains. We risk making inaccurate interpretations of child functioning if we just rely on domain-specific test scores. Neisworth and Bagnato (1996) hold that "Test data are of little use and seriously prone to error until they are interpreted and translated with reference to the child's functioning across social contexts and then linked to plans of instruction and therapy" (p. 52). From this perspective and a review of numerous published recommended practices regarding assessment of young children, they developed four major standards to guide our practice. These are presented in Table 3–2.

A context-based approach facilitates the review of child functioning across settings while reducing erroneous interpretations of child performance that might occur if assessments were limited to clinical testing. Each stage in the assessment process follows a natural progression of data gathering and should build on the previous stages. The approach taken during the initial planning for an assessment determines the extent to which it will provide context-based information or follow a more traditional clinical model. Careful attention to the planning stage in the assessment process can reduce the production of unneeded or unwanted information, as well as eliminate gaps in information. The remainder of this chapter presents an organizational structure for use during the planning stage of assessments and brief descriptions of the other four stages. Chapters 11 and 12 present case studies using the structure.

TABLE 3–1 Guiding Practices of the Context-Based Assessment Model

Guiding Practice One	Understanding why we are conducting an assessment is essential to obtaining useful results, although we must remain open to unanticipated findings.
Guiding Practice Two	All of the systems in a child's life influence test results. The child who is impoverished, malnourished, drug-addicted from birth, homeless, or whose mother is a single teen deserves consideration given to these circumstances and the differences they are likely to make in a child's performance.
Guiding Practice Three	Comprehensive planning and assessment incorporate information about the child's motivation to learn new tasks across developmental domains and behavioral settings, not just current abilities.
Guiding Practice Four	Understanding how a child spends her day initiates the assessment process from the perspective of the child and family.

TABLE 3–2 Standards to Guide Assessment Practices

Standard	Guidelines
Standard 1: Treatment Utility Assessment must be useful for early intervention and education.	■ Assessments should be planned around specific feasible goals and objectives for the child and family. ■ Assessment information should provide guidance in the selection and use of instructional methods and materials. ■ Assessments should contribute to determining the efficacy of intervention efforts.
Standard 2: Social Validity Assessment must be judged as valuable and acceptable.	■ Assessments must have goals and objectives that are considered worthwhile and appropriate to the child's family. ■ Assessment instruments and approaches must be acceptable to the participants. ■ Assessments must be capable of revealing the social significance of change, not merely documenting improved test scores.
Standard 3: Convergent Assessment Assessment must be based on a wide foundation of information.	■ Assessments should involve several types of assessment materials and approaches. ■ Assessments should include the collection of information from multiple sources, especially family members. ■ Assessments should be conducted over multiple occasions.
Standard 4: Consensual Validity Assessment-based decisions must be reached through team member consensus.	■ Team members should collaborate to achieve consensus on assessment decisions.

Source: Adapted from "Assessment for Early Intervention: Emerging Themes and Practices," by J. T. Neisworth and S. J. Bagnato, in *Early Intervention/Early Childhood Special Education: Recommended Practices* (pp. 23–57), by S. L. Odom and M. E. McLean (Eds.), 1996, Austin, TX: Pro-Ed.

Stage One: Planning

The planning phase of the assessment process consists of four components: (1) establishing basic family context; (2) identifying family resources, priorities, and concerns; (3) identifying the primary questions to be addressed in the assessment; and (4) selecting the assessment techniques and instruments consistent with these questions. Each component is interdependent upon the others. It is likely that in a thorough assessment process, these components, especially identification of desired outcomes and selection of techniques and instruments for use in the assessment process, will require adjustments. As professionals learn more about a particular child through assessment, they become better able to target additional areas of interest and become more specific in their concerns. A form that can be used in this process is presented in Figure 3–2.

Establishing Basic Family Context

To begin the process, we should consolidate basic identifying information about the child and family on a single form. This includes the child's birth date, chronological age, adjusted age if premature, and overall health. A primary contact and her relationship

FIGURE 3–2 Context-Based Assessment Identification Sheet

Child's name _____

Primary adult contact _____

Relationship to child _____

Work phone _____ Home phone _____

Street address _____

City, State, Zip _____

E-mail _____ FAX _____

Today's date   Yr. ___ Mo. ___ Day ___

Birth date   Yr. ___ Mo. ___ Day ___

               Age ___ Yrs. ___ Mo. ___ Days ___

Premature?

Yes ☐   No ☐

Number of weeks ___

Adjusted age   Yrs. ___ Mo. ___ Days ___

Overall health of child:

Mother:

Name _____

Street address _____

City, State, Zip Code _____

Phone _____

Living with child? ☐ Yes ☐ No

Father:

Name _____

Street address _____

City, State, Zip Code _____

Phone _____

Living with child? ☐ Yes ☐ No

Others in home:

Names	Ages	Relationship
_____	____	_____
_____	____	_____
_____	____	_____
_____	____	_____
_____	____	_____

Other relevant information:

(continued)

FIGURE 3–2 Context-Based Assessment Identification Sheet (Continued)

Identifying Family Resouces, Priorities, and Concerns

What are the priorities and primary areas of concern related to the child for the family?	What efforts have already been made to address these concerns?

What resources are available to assist the family in addressing these priorities and concerns?

FIGURE 3–2 Context-Based Assessment Identification Sheet (Continued)

Structuring the Assessment

Primary Questions	Assessment Techniques
1.	1.
2.	2.
3.	3.
4.	4.
5.	5.
6.	6.

with the child is recorded. The parents are identified and all persons living in the same home with the child can be identified by age and relationship. Any other general relevant information can be included here.

Identifying Family Resources, Priorities, and Concerns

The planning process begins with the identification of family concerns related to the child's development. Making this the initial task of the assessment process should assist professionals in developing a comprehensive assessment plan that gives a high priority to matters of greatest concern to the family. Parents can use this time as an opportunity to describe the concern that is triggering the need for an assessment as they see it. When we place an emphasis on defining troubling behaviors, rather than on pursuing pathological labels for the child, we can more easily separate the problem from the child (Stacey, 1994). The child and his family may be experiencing difficulties associated with the problem, but neither the child nor his family should be defined by the problem.

If a five-year-old child has cerebral palsy, professionals are tempted to define that child primarily by her physical condition. Her parents, on the other hand, may view her quite differently. She is their daughter who needs assistance coping with a variety of problems, such as limited voluntary muscle control, persistent primitive reflexes, and difficulties in producing clear speech. The task for us shifts from explaining her limitations with a diagnostic label to finding a means of improving her functioning in light of the physical problems she is facing. Most often families have already been working to address these concerns. Although they might not have had success, they have been trying. It is appropriate to identify and acknowledge what has gone on before this assessment. We can avoid recommending that parents try something that they feel has already been well tested, explore adjustments to earlier efforts, and so forth.

Techniques that we use to identify family resources, priorities, and concerns should be thoughtful and respectful of parental preferences, including the acceptance of a lack of information when parents prefer not to discuss some matters. Interviews typically provide the best means of gathering information from parents in planning an assessment. Information gathered during a parent interview can be used to identify the parents' desired outcomes for the assessment and the child's primary behavior settings and schedule. Chapter 4 provides information about conducting such interviews and using other specific techniques for this initial part of the assessment process.

Structuring the Assessment

The third component in the planning stage is the identification of the primary questions to be addressed in the assessment. In some instances assessments have a specific outcome that is agreed upon by everyone. For example, parents and professionals all might want to determine a child's eligibility for participation in a particular early intervention program. In other cases, desired outcomes of assessment can vary greatly depending on who is being asked. For example, when a child is exhibiting autistic-like behaviors, a parent might want to know how to form a relationship with the child, a psychologist might want to diagnose the child's condition, and a teacher might need specific strategies to work with the child in a group setting. In order to complete this component of the process, assessment teams should address the three basic questions presented in Figure 3–3.

Persons conducting an assessment should ask the family to identify the primary settings in which the child spends her time and approximately how much time is spent in each setting. It may be useful to categorize behavior settings according to home, center, and community settings. However, not every child will have behavior settings in all three categories. An infant's primary behavior settings might just include home settings. A preschool child is more likely to have a balance across all three categories. The use of bedroom, bathroom, and kitchen/dining

FIGURE 3–3 Basic Questions to Begin the Assessment Process

1. What were the initiating factors that led to the request for an assessment (include behavioral descriptions of child in several settings)?
2. Who is seeking information from the assessment (can be several individuals and/or agencies)?
3. What are the desired outcomes of the assessment according to each individual or agency seeking information?

area locations might be more functional for infants. Past, current, and possible future behavior settings can be identified if relevant to the desired outcomes. Examples of typical behavior settings in each of the three categories suitable for many preschool children are presented in Table 3–3.

A medically fragile child's primary behavior settings might better be classified according to hospital, home, and clinic. If breakfast, lunch, dinner, and snack times are all identified and described separately, each would represent a smaller percentage of time than if we categorize them together as mealtime.

In addition to primary behavior settings, there are likely settings that might be of interest or concern to the assessment team that are only occasionally visited by the child. A relative's home and shopping malls are examples of such places. These should be mentioned during the planning stage if they are of sufficient concern to any member of the assessment team, particularly the parents.

Selecting Assessment Techniques and Instruments

Finally, the assessment team identifies how to address each of the primary questions, selecting appropriate procedures and/or instruments. It might be helpful to consider which of the following four components each question targets: **critical events, personal interactions, developmental functioning,** and **environmental analysis.** Some questions will be specific to one behavior setting (e.g., reaction to immersion into water during bath time would be a critical event in the home setting), whereas other questions are relevant across all behavior settings (e.g., developmental functioning, skills in communication, how a child uses unstructured free time).

Finding A Better Way

The case of a four-year-old child with hearing disabilities who lived in a rural community demonstrates the flaws of an approach that omits communication among the professionals. After evaluations by several different professionals who served as the child's multidisciplinary "team," the parents received individual recommendations from each professional. The child's program of intervention became a hodgepodge of services that involved conflicting approaches to communication development. She was put on a bus at 6:00 A.M. and returned home after 5:00 P.M. three days a week in order to receive services from an oral/aural therapy program in the morning, was then transported to a comprehensive development center where signing skills were encouraged, and the family received home-based parent training in the evenings that relied on a total communication program. The parents, eager to give their child the best possible services, followed up on each separate recommendation that had been given to them. They had no one to explain the conflicting nature of the recommendations, discuss the pros and cons of each for their particular child in the context of the other recommendations, or assist them in gaining greater understanding of the basis for the recommendations. Fortunately, this schedule did not go on very long before those involved in providing the services discovered the long day of inconsistent interventions and worked with the parents to develop a more reasonable plan for the child.

TABLE 3–3 Examples of Behavior Settings

Home	Center	Community
Mealtime	Group time	Playing in the neighborhood
Bath	Snack time	Attending church
Bedtime	Free play in centers	Visiting the zoo
Morning routine	Lining up	Waiting in the doctor's office
Taking medicine	Using the bathroom	Playing at the community park
Being read to	Teacher-directed activities	Visiting a friend's house
Watching TV		Visiting play area at fast-food spot

Critical events include routines, personal interactions, and opportunities for play that the child experiences throughout the day. They can also include the child's tolerance for changes in routine, visitors to the classroom, and other events that stray from the standard routines. Examples of typical critical events for a four-year-old who attends preschool include independent play with peers in centers, snack time and mealtime, departure time, and transitions from one activity to another. A preschool teacher concerned about a child's aimless behavior during independent play should target independent play as a critical event. The assessment technique likely to produce the most meaningful information for the teacher would be detailed observations of the child during independent play opportunities at the preschool. Interviews with the parents and other caregivers that include questions about the child's independent play behaviors in other settings (e.g., community park, at home, in the church nursery) could provide additional insights.

Assessment of **personal interactions** can focus on specific interactions (e.g., parent-child interactions, teacher-child interactions, interactions between two specific children) or we can direct assessments toward clusters of interactions (e.g., child-to-child interactions, child-to-adult interactions, child-to-group interactions). When a child is frequently acting out, either at home or in a center-based program, observation of personal interactions becomes a significant element of the assessment process. A child exhibiting scattered developmental skills might also be better understood after assessing his personal interactions. For example, if one adult reports that the child can feed himself, whereas others have been unable to see this behavior in the child, analyses of the interaction patterns might reveal the cause for the discrepancy. The child's tolerance for turn taking or sharing and the frequency that he chooses to play in isolation are other potential targets for assessment under personal interactions.

The team can specify domains of **developmental functioning** that need to be assessed, selecting appropriate techniques based on child characteristics (e.g., age, functioning level). Today there is a wide array of assessment instruments and guides designed to help determine a child's developmental functioning level, including play-based approaches, developmental checklists linked directly to curricular materials, criterion-referenced assessments, work-sampling systems, and standardized tests that render norm-referenced scores. Which is suitable for a specific child and a specific desired outcome of the assessment will vary.

When the assessment team decides which approaches to use they should avoid two common pitfalls. The first pitfall to avoid is using the same developmental scale on every child simply because it is the one preferred by the examiner, rather than because it offers a good match with the primary questions for a particular child. The second is using standardized instruments biased against children who have physical or sensory disabilities, cultural or linguistic differences, or who have experienced childhood trauma, without regard to the impact such disabilities or experiences are likely to have on that child's test performance.

We must particularly try to avoid these pitfalls interacting during the assessment process. For example, the appropriateness of a testing instrument for a child with severe physical limitations must be weighed against an agency's policy to administer the same test to all children enrolled in their program. In general, early interventionists and parents who are seeking specific suggestions for program planning are much better served through the use of play-based approaches or criterion-referenced instruments linked to curriculum building than by the use of standardized instruments that generate inappropriate developmental quotients.

Environmental features can be targeted for assessment independently as well as in conjunction with child behaviors. For example, we would need to assess the preschool environment of a child with visual impairments to determine its consistency with features helpful to the integration of children with visual impairments. We should also consider how well the child is actually coping within her environment (e.g., the tactile sign over her cubby is too high and she is unable to reach it). The team should base their decisions about what to assess on the desired outcomes identified during the first component of the planning process.

Stage Two: Assessing

The actual assessment is the second stage in the process. Environmental assessments and child assessments occur during this stage. As data from assessments become available, adjustments to the assessment plan will also likely be needed. For example, an assessment plan for a four-year-old with poor expressive language and frequent tantrums should include a hearing test to rule out the possibility of a hearing loss as the root of both problems. Otherwise, the assessment is likely to emphasize language development and behavioral patterns across settings and conditions. If we discover that the child does have a moderate hearing loss, we should revise the plan to focus more on the hearing loss and the most beneficial means of enabling the child to communicate. Assessments of effective means for reducing tantrums should now center on reducing frustrations linked to communication problems rather than on how to reduce tantrums through social-emotional considerations.

Parental perceptions of child performance can be most helpful when a professional is analyzing a child's behavior. Parents and extended family members observe children from birth for signs of typical development. They naturally anticipate the emergence of developmental milestones from the first smile forward. It is the interpretation of their observations that can become the bridge of communication between parents and professionals. Since parents' interpretations may be based on previous experience and knowledge of child development patterns from siblings or other relatives (e.g., he talks like his brother did, so I guess he's doing fine), professionals should ask parents to describe their child's specific behaviors to clarify their meaning. Discrepancies between parental report and professional observation should be discussed before assessment results can be considered complete. If a child actually demonstrates inconsistency of performance across settings or people, that can become an interesting component of the assessment.

Stage Three: Interpreting

When the data gathering is completed, those involved in the assessment begin the third stage by interpreting results and formulating recommendations. As assessments are completed, the team analyzes and interprets the results based on the identified desired outcomes. A return to these outcomes as a structuring focus of the final analysis helps us ensure the productivity of our results. When we still have no answers for certain desired out-

Know The Facts

Assessment results do have a significant impact on the lives of young children and their families. Children become eligible for publicly supported services on the basis of assessment results. They can receive special accommodations and modifications in the classroom and on standardized tests based on assessment results. They gain access to many free related services, including expensive augmentative communication systems, physical and occupational therapy, mental health services, transportation, and a number of other services as needed. The assessment process serves as the gatekeeper.

comes, we must either acknowledge our limitations or return to the planning process and continue data gathering. It may be desirable to initiate interventions even when further assessments are needed. For example, parents and physicians might need to continue exploring the causes of a child's problems after the teacher has ample data to initiate an intervention program. Such information might influence the parents' decisions about having additional children, the doctor's methods of treatment, and even what we know about the life expectancy of the child.

Stage Four: Evaluating the Assessment

The assessment process is not complete until we evaluate the effectiveness of the process. This evaluation is achieved by matching the assessment findings with the desired outcomes indicated during the planning stage, and ascertaining the satisfaction both parents and professionals felt about the results. If a preschool teacher, frustrated with a child's acting out behavior, asks for some very specific suggestions as to how to handle the child in her class, and receives diagnostic labels instead, the assessment failed to reach her desired outcomes. If what the teacher gets as the result of her request is a report verifying that the child has a behavior disorder, her dissatisfaction with the assessment results is guaranteed. If the diagnostic information is accompanied with further clarification that the disruptive behaviors are due to unstable home conditions and general suggestions for interventions in the preschool class are provided, she at least knows how to begin addressing the situation.

When the assessment process includes classroom observations, experimentation with various intervention techniques, and parental interviews, the recommendations are likely to be of far greater benefit to the teacher and the child. A final report with detailed intervention strategies based on direct observations in the setting as well as child assessments and study of the home environment matches the desired outcome of the assessment, whereas a diagnostic description of the child's behavior is off the mark. If the parents' top priority is related to the child's feeding and language development, an assessment that emphasized cognitive or motor development would be unsatisfactory regardless of how accurate the results were.

Special Considerations for Assessing Infants, Toddlers, and Preschool Children

The assessment of infants, toddlers, and young children requires age-specific understanding and skill. In fact, we must use practices that contradict what is acceptable and appropriate for assessing children at older ages. The role of the parents in the process of assessing infants is quite different from that of typical school-age child assessments. During the assessment of infants it is often preferable to have one or both parents present. In the case of transdisciplinary assessment, we encourage parents to be actively involved in the assessment process. Assessment of school-age children is most often conducted in a school-based setting without the parents present. Such separation of the parents from the assessment process for school-age children enhances the meaningfulness of the results, whereas it diminishes the accuracy of assessment for preschool-age and younger children. The following sections identify practices to avoid and adopt when assessing infants, toddlers, and young children.

Practices to Avoid

There are common practices in the assessment of children in special education that we must avoid when working with infants and young children.

Greenspan and Meisels (1994) note four specific practices that can compromise our ability to get an accurate picture of an infant's or young child's abilities. These practices to avoid include (1) forcing the separation of children from parents or familiar caregivers, (2) using a strange examiner to test a young child, (3) limiting assessments to easily measured developmental skills, and (4) using formal testing as the cornerstone of our assessment.

Forcing Separations

We should not require young children to separate from their parents or familiar caregivers for an assessment. We want the child to be relaxed and comfortable as we explore the child's abilities and gather information that will help us design effective interventions. There is no value in causing the child distress by forcing this separation. We can gain far greater information about the child when he is not distracted by the absence of a reassuring parent or caregiver. Observation of the child as he interacts with a parent or familiar adult can give us information about the child's abilities and preferences that would likely exceed what we could gain from traditional testing with the parent out of the room.

Strange Examiners

We cannot expect a young child to perform for a strange examiner as she might with someone familiar to her. The child might be anxious about a stranger's intentions, distracted by the novelty of a new face, uncertain why she is expected to cooperate with this unknown adult, or unwilling to try the tasks the examiner has in mind. These are typical reactions that we can expect from young children put in the position of being tested by a stranger. They certainly can influence the child's performance and, therefore, the results of any assessment, regardless of the techniques used. Although a strange examiner using a play-based approach might trigger less anxiety than one expecting to administer a traditional standardized test, the child might still be appropriately hesitant about interacting with this new adult.

Reliance on Easily Measured Skills

The isolation and assessment of a child's performance in developmental skills does not provide a complete picture. Isolated cognitive, motor, or language skills are easy targets for us to use in our assessments. Test items such as stacking blocks, repeating nursery rhymes, or putting together a puzzle are easy to present to a child, simple to score, and produce consistent results. They do not give us much insight as to how a child organizes her world, or how she prepares herself to act and react in the environment. When the assessment is merely a litany of isolated tasks on which the child displays competence or incompetence, we have no description of how or if these skills are put to use in the context of the home, preschool or child care settings, or the playground at McDonald's. We might know that a child has an expressive vocabulary of fifteen words, and pointed correctly to pictures representing words up to the twenty-four-month level for receptive vocabulary. We do not know if that child communicates effectively with his peers, manages the tasks associated with friendship well, uses his language skills in problem solving, or if he enjoys the pleasures of imaginary play through the creation of "scripts" that he then orchestrates and performs. There is much more to know that is not so easily standardized into tidy kits and lists of tasks divided by age levels.

Formal Testing as the Cornerstone

The focal point of an assessment must not be the score a child makes on formal tests. There is a tendency to treat test scores as having more significance than other sources of data, such as observations, parent and caregiver reports, or work-sampling approaches to assessment, when the latter may be more meaningful than the former. Formal tests can be included in the assessment process, but should not be the pivotal data source upon which we make major decisions. Formal tests offer single points of data that are static in their very nature. They offer a snapshot, not a video of the child. Although they are quicker and simpler than other forms of assessment and are held in higher esteem by many professionals, formal tests do not convey some higher truth about a child than that which can be discovered through thoughtful observation, interactive play, and functional analysis of child behaviors through the manipulation of contextual variables.

Practices to Adopt

In addition to the practices that we must avoid, there are other practices that we should follow. Greenspan and Meisels (1994) have recommended the adoption of eight principles of assessment that represent a "new vision" of developmental assessments. With these principles, presented in Figure 3–4, Greenspan and Meisels present a challenge to the field to reconsider many of its assessment practices. Their challenge targets some of the most fundamental elements of traditional assessment. These recommendations are the foundation for the five sections that follow.

Assessment Focuses on Functional Abilities through an Integrated Model of Infant and Child Development

The adoption of an integrated model of infant and child development represents a radical departure from the established domain-specific assessments prevalent in the field of early childhood special education for many years. We are trained in professions that reflect to a certain extent domain-specific arenas, such as speech and language pathology, physical therapy, or special education that emphasizes

FIGURE 3–4 Eight Principles of Vision to Guide Our Assessment Practices

- Adoption of an integrated model of infant and child development;
- Pursuit of multiple sources of data and assessment techniques;
- Involvement of parents from the preliminary data gathering and planning throughout the assessment process;
- Knowledge of child development;
- Emphasis on the child's functional capacities and how he organizes his experiences, reflecting an integration of emotional and cognitive abilities;
- Recognition of abilities and strengths of the child as well as needs;
- Collaboration that includes family members and all assessors; and
- Acknowledgment that assessment is an ongoing process that continues to occur throughout intervention.

Source: From "Toward a New Vision for the Developmental Assessment of Infants and Young Children," by S. I. Greenspan and S. Meisels, 1994, *Zero to Three, 14,* pp. 1–8.

cognitive and social development. This pattern of specialization has long been the standard of practice as we test by developmental areas, write intervention plans by developmental areas, and contribute our own expertise to multidisciplinary teams. However, this compartmentalization of infant and child behaviors is not really possible. Our attempts to separate language development from cognitive development from motor development from socioemotional development are futile. The overlapping, dependent nature of all areas of development is the reality. One of the advantages to a transdisciplinary model of assessment is the opportunity it gives early interventionists to move toward an integrated model of development, while tapping traditional discipline-specific expertise. The organization of this text is based upon the premise that an integrated model of infant and child development is preferable as we strive to get to know children through the process of assessment.

We can use the orientation of an integrated model of development to consider a child's functional behaviors rather than being restricted to isolated domain-specific skills. We can consider how a child communicates with his peers and how these means of communication influence his social relationships. We can look at how the child uses language to solve problems, think ahead, or convince a friend to play with him. We do not have to stop at the measurement of mean length of utterances, the ability of a child to repeat back to us, or the child's ability to recognize words and point to the matching picture. The child's functional use of language as a means to communicate, think, and relate to others is far more interesting and worth knowing.

Assessment Is Ongoing, Based on Multiple Sources of Data, and Varied in Technique

We cannot rely on one test, one observation, one interview, or one teacher's opinion to develop a complete understanding of a child. We need to have information that includes descriptions of (1) the child's behaviors across a range of settings; (2) the child's interactions with parents, siblings, peers, and other adults; (3) the child's performance in comparison to other children; and (4) the child's persistence and motivation to engage in play and other meaningful activities. In order to acquire this much information about a single child, we must tap all the resources available to us through parent and caregiver inter-

views, observations across time and settings, systematic monitoring of child performance over time, and standardized tests, as needed. The intention of this recommendation is not to increase standardized testing; rather, it is to end the overreliance on a single source of data that is based on a single sample of a child's behavior to give us an understanding of a child.

Assessment Involves Parents throughout the Assessment Process

Parents have the biggest stake in the outcomes of our assessments and the resulting recommendations for intervention that may follow. Their participation throughout the process, from the initial stage of planning through the evaluation of the process, gives our work greater significance to them as the ultimate decision-makers for the child. We can look to parents as a source of accurate information about their child's behavior. For example, a six-month-old who routinely babbles and enjoys imitating sounds with her parents may not utter a sound in an unfamiliar setting or while actively engaged in visual and motor tasks during a cognitive assessment. The examiner might note such behavior and express concern about the child's hearing and/or language development to the parents. If the parents point out that this silence is atypical, such reports can outweigh the limited time upon which the concern is based. Parental reporting and their observations in natural settings can provide a more accurate picture of the child's language abilities than did her performance during one forty-five-minute examination period. There is no need to follow up here with language and hearing assessments that would convey to the parents that the forty-five-minute sample of child behavior has more meaning than their observations of their own child.

Cultural sensitivity is also vital to any efforts to assess a young child. Whether the child and family is from a dramatically different culture from that of the persons responsible for the assessment, or those differences are relatively minor, we need to acknowledge the powerful influence culture and language have on the developing child (Lynch & Hanson, 1996). The patterns of language usage in the home can vary across ethnic groups within the same community (Heath, 1983). In some instances, a pattern or oral tradition in storytelling is evident. This contrasts with the standard in typical white middle-class homes, where question-and-answer patterns are prevalent (e.g., what color is your shirt, how many cookies did you eat, what is the girl in the story going to do next). Although one pattern is more closely linked to the standards and expectations that the children will encounter in school, one cannot be presumed to be superior to the other. They are different, and will produce different language skills in the young children who experience them. Testing will likely reflect these differences, especially if the testing is based primarily on one of the patterns and excludes skills developed through the alternative pattern.

Assessment Requires Knowledge of Child Development

Professionals need a thorough knowledge of infant and child development before they begin conducting assessments at this age level. Regardless of the training one has in assessment practices and competence in the assessment of school-age children, without an understanding of infants and young children, that expert will be ineffective. Families and other professionals rely on the professional's knowledge and understanding of infants and young children to prevent the misinterpretation of behaviors. We can use this knowledge to prevent others who may be less familiar with young children from overemphasizing any one observation or test result.

Typical characteristics of infants, toddlers, and preschool children can influence the quality and accuracy of assessment results. Their normal activity level and distractibility can render any standardized test subject to interpretation. Children in this age span have little control over the variable states in and out of which they fluctuate. The child may be alert and ready to go at the outset of an assessment, but move into the tired and fussy state before we finish. The baby's state must be given consideration because moving forward with an assessment when the baby's state is no longer alert and ready to engage is futile. Even though we may have succeeded in completing the assessment, we can have no confidence in the accuracy of the results. Similarly, the attention span of infants and young children will fluctuate. In some instances, the child may wish to continue engaging with a toy when we want to direct his attention to another task. Our insistence on his shifting attention from the preferred toy to something new can backfire, and again, leave us wondering how accurate our results are. Sometime between six and nine months of age, infants are likely to develop a healthy wariness of strangers. This wariness means that we are likely to obtain more accurate results with a parent present, even participating in an assessment, than we are if we forced the separation and waited for the child to calm himself. Inconsistent performance in unfamiliar environments is another influencing factor for young children.

A preschool child may not easily control his desire to be up and moving when we ask him to sit with us to take a test. His inability to sit still for us on that occasion does not mean that the child is always (or even often) unable to sit still and engage in the tasks we had in mind. We should not be tempted to draw incorrect conclusions about the child's overall ability to sit and attend because the child was not on our schedule.

When a toddler is fussy, we cannot discuss with her the irrationality of her mood. Rather, it is the adults' responsibility to explore all the possible causes of the fussiness, and finally resign ourselves to let her work through the mood as she will. If the fussiness coincides with our scheduled assessment, it does not mean that the child is always fussy, or incompetent on the tasks we presented to her that she refused to do, or that she does not like the activities we presented to her. It simply means that she is a toddler, and quite naturally has variable mood states that she has less control over than we hope she will have as an adult, or even as a six-year-old.

Assessment Entails Identification of Abilities and Strengths as Well as Needs

The same information about a child can be conveyed through positive descriptions that describe what skills the child has mastered or negatively by making chronological age comparisons and listing the age-appropriate skills that the child is missing. Figure 3–5 shows two differing descriptions of the same child. The first statement has a tone of negativity, age comparisons, and defining labels. We really do not need to be told that a four-year-old has an age equivalency of twelve to fifteen months. We understand that a four-year-old with a speaking vocabulary of seven words is delayed and well behind his age mates in language development. The second statement provides the same information, but with a positive tone. What skills Seth does have are effectively combined to create for him a functional means of expressive communication.

FIGURE 3–5 Positive and Negative Descriptions of the Same Child

Negative Description	Strengths-Based Description
Seth is a four-year-old with a severe expressive communication disorder. He is unable to speak in complete sentences, or even put together two-word phrases. His expressive vocabulary consists of fewer than ten words that can be understood consistently. Essentially, he has no effective means of expressive communication other than idiosyncratic sounds and gestures. Developmentally, his expressive communication skills are at the twelve- to fifteen-month level.	Seth has a speaking vocabulary of seven words. He uses sounds and gestures to communicate and becomes frustrated when his attempts at communication are not understood. As a four-year-old, Seth needs to have a functional means of communication that can be used at home or in his preschool setting. He can consistently point to objects and pictures of some objects when their names are called. This skill can be used to establish an alternative means of expressive communication for Seth. The pointing to selected objects and pictures as a means of expressive communication should be integrated into all of Seth's settings as much as possible.

The intention is not to deny or cover up the nature or severity of a child's disabilities. Rather, it is to see the child, within his own context, as having some skills. These skills, regardless of how far below his chronological age by normal standards, do represent a point from which to build for him. The three-year-old who has recently pulled-to-standing for the first time is ready to begin cruising around the room and might be walking before we know it. He also happens to be approximately two years delayed in achieving this skill. The fact that his gross motor development is delayed is obvious, but has little meaning for us as we plan an intervention based on what he can do rather than what he cannot do.

Closing Thoughts

This chapter presented the context-based approach to assessment and special considerations for the assessment of young children. The context-based structure is designed to be as consistent as possible with the special considerations for assessment of young children. The process is both fluid and circular in nature.

The use of a context-based structure can result in outcomes and findings far different from the traditional assessment reports that emphasize test scores and eliminate as much context as possible from interpretations of a child's behavior. The beginning questions provide the outline for summarizing findings and recommendations. If answers to these questions still remain, then the assessment process must continue. However, it may be important to begin or continue services even when all the answers cannot be determined.

▪▪ For Your Consideration

1. When and how should parents be involved in the assessment process?

2. What does it mean to use a strengths-based orientation to summarizing assessment results?

3. If you were responsible for structuring initial child assessments for children between the ages of two and one-half and five as part of a Child Find system, what policies and procedures would you adopt?

4. What part should environmental analysis play in the assessment process for preschool-age children?

CYBERSOURCES

Check out the following Web sites for more information related to the ideas presented in this chapter.

National Association of School Psychologists

http://www.nasponline.org/index2.html

Division for Early Childhood Education, Council for Exceptional Children

http://www.dec-sped.org/

National Association for the Education of Young Children

http://www.naeyc.org/

Zero to Three (national clinical infant programs)

http://www.zerotothree.org/

Connect for Kids

http://www.connectforkids.org/

 For additional resources on assessment, visit us on-line at www.earlychilded.delmar.com

CHAPTER 4

Assessment through Collaboration with Families

Chapter Objectives

After reading this chapter, you should be able to:

1. Describe a strengths-based approach to gathering information about family resources, priorities, and concerns.
2. Understand a variety of techniques that can be used to gather information from families, including focused interviews.
3. Identify appropriate assessment instruments available to assist in gathering information from parents about resources, priorities, and concerns.
4. Explore the issues involved in cross-cultural parent-to-professional relationships through culture-identity models.

Chapter Overview

The family-focused standard of practice in early intervention is now an unequivocal expectation. Federal legislation, rules and regulations, and state and local implementation policies all include such a standard. Further, there is an expectation that assessments be conducted in a manner that is sensitive to cultural differences of families. Approaches to achieving these standards have evolved over the past fifteen years. Long before early interventionists became interested in family assessment, social workers and psychologists had been studying families and family dynamics, and assessing and treating families with dysfunctional patterns of interaction.

When the standard requiring family involvement in assessments was first introduced, it was apparent that the existing family assessment instruments used in family therapy were not well suited for this new arena of family assessment. Therefore, the need for early interventionists to comply with the law triggered the development and marketing of a flurry of family assessment tools designed to compile family strengths and needs. These tools typically took the form of parent questionnaires covering needs, sources of support, the nature of relationships between family members, and other personal matters. However, not all of the items on these instruments were closely linked to the intervention programs that were available to children and their families. They often included items outside the traditional realm of early intervention, such as questions regarding the quality of the relationship between the parents. Parents found it difficult to articulate what their "strengths" and "needs" were, although they were interested in being heard and given a bigger part in early intervention planning. Language in the federal legislation changed from strengths and needs to resources, priorities, and concerns. Concurrently, professionals began to question the wisdom of using assessment tools that might push families to reveal more than they needed to share with early interventionists (Slentz & Bricker, 1992).

After more than a decade of struggling to implement this standard, professionals now appreciate that it has more to do with attitude and relationships with parents, and awareness and sensitivity to cultural differences than to the use of multiple family assessment tools. Family assessments, in a broader sense, can and should be left in the hands of professionals trained in family counseling.

Since data gathering by early interventionists typically occurs at the beginning point in a parent-professional relationship, the process can provide the opportunity to define the relationship as collaborative rather than hierarchical in nature. The opportunity for collaboration exists at two levels. The first is in basic planning and implementation of the assessments of the child. The second is in gathering appropriate and relevant information about the family, particularly resources, priorities, and concerns as related to the child and her development. This chapter includes a brief review of the rationale for family collaboration in assessment; the ways parents can contribute to child assessments; the techniques useful to the process of identification of family resources, priorities, and concerns; and the societal challenges to family-professional collaboration.

Rationale for Family Collaboration in Assessment

Research on the effectiveness of early intervention has consistently led to results that document the importance of environmental influences on child development. Programs that restrict their efforts to a child-focused perspective, failing to address the concerns of the family or adjusting to varying conditions present in a child's home, will also be limited in their long-term impact. Early intervention programs that are primarily child-focused have severely limited success in comparison to those operating with family-focused models (Silber, 1989). The shift in programming from child-focused to family-focused intervention has been evident in the federally funded Head Start programs for many years. The importance of using a family-focused intervention strategy is now stressed in the federal laws that support early intervention services for young children with special needs. Since programming and intervention have shifted from child-focused to family-focused, then it follows that we need to adopt practices that foster a collaborative partnership with parents, and employ a system to identify family resources, priorities, and concerns that can be of some benefit to the family.

As discussed in chapter 1, the child is part of the family system. The child's participation in early intervention will have effects on other members of the family. The provision of services might reduce the anxiety and worry a parent feels, increase the stress placed on family transportation resources and schedules, or trigger any combination of helpful and stressful effects. One family member might object to the initiation of intervention services, while others dispute what the nature of the services should be like. For some, the initiation of intervention services represents the first acknowledgment that their child has a disability, whereas others might have been fighting to get services for their child for several years. The parents of children with disabilities will develop attitudes, values, and behaviors that are constructed from their personal life experiences. Likewise, professionals will establish their own attitudes, values, and behaviors that reflect their personal life experiences.

The accuracy of information regarding child development that is supplied by parents is highly consistent with formal assessments (Diamond & Squires, 1993). Although professionals come equipped with a variety of standardized measures, the parents spend far more time across far more settings with the child than does any professional. The parents put the child to bed, are there when the child awakens, feed the child, play with the child, and take the child on outings over days, weeks, months, and years. They will always know their child in a way that is beyond the capacity of a professional to know that child. However, there will inevitably be discrepancies in how the parents view the child and assessment results. The explanations for these discrepancies may be as simple as the child has not yet generalized a skill across multiple settings or people. It may be far more complex, but the parents' perspective must be acknowledged and honored, rather than assumed to be inaccurate.

Any techniques we use in the process of gathering information from the family should identify, build on, and reinforce existing and potential family strengths and resources. Practices that foster enablement and empowerment of families serve the

child and the family better than traditional help-giving models that might actually diminish a family's ability to solve problems and secure resources (Dunst, Trivette, & Deal, 1994).

A strengths-based model of family-centered assessment and intervention is based upon five basic considerations (Dunst, Trivette, & Mott, 1994). First is the recognition that all families have unique strengths that reflect their own beliefs, cultural background, ethnicity, and socioeconomic background. Second is the consideration that a failure to demonstrate competence by a family or member of a family is not an indicator of deficits within a person or family; rather, it can be attributed to a lack of opportunity to display competence. Enabling experiences are those experiences that create the opportunities for competence to be displayed. The third consideration is use of an approach to working with families that is based on the aspects of their functioning rather than targeting areas for "fixing." Fourth, models of promotion and enhancement should replace either treatment or prevention models. The goal shifts to the enhancement of human development rather than prevention or treatment of pathology. The fifth consideration is that it is crucial that the family members feel a sense of responsibility for any behavior change that leads to improved management of their affairs. When a person has such a sense of control, he or she is empowered.

A similar view is expressed by Lambie and Daniels-Mohring (1993) when they refer to approaching family members with the belief that they are resourceful. When professionals view the family as resourceful, they recognize that the need for additional resources is secondary and temporary. A resource model of family functioning assumes that families interact with history, culture, ethnicity, social class, politics, interpersonal relationships, individual quirks, and more in a process of continually creating their norms. School professionals can frame their view of the family with this in mind and recognize the impact of context. Seeing context as significant, the professional is better able to make sense of family observations.

Early interventionists can have a greater impact by assisting parents in the management of their child's needs, than by taking charge of the child's needs. Many parents will have the resources and skills needed to assume the responsibility of caring for their child. However, for those who are facing social or economic challenges that make the tasks more daunting, family enablement is vital to providing effective early intervention.

Families are the decision-makers, and are, therefore, equal partners with professionals in the early intervention process. However, it is not likely that a young teen that grew up facing poverty, social isolation, abuse or neglect, and no structure in her home will automatically be transformed into a wise and nurturing parent by becoming a mother. The goal of family collaboration is to render services that assist families in becoming as strong and secure as possible, rather than to meet the needs of children while they are temporarily eligible for our programs. We must remember that most often the ongoing consistent influence in a child's life is her family. This will remain true regardless of whether her family is faced with challenges as common as divorce, as devastating as homelessness or chronic drug abuse by a parent, or as sensitive as adjusting to a new cultural and linguistic environment.

Family Collaboration in Child Assessments

Often the beginnings of a relationship can set the tone for years to come. Since assessment of the child is typically one of the first tasks to be accomplished when that child is referred for early intervention, the process should incorporate the opportunity to establish a collaborative partnership with the parents. If professionals take charge during the child's assessment with little or no input from the family, they have already established unequal roles for themselves and the parents. Rather, the process should be characterized by giving much attention to the parents—what questions they want answered, what they have to say about their child's development, and what role they hope the professionals can play in helping them with their child. As Dale (1996) points out, partnerships can have an internal power balance, predisposing members in the relationship to varying degrees of equality and predefined role relationships. It is too comfortable for professionals to slip into authority roles in their working relationships with parents. Likewise, parents, already familiar with the typical professional-to-client relationship, expect the professional to be in control. We must learn to structure our interactions with parents and other family members in a way that neither shatters their confidence in us, nor undermines an equitably negotiated partnership.

Parents can provide rich descriptions of how children influence their daily routines. These descriptions can then become the basis for forming a picture of the child (Bernheimer, Gallimore, & Kaufman, 1993; Bernheimer & Keogh, 1995). Although it is possible that interventionists will see the child differently from the parents, knowing how the parents view the child within the context of the daily routine is equally important and valid. Bernheimer and colleagues suggest that parental views of child characteristics that can influence family functioning should be explored, including temperament, behavior, readability, caretaking demands, feeding and sleeping behaviors, and self-help skills. Does the child's temperament influence when and how the mother shops for groceries, or visits with friends who also have young children? Does feeding the child require an unusual amount of time or special equipment? Is the child starting to gain independence in any areas of self-help? The answers to these and many other questions will naturally emerge when family members begin describing daily routines. The early interventionist can ask for further specificity about particular developmental skills as the conversation unfolds. For example, the mother of a two-year-old might mention that the child has become very opinionated about what she wants to wear. This could open the door for discussion of how the child communicates these preferences—are words used, gestures, pulling things out of her drawers, screaming, lack of cooperation in dressing, or some other means that the parent is able to translate. This information could then lead to a discussion of the child's communication skills across multiple other points in the daily routine. Child traits that are closely linked to family functioning, such as the child's responsiveness to caregivers, temperament, frequent behavior patterns, caregiving demands, consolability, and motivation can also be the target of an observation, if they are traits of particular concern to the parents.

When professionals plan to conduct child observations as a part of their assessment, parents can provide a wealth of information to increase the amount of information that can be obtained. Guiding questions that can be used with parents and family members, teachers and significant others, and in preliminary child observations include questions regarding what the child enjoys, whether the child tends to engage in easy or difficult tasks, if a physical or sensory disability seems to limit the child's behaviors, and so forth. Parents can give descriptions of the child's typical reactions to various play situations, stimulus materials, and settings that far expand the professional's opportunities to observe the child across multiple conditions.

When professionals also need more structured approaches to assessment they can still use the parents as informants. Historically and currently, many standardized assessment instruments for use with young children are based on parental report. Selected examples are presented in Table 4–1.

Findings from these assessments should be combined with observations and informal parent reports to create the most complete picture of the child possible. The subjective meaning of words we might use with parents or other professionals when asking them to categorize a child's behavior such as *frequently* or *often* can confuse our findings. Misbehavior might be defined quite loosely by one parent and far more stringently by the other. What might seem to be frequent tantrums to one parent is a fairly normal level for another. The child's behavior is identical, but the adult descriptions of it far different. These points of confusion in meaning can be reduced when parents have the opportunity to describe the child's behaviors, not simply react to questionnaires.

Family Constructs

Although it is beyond the task of early interventionists to assess comprehensive family functioning, it is helpful to have a basic understanding of critical family constructs as we develop working relationships with families. These constructs include communication, conflict, problem solving, bonding/cohesion, affect and emotion, intimacy, differentiation and individuation, triangulation, and stress (Bray, 1995). Definitions of these constructs are listed in Table 4–2.

There are families facing multiple challenges that can interfere with the parents' ability to work as partners with early interventionists. A comprehensive assessment of family functioning is not likely to make those challenges disappear. Rather, we must concentrate on those matters linked to our ability to offer the child an effective program and refer the family to more suitable sources of support for other needs and concerns.

A context-based perspective can give us additional insights into some of the issues families with young children with special needs may be facing as

we establish collaborative relationships with them. Potential issues for families with children who have special needs occur at micro-system, meso-system, and exo-system levels. The micro-system-level concerns are related to how well parents cope with their child with disabilities, the potential emotional responses (e.g., depression, guilt, or blame) that may influence overidentification with the child or complete disengagement, parental expectations of siblings, and sibling reactions to the special needs child. The meso-system incorporates the roles and emotional reactions of extended family members, friends and neighbors, and work and recreation associates, interactions with medical and health care workers, contact with other parents, and other available resources within the local community. Exo-systems that influence family functioning include health care systems, social welfare, education, and mass media, which affect public attitudes toward disabled populations. At the level of macro-systems, ethnic/cultural, religious, and socioeconomic factors exert control over how a family interacts with service delivery systems, and economic and political elements dictate what resources are available to families of children with disabilities.

The adoption of a social constructivist perspective in collaboration with families makes the family members' perspectives of themselves significant. Parents respond to their children (with or without disabilities) based on their personal beliefs, goals, and values as derived from their own life experiences. In an effort to understand the family within a sociopolitical and cultural context, Mailick and Vigilante (1997) have conceptualized a family assessment wheel for use in family therapy. The assessment wheel is based upon a social constructivist framework, which puts the family members' views of their lives at the hub of the wheel.

At the outermost portion of the wheel are five concentric circles that represent elements affecting virtually all families. The outside circle represents culture as it has an "overarching influence on all aspects of family, community, and societal life" (p. 363). It is followed by a circle representing social pathology and risk factors. Factors such as racism, poverty, and societal attitudes regarding sexual preferences will have varying influences on families. Negative societal conditions can lead to either group cohesiveness and stability or disorganization pathology. The third circle is that of cohort experiences. Mailick and Vigilante note, "family members develop attitudes,

TABLE 4–1 Selected Standardized Assessment Instruments Based on Parent or Caregiver Report

Instrument	Ages	Domains	Description
Ages and Stages Questionnaire (ASQ), 1995	4 to 48 months	Communication Gross motor Fine motor Problem solving Personal-social	Parent questionnaires for use at specific ages to monitor the infant's development across these domains; each questionnaire contains 30 simple questions with response options of "yes," "sometimes," "not yet" and space for general parent concerns; scores in each domain can be compared to a recommended cutoff score for referral for in-depth evaluation; Spanish version is available
Developmental Observation Checklist System (DOCS), 1994	0 to 6 years	Language Cognition Social Motor Overall Adjustment Behavior Parent stress	Multidimensional screening system including language, social ability, parental stress, parent support, fine/gross motor, child adaptability, cognitive, overall development, play, parent-child interaction, and environmental impact; parents complete three checklists: (1) developmental checklist that covers motor, social, language, and cognitive development with "yes" or "no" responses; (2) adjustment behavior checklist with 25 items rated from "very much like" to "not at all like" on 4-point scale; and (3) parental stress and support checklist with 40 items rated "highly agree" to "do not agree" on 4-point scale; scoring includes standard scores and percentile ranks for all checklists
Social-Emotional Early Childhood Scales (SEEC), 1998	0 to 5 years 11 months	Social-emotional	Identifies strengths and weaknesses in interpersonal relationships, play and leisure time, and coping skills; parents are interviewed regarding child's performance on age-appropriate items and each is scored as "usually performs," "sometimes or partially performs," "never performs," "no opportunity," or "don't know"; scores include standard scores, percentile rank, and stanine for the three scales and an overall composite
Receptive-Expressive Emergent Language Test-2 (REEL-2), 1991	0 to 3 years	Receptive and expressive language	A 132-item checklist that uses observational information reported by parents; items organized in age levels and scored a plus for typical behavior, a minus for behavior that has never been observed, and a plus-minus for emerging or partly exhibited items; scores include a "receptive," "expressive," and "combined language age" and a "receptive," "expressive," and "language quotient"

59

TABLE 4–2 Family Constructs

Construct	Meaning
Communication	The verbal and nonverbal exchange of information, including explaining and clarifying wants, needs, and desires; attending to others and responding appropriately; seeking the views of others; providing appropriate attention to all family members; developing shared and common meanings through clear and direct verbal exchanges
Conflict	Mild disagreement and criticisms to verbal and physical assaults; can increase in intensity when all parties reciprocate negative interactions, but can decrease when one or all parties work to decrease the conflict; can be seen in cyclical pattern: perceived critical statement triggers defensive response, which is perceived as critical response triggering another defensive response; cycle can be altered when response to a perceived criticism is supportive or empathic, triggering a noncritical, neutral or supportive statement in return
Problem solving	Ability to identify and discuss issues, plan alternative resolutions to problems; related to good skills in communication and negotiation
Bonding/Cohesion	Extent to which family members consider themselves close or distant from one another; continuum ranges from overinvolvement (enmeshed) to disengaged (disconnected); includes family support and interest in shared activities and friends
Affect and emotion	Expression of affection and response to affection between family members; mood or emotional tone of the family
Intimacy	Dyadic process of voluntary closeness while maintaining distinct boundaries of self; includes trust, love-fondness, self-disclosure, and commitment; isolation represents opposite end of continuum
Differentiation and individuation	Ability to function autonomously without an undue feeling of responsibility or limitation from significant others; ability to separate and control emotional reactions from cognitive capacities; unresolved emotional attachments associated with emotional fusion at other end of continuum, which is associated with tendency to take too much responsibility for others while avoiding responsibility for self
Triangulation	Two people use a third person in attempts to cope with anxiety and emotional fusion through diversion, collusion, or scapegoating; reduces stress of first two people but usually increases stress of third person; associated with poor problem-solving skills
Stress	Process and product of family interactions and context in which family is living; triggered by undesirable negative life events and routines of daily living; can be caused by family processes associated with conflict and hostility; leads to biopsychosocial responses of individual family members

Source: Adapted from Bray, J. H. (1995). Family assessment: Current issues in evaluating families. *Family Relations, 44,* p. 469–477.

values, and behaviors relative to the time and space experiences of the age in which they live" (p. 363). Family developmental needs is the fourth concentric circle. This circle could be of particular importance to families with young children with disabilities. The inside circle represents the family situation and why services are being sought. Between these circles and the family at the hub are five spokes that represent domains of individual family experiences, including relevant family events, family organization, communication patterns, access to institutional resources, and specific aspects of culture and values.

The availability of sources of support provides a key to family functioning. The ability of a family to continue functioning effectively regardless of the number of stress factors present, the family composition, and the severity of a child's disability is based on the available social support systems. Three components of social networks that influence their effectiveness are (1) network size, (2) network density, and (3) boundary density (Kazak & Marvin, 1984). Network size pertains to the number of different types of support available (e.g., spiritual, medical, psychological). Network density refers to the extent members of a support network are known to each other. Boundary density is a measure of the number of network members shared by both parents. Reciprocity and dimensionality are two additional network characteristics that may be of interest to persons assisting families in the identification of strengths and needs (Kazak & Wilcox, 1984). Network reciprocity is related to the equal exchange of support by network members. For example, taking turns baby-sitting with a friend might produce a significant imbalance if one of the children is harder to care for than the other. Dimensionality addresses the number of functions provided through each relationship. An intimate relationship, such as that of a spouse, should provide support to offset needs across multiple dimensions. Families can also seek external resource networks to find supportive links they need outside their social network. Social support systems can vary in regard to the levels of satisfaction family members derive from them and the frequency of contacts made within the network. The pursuit of early intervention for a young child with developmental delays would be such action. Participation in parent support groups and disability advocacy councils are also external resources that can provide meaningful support structures to families.

Identifying Family Resources, Priorities, and Concerns

The determination of what is specifically included in the process of identifying family resources, priorities, and concerns should be done on an individual basis with the focus remaining on the child. The underlying purpose is to identify family strengths, resources, needs, and concerns relevant to the family's ability to enhance the child's development. Slentz and Bricker (1992) suggest that we consider the assessment process as family-guided rather than family-focused, noting that the focus is actually on the child, not the family. Family issues and outcomes will arise naturally as a part of the IFSP process rather than being targeted directly as an intervention priority.

Professionals have a responsibility to gather relevant data in a nonintrusive manner. Asking families about personal issues and feelings simply because those topics are part of a questionnaire that we are using, when the information will never be put to any real use, is unnecessary, and can be harmful to the family and our relationship with them. Professionals soliciting information from parents should always begin with an explanation of why the information is needed and how it will be used. Adherence to this procedure can significantly reduce the intrusive questions we may think we need to ask, but are unable to justify even to ourselves. Additionally, we must always assure parents of their right not to provide information that they consider intrusive. Our goal should be to establish a direct link between the data we obtain from the family and the intervention strategies that we will use for the child.

Information about a family's resources, priorities, and concerns can best be obtained initially through a brief informal interview and needs assessment. As relationships between family members and interventionists mature, the process of data gathering from the family should become an ongoing process, much like assessment of the child is an ongoing process. We can use interviews to determine the perception parents have about specific events and to identify their priorities for services. Simply asking the parents to describe what a typical day is like for their family from waking until bedtime is an effective beginning. The stories that can emerge from this simple starting point can lead to discussion of family problem solving and compromise when the car breaks down, or a child is sick. Thus, it can lead to the discovery of much more useful data that can be linked to the family's lives than direct intrusive questions. Ten accommodation domains (Keogh, Bernheimer, Gallimore, & Weisner, 1998) can be addressed through the exploration of daily routines with families. These are presented in Table 4–3.

Although many parents seem to prefer a loosely structured interview process to identify family issues (Summers et al., 1990), some might prefer to complete questionnaires or checklists or have a structured interview designed to cover set topics (Davis & Gettinger, 1995). Davis and Gettinger found that some parents prefer the structured interview because it might decrease the chance that something important would be overlooked. Parents preferring the informal interview process expressed appreciation for the opportunity to have a free exchange of ideas and information centered around their child without the lengthy process a structured interview can involve. Parents who preferred to complete questionnaires outside of an interview format appreciated the opportunity to be reflective, progressing at their own pace, providing only that information which they consid-

ered relevant, and found it the most efficient use of their time. Matching parental preference for assessment to the procedures followed is a simple accommodation early interventionists can make rather than using the same approach for every family. Davis and Gettinger report that a majority of parents prefer an unstructured interview format to that of written questionnaires or structured interviews, including some who initially indicated an alternative preference.

The focused interview format described by Winton (1988) and Winton and Bailey (1988) provides a moderately structured interview procedure. The interview is organized into a five-phase structure, and takes place after other assessment procedures have been completed. The phases are summarized in Table 4–4. The ultimate goal of the focused interview is to generate family outcome statements that are the result of collaborative efforts between the interventionist and the family.

Available questionnaires and checklists include both standardized tools and less formal self-evaluative checklists and scales. Some instruments are specifi-

TABLE 4–3 Accommodation Domains Addressed through Daily Routines of Families

Domain	Examples
■ Family subsistence	Who works Hours of work
■ Services	Transportation sources Availability and frequency of services
■ Home/neighborhood safety and convenience	Quality and accessibility of play areas Home security Safety from community or family violence
■ Domestic workload	Who is available and how much needs to be done
■ Child care tasks	Any unusual demands in child care
■ Child peer groups	Availability of playmates
■ Marital roles	Decision making Distribution of child care and household chores
■ Instrumental/emotional support	Informal social networks Church
■ Father/spouse role	Involvement with child Emotional support for mother
■ Parent information	Sources of information about disability and community resources

Source: Adapted from Keogh, B. K., Bernheimer, L., Gallimore, R. G., and Weisner, T. S. (1998). Child and family outcomes over time: A longitudinal perspective on developmental delays. In M. Lewis & C. Feiring (Eds.). *Families, Risk, and Competence* (pp. 269–288). Mahwah, NJ: Erlbaum.

TABLE 4–4 Focused Interview Format

Phase	Description
Preliminary	The interviewer talks with the parents to identify high-priority needs and any difficulties in parent-child interactions, and to specify child characteristics that have potential impact on the family.
Introduction	The interviewer should reduce the parents' anxiety and establish an appropriate listening environment. The interviewer should confirm the purpose and length of the interview, and discuss matters of confidentiality.
Inventory	Most of the talking should be done by the parents. The interviewer can begin the conversation with an opening statement or question, allowing the parents to direct the conversation to their concerns.
Summary	The interviewer confirms with the parents the prioritizing of concerns and goal setting.
Closure	The parents get an opportunity to express any concerns regarding the interview, and the interviewer acknowledges the role of the parents in the assessment process.

Source: Adapted from Winton, P. J., & Bailey, D. B. (1998). The family-focused interview: A collaborative mechanism for family assessment and goal-setting, *Journal of the Division for Early Childhood, (12),* 195–207, and Winton, P. J. (1998). The family-focused interview: An assessment measure and goal-setting mechanism. In D. B. Bailey, & R. J. Simeonsson (Eds.), *Family Assessment in Early Intervention.* Columbus, Ohio: Merrill.

cally designed to identify family strengths, needs, resources, and sources of support rather than assess current functioning. Other instruments are designed to determine current family functioning in specific domains, such as stress (e.g., Abidin, 1986; Holroyd, 1974), life events (e.g., McCubbin & Patterson, 1987), or family adaptability and cohesion (e.g., Olson, Portner, & Lavee, 1985).

Those instruments designed to provide helpful information about family strengths, needs, resources, and sources of support are most useful in the IFSP process. More specific measures might be identified as a second level of assessment, if, during the assessment process, specific areas of concern emerged for the family. Unless an early intervention program includes trained staff and necessary resources to address the needs identified through such specific testing, it should not be pursued (Slentz & Bricker, 1992). Table 4–5 lists a variety of instruments that can be useful in the identification of resources, priorities, and concerns.

Other scales designed to assess sources of support and resources are included in Table 4–6.

Sociopolitical Influences on Families

At any given time in history there are critical issues influencing the needs of a society. The children and their families who are in need of early intervention are representative of the society in which they exist, and, therefore, also have these needs. Many of the serious concerns of the past (e.g., polio, scarlet fever) are no longer such grave threats to children in the United States. New issues emerge as solutions to existing problems are found. The issues challenging families today are complex, ranging from the detrimental effects of cocaine use by pregnant women and mothers to the miraculous survival of extremely premature, low-birth-weight babies through recent technological advances. We must strive to have collaborative partnerships with all families while accepting the reality that some parents will not be available to us as partners. The reasons for their unavailability include sociopolitical as well as personal and emotional issues.

When cultural differences interfere with the collaborative process, parents may consider that it is the

TABLE 4–5 Instruments to Identify Family Resources, Priorities, and Concerns

Title	Description
Family Functioning Style Scale Dunst, C. J., Trivette, C. M., & Deal, A. G. (1988). *Enabling and empowering families: Principles and guidelines for practice.* Cambridge, MA: Brookline.	Assesses 12 qualities of strong families organized into 3 categories: family-identity measures, information-sharing measures, and coping/resource mobilization measures; scale contains 26 statements to which responses are made using 5-point scale ranging from "not at all like my family" to "almost always like my family"; scale produces subscale scores for each family strength as well as an overall family strengths score; scores can be plotted to form a profile of family functioning style
Family Needs Scale (Dunst, Cooper, Weeldreyer, Snyder, & Chase, 1988) Dunst, C. J., Trivette, C. M., & Deal, A. G. (1988). *Enabling and empowering families: Principles and guidelines for practice.* Cambridge, MA: Brookline.	Scale has 41 items organized into 9 categories (financial, food and shelter, vocation, child care, transportation, communication, etc.); each item is rated by parents on 5-point scale ranging from "almost never a need" to "almost always a need"; parents are asked to read the 41 items and respond according to scale or indicate "not applicable" Instrument is dependent on reading skills of parents or must be read to them; was specifically developed for use in intervention programs, and is to be used to prompt discussions about responses to define nature of family's needs—however, intervention programs unable to respond to these needs after they are identified should avoid unnecessary intrusion some of these items might cause
Family Needs Survey (Bailey & Simeonsson, 1985) Frank Porter Graham Child Development Center University of North Carolina at Chapel Hill Bailey, D. B., & Simeonsson, R. J. (1988). Assessing needs of families with handicapped infants. *Journal of Special Education, 22,* 117–127. Sexton, D., Burrell, B., & Thompson, B. (1992). Measurement integrity of the Family Needs Survey. *Journal of Early Intervention, 16,* 343–352	Statements covering 6 broad areas (Needs for Information; Needs for Support; Explaining to Others; Community Services; Financial Needs; Family Functioning) to which parents respond on 1–3 scale with "definitely do not need help with this," "not sure," or "definitely need help with this"; total of 35 statements; 1 open-ended question that asks what greatest needs are currently; for the open-ended question parents can use needs included in the 35 statements and/or identify needs not mentioned on the form The format is easy to follow assuming that a person can read English. Although the statements could be read to a nonreader or translated for a non-English-speaking parent, quality of responses may be affected. Content of the instrument based on established needs of parents with young children with disabilities. The routine collection of this information by an early intervention program when there is no direct usefulness or applicability to the intervention efforts should not occur. The instrument includes an open-ended question regarding parental needs, so parents are free to identify needs not included in the statements. The response choices are limited and do not permit the identification of priority needs; however, open-ended question does.
Family Resource Scale Dunst, C. J., & Leet, H. E. (1987). Measuring the adequacy of resources in households with young children. *Child: Care, Health, and Development, 13,* 111–125.	Measures extent to which households with young children have adequate resources; 31 items that address both physical and human resources (food, shelter, transportation, time to be with family and friends, health care, money to pay bills, child care, etc.); respondent uses 5-point scale ranging from "not at all adequate" to "almost always adequate" to indicate adequacy of each resource; items rated as inadequate can be used to identify household needs; modified version available for teen mothers

TABLE 4-5 Instruments to Identify Family Resources, Priorities, and Concerns (Continued)

Title	Description
Family Strengths Inventory Family, Infant and Preschool Program, Western Carolina Center, 300 Enola Rd., Morganton, North Carolina 28655 ATTN: Community Resource Services	Has 13 items measuring 6 qualities of strong families and aspects of interpersonal and intrapersonal relationships; respondent uses 5-point scale based on the degree to which the characteristic is present in her family; yields a total score reflecting overall family strengths; however, analysis of responses to individual items through follow-up interviews provides more useful information
Family Strengths Scale Family, Infant and Preschool Program, Western Carolina Center, 300 Enola Rd., Morganton, North Carolina 28655 ATTN: Community Resource Services	Contains 12 items that assess family pride (loyalty, optimism, trust in family) and family accord (ability to accomplish tasks, deal with problems, get along together); respondent indicates the extent to which each quality listed is present in his family; items cover strengths such as trust and confidence, ability to express feelings, congruence in values, and beliefs, respect, etc.
How Can We Help? (Child Development Resources, 1988) Child Development Resources, P.O. Box 299, Lightfoot, VA 23090-0299	Instrument has 2 parts—first part has 7 open-ended questions and the second part is checklist of needs subdivided into 6 categories (information; child care; community services; medical and dental care; talking about the child; planning for the future/transition); possible responses include "we have enough," "we would like more," or "not sure"; format includes space for additional items to be added in each of the 6 categories as well as another open-ended question at end of form; parents complete by responding only to those questions they feel would be helpful for the intervention staff; open-ended questions appear first followed by checklist responded to by marking in appropriate response column and/or adding additional items; one final open-ended question follows the checklist
Parent Need's Survey (Seligman & Darling, 1989) Seligman, M., & Darling, B. R. (1989). *Ordinary families, special children: A systems approach to childhood disability.* New York: Guilford Press.	Includes 26 statements about needs that parents of young children with disabilities may have; possible responses to these items are: "I really need some help in this area"; "I would like some help, but my need is not that great"; or "I don't need any help in this area"; instrument includes space for needs not addressed; parents read statements and mark corresponding response they wish to make
Personal Projects Matrix Little, B. R. (1983). Personal projects: A rationale and method for investigation. *Environment and Behavior, 19,* 273–309.	Respondent asked to list up to 10 personal projects that occupy time or energy; then to rate enjoyment, difficulty, stress, positive and negative impact of each according to its importance, and progress toward reaching goal
Support Functions Scale Dunst, C. J., Trivette, C. M., & Deal, A. (1988). *Enabling and empowering families: Principles and guidelines for practice.* Cambridge, MA: Brookline.	Measures person's need for different types of assistance; 20 items that cover 4 types of support needed (financial, emotional, instrumental, e.g., child care, and informational); respondent uses a 5-point scale ranging from "never have a need" to "quite often have a need;" items rated "sometimes," "often," or "quite often" (have a need) should be followed up with an interview to pinpoint needs

TABLE 4–6 Social Support Scales

Title	Source	Description
Exercise: Social Support	Summers, J. A., Turnbull, A. P., & Brotherson, M. J. (1985). *Coping strategies for families with disabled children.*	Exercise in which respondent answers 4 questions aimed at identifying roadblocks toward obtaining social support and developing steps to overcome these roadblocks; all questions are open-ended; both practical (e.g., lack of transportation) and value (believing that you should not burden others) roadblocks are to be identified as a part of the exercise Published in Johnson, B. H., McGonigel, M. J., & Kaufmann, R. K. (Eds.). (1989). *Guidelines and recommended practices for the individualized family service plan.* National Early Childhood Technical Assistance System and Association for the Care of Children's Health.
Family Support Scale	Dunst, C. J., Trivette, C. M., & Deal, A. G. (1988). *Enabling and empowering families: Principles and guidelines for practice.* Cambridge, MA: Brookline.	Respondent rates sources of support as to their helpfulness in raising a young child, including parent, spouse or partner, friends, neighbors, co-workers, church, professionals, and social groups or organizations, using a 5-point scale ranging from "not at all helpful" to "extremely helpful"
Inventory of Social Support	Dunst, C. J., Trivette, C. M., & Deal, A. G. (1988). *Enabling and empowering families: Principles and guidelines for practice.* Cambridge, MA: Brookline.	Matrix format intended to determine who provides help to a person as well as the nature and quality of that help; first respondent indicates the frequency of contact (including face to face, group setting, and telephone contact) he has had with 18 possible support providers (with room available to add 2 additional persons or groups); then the respondent indicates to whom he goes to receive help for 12 different needs
Perceived Support Network Inventory	Oritt, E. C., Paul, S. C., & Behrman, J. A. (1985). The perceived support network inventory. *American Journal of Community Psychology, 13,* 565–582.	Uses a 3-step assessment process to identify members of a family's personal network and the quality of the relationships; respondent first lists everyone she would routinely seek help from, then describes the type of support she would ask for, and finally rates a number of qualitative aspects of support exchanges
Personal Network Matrix	Dunst, C. J., Trivette, C. M., & Deal, A. G. (1988). *Enabling and empowering families: Principles and guidelines for practice.* Cambridge, MA: Brookline.	Divided into 3 parts designed to assess frequency of contacts and qualitative information about the support network available to a person
Psychosocial Kinship Inventory	Pattison, E. M., DeFrancisco, D., Wood, P., Frazier, H., & Crowder, J. (1975). Psychosocial kinship model for family therapy. *American Journal of Psychiatry, 132,* 1246–1251.	Used to identify members in personal network and assess 11 dimensions of support for each person in network (kind of feelings/thoughts toward person; strength of feelings/thoughts; help provided by that person; degree of emotional support provided; frequency of contact; degree of stability of relationship; physical proximity; kind of feelings/thoughts believed held by person toward them; strength of feelings believed held; help provided to person; emotional support provided; each dimension is rated on a 5-point scale

professionals who are not available to them as collaborative partners. In either case, the professional has the burden of responsibility to initiate acceptable solutions. Many sociopolitical issues can severely hamper the availability of a parent to work as a collaborative partner on behalf of a child. A sampling of such issues explored in this chapter includes health issues, economic issues, community and domestic violence, maltreatment of children, and technological advances.

Health Issues

The dangers associated with alcohol consumption during pregnancy have been a point of discussion for many centuries (Rosman & Oppenheimer, 1985). The term *fetal alcohol syndrome* relates to the characteristics of a child exposed to the injurious effects of alcohol during fetal development (Jones & Smith, 1973). In order for a child to receive this diagnosis he should show signs in each of three categories: (1) pre- and/or postnatal growth retardation; (2) central nervous system involvement; and (3) characteristic facial disfigurement (microcephaly, microphthalmia, flat or absent philtrum, thin upper lip, and/or flattening of maxillary area (Rossetti, 1990). Reports indicate that approximately 1 out of every 750 babies born has fetal alcohol syndrome (Centers for Disease Control, 1984). Some children may exhibit partial features of the syndrome, and are more accurately diagnosed as "suspected fetal alcohol effects" (Clarren & Smith, 1978).

Confounding the impact of alcohol use on a developing fetus is the fact that heavy drinkers have a higher frequency of tobacco, marijuana, and drug usage (Rosman & Oppenheimer, 1985). Each factor alone has been associated with specific neonatal outcomes. For example, marijuana use has been linked to birth weight 300 grams lower in offspring than seen in the offspring of nonusers (Hingson et al., 1982). The impact for a child whose mother used multiple substances during pregnancy is even greater. Additionally, poor nutritional habits often accompany maternal alcoholism, and the fetus is totally dependent on nutrients provided by the mother. Alcohol consumption by the mother is toxic to the fetus and appears to result in a reduction of nutrient absorption independent of maternal eating habits. A poor nutritional environment, combined with decreased nutrient absorption, compound fetal risk for growth retardation (Phillips, Henderson, & Schenker, 1989).

The number of newborns exposed to prenatal drug abuse is estimated at 375,000 per year (Schneider,

Griffith, & Chasnoff, 1989). The damage caused by cocaine and crack-cocaine, which have grown in popularity, far exceeds previous withdrawal symptoms seen in the newborn nursery. The characteristics of babies born exposed to cocaine, include poor body-state regulation, poor feeding, tremors/trembling, stiffness/rigidity, chronic irritability, difficulty sleeping, and poor visual orientation. Since these conditions last well beyond the first few weeks of life, they are more indicative of lasting changes in the central nervous system, than withdrawal symptoms (Schneider, et al.). Strokes and seizures, small head size, missing bowels, and malformed genitals in babies have all been related to crack-cocaine-addicted mothers. These children continue to exhibit multiple problems as they enter school, such as poor abstract reasoning and memory, poor judgment, inability to concentrate, inability to deal with stress, frequent tantrums, and violent acting out.

Cocaine easily passes into the fetal circulatory system and remains there longer than in the maternal system. Chemical properties of the drug have led to speculation that the fetus is continually exposed through the amniotic fluid, following a single use of the drug by the mother. Screening tests are available to determine exposure of a newborn to cocaine as well as other drugs (e.g., opiates, amphetamines, barbiturates, phencyclidine, and marijuana). The urine-screening test is relatively low cost (between eighteen and twenty-five dollars for cocaine), but requires confirmatory testing, since both false positive and false negatives are possible. False positives will occur if a test reacts positively to substances other than the drug; however, no such cross reactants with cocaine are known other than derivatives of the drug (Brayden, 1990). Laboratory technician error might also cause false positives or false negatives. False negatives could also result from "doctored" urine samples, or the amount of time elapsed since drug usage. The screening test is also limited in that it cannot reveal how much of the drug is present in the infant's system. Decisions that follow a positive screen have serious long-term implications for the newborn child. Some of these children become "boarder babies," residing for extended periods in a hospital setting. Some make their way into foster care, and others are simply released into the care of their drug-addicted mothers.

The abuse of drugs or alcohol by pregnant women can mean double risk for the child. First, the child's fetal development can be impacted. Second, if the adult patterns of behavior continue after the child's birth, the child's home environment will be jeopardized. This can put the child at danger in terms of malnutrition, safety and quality of supervision provided, and the availability of a stimulating, nurturing caregiver with whom to talk and play. This second set of dangers can also be triggered by a father who is abusing drugs or alcohol.

The parent-professional partnership for children living under these conditions is jeopardized in several ways. The parent may literally be unavailable, have no means of being contacted, and be inconsistent and unreliable at keeping appointments. Professionals may find it difficult to work collaboratively with an adult whom they perceive as responsible for the child's disabilities and who is continuing to cause harm to the child. However, for any intervention program to be effective it must involve a family-centered approach that provides parents with assistance in becoming and remaining drug-free coupled with training in the care and management of their child.

Acquired immunodeficiency syndrome (AIDS) is a disease caused by a virus that can damage the brain and destroy the body's ability to fight off illness. The virus causing AIDS and related disorders has several names: HTLV-III (human T-cell lymphotropic virus type III), LAV (lymphadenopathy associated virus), ARC (AIDS-related complex), and HIV (human immunodeficiency virus). It is possible for an individual to be infected and transmit the related virus without displaying any symptoms. Although AIDS cannot be spread by casual contact in schools or other public places, it is a concern to all professionals working with children. AIDS is primarily spread in three ways: (1) having sex with an infected person; (2) sharing drug needles and syringes with users of heroin, cocaine, and other illegal drugs; or (3) infecting infants in utero, perinatally, or postnatally. On rare occasions AIDS has been transmitted through blood transfusions. According to cumulative figures based on all known AIDS cases published in 1987, 2 percent of AIDS cases were the result of blood transfusions, and 1 percent occurred in persons with hemophilia who received blood-clotting factors. Since March 1985 all blood donations are screened for the AIDS virus, and no donations are accepted from high-risk individuals, reducing the likelihood of spreading the disease through transfusions. However, one out of every thirty-seven individuals with hemophilia has AIDS (Hutchings, 1988).

For early interventionists, the greatest concern is transmittal of the disease during pregnancy and the newborn period. Transmittal from an infected mother can occur in utero through transplacental passage of the virus, during labor and delivery when the infant may be exposed to maternal blood and vaginal secretions, or postnatally through breastfeeding (Hutchings, 1988). It is estimated that the biological parents of 25 to 33 percent of infants born with AIDS will not care for them (Tourse & Gundersen, 1988).

Perinatal transmission of HIV is the predominant means by which children become infected, accounting for 90 percent of cases seen in children (Centers for Disease Control and Prevention, 1998). The incidence of perinatal AIDS peaked in 1992, showing an 80 percent decline for infants and a 66 percent decline for children ages one to five years through 1997. The introduction of the drug zidovudine has been credited in this decline (Lindegren et al., 1999). Through June 1998, the incidence of perinatally acquired AIDS for forty-eight states, Puerto Rico, the District of Columbia, and the U.S. Virgin Islands was 7,512 children. Fifty-eight percent of these cases were reported from four states—New York (27 percent), Florida (16 percent), New Jersey (9 percent), and California (6 percent).

A disproportionately high number of pediatric AIDS occurs in minority populations. Although 15 percent of the total U.S. child population is black, 35 percent of all childhood cases involve black children, and 23 percent are Hispanic, who comprise just 10 percent of the total population. Figures from 1988 indicate that an HIV-infected mother delivered one out of every sixty-one infants born in New York City. The risk to infants increased because the proportion of AIDS cases in women has increased.

The early symptoms of HIV infection in infants and children include failure to thrive or weight loss, chronic or reoccurring diarrhea, persistent or reoccurring fever, and persistent and severe oral fungus infection. Additional conditions that appear include reoccurring bacterial infections, encephalopathy (developmental delay), lymphoid interstitial pneumonitis, and heart, liver, kidney, and skin involvement (Hutchings, 1988). Neurologic impairments may also appear, including ataxia, spasticity, paralysis, cortical atrophy, calcifications of basal ganglia, dementia, and slowing of brain electrical activity (Bale, 1990).

Since the majority of AIDS-infected children come from families with multiple problems, including drug abuse and poverty, effective intervention to meet their medical needs must take on a family-focused approach. The nature of the disease dictates that we view it from a context-based perspective. Dokecki, Baumeister, and Kupstas (1989) emphasize the social and political aspects, and have identified recommendations that reflect a philosophy of community- and family-based care, including increased availability of voluntary antibody screening and testing programs, ongoing developmental monitoring of young children who have or who are at risk of having HIV infection, and reduction of resistance from early interventionists to work with children infected with HIV.

Economic Issues

Child- and family-related issues are favorite topics of politicians, ranging from presidents (and presidential candidates) to local city and county officials. Most recently, programs such as Head Start, Medicaid, and increased federal support to ensure adequate child care for the children of working women have been highlighted. The special education legislation described in chapter 1 reflects a politically favorable stance on issues pertinent to children with disabilities. However, political rhetoric and actual legislation intended to support family structures and protect children have not always achieved their goals. Dukes (1976) points out the negative impact studies related to effective child-rearing practices have had on attitudes toward the African American population by creating a myth regarding the inadequacy of child-rearing practices among poor and minority groups. The impact of this myth has resulted in three negative outcomes for these families. First, it has misplaced the focus on the child and family as elements that foster pathogenic retardation. Second, families of low socioeconomic status (SES) are viewed and treated as the inferior element of American society. Third, the dynamics of the American social stratification system work to keep an inordinate number of these families at the bottom of the economic ladder, thus limiting their chances for a better life.

The ramifications of being in poverty in America today are overwhelming. Housing, adequate nutrition, transportation, and employment all become unobtainable when an individual or family faces extreme poverty. Public policy makers have attempted to respond to the needs of poor children through passage of income support programs (e.g., Aid to Families with Dependent Children), health care (e.g., Medicaid), protection from abuse (e.g., Child Abuse Prevention and Treatment Act, Adoptions Assistance and Child Welfare Act of 1980), nutritional assistance (e.g., Special Supplemental Food Program for Women, Infants

and Children), and child care (e.g., Head Start). However, the number of children and families who qualify for many of these programs far exceeds the numbers who actually receive benefits (Washington, 1985). Only 15 percent of the eligible children participate in Head Start programs. Approximately six million women, infants, and children are eligible, but do not receive WIC program benefits. If these programs were to serve a higher percentage of the eligible population, budget constraints would have to result in adjusted eligibility standards or significant budgetary reallocations.

The impact of extreme poverty is particularly evident in the homeless population in America today. Although determining the actual number of homeless individuals is impossible, several attempts to gather such data have been undertaken. One of the fastest-growing segments of the homeless population is family units with children, constituting approximately 40 percent of the population (Shinn & Weitzman, 1996). In rural areas, families, single mothers, and children are the largest group of homeless people (Vissing, 1996). Disproportionate numbers of nondominant population groups are seen among the homeless population with 49 percent African American, 32 percent Caucasian, 12 percent Hispanic, 4 percent Native American, and 3 percent Asian (U.S. Conference of Mayors, 1998). The definition used influences the estimate of homeless individuals and can explain some of the widely varying numbers (e.g., 350,000 estimate from the Department of Housing and Urban Development (HUD) as contrasted to 1.5 million estimated by advocates for the homeless) (Rossi, 1989). Regardless of the actual numbers, homelessness and extreme poverty are significant social problems that inflict lifelong disabilities on many young children in America today.

Substandard housing is a crisis affecting more than one out of every eight children, but has its most significant impact on minority children. The ratio jumps to about one in four for African American and Hispanic children. A description of a walk to a nearby "playground" for the preschoolers participating in the program for homeless families depicts a harsh reality (Ayers, 1989).

There is a vacant lot cluttered with wrecked automobiles and broken glass. In an alley with a chain-link fence is a battered, broken-down delivery truck, a pile of old tires, and, incongruously, a huge white yacht on cinder blocks with an American flag flapping at the stern. Maurice says, "Don't step on that man," as the little line of walkers snakes past someone passed out on the sidewalk. The street is littered with garbage, and a block away two hookers lean in a doorway smoking. The walkers pass by a group of men playing cards on the sidewalk, using a little box for a table, and everyone calls out friendly greetings. They pass a fried-chicken restaurant and a little bodega, then two deserted buildings whose broken doors and gaping windows stare back at the children. It is a whole landscape of abandonedness. The playground is under an enormous bridge and is littered with broken fences and scattered glass. There is a lot of traffic noise and no sunlight. Somehow the children see beyond it and fashion the games all children play: tag, chase, and their favorite, hide-and-seek. (p. 104)

These issues and concerns facing American society point to the need to view children from the contexts in which they exist. The reality of providing preschool services to homeless children demands acknowledgment of their condition. To run such a preschool "just like any other preschool" would clearly fail to meet the needs of these children and their families. The preschool teacher in the program describes her intake procedure, "I try to build up a sense of trust first. They're supposed to fill out a lot of forms, but I try not to start with that. I try to start with a kind word or just talk about the kids" (Ayers, p. 101). The temptation to look at the child in isolation, apart from his home environment, is no longer an effective option for early intervention programs. The number of children needing such services is increasing, while the nature of their needs is expanding.

Community and Domestic Violence

Some families are exposed to community violence on a routine basis. Other families experience violence within their own homes. This domestic violence refers to incidents of violence between parents or other adult partners with an intimate relationship (Fantuzzo & Mohr, 1999). Children are exposed to this form of violence by witnessing it, hearing it, attempting to intervene, or seeing the damage caused from the violence. Although there are no reliable national prevalence figures regarding the number of children exposed to domestic violence, it is apparent from crime reports, 911 calls, and population-based surveys that many households that include children have experienced domestic violence. Some parents even chose to become homeless in an effort to escape domestic violence (U.S. Conference of Mayors, 1998).

It is clear that exposure to domestic violence is linked to negative behaviors in children of all ages (Osofsky, 1999). Infants and toddlers are equally affected by witnessing violence as older children. Although violence can occur in any community, there is a higher prevalence of incidents of violence in communities with inadequate housing, poverty, and high rates of drug usage (Groves, 1997). Characteristics associated with infants and toddlers who have been exposed to domestic violence include excessive irritability, immature behavior, sleep disturbances, emotional distress, fear of being alone, and regression in toileting and language (Osofsky & Fenichel, 1996; Zeanah & Scheeringa, 1996). It will disrupt the child's development of trust and security that lead to exploratory behavior and eventually autonomy (Osofsky & Fenichel). The child will seek to avoid associations with the violence (e.g., location), have diminished responsiveness, and increased arousal.

The need to incorporate a family-centered approach to these children is readily apparent when one considers that a strong positive relationship with a competent, caring adult is the most important protective resource to help the child cope with domestic violence (Groves & Zuckerman, 1997; Osofsky & Thompson, 2000). The protective benefit of parenting is also apparent when children are exposed to community violence (Hill, Levermore, Twaite, & Jones, 1996). However, the impact of either community or domestic violence on the adults in a child's life can reduce their capacity to provide positive parenting. "There are two basic aspects to the problem: (1) parents may be unable to protect their children and keep them safe; and (2) parents themselves may be numbed, frightened, and depressed, unable to deal with their own trauma and/or grief, and emotionally unavailable for their children" (Osofsky, 1999, p. 40). Parents will need to cope with their own trauma before they can begin to respond to a young child's need for an emotionally available parent. Parents might choose to cope with community violence by accepting it as a part of the everyday routine, failing to realize the debilitating effects exposure to violence can have on a child. When schools and community centers become additional sources of violence and fear rather than the intended sources of support, there are even fewer resources for the parents to use.

Maltreatment of Children

Sometimes children are not merely exposed to violence but are the targets of it. This violence comes at the hands of their parents or other trusted adults within their own homes. Physical abuse, along with sexual abuse, neglect, and emotional abuse comprise the broad category of maltreatment toward children. Although the actual prevalence of child maltreatment is difficult to determine, the problem is substantial. For example, during 1994, out of nearly three million reports of possible abuse or neglect, over one million children had experienced maltreatment (English, 1998). There are reports that indicate that one-third of the victims of child abuse are less than one year old (Children's Defense Fund, 1993). Factors associated with child maltreatment include characteristics of the caregiver, socioeconomic factors, and child characteristics. Individual traits of adults prone to the maltreatment of children include low self-esteem, poor impulse control, aggressiveness, anxiety, and depression. There is also a link between domestic violence and child maltreatment, with mothers who are victims of domestic violence more likely to physically abuse their children and fathers who batter their wives more likely to abuse their children as well (Giles-Sims, 1985; Petchers as cited in English). Approximately 50 to 80 percent of families involved with child protective services also have a substance abuse problem (Kienberger-Jaudes, Ekwo, & Van Voorhis, 1995).

Child maltreatment is seen at all economic levels, but at a disproportionately high rate from families living in poverty and from single-parent homes, particularly severe neglect and severe violence (Sedlack & Broadhurst as cited in English). However, most poor people do not abuse their children. The link between poverty and maltreatment appears to be connected through interactive factors, such as unrealistic expectations for child development, depression, isolation, substance abuse, domestic violence, and unemployment. The children at risk for maltreatment live in poor households that are confounded by disorganization and social isolation. The victims of maltreatment are most frequently younger children, girls, premature infants, and children with irritable temperaments.

The types and extent of damage caused by maltreatment varies with the age of the child, the intensity and duration of the abuse, and the nature of the abuse. Fatalities occur most frequently when the victim is young, with 85 percent of maltreatment-related fatalities between 1993 and 1995 involving children under five years of age (Lung & Daro as cited in English). Between 1990 and 1994, 5,400 children within the United States died as a result of abuse or neglect (U.S. Department of Health and Human Services, National Center on Child Abuse and Neglect, 1996). For those who survive, research data tend to be associated with those children who have been placed in treatment programs, likely representing the most severe behavioral problems. Those who experience neglect may experience nonorganic failure to thrive resulting in growth retardation. Aggression, poor peer relations, and a reduced ability to show empathy for others are just some of the developmental problems these children might exhibit. Resilience again seems connected to the availability of a supportive, caring adult with whom the child can form a trusting relationship.

The model of intervention for cases of child maltreatment in the United States is family preservation, designed to keep families intact. However, this approach is not without critics. Some feel that this model actually works against the best interests of children (McCroskey & Meezan, 1998). They believe that children should be removed from their parents when those parents are unable to ensure their safety. However, most experts concur that a system of family support or more intense family preservation systems used to assist the family in achieving a home safe for the child is preferable to removing the child into permanent state custody.

Technological Advances

Any infant born weighing less than 2,500 grams (approximately 5.5 pounds) is defined as low-birth-weight. Those below 1,500 grams (about 3.3 pounds) are considered very-low-birth-weight. The survival of low- and very-low-birth-weight infants has been steadily increasing since the development of neonatal intensive care units (Rossetti, 1986). Figures from the San Francisco metropolitan area presented in Table 4–7 document the point. Survival percentages for children with even lower birth weights rose as well. The incidence of infants below normal weight is higher for nonwhite infants than for whites. The 1983 percentage of very-low-birth-weight infants (less than 1,500 grams) was 0.9 for whites, while rising to 2.54 for nonwhites.

Survival rates have not improved without significant costs. Of those infants surviving, those who weighed less than 1,000 grams spent an average of eighty-nine days in a neonatal intensive care unit. The average stay for those below 1,500 grams is fifty-seven days. For those between 1,501 and 2,000 grams the average stay is twenty-four days (Rossetti). Financial resources and insurance policies are quickly

TABLE 4–7 Survival Rates of Low-Birth-Weight Infants (1,251–1,500 grams) Born in Metropolitan San Francisco

Time Period	Number Born	Number Survived	Percent Survived
1965–1969	35	21	60.0%
1976–1981	104	97	93.3%

Source: From Rossetti, L. M. (1986). High Risk Infants: Identification, Assessment, and Intervention. Boston, MA: College-Hill Press.

exhausted for a family confronted with the expenditures of a very-low- or low-birth-weight infant. Many are technology-dependent for their continued survival (e.g., respirators, intravenous nutrition, kidney dialysis). These children have become the "million dollar" babies (Fackelmann, 1988). Many parents are unable or unwilling to make renovations to their homes and/or assume twenty-four-hour-a-day nursing of their child. Many teenagers, who are at high risk to deliver low-birth-weight infants, make the choice to abandon their infants. These children become stranded in the hospitals. Even if Medicaid picks up a portion of the costs, the hospitals are running up enormous bills for these children. For example, one abandoned five-year-old cost Cardinal Glennon Hospital in St. Louis two million dollars (Fackelmann). Although home-based care would often be much less expensive than hospital-based care, Medicaid and/or insurance requirements have forced the parents to keep the child in the hospital. These children are at high risk of developing secondary disabilities that will require additional care well beyond early childhood.

Cultural Differences between Professionals and Families

The theme of this text is that assessment must be context-based to be valid and to offer the best benefit to the child and family. Exploring and understanding that context is of far greater value than the outcomes of any standardized clinical assessments. The adoption of context-based assessment practices is vital to changing the long-standing pattern of discrimination and bias toward oppressed children manifested on standardized tests (Stacey, 1994). Use of contextual assessment practices for children in oppressed groups is absolutely vital if one wishes to alter the history of their mistreatment and misrepresentation through standardized tests and

traditional assessment practices. This premise applies equally to our judgment of families and their child-rearing practices. It will be possible for early interventionists to practice context-based assessment only if they do not hold to ethnocentric perspectives toward the values and beliefs of families who are not from the same cultural group.

There are many different cultural groups within the United States today. Within these groups, members share customs, language, religious beliefs, family val-

Know The Facts

The Western belief that mothers and babies sleeping together is abnormal, disruptive for the parents as well as the child, and undesirable conflicts with beliefs held by cultural groups who consider abandoning an infant to an isolated crib particularly harsh and developmentally inappropriate (Bhavnagri & Gonzalez-Mena, 1997). Infant sleeping routines in 169 societies studied by Barry and Paxson did not include a single group that put their children in a separate room to sleep. Study of fifty-six world societies by Whiting, Kluckhohn, and Anthony included only five with patterns similar to those in the United States.

Our views toward sleep routines are reflective of larger societal values that emphasize independence and autonomy. We cannot start too soon becoming a "rugged individualist." Other cultural groups place a greater premium on relationships and consider having the child sleep with the mother a means to help the child establish a secure base that will enable him to achieve independence and autonomy at the appropriate time. Privacy and individuality are not goals toward which all cultural groups strive.

ues, and historical perspectives. Traditionally, we have identified majority and minority cultural groups, with whites as the majority and all other ethnic groups as minorities. Alternate terms of dominant and nondominant, which relate to a group's degree of "social power" as used by Gushue (1993), offer a more accurate choice of words for our purposes. There can be many segments of the population who represent nondominant groups, but who might ethnically fit in the dominant group. Members of cultural groups can take on an ethnocentric perspective, holding to the view that their beliefs and views toward child-rearing and early intervention are the only correct ones. Often they contend that these views are proven through research, unaware that the vast majority of child development theory and research has been associated with middle-class children of European extraction who live in the United States, and may not represent child development as it occurs in many other cultures now or historically (Bhavnagri & Gonzalez-Mena, 1997).

When people are able to abandon their ethnocentric perspectives, they begin the process of going through stages of understanding from awareness of cultural diversity, to cultural competence, and finally to cultural sensitivity (Smith, 1993). Recognition of cultural diversity, coupled with awareness that there are many different perspectives and belief systems, is the most basic level of cultural awareness. Cultural competence indicates that a person has achieved an understanding of cultural differences and has the competence to be of

help. The early interventionist who has achieved a level of cultural sensitivity understands and respects the beliefs and values of other cultural groups, without aiming to transform the family into valuing her own goals.

The extent to which professionals working in early intervention have achieved a level of cultural identity that enables them to work with diverse groups varies. It can be dangerous to reduce a family's culture down to generalizations and characterizations of the group as a whole. The diversity of cultures now present in U.S. public schools further makes such an approach to understanding diversity futile. Nevertheless, we must assume responsibility for exploring the nature of the cultural backgrounds of children in schools. Racial- and cultural-identity development models have emerged from the field of counseling that address dynamics that can arise in multicultural counseling (Gushue, 1993). These models give consideration to the responses an individual has to his or her membership in a dominant or nondominant cultural group. Within these models there are positive stages of psychological development moving toward cultural identity. Drawing primarily from the work of Helms (1984, 1990) on racial identity, Gushue has developed a model of cultural identity. The model includes four developmental stages of cultural identity for members of nondominant groups, shown in Figure 4–1. Issues revolve around a person's own beliefs about his or her own culture, and the attitudes held toward persons from the dominant cultural group.

FIGURE 4–1 A Nondominant-Culture-Identity Development Model

Awareness
Critical interest and pride in own culture and critical acceptance of dominant culture; continuing resistance to political marginalization and complete assimilation

Resistance
Active rejection of dominant culture, including resistance to values and politics paired with an exclusive focus on and pride in one's nondominant culture

Dissonance/Introspection
Increasing interest in one's own culture as one begins questioning uncritical adoption of the dominant culture's ways and values

Conformity
Idealization of dominant culture and naive adoption of its values; tendency to belittle of one's own nondominant culture

Source: Adapted from "Cultural-Identity Development and Family Assessment: An Interaction Model," by G. V. Gushue, 1993, *The Counseling Psychologist, 21,* pp. 487–513.

Gushue also outlines six developmental stages for members of the dominant group to achieve cultural identity. These stages, shown in Figure 4–2, are based on the premise that members of the dominant culture begin their development within the racist context of that dominant society rather than in a neutral position. The process begins through contact with members of nondominant groups, and the awareness that they have customs, beliefs, and child-rearing practices that seem deviant simply because they are different. When the individual is willing to reevaluate his own beliefs and those of the different culture, the developmental progression can begin. Within the model, the first three stages represent the "abandonment of racism." Those who progress through these stages can choose to complete some or all of the final three developmental stages, achieving a multicultural perspective. It can be predicted that interactions between members of dominant and nondominant groups are influenced by where each individual is in her personal development of cultural identity.

Cultural-identity models differ from models of acculturation in that they focus on an individual's attitudes regarding two cultures—the dominant culture and the nondominant culture. In contrast, models of acculturation are based on determining where an individual is on a continuum of beliefs and values, attitudes, knowledge, and behavior between a dominant and nondominant culture. Models of acculturation do not include positive developmental stages of cultural understanding as found in the cultural-identity models. For some families, the goal is to achieve acculturation into the dominant culture as quickly as possible. Others are highly resistant to acculturation, as it represents the negation of their own cultural identity.

Factors that influence speed and depth of acculturation include availability of support systems, the degree of harmony between the two cultures, and access to extended family (Landau-Stanton, 1990). Socioeconomic factors also play a role in the acculturation process (Hines, 1988). The concept of a single profile that defines all families from a cultural group is unrealistic. Although we need basic knowledge regarding the characteristics and beliefs of specific cultural groups with whom we work, every family has a unique set of standards, beliefs, practices, and family goals. Early interventionists cannot memorize a litany of characteristics associated with specific cultural groups and

FIGURE 4–2 A Dominant-Culture-Identity Development Model

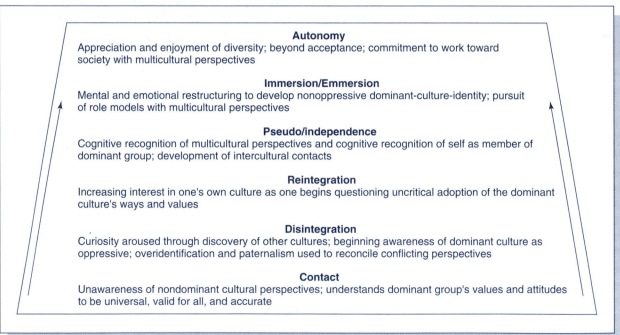

Autonomy
Appreciation and enjoyment of diversity; beyond acceptance; commitment to work toward society with multicultural perspectives

Immersion/Emmersion
Mental and emotional restructuring to develop nonoppressive dominant-culture-identity; pursuit of role models with multicultural perspectives

Pseudo/independence
Cognitive recognition of multicultural perspectives and cognitive recognition of self as member of dominant group; development of intercultural contacts

Reintegration
Increasing interest in one's own culture as one begins questioning uncritical adoption of the dominant culture's ways and values

Disintegration
Curiosity aroused through discovery of other cultures; beginning awareness of dominant culture as oppressive; overidentification and paternalism used to reconcile conflicting perspectives

Contact
Unawareness of nondominant cultural perspectives; understands dominant group's values and attitudes to be universal, valid for all, and accurate

Source: Adapted from "Cultural-Identity Development and Family Assessment: An Interaction Model," by G. V. Gushue, 1993, *The Counseling Psychologist, 21,* pp. 487–513.

simply apply them as needed. Rather, there needs to be an interactive understanding of the process.

Early interventionists first need to reflect on their own cultural identity and their attitudes toward other cultural groups. They then need to be understanding of the developmental stages of cultural identity parents from the same or different cultural groups are currently experiencing. Such awareness and sensitivity can be paralleled with the need to understand the grieving process that parents might be experiencing. It is not the task of the early interventionist to evaluate, diagnose, or provide counseling for parents who might be experiencing a stage of anger. It is our task to understand that the anger expressed by these parents should not be taken personally or held against them.

Closing Thoughts

Both the family and the professional contribute to the effectiveness of early intervention. The language and words we use convey the attitudes and beliefs to which we hold. Whether we define our goals for children and their families as enabling the child and family to overcome identified deficits, striving to promote excellence, or helping children overcome challenges, we convey our intentions. Teachers are motivated to set goals based on the perceptions of social norms (Graue & Marsh, 1996). In one school setting, the teachers promote high standards and expectations, whereas teachers in a contrasting setting define children by their limitations, setting equally limiting goals. The goals and standards that professionals hold are not without social context. If we aim to have collaborative partnerships, we are far more likely to reach that goal than if we set the goal simply to get the parents to attend our meetings, reveal personal data to us, and sign our forms.

For Your Consideration

1. How can professionals gathering information from families ensure that they approach the task using a strengths-based orientation?

2. What instruments can be used to gather information from parents about their child?

3. Which approach is most likely to get a useful response from the parent during an interview and why?

   a. Are you unable to discipline your child effectively?

   b. Tell me what happens when David acts up.

4. When there appear to be cultural differences interfering with a professional's communication with a parent, what steps can be taken to improve communication?

CYBERSOURCES

Check out the following Web sites for more information related to the ideas presented in this chapter.

Connect for Kids Celebrating Families calendar and other family-related information

http://www.celebratingfamilies.org/

Family and Advocates Partnership for Education

http://www.fape.org/

Federation for Children with Special Needs

http://www.fcsn.org/

Family Involvement Network of Educators

http://gseweb.harvard.edu/hfrp/projects/fine.html

Parent Advocacy Coalition for Educational Rights

http://www.pacer.org/

Cultural Orientation Resource Center

http://www.cal.org/rsc/

National Association for Bilingual Education

http://www.nabe.org/

National Alliance of Black School Educators

http://www.nabse.org/

National Indian Education Association

http://www.niea.org/

Quality Education for Minorities Network

http://qemnetwork.qem.org/index.html%20

 For additional resources on assessment, visit us on-line at www.earlychilded.delmar.com

CHAPTER 5

Approaches and Techniques Used in Child Assessment

Chapter Objectives

After reading this chapter, you should be able to:

1. Identify differing theoretical perspectives toward child development and discuss the relationship between them and assessment practices.

2. Define the models of teaming used in early childhood special education.

3. Distinguish between norm-referenced and criterion-referenced assessment.

4. Match an observation strategy with the type of information to be obtained from an observation.

Chapter Overview

Just as there are many purposes for conducting an assessment, there are many valid approaches and techniques to use in the process. Who the examiners are and their connections to the family and to intervention programs vary as well. The effectiveness of any technique hinges on an examiner's theoretical orientation, her ability to establish rapport with the child and family members, as well as her skill in selecting and using techniques appropriate to the stated purpose of the assessment. Techniques that might seem simple enough, such as child observations, require practice and reflection. Practices that offer more freedom and flexibility, such as play-based assessment, are appealing, but can be time consuming and hard to summarize. Team-based and family-centered assessment models present unique managerial challenges associated with legal deadlines and payment restrictions for personnel participation in team meetings.

This chapter begins with a review of influences that are present in the assessment process, including theoretical perspectives and beliefs about the causes of particular conditions. The second portion of the chapter covers information about persons and techniques that are involved in the assessment process. Topics related to persons include levels of specialization, models of teaming, and direct and indirect assessment. Techniques covered are norm-referenced to criterion-referenced assessment, standardized assessment to assessment with accommodations, product-oriented to process-based assessment, and naturalistic observation to clinical observation. These techniques are not mutually exclusive and do not always have precise distinctions, but do offer a means of organizing the discussion of the complex process of assessment.

Influences on Assessment

Although we might not always be aware of it, theoretical perspectives about child development as well as beliefs about the underlying causes of disabilities influence the process of assessing young children with special needs. To illustrate, the criteria one uses to diagnose a child as having Attention Deficit/Hyperactivity Disorder (ADHD) can make a substantial difference in the number of children so diagnosed, giving us estimates as variable as 1 to 20 percent of the child population (Cohen, Riccio, & Gonzalez, 1994). The beliefs held by the diagnostician about the causes of ADHD (e.g., the presence of an underlying neurological dysfunction as the cause of ADHD versus a reliance exclusively on behavioral standards; the pervasiveness of the symptoms across all settings versus situational-specific symptoms) influence her understanding of the definition and the instruments she chooses to apply in the diagnostic process.

The wide array of tests, assessment systems, and diagnostic tools available for use with young children with special needs today reflects the evolution and diversity of the theoretical orientations evident in the field of early childhood special education. Persons responsible for assessments are likely to select approaches and assessment instruments that are most compatible with their theoretical biases and beliefs.

It would be difficult, if not impossible, to conduct assessments free from these influences. It would even be undesirable to think that we would enter into the task of assessing children and planning interventions for them free from a solid theoretical orientation. Indeed, it is important that we acknowledge the power our theoretical beliefs can have over the choices we make in the assessment process and the interpretations we make of child performance. We need to balance between having a strong theoretical orientation and allowing that orientation to limit our vision and understanding of the child and his family. When we find ourselves in disagreement with other professionals or parents regarding the techniques to use or the conclusions to draw from assessments, it is likely that we can identify some of these factors at the root of the dispute. Perhaps this awareness can help us realize how we have reached such disparate findings and provide a means to respect one another's conflicting opinions.

A discussion of differences in these perspectives might open lines of communication, even though it will not eliminate the conflict or the disputes in our interpretation of children's behavior.

Theoretical Perspectives

How we believe children develop and learn influences our understanding of the very nature of the assessment process. Specifically, our beliefs influence what we want to know about the child, how we obtain that information, and finally, how we analyze and interpret that information. Four theoretical perspectives of child development that influence assessment practices in early childhood special education today are maturational/developmental, behavioral, constructivist, and transactional. The key principles of these four perspectives are summarized in Table 5–1. These particular theoretical perspectives also reflect an evolution and expansion of assessment practices from primarily norm-referenced to the diverse array of criterion-referenced instruments, observational tools, and play-based systems available today. Developers of commercially available instruments strive to base their product on a particular theoretical perspective toward child development and learning. However, instruments based on differing theoretical perspectives often have similar test items (Fewell, 1983). Theoretical differences may be reflected more in the scoring procedures and analysis of test outcomes or in the style of item presentation than in test content.

Early childhood experts have criticized maturational/developmental milestones-based assessment instruments for their heavy reliance on motor performance across all domains. Children who have advanced scores on such scales do not necessarily go on to excel in school achievement, nor does poor performance mean a child is cognitively impaired or even temporarily delayed. Professionals have not found a reliable means to assess cognitive functioning apart from motor and language behaviors during infancy and the preschool years. Therefore, there is a high incidence of errors when developmental scales are used to predict future cognitive performance of children. Often lags or advanced performance can be explained by the naturally occurring developmental spurts and plateaus associated with motor and language milestones.

The failure of maturational/developmental theorists to incorporate the potential interactive impact of environmental influences on the development of the

Know The Facts

The limited number of items on many tests designed for infants and toddlers can cause big swings in scores. Percentile rankings on the Cognitive Subtest of the Developmental Assessment of Young Children (Voress & Maddox, 1998) fluctuate even when the actual number of items missed seems to be very low. A raw score of 14 places a nine-month-old infant at the 61st percentile. A drop of 2 points down to a raw score of 12 (missing just two items) moves the infant down to the 42nd percentile. Even more dramatic fluctuations occur across age groups. The raw score of 14 places a 10- to 11-month-old at the 34th percentile, and a 12-month-old with the same raw score drops to the 13th percentile. These numbers do not suggest that this particular test is one to be avoided, but they do illustrate the challenge involved in standardizing assessments of infants and toddlers in particular. Rapid growth and development combined with the individuality of developmental patterns make the task particularly challenging.

growing child is another limitation of assessments based exclusively on this theoretical orientation. Yet, the tradition of interpreting a child's performance primarily on the basis of her chronological age continues today. Popular norm-based tests have long been the backbone of the special education assessment process for older children. Developers of recently normed early childhood instruments do strive to use norm groups that represent the diversity of the American population. However, the notion that a standardized test allows us to assess any child fairly and accurately without giving consideration to their individual lives is inconsistent with a context-based approach to assessment. No matter how representative norm groups are of the geographic, socioeconomic, and racial composition of our country, these tests do not offer any specific means to understand how an individual's environment has had an ongoing interactive effect on his development and, therefore, his performance.

Although it can be useful to have an idea of how a child compares to children his own age, it is our responsibility to interpret scores within the child's

TABLE 5–1 Theoretical Perspectives of Child Development

Theoretical Perspective	Key Theorists	Principles	Assessment Implications	Examples of Assessment Instruments/Techniques
Maturational or developmental	Gesell (1925)	Maturation of the nervous system and physical growth govern a child's physical, psychological, cognitive, and social development. Child's development and growth are biologically set, not particularly subject to environmental influences. The ages at which normal children reach developmental milestones such as rolling over, creeping, crawling, sitting independently, standing, walking, and stacking three blocks in a tower are identified. Children who are unable to perform these skills at the expected ages are considered to be experiencing developmental delays.	Child's chronological age serves as a reference point in setting expectations and assessing functioning without concern for the child's background and life experiences.	Gesell Developmental Schedules (Gesell, 1925; Gesell & Amatruda, 1947) Bayley Scales of Infant Development (Bayley, 1969, 1993) Denver Developmental Screening Test (Frankenburg & Dodds, 1970, 1990; Frankenberg, Dodds, Archer, Shapiro, & Bresnick, 1992) Battelle Developmental Inventory (Newborg, Stock, Wnek, Guidubaldi, & Svinicki, 1984)
Behavioral	Watson (1913, 1919)	All behavior is learned. Development and learning occur not simply as the result of maturation, but rather as a child engages in behaviors that are followed by consequences; if these consequences reinforce a behavior frequently enough, it becomes a learned behavior. The age at which learning takes place is less significant than how it takes place.	Emphasis is on what skills the child has acquired, and which ones remain to be learned. Criterion-referenced instruments and some observational systems are compatible, avoiding comparison of children to norms. Many of these instruments do provide age approximations to have greater market appeal.	Brigance Early Preschool Screen (Brigance, 1998a) Brigance Preschool Screen (Brigance, 1998b) Brigance K & 1 Screen-Revised (Brigance, 1997) Functional behavioral assessment (e.g., O'Neill et al., 1997)

(continued)

TABLE 5–1 Theoretical Perspectives of Child Development (Continued)

Theoretical Perspective	Key Theorists	Principles	Assessment Implications	Examples of Assessment Instruments/Techniques
Constructivist: cognitive stages	Piaget (1952)	Development is broken down into hierarchical stages.	Provides useful alternatives in the assessment of minority and bilingual children—freedom from age scores, process-based.	Infant Psychological Development Scales (Uzgiris & Hunt, 1975)
		Stages and abilities associated with each are invariant, sequential, and qualitatively different from one another.		Albert Einstein Scales of Sensorimotor Development (Escalona & Corman, 1966)
		Although there are approximate age levels associated with each of the stages, the theoretical emphasis is on the sequence—abilities associated with each stage have more meaning than does the age of skill acquisition.	Debates usefulness of Piagetian-based scales for children with special needs, with some in strong support (Fewell, 1983).	Observation of Behavior in Socially and Ecologically Relevant and Valid Environments (OBSERVE; Dunst & McWilliam, 1988)
		Development occurs as a result of interactions with the environment coupled with natural physical and neurological maturation.	Instruments helped lay the groundwork for the development of play-based approaches.	
		Importance is placed of the child's interactions with environment as it contributes to progression through the cognitive stages.		
Constructivist: social constructivism	Vygotsky (1978, 1993)	Considers the importance of people and culture in a child's development; culture and people around a child determine how a child learns.	Uses a scoring system that gives partial credit for emerging skills.	Play-based models of assessment (e.g., Linder, 1993a; Flagler, 1996)
		It is the people in a child's life who give that child language by providing him with words and labels for the objects and events in his life.	Children would not be required to demonstrate all skills associated with one stage of development before being exposed to more advanced ideas (scaffolding).	Kaufman Survey of Early Academic and Language Skills (K-SEALS; Kaufman & Kaufman, 1993)
		It is through language that children acquire the ability to think.		Dynamic assessment (Kahn, 2000)
		Social connections to people enable children to develop language, and language, in turn, enables them to communicate, formulate and express ideas, asks questions, and conceive and develop solutions to problems.		

TABLE 5–1 (Continued)

Theoretical Perspective	Key Theorists	Principles	Assessment Implications	Examples of Assessment Instruments/Techniques
Constructivist: social constructivism (*continued*)		The most debilitating consequence of a child's having a disability is how the disability might alter the extent to and manner in which the child is able or allowed to participate in the social world around him.	Interactive assessments follow a test-teach-test format, where gain scores become the primary focus rather than static performance on a single administration of a test.	
		The distance between a child's actual developmental level and her potential development, known as the zone of proximal development reflects how learning precedes development.		
Transactional	Sameroff and Chandler (1975)	Based upon the interaction of a child's genotype and the nature of the environment provided by the child's caregiver.	Child is viewed within his environment, not in isolation.	Observations of parent-child interactions
		There is an ongoing progressive interplay between the child and her environment, with a mutual influence on one another.		Diagnostic Classification of Mental Health and Developmental Disorders of Infancy and Early Childhood (Zero to Three, 1994)
		There is a continual evolution of the child's environment as well as development and change in the child.		
		The child will bring to the environment many traits such as temperament, physical attributes, and genetic information. Caregivers, family members, and others with whom the child has contact will react based on these traits. In turn, the child will continue to interact with the people in her life, triggering reciprocal influences.		
		Risk factors to which a child is exposed interact with the natural and quality of child care.		

context. We cannot give the same standardized test to children from wealthy suburban areas, rural pockets of poverty in Appalachia, an urban inner city, migrant farm families, or pockets of immigrant non-English-speaking communities and assume that their having been "represented" in the norm group makes these differences irrelevant. Children with no siblings, five siblings, two birth parents, a single mother who is a fourteen-year-old school dropout, no books in the home, or a wealth of books and other resources in the home simply do not come to the assessment process with equal experiences. Were such a variety of children all to achieve the same score on a standardized test, we would certainly need to interpret the score's meaning from the context of the child.

Criterion-referenced testing has no better means of incorporating the child's context into the assessment process than does norm-referenced testing. However, the intended purpose of these assessments is simply to identify what skills a child has and which ones should follow next in a logical sequence. The addition of age approximations to these instruments seems to broaden their market appeal while increasing their distance from context-based perspectives of the child. The responsibility to give the test results meaning within the child's context again rests in the hands of those using these tools. Criterion-referenced tests do offer an efficient means to plan programs, communicate with parents about the child's development, and document a child's progress to monitor the effectiveness of early intervention.

The constructivist perspective currently popular in early childhood education and early childhood special education has developed primarily out of the combined influence of the cognitive stages theory of Piaget and the social constructivism of Vygotsky. Piaget's (1952) cognitive stages theory of child development is based upon a series of hierarchical stages of development, summarized in Table 5–2.

How Assessments Are Done

Assessments of infants, toddlers, and preschool children can be completed in many ways. There are differences related to the number and types of people involved and the ways in which these people work together and how they gather information about the child. There can also be variety in the nature of assessment tools and strategies. For the purposes of dis-

Finding A Better Way

Als (1986) offers a synactive model for premature newborns that has a theoretical orientation similar to the transactional perspective. In this model, she describes the reciprocal relationship between newborns that are in a neonatal intensive care unit (NICU) and their care. The infant is not viewed as a passive recipient of care, but rather as an individual who is actively seeking to influence the nature of that care. Caregivers develop individualized behavior-based care plans to maximize the benefit. Physiological and behavioral distress signs such as heart rate, respiration, skin color, vomiting, gaze aversion, and state of arousal serve as a means of communication for the infant. In Als's model, the caregiver strives to understand the infant's efforts to communicate and offer appropriate individualized responses. Sensory stimulation may need to be kept to a minimum for a very fragile infant, whereas a stable infant should be ready to welcome greater sensory input. This individualization of need includes such basics as amount of lighting and noise in the room, frequency of caregiving routines that require handling and positioning, and amount of bed space and swaddling provided. Research findings have consistently demonstrated that this model of intervention produces fewer days on ventilation and oxygen support, shorter hospital stays, and significantly reduced hospital costs (Gorski & VandenBerg, 1996). The implications for care and management of an NICU are contrary to a model of intervention that is based on universal routines and protocols.

cussion, these variables have been divided into two sections. The first section includes information related to people involved in the assessment process, including levels of specialization, models of teaming, and direct and indirect assessment. The second contains information about techniques used in the assessment process. Figure 5–1 offers a visual illustration of the persons and techniques described in this chapter. Each technique runs on a continuum of options. Since it would be impossible to discuss every possible point along these continua, you are encouraged to envision examples of assessment techniques in addition to the examples included in the text.

TABLE 5–2 Piagetian Stages of Development

Developmental Stage	Developmental Accomplishments	General Characteristics
A. Sensorimotor Period (0–2 years)		
I. Use of reflexes (0–1 month)	Learns to use reflexes in new behavior patterns (e.g., sucking nipple, expands to sucking other objects) Cries when another infant is crying	Predominated by reflexive behavior—blinking, sucking, startled by loud sounds, motor reflexes
II. Primary circular reactions (1–4 months)	Hand-to-mouth coordination Visually attempts to follow objects as they move outside visual range Repeats own sounds and movements after adult imitations Plays through continual repetition of patterns of movement and/or sound	Trial-and-error explorations repeated until they become habits Focus of attention is on infant's own body Integration of sensory and motor behaviors to beginning interaction with the environment
III. Secondary circular reactions (4–8 months)	Repeats patterns of behavior that produce pleasurable effects Restores visual contact when objects are out of sight by anticipating reappearance or removing material covering object Imitates sounds and simple gestures that infant is capable of producing Plays through repetition of interesting actions using objects in the environment	Awareness that his own behavior can have an effect on the environment Repetition of actions that produce pleasurable effects on the environment
IV. Coordination of secondary schemes (8–12 months)	Creates series of behaviors to achieve goals Touches adult's hands in order to initiate or continue an interesting activity Studies objects in a manner reflecting appreciation of three-dimensional attributes Obtains objects that he has watched be hidden Imitates novel sounds that are similar to previously produced sounds Imitates novel movements that include actions similar to previously accomplished ones	Behavior becomes goal directed Application of previously learned behaviors to new situations

(continued)

TABLE 5–2 Piagetian Stages of Development (Continued)

Developmental Stage	Developmental Accomplishments	General Characteristics
V. Tertiary circular reactions (12–18 months)	Seeks novel ways to desired goal	New behaviors learned through trial and error
	Locates objects hidden in a series of observable displacements	Actions and thoughts are flexible
	Hands objects to adult to initiate or repeat a desired action	Many cognitive and motor alternatives used in problem solving
	Imitates novel sound patterns and words not previously heard	
	Imitates novel movements not previously performed	
	Substitutes objects during play (e.g., toy dishes for real ones)	
VI. Combination of new means through mental combinations (18–24 months)	Uses foresight to invent new behaviors (purposeful problem solving)	Use of insight rather than trial-and-error problem-solving strategies
	Locates objects that are hidden (object permanence)	Use of symbolic language to refer to absent objects
	Able to infer a cause when only the effect is seen and to understand the effect when just the cause is known (cause-effect relationship)	
	Imitates complex verbalizations; reproduces previously heard sounds and words from memory (vocal imitation)	
	Imitates complex motor movements and reproduces previously seen actions from memory (motor imitation)	
	Plays using one object to represent another (e.g., box for a cash register) (symbolic play)	

TABLE 5-2 (Continued)

Developmental Stage	Developmental Accomplishments	General Characteristics
B. Preoperational Thoughts (2–7 years)	Initially speaks in collective monologues (in the presence of others but not addressed to them for communicative purposes; thinking out his actions aloud)	Socialization of behavior as seen in verbal exchanges and play in games with rules
	Advances to socialized intercommunicative speech	Behavior and thinking are egocentric (child cannot see viewpoint of another)
	Thought processes characterized by centration (fixing attention on a limited perceptual aspect of an object)	Unable to understand or conceptualize transformations of objects (just sees an initial and final element when objects are transformed)
	Lacks reversibility (following a line of reasoning back to where it started) in thought processes	Initially thought is slow, plodding, inflexible, dominated by perceptions, and remains irreversible; gradually as egocentrism diminishes, decentering and attendance to simple transformations increase reversibility of thought
	Gradually develops a beginning understanding of conservation (conceptualization that the amount or quantity of matter stays the same regardless of changes in shape or position)	Skills in conservation developed sequentially: Number Age 5–6 Mass Age 7–8 Area Age 7–8 Weight Age 9–10 Volume Age 11–12
C. Concrete Operations (7–11 years)	Becomes a social being	Reasoning processes become logical—makes cognitive and logical decisions as opposed to perceptual decisions
	Decenters perceptions	
	Attends to transformations	Egocentrism diminished as child uses social interaction to verify or deny concepts
	Attains reversibility of operations	
	Improves operations of seriation and classification	
D. Formal Operations (11–15 years)	Able to deal with complex verbal problems, hypothetical problems, or problems involving the future	Cognitive structures reach maturity

FIGURE 5–1 Assessment Persons and Techniques

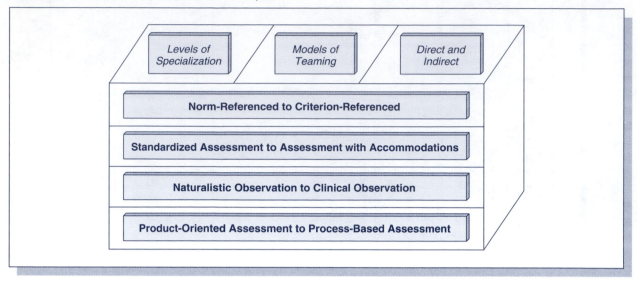

Persons Involved in Assessment

Levels of Specialization

The pattern of generalist to specialist is evident across several different disciplines involved in the assessment of infants, toddlers, and preschool children. These disciplines include education, health and medicine, psychology and mental health, and social work and human services. We are most likely to see generalists involved at the initial point of contact with a family. These generalists include pediatricians, health department nurses, social workers, child care workers, preschool and kindergarten teachers, Head Start teachers, and so forth.

These generalists routinely interact with children and their families, often conducting simple screening assessments that provide quick looks at the developmental progression of the children in their care. For example, well-child checkups, whether through a private pediatrician or a health department, usually involve parents completing a simple developmental questionnaire that includes a few questions about the child's ability to perform age-appropriate tasks. The Denver Prescreening Developmental Questionnaire-Revised (Frankenburg, et al., 1992) is an example of such a questionnaire. Further, a well-child medical examination will include observations of physical development, integration of primitive reflexes, height, weight, and head circumference. As the child gets older it expands to include communication skills, cognitive alertness, and social and emotional patterns. Vision screenings are often offered by nurses through a local health department and may be as convenient as the local shopping mall. Teachers working with young children monitor individual development in a variety of ways, both formally and informally. When generalists find cause for concern as a result of their assessments, they refer the child and family to a specialist for further assessments.

Specialists who commonly get involved in the assessment of young children with developmental delays include physical therapists, speech and language pathologists, audiologists, vision specialists, occupational therapists, psychologists, nutrition specialists, special educators, and medical specialists, such as pediatric neurologists. These individuals provide a higher level of expertise in a more restricted arena of child or family functioning. As the severity of a problem increases, the number and level of specialists involved in assessments also increases.

A pediatrician might be concerned about a nine-month-old who is continuing to display primitive reflexes rather than developing normal voluntary motor control. She makes a referral to a pediatric neurologist. The neurologist conducts a number of assessments, focusing on both current functioning of the child and possible diagnostic explanations of the lack of motor development. She may need to make even further medical referrals to a geneticist for assistance in the search for an accurate diagnosis.

Additionally, if she is concerned about the child's developmental progress, she will make further referrals to a physical therapist, a speech and language pathologist with expertise in oral-motor feeding problems and prespeech development, and an early intervention specialist. Each of these persons will also begin with assessment of the child to determine present functioning and to identify the best means of intervention. The specialists then report their findings to the referring generalist, and the child's parents. Results may also be shared among specialists, depending upon the model of teaming being used. In most instances, these specialists will supplement the work of generalists rather than replace them as primary service providers. A child will continue to see a pediatrician or family practice physician for general health needs even after a geneticist has determined that the child has Down syndrome.

Models of Teaming

The continuum seen in models of teaming goes from the generalist operating in an isolated rural area to multiagency teams of specialists working collaboratively. This wide variance can be attributed to differences in community resources, preferences of service providers for one delivery system over another, sources of funding, availability of specialists, or the extent of a child's disabilities. The practical realities of delivery systems and current models of funding present obstacles to the widespread adoption of a transdisciplinary model described below, which requires the simultaneous presence of multiple professionals during an assessment session. However, special education legislation does require that the evaluation of infants, toddlers, and preschool children to determine eligibility for services involve professionals from multiple disciplines working together as a team in some fashion.

Outside of the special education system, parents might seek an assessment of their young child from a person with expertise in a single discipline. For example, an audiologist might be consulted when a toddler has had chronic middle ear infections to determine if there is temporary or permanent loss of hearing. If the results show that the child has normal hearing, that would likely be the end of it. If the audiologist did detect a hearing loss, in addition to the medical personnel that would be consulted regarding possible treatment, a number of professionals would likely become involved (e.g., speech and lan-

guage pathologist, deaf educator, and/or early interventionist). In another instance an infant might have experienced a seizure, causing the pediatrician to refer the child to a pediatric neurologist for evaluation. If the neurologist determines that the seizure is not symptomatic of more serious problems, she will likely treat the child without the involvement of other professionals. However, if the pediatric neurologist determines that the seizure is one symptom among many that indicates the child has extensive brain damage, she will probably make multiple additional referrals. At this point the infant and family should be referred to the Part C service delivery system in their state. Through Part C services, the infant and family should have a team of professionals involved in an eligibility evaluation and assessment for program planning.

Today many early interventionists base programs on a team approach. Very young children with disabilities often present a variety of problems requiring knowledge and expertise from multiple disciplines. Children with motor delays may need physical therapists, occupational therapists, speech and language therapists, as well as early interventionists. Additionally, the parents and caregivers of this child might need training in proper handling and positioning techniques. If there are particular concerns about the child's ability to eat, gain weight, or tolerate a textured diet, a nutritionist could be added to the team. The determination of who comprises the team of professionals for early intervention is best made on an individual basis. Although the basic composition of teams may be fairly consistent for children with similar disabilities, every child presents a unique picture with needs originating out of their home and community environments.

Three models of the team process are identified in early intervention literature—multidisciplinary, interdisciplinary, and transdisciplinary. Whereas there are distinctions made between these models in textbooks and research journals, the words are not always used with such precision in legislation or actual practice. For example, Part C requires that each child receive a multidisciplinary team evaluation to determine eligibility for services. In this case, the emphasis is on the inclusion of two or more disciplines in the process, not the model of communication used by the team. Any one of the three models would meet the requirement. Terms used generally reflect local preferences and resources, combined with funding and reimbursement options available within a specific community. *Multidisciplinary team* is used both as a general term to indicate any team comprised of the child's parents and professionals representing a variety of specialties and as a particular type of team described below.

Multidisciplinary Teams   The multidisciplinary team approach emerged from the medical model. Specialists who have expertise in the areas suspected of causing medical difficulties for a patient receive a referral and examine the patient independently. Each professional with expertise in relevant developmental areas performs separate examinations on the patient. Each team member sees the child individually, writes up a report, and makes recommendations for the patient. No discussion, debate, comparison of results, analysis or interpretation of findings, or mutual development of recommendations across disciplines takes place in this medically oriented multidisciplinary process (Bennett, 1982; Fewell, 1983). Such an assessment model for young children can leave parents with multiple, conflicting recommendations.

Even when a multidisciplinary team channels all of the assessment results to one professional, who then summarizes the findings and makes recommendations for the parents, there are flaws in the multidisciplinary model. The biases of the person responsible for summarizing results will influence his interpretation of the findings. Additionally, this person might be put in a position of trying to help the parents interpret medical test results and make decisions about the child's future without an adequate background. Finally, the professionals do not get to interpret their own findings with an awareness of the other assessments of the child.

The potential composition of an *interdisciplinary team* is identical to that of a multidisciplinary team. The difference between the two lies in the formality of communications and group decision making (Fewell, 1983). Members of an interdisciplinary team come together informally during the assessment process and formally when the process is complete to make decisions regarding services. The interdisciplinary team may be hampered by communication difficulties across disciplines. Professionals who are familiar with the language associated with their particular area of expertise may have difficulty understanding and being understood by professionals from other disciplines. Professionals might also disagree as to what the priority areas for intervention are, or the best approaches for intervention to recommend.

The addition of a formal system of communication into the model does not ensure that cooperative group decisions will be reached regarding the recommendations for a child and his family. However, the parents are at least not left in isolation with the conflicting choices before them. Professionals should openly discuss contradictory findings or recommendations with parents, providing them with resources that offer additional information about the issues at hand, various intervention options, and the names of other parents willing to talk to them. If participants of interdisciplinary teams follow these policies, they can facilitate informed parental decision making and avoid placing the parent in the middle of a battle between two or more professionals.

As with the interdisciplinary model, team membership on the *transdisciplinary team* is similar to the multidisciplinary team. How the team functions, however, is very different. Although some initial assessments and ongoing medical procedures will always necessitate separate clinical evaluations (e.g., genetic evaluations), a significant portion of the educational and therapeutic assessments typically conducted on infants and young children with disabilities can be performed using transdisciplinary teams. Such assessments can be conducted as **arena assessments,** allowing all team members the opportunity to plan, observe, and analyze the assessment process.

In an arena assessment, the actual handling and interaction with the child is limited to one or two individuals (McGonigel, Woodruff, & Roszmann-Millican, 1994). The person who is interacting with the child conducts an assessment of the child in her own discipline as well as asking the child to perform tasks relevant to other disciplines. Professionals from the various disciplines involved observe the child's performance and ask the one conducting the assessment for additional information regarding unobservable child characteristics. Parents can also participate in the arena assessment, as observers or as one of the persons responsible for interacting with and handling the child.

Team members using a transdisciplinary model need to reach agreements in five areas presented in Figure 5–2. Without such commitments, transdisciplinary teams face the same limitations found in the interdisciplinary model. One potential drawback to the transdisciplinary approach is the time commitment that can be required of numerous professionals. The model requires that all involved professionals attend meetings to plan the assessment, participate or

FIGURE 5–2 Five Agreements of Transdisciplinary
Teams

1. Acceptance of differences in skills
2. Acceptance of differences in approach
3. Willingness not to try to know everything
4. Ability to call on others for assistance and
   ongoing knowledge
5. Nonthreatening opportunities for discussion
   of these areas

Source: From "The Role of the Pediatrician with Young Exceptional Children and Their Families," by J. Howard, 1982, *Exceptional Children, 48,* pp. 296–304.

observe throughout the assessment, and attend a postassessment meeting to summarize results and determine recommendations. Such an approach can be expensive as well as time consuming, since multiple professionals are simultaneously present and focused on a single child for an extended period. However, the rewards are substantial for this increased investment through improved communication and collaborative formulation of recommendations regarding needed services for children and their families. Although it increases professional time commitments for a single child, the model can reduce the time and stress for the child and parents. The number of separate appointments is reduced as is the number of people who are directly handling the child who are strangers to the child.

The advantages of such a model of intervention are particularly evident when children present problems that overlap traditional boundaries for service delivery. For example, a child with prespeech and feeding difficulties can profit more when a speech and language therapist works with an occupational therapist and a physical therapist to plan an intervention than when each works in isolation. Transdisciplinary programming can be helpful in reducing the gaps in a child's services if no single person feels adequately trained to address an area of need. As team members, professionals can assist each other in the pursuit of solutions to problems that the children and/or families are facing. The types of information that can be obtained through arena assessments of infants are shown in Table 5–3.

The arena assessment model incorporates family members as part of the assessment team. Before the actual assessment, one team member is designated as the facilitator, and another serves as the coach. The role of the facilitator is to interact with and handle the child, while the coach offers assistance and provides reminders or additional suggestions from other professionals observing the assessment. All team members participate in the process. The facilitator provides the "hands" for the "brains" of the team members who are observing. The facilitator acts in concert with the observers as they prompt her, offer reminders, and make on-the-spot suggestions as the assessment is progressing. The parent(s) can work with the facilitator interacting with the child or remain an observer. Often a parent(s) will join the play situation as needed.

Direct and Indirect Assessment

When we assess a child by having face-to-face contact in a testing situation or observing the child firsthand, it is direct assessment. However, we may be interested in how a child performs across a variety of behavioral settings and times that are not available to us. In such cases, we can use information from an intermediate source. Most often indirect assessments involve obtaining information from parents and caregivers about the child's abilities through interviews or questionnaires. Examples of indirect assessments include the Vineland Social-Emotional Early Childhood Scales (SEEC; Sparrow, Balla, & Cicchetti, 1998) and Ages and Stages Questionnaires: A Parent-Completed, Child-Monitoring System (Bricker et al., 1995). The SEEC uses a caregiver interview format to determine developmental levels of interpersonal relationships, play and leisure time, and coping skills. The Ages and Stages Questionnaires are a series of brief checklists that parents complete to monitor the developmental progress of their infants and toddlers.

Techniques Involved in Assessment

Norm-Referenced to Criterion-Referenced Assessment

Assessment instruments based on comparisons of a child's performance to samples of other children within specified age levels are **norm-referenced.** The emphasis in norm-referenced testing is on how children compare to other children rather than on which specific skills they have mastered. Norm-referenced instruments produce standardized scores such as age equivalents, developmental quotients, grade equivalents, percentiles, or other standardized

TABLE 5–3 Types of Information Obtained through Arena Assessments of Infants

Area of Functioning	Examples
Behavior and style	■ Appearance ■ Rhythmicity ■ Frustration tolerance ■ Attention
Object interaction and cognition	■ Symbolic object use ■ Planned problem solving ■ Discrimination
Social/emotional	■ Reaction to strangers ■ Affective range ■ Attachment/separation behavior ■ Play style
Communication	■ Frequency/duration ■ Quality of speech ■ Mode of communication
Sensorimotor	■ Tactile responsivity/sensitivity ■ Primitive reflexes ■ Tool use ■ Sucking/drinking/chewing
Self-help	■ Feeding ■ Dressing ■ Toileting

scores such as *z*-scores or *T*-scores (described in Chapter 6). They are commonly used in the process of determining eligibility for special education services, placement decisions, and program evaluations. Such tests may be of limited value for daily program planning or development of specific intervention strategies.

The group of children used to establish the level of difficulty of each test item is known as the **norm group.** The test is supposed to be used to assess the abilities of children who match (were represented by) the norm group. The more children of diverse ethnic groups present in the norm group (e.g., five-year-old males of Asian decent living in the southwest in a median income bracket), the more representative the norm group is for a particular child who is a member of that group. The director of a migrant Head Start program would not want to measure program effectiveness with a language development assessment instrument normed exclusively with

upper-middle-class children residing in one large metropolitan area. However, the director of an exclusive preschool in Manhattan might find such a test ideal as part of admission testing.

Since most standardized tests intended for nationwide use are developed with norm groups that reflect the most recent U.S. Census available, they tend to represent white middle-class children best. Regional tests or tests normed on special populations (e.g., children with visual impairments) offer exceptions to this generalization. The 2000 census reflects changing demographics that eventually will become reflected in the norm groups used to standardize new tests and revise current ones that are based on older census data.

Critical factors regarding the norm group that we should consider in the process of selecting assessment instruments for a particular child are the extent to which the child is represented by the sample and the extent to which we need to compare that particular child to the types of children who are represented by the sample. Other factors to consider are the overall size of the sample, distribution of characteristics evenly across age and gender groups, and recency of the sampling.

Criterion-referenced assessment focuses on what specific skills a child has mastered rather than group or norm comparisons. When criterion-referenced testing is used, the examiner presents the child with a variety of tasks to perform and notes which ones the child can perform. The results of such testing may not be helpful in determining a clinical diagnosis or developmental quotients associated with eligibility criteria for early intervention. However, teachers can use such results to develop individualized program plans and monitor the child's progress. Examples of criterion-referenced assessments that are directly linked to a curriculum, including objectives and activities for intervention, are the Hawaii Early Learning Profile (HELP; VORT Corporation, 1995, 1997); the Assessment, Evaluation, and Programming System for Infants and Children, Volumes 1–4 (AEPS; Bricker, 1993; Cripe, Slentz, & Bricker, 1993; Bricker & Pretti-Frontczak, 1996; Bricker & Waddell, (1996); the Carolina Curriculum for Infants and Toddlers with Special Needs (Johnson-Martin, Jens, Attermeier, & Hacker, 1991); and the Carolina Curriculum for Preschoolers with Special Needs (Johnson-Martin, Attermeier, & Hacker, 1990). The idea behind each of these assessments is to pinpoint what skills the child has accomplished, what skills are emerging, and where to begin intervention on the basis of individual performance.

When we select a commercially available assessment and curriculum package, there are several risks involved. First, if the particular instrument being used does not accurately reflect a child's experiences or opportunities for learning, a child's potential to learn the skill may still be unknown. For example, a criterion-referenced instrument might include the ability to place objects appropriately according to prepositions (put the block in the cup, under the cup, behind the cup, etc.). If a child had not previously been exposed to these concepts, failure could be the lack of opportunity to learn the material rather than lack of competence.

If we use criterion-referenced instruments to monitor the progress of children, we must be certain the instrument is consistent with the intervention we have been providing. Staff of a therapeutic nursery focused on social and behavioral needs of children from abusive homes should not monitor child progress with an instrument that primarily covers reading readiness skills. We might find that the child appears to have gained no new skills because of the bad match between the intervention and the assessment tool. Such inaccurate results could lead interventionists to the erroneous conclusion that their intervention program is ineffective.

Another risk of criterion-referenced testing also relates to the match between test items and the curriculum, where the test becomes the curriculum. It is an easy temptation for interventionists to select a commercially available program and let it become the curriculum for all children, without due consideration to individual needs and parental priorities. Although the problem of evaluating a child's progress on skills to which he has not been exposed has been eliminated, the planning of an appropriate program may have been the cost. Criterion-referenced tests have much to offer early interventionists, however, they should be reviewed for each individual child before the content of the test is adopted as the curriculum.

A related procedure, particularly useful in the assessment of children with severe disabilities is **task analysis.** Task analysis involves the division of a skill into smaller subskills. The procedure is used in assessment as well as instruction. For assessment purposes, we can use task analysis to determine which subskills of a task a child has already mastered. From such an assessment it is easy to know what skills to work on with the child. There are two approaches that can be taken in task analysis: **skill sequencing** and **chaining of responses.**

Skill sequencing involves the identification of a sequence of skills that lead to mastery of a more advanced skill. For example, independent toileting involves skills related to muscle control, ability to anticipate and take action, dressing and undressing, sitting balance, ability to follow a multiple step process without distraction, and general hygiene. Chaining of responses involves the identification of specific behaviors as they occur during the completion of a task. Table 5–4 provides examples of skill sequencing and chaining of responses for toileting. Each of the subskills could be further task analyzed into additional sub-subskills. The task analysis should be as detailed as needed to isolate specific subskills a child is unable to perform. For interventionists struggling to help a child achieve success on a particular skill, task analysis can enable the child and the teacher to see progress in small increments. The AEPS, developed

TABLE 5–4 Examples of Two Types of Task Analysis

Skill Sequencing for Toileting	Chaining of Responses for Toileting
1. Muscle control	1. Become aware of the physical need to urinate
2. The ability to anticipate and take action	2. Locate and go to an appropriate bathroom
3. Dressing and undressing	3. Remove clothing as necessary
4. Sitting balance	4. Sit or stand in the appropriate location
5. Ability to follow a multiple-step process with distraction	5. Release muscle tension of bladder and urinate
6. General hygiene	6. Wipe off excess urine (for females)
	7. Stand up (for females)
	8. Get dressed
	9. Flush toilet
	10. Find sink and wash hands, using soap
	11. Dry hands
	12. Exit bathroom

by Bricker and colleagues, uses a task analysis approach to match the child to appropriate instructional objectives and activities. The effective use of task analysis for program planning also requires the identification of the necessary prerequisite skills (e.g., cooperativeness in going to the toileting area).

Standardized Assessment to Assessment with Accommodations

Standardized tests have specific procedures that must be followed for test results to be considered valid. Some tests provide the examiner with exactly what to say throughout the test. Other tests require the presentation of subtests in a specific order with specific restrictions (e.g., timed portions). Standardized tests have specific instructions for establishing starting and stopping points.

Since all of the standardized procedures of test administration are used in the establishment of test norms, an examiner must adhere to them for proper test administration. If she deviates from them, the results are no longer comparable to those obtained from the norm group and the scores are not valid. However, for some children following standardized procedures can produce equally invalid results. If a test requires that a child look at a picture and point to some specific part of it, a child unable to see the picture due to visual impairments simply cannot do it. A child who is unable to speak cannot recite a nursery rhyme, even if he is familiar with it, has the words memorized, or could trigger assistive technology to

repeat the rhyme. Other testing procedures that present difficulties for children with disabilities may be subtler. For example, timing the speed at which a performance item is completed for a child with physical disabilities could result in an unfair and inaccurate assessment of cognitive potential.

Some examiners do deviate from standardized procedures when testing children with disabilities. Sattler (1992) points out that some deviations appear to be minor and would not preclude the use of standardized norms. For example, children who are physically unable to point can use eye gaze to indicate choices, and examiners can read test items to a child with visual impairments. Even modifications of this nature must be done with extreme caution. Hoffmeister (1988) notes how such modifications in testing children with severe hearing impairments fail to account for the developmental differences that these children may experience. The tests, based on a norm group of children with intact hearing, may assess cognitive functioning as reflected by auditory, visual, and motor skills, whereas the child who is deaf develops his cognitive understanding primarily through visual and motor skills. Simply using sign language throughout the test will not resolve the poor match between the child being tested and the norm group.

Children who do not present a close match to the norm group simply should not be given a test other than for the sole purpose of comparing the child to the norm group. For example, a child who is blind might be viewed as physically delayed when compared to a sighted population, but when compared to other children with visual impairments the motor delay is not apparent. Proper interpretation of the child's performance on a test normed with a sighted population is that he is delayed in motor development (as expected for children with visual impairments), but does not necessarily indicate a separate motor impairment. Although we should provide intervention to reduce the motor delay, it would be a misdiagnosis to indicate that the child had a motor impairment in addition to the visual problem.

A technique known as **testing-of-limits** can be used to explore the child's abilities beyond those exhibited during a standard test administration (Sattler, 1992). To avoid compromising the integrity of the standardized instrument, we should not use testing-of-limits until the entire test has been given under the standardized procedures. Following the standardized test administration, there are five actions that examiners can try as part of this technique summarized in Figure 5–3. One possible drawback to the use of testing-the-limits is the potential invalidation of any future retesting of the child using the same instrument. Additional adaptive assessment strategies are shown in Table 5–5.

Some tests are developed so that they can be easily altered for use with children who have disabilities. Adaptive-to-disability scales allow a child to use alternative senses and responses to attempt test items. Scales are available that give the examiner the responsibility of determining if and when modifications of items and procedures are appropriate, such as the Battelle Developmental Inventory (Newborg et al., 1984). Some tests provide guidelines for the alteration of test items or the response required. Such modifications are similar to Sattler's suggestion that an examiner wishing to test-the-limits might change the modality required.

Adaptive-to-disability assessment techniques can involve the use of instruments specifically designed for and standardized on groups of children with specific disabilities. However, there are very few such norm-referenced instruments that can meet the technical standards set for quality in today's market for infants and very young children. The Bayley Screener is a unique example with its clinical standardization sample. The Universal Nonverbal Intelligence Test (UNIT; Bracken & McCallum, 1998) is a recent addition to the cognitive assessment market for children who may face a disadvantage on traditional measures of intelligence. The UNIT is a nonverbal test suitable for children between the ages of 5 years and 17 years who have speech, language, or hearing impairments; color-vision deficiencies; different cultural or language backgrounds; and children who are nonverbal. The standardization sample included a wide variety of

---

FIGURE 5–3 Testing-the-Limits Accommodations

1. **Providing additional cues:** The examiner can return to failed items and let the child attempt them again with additional help, such as providing the first step in problem solution, or increasing the structure.

2. **Changing modality:** The examiner can change the modality that is involved in problem solution. For example, moving from oral to written problem solution or from written to oral might change the level of difficulty of the task for some children.

3. **Establishing methods used by the child:** Learning how the child went about solving the problem could provide as much information as the fact that he missed it or passed it. Ask the child to explain how he got his answer. If he is unable to explain it, he might be able to show how he found his solution to the problem.

4. **Eliminating time limits:** For those children whose performance was hampered by the time limits on a test, readministration of timed items with no time limits can give the examiner needed information about the child's ability to accomplish specific tasks.

5. **Asking probing questions:** If a child gave responses that the examiner wanted to explore further but could not while following a standardized testing procedure, he might want to return to those items upon completion of the test. He can give the child an opportunity to tell more about his response.

Source: *Assessment of Children* (revised and updated 3rd edition), by J. M. Sattler, 1992. San Diego, CA: Jerome M. Sattler, Publisher.

TABLE 5–5 Testing Accommodations

Accomodation	Examples
■ Alter the properties of materials and objects used during the assessment process	■ Change size of objects; increase differences between items such as colors, sizes, sounds; add texture to flat surfaces
■ Increase the ways in which a child can respond	■ Directed eye gaze to communication board, microswitches, selection from multiple options
■ Remove items that bias performance	■ Put together a puzzle within a time limit for child with physical disability that involves arms and hands, with adjusted score
■ Expand scoring to include some partial credit	■ Score 0, 1, 2 for emerging skills instead of wrong or right
■ Alter the sequence of tasks	■ Present all tasks associated with color recognition together instead of distributed across age levels with other items in-between
■ Present similar items from multiple scales	■ Vary letter recognition to a pointing task, an oral response, or a written task on different tests
■ Use a test-teach-test approach	■ After testing numeral recognition, spend a few minutes "teaching" the numerals that were not known, noting child's response to instruction; then retest for short-term retention

children receiving special education services with percentages approximating numbers of children served in each disability category. Another example is the Autism Screening Instrument for Educational Planning (Krug, Arick, & Almond, 1993). The standardization sample for this instrument included children previously diagnosed with autism or severe mental retardation and typically developing children. Instruments specifically designed for use without modifications have the advantage over testing-the-limits procedures in that they produce a valid score, and future use of the same test is not compromised.

Product-Oriented Assessment to Process-Based Assessment

A **product-oriented** approach to assessment involves giving the child a battery of tests that produce scores or other final products. Screening and diagnosis procedures are typically product-oriented assessments. Testing of this nature can give parents and professionals information about how the child compares to other children, and help them in making

placement decisions and determining general instructional levels. Product-oriented assessment gives us a test score, a percentile, a "yes" or "no" for referring the child for further testing and diagnostics, an age equivalent, a developmental quotient, or some similar summative result. The results of product-oriented test assessments are easy to communicate, but are at risk of being meaningless and misleading if we use inappropriate or biased instruments.

In contrast, **process-oriented assessment** involves the study of the child's interactions with the examiner and/or others as well as responses to environmental stimuli. Examiners find process-oriented assessment particularly useful in estimating the abilities of children with severe impairments. It provides a focus on changes in child behaviors, such as smiling, eye gaze, heart rate, surprise, communicative intentions, or other subtle indicators that have no significance in product-based assessment. Play-based assessments and interventions (e.g., Linder, 1993a, 1993b) focus on the nature and quality of child play as well as child performance. **Portfolio assessment** (e.g., Shores & Grace, 1998), which involves the compilation of samples of children's work, offers another process-based approach that can be used with preschool-age children. The child's progress over time across a variety of activities is documented in the portfolio. **Work sampling systems** (e. g., Harrington, Meisels, McMahon, Dichtelmiller, & Jablon, 1997a, 1997b) combine a variety of systematic observations, anecdotal records, and work samples to develop narrative summaries of child functioning across a variety of curricular areas.

Interactive approaches to assessment developed from Vygotsky's theoretical perspectives emphasize process-based data gathering rather than the production of test scores. The emphasis is placed on identifying and strengthening emerging skills rather than on identifying and eliminating deficiencies. Four characteristics shared by differing interactive approaches to assessment are that the examiner (1) plays an active role rather than passively monitoring the child's performance; (2) engages with the child in collaborative interaction at some point during the assessment; (3) deliberately changes the nature of what is being tested; and (4) focuses on the broad goal of assessing potential rather than being concerned only about current performance (Haywood, 1992). The interactive approach known as dynamic assessment (Kahn, 2000; Lidz & Elliott, 2000) is based upon theories of cognitive modifiability developed by Feuerstein and Vygotsky's work related to the mediation of learning that occurs in a sociocultural context. The approach involves a cycle of test-probe-teach-test. Table 5–6 provides further descriptions of interactive approaches.

Product-based assessment techniques have limited use with children who have very restricted response repertoires. The need for alternative approaches to assessment that do not rely on voluntary muscle control or speech production is readily apparent when we face the challenge of assessing a two-year-old with severe motor impairments who is nonverbal. The result of testing children in a non-adapted manner can yield results that depress the estimate of the child's cognitive ability. If caregivers and interventionists accept these assessments, they may assume lower cognitive expectations for the child. Lowered expectations can then lead to a depressed performance by the child. Such a prognosis that can lead to a "syndrome of learned incompetence" (Kearsley, 1979) is known as **iatrogenic** retardation. An iatrogenic condition is one that is the result of treatment. For example, a visual impairment may be the result of prolonged administration of oxy-gen to a premature infant. Likewise, a cognitive impairment may be the result of programming at an inappropriately low level for a child who is unable to speak or move. Kearsley used the term is his work with high-risk infants who were diagnosed as mentally and motorically retarded.

The prerequisite motor competence and dependence on cooperative behavior can make standarized instruments inappropriate for infants with sensory or motor impairments. Alternative measures, such as the perceptual cognitive processing procedures developed by Zelazo (1979, 1982a, 1982b), can be a more reflective and accurate interpretation of child functioning during infancy. There is a need to use unconventional means to assess many infants who are severely physically limited (Zelazo & Weiss, 1990). The process-oriented approach to assessment can be time consuming, both in terms of assessment time and in time spent analyzing and interpreting the results. However, for the infant or young child with severe impairments, it may be the only method available that is fair.

Naturalistic Observation to Clinical Observation

Observation is an essential technique used in assessment that can involve gathering both qualitative and quantitative data about a child's behavior. Brandt (1975) has identified four perspectives used in research involving observation, summarized in Table 5–7. These same four perspectives have direct application to observations that we make for child assessments. The intended purpose of an observation influences which behaviors we observe and the appropriate perspective for us to take. For example, if a physician is concerned with the effectiveness of a medication that has been prescribed to reduce hyperactivity, an ethological approach to observation could be appropriate—recording the frequency and duration of motor movements only. However, the parent might be concerned with the impact the medication is having on the child's social development. In such a case, we would use an ecological approach or interaction analysis.

When we use observations for assessment, we need to focus initially on the actual events and behaviors, rather than the subjective interpretations of those behaviors. Consider the scenario of observing one child kick another. A premature interpretative recording of such a behavior might read:

> Joe and Jack were <u>enjoying</u> the time they have together playing with the blocks. <u>They are good friends.</u>

TABLE 5–6 Examples of Interactive Testing

Approach	References	Description	Instruments
Test-teach-test	Campione & Brown, 1987	Focuses on observing a child's learning efficiency and her ability to transfer skills from one task to another. Pre- and post-test performance, combined with the number of hints a child needed to accomplish the task taught between the test administrations, do provide a quantitative measure for this approach.	Learning Potential Assessment Device Preschool Learning Potential Assessment Device
Dynamic assessment	Feuerstein, 1979 Feuerstein, Miller, Rand, & Jensen, 1981 Kahn, 2000 Lidz & Elliott, 2000 Lidz & Thomas 1987 Tzuriel & Klein, 1987; 1988	Introduces new cognitive tasks to the child in such a way that the child must use problem-solving strategies to understand and complete the tasks before him. Involves documentation of the amount of instruction and the rapidity with which the child comes to understand the task.	Mediated Learning Experience (MLE) and Rating Scale Children's Analogical Thinking Modifiability

TABLE 5–7 Observation Perspectives Used in Research

Perspective	Description	Use
■ Ecological psychology	■ The study of naturally occurring behavior in everyday settings	■ Observer begins with as few preconceptions as possible, hoping to discover the "stream of behavior" that may have been previously unrecognized
■ Ethological	■ Observation in a natural setting with relatively few preconceptions	■ Restricted to those behaviors that are clearly observable—motor patterns and discrete actions
■ Interaction analysis	■ Categorization of behaviors observed during interactions	■ Predetermined if the observer is using a checklist or rating sheet, or the observer can create his own categories based on data analysis
■ Behavior modification	■ Typically focuses on the specific behavior of a child who is the target of the observation	■ Observers determine what elements of a behavior setting serve as reinforcers for the child, and the effectiveness of adjusting those reinforcers to increase desired behaviors while decreasing undesired behaviors

Source: From "An Historical Overview of Systematic Approaches to Observation in School Settings," by R. M. Brandt, in *Observation of Pupils and Teachers in Mainstream and Special Education Settings: Alternative Strategies,* by R. A. Weinberg and F. H. Wood (Eds.), 1975, Minneapolis: University of Minnesota.

When the teacher announced that it was time to clean up, both boys <u>became angry</u> because they <u>were disappointed</u> that playtime was over. Jack <u>showed a lack of responsibility and immaturity</u> by leaving the play area. This behavior <u>made Joe so mad that he lost all control and started abusing Jack. Jack and Joe will not be allowed to play together again since they treat each other so badly. Joe has been unable to adjust in this setting and needs a program designed to serve children with severe emotional disturbance.</u>

The underlined portions of the passage are unobservable interpretations of the children's behaviors. The last two sentences are conclusions drawn by the observer based on her interpretation of the situation. An appropriate objective recording of the same scene, depicting what was *actually observable,* might read:

Joe and Jack were playing with the wooden blocks. They were smiling and talking quietly together. The teacher announced that it was time for the boys to clean up the blocks. Jack walked away from the block area. Joe ran after Jack, grabbed his shoulder,

and shouted to him, "Come back!" Then he kicked Jack in the shin and ran back to the block area.

This recording of the scene includes no interpretations of child behavior. It leaves room for investigation into the possible causes for each child's behavior. Observers can give the children an opportunity to clarify behavior and discuss feelings during the interaction, enabling the observer to make a more accurate analysis of the witnessed events.

Even when observers are careful to record actual behaviors there can be disagreement between multiple observers. Cautions should be made to distinguish *emic,* or insider views, from *edic* observations, that is, those from an outsider's view. Although an outsider may be unaware of certain dynamics or the characteristics of an ongoing relationship, the insider may be unable to free herself to observe from an unbiased perspective.

Observations that exclusively target the child, ignoring the context of behavior, can lead to confusing and inaccurate conclusions. An observer might carefully note that, when asked to draw a picture, a child drew the entire picture in black, indicating the child's overemphasis on the dark side of life and depression. The reality might have been that (1) he was given only black and brown crayons; (2) the black crayon was newest, still having a sharp point, while all the others were worn down; or (3) recently the child had participated in an art workshop in which one of the activities had been to draw an entire picture in one color and the child was simply recreating this experience for himself. Single observations taken out of context can give us inaccurate perceptions. Only through multiple observations across time, settings, and people, combined with behavioral reports about the child from parents and other caregivers, can we get a realistic picture of the child.

The observation of children in their naturally occurring play interactions under normal routines is a common part of child assessments. Observations in natural environments can involve the observation of an entire behavior setting and all that occurs within that setting over a given period. We can conduct such a comprehensive observation, including all individuals and aspects of the behavior setting, or restrict it to certain individuals and aspects of the setting. A global observation can guide us in planning future focused observations relevant to a specific child.

Through focused observations, we can look for specific exchanges or types of behaviors. For example, a child who has been having an unusually high number of temper tantrums might be observed in a natural environment over the course of the day. The behavior that is the focus of the observation is tantruming. The observer would note the times when a tantrum occurred, what preceded each one, how long each lasted, what followed the tantrum, and its nature. The observer can combine such information with other data available about the child for analysis and intervention planning. Direct observations are the primary components of several of the most innovative approaches to assessment in use today, including functional assessment of behavior (e.g., O'Neill et al., 1997) and diagnosis of mental health and developmental disorders in infancy and early childhood (Greenspan, 1992).

The techniques used to gather data in natural environments depend upon the stated purpose and intended outcomes of the observation. Each is described along with appropriate uses and possible drawbacks in Table 5–8. Sample forms that can be used to record frequency counts are shown

in Figures 5–4 and 5–5. A sample form to record the duration of behaviors is shown in Figure 5–6.

Running records produce a great deal of information that is not initially organized in any meaningful way. We can convert the information into useful data, through the development of categories. These can emerge from our notes or we can adopt a set of categories that we believe will be useful in advance. Figure 5–7 shows examples of behavioral categories useful for observations related to communication and social peer interactions.

Whether we create categories from running records, or adopt categories available from commercial assessments, we need a clear understanding of what behavior is and is not included in the category. There are a number of systems that provide categories for observation available today. For example, the Early Screening Project (Walker, Severson, & Feil, 1995) uses the observation of target children in preschool settings who display either externalizing or internalizing behavior problems. The authors provide written behavioral descriptions for the negative and positive categories of behavior to observe as well as a training videotape. For the negative categories, antisocial and nonsocial behavior, there are four types of behavior, including (1) a negative reciprocal social exchange, either verbal or physical; (2) disobeying established classroom rules; (3) tantruming; and (4) solitary play. An example of these descriptions follows:

> **Tantruming.** When the child is yelling, kicking, and/or sulking following a negative social interaction. For example, when the teacher does not allow the target child to play with a toy, the child starts to whine and jump up and down. Frequently, a tantrum will escalate and may require physical intervention by the teacher. (Walker et al., p. 37)

Observations in natural settings provide a context through which to perceive a child's actual functioning and real behaviors. Sometimes, however, a natural observation is not possible or does not offer an efficient source of data. In such cases we can use a controlled observation within the natural environment. We can "arrange" the environment as needed to monitor areas of concern. The use of imposed structure enables us to create situations that may not otherwise happen during a scheduled observation and make comparisons of child behavior as we manipulate the setting. A structured observation allows us to target specific circumstances for observation,

TABLE 5–8 Natural Observation Techniques

Observation Technique	Task of Observer	Uses
Running Record	Record everything that occurs within a given time period by taking notes; can use audio and/or video taping to allow review	Useful to get picture of what is happening generally and the sequencing of events; is of the most use at the initial stages of assessment; if the purpose of the observation is to make a placement decision, to conduct a program evaluation, to identify areas of child functioning that warrant further study for a specific child, or to initiate an environmental assessment
Event Sampling	Record specific predefined behaviors as they occur; note environmental variables such as time of day, physical setting, other persons present, and physical condition of the child	Provides focused look at particular critical events (e.g., transitions, center-based free play; meals) for specific children or types of behaviors (e.g., symbolic play, initiation of conversation with a peer)
Frequency Counts	Record the number of times a predefined behavior occurs in a given amount of time	For the observation of behaviors relatively short in duration (number of times child hits, number of toileting accidents, number of verbal outbursts directed to peers) during a specific period; comparisons of behavior frequencies across times and behavior settings can offer additional information; confirm or refute teacher perception of frequency of a behavior
Duration Recording	Record the length of time a predefined behavior occurs during an allotted period	Useful for the measurement of behaviors that vary in length (e.g., length of time child plays alone, number of minutes child cries each day, amount of time on task, time spent wandering aimlessly around room, time engaged with specific toys, time spent in the imaginary play area) observers can use this technique to determine patterns of child behavior and to set target goals for intervention
Category Sampling	Record all behaviors associated with a broad category of skills encompassing many different behaviors; recording the number of times a child initiates interactions with peers might involve observing eye contact, smiles, speaking, and touching. Examples of other categories include physical contact, number of times the child displays helping behaviors, and child-demonstrated creativity and originality	Can show patterns of interaction, motivation, cooperation, social relationships, problem-solving strategies; offers comprehensive look at child behavior integrated into the context of the setting, but can be challenging to define and achieve accuracy and agreement between observers

FIGURE 5-4 Frequency Count Observation Recording Form

Individual Child Form for Two Target Behaviors

Child's Name _____

Time of Observation

Start _____ Stop _____ Length of Observation _____ Date _____

Observer's Name & Role _____ Location of Observation _____ Description of Setting _____

Behavior	Count	Notes
1.		
2.		
3.		
4.		
5.		

FIGURE 5–5 Frequency Count Observation Recording Form

Group Form for One Target Behavior

Target Behavior _____

Time of Observation _____

Start _____ Stop _____ Length of Observation _____ Date _____

Observer's Name & Role _____

Location of Observation _____

Description of Setting _____

Child's Name	Count				Notes
1.					
2.					
3.					
4.					
5.					

FIGURE 5–6 Duration Recording Observation Form

Date _____

Time: Start _____ Stop _____ Length of Observation _____

Child's Name _____

Location Description _____

Observer's Name & Role _____

_____

Target Behavior A

Comments	Start	Stop	Duration

Total Duration of Behavior A _____

% of Time during Observation _____

Target Behavior B

Comments	Start	Stop	Duration

Total Duration of Behavior B _____

% of Time during Observation _____

FIGURE 5–7 Examples of Behavioral Categories for Analyzing Running Records

Category	Positive	Negative

Initiations to Peers
  Verbal
  Physical
  Nonverbal
  Gestures		

Responses to Peers
  Verbal
  Physical
  Nonverbal
  Gestures		

Initiations to Adults
  Verbal
  Physical
  Nonverbal
  Gestures		

Responses to Adults
  Verbal
  Physical
  Nonverbal
  Gestures		

whereas we might not be around to catch a specific behavior when it occurs naturally.

Structured observations can involve **simulated** or **staged situations,** and **role-play situations.** Structured observations that use simulated or staged situations involve the arrangement of a behavior setting that creates opportunities. A teacher, wanting to observe how a child reacts when all the materials needed to complete an activity are not immediately available, might set out everything needed except one item. The child might ask to borrow from another child, grab from another child, use physical gestures to get assistance from the teacher, begin shouting that he needs the missing item, or wait passively for help. Such an observation can give us insight into the child's approach to problem solving, peer relations, motivation to complete an activity, and use of expressive language.

Use of role-play for a structured observation gives the child an opportunity to show us how she would behave in a specific situation, such as if another child asked her to play house, or if her best friend damaged her favorite toy. Role-playing does require that a child think about the behavior she will exhibit, and, therefore does not have the spontaneity of a natural observation. Although setup of role-play observations may not offer the context-based validity of naturally occurring events, they do provide the opportunity to target a specific condition for observation. Role-playing can also be designed to target behavior settings for which natural observations are impossible (e.g., grandmother's house five hundred miles away, the doctor's office, the neighborhood playground). They can be manipulated and controlled so as to include those elements of interest to the observer at the moment.

Often formal assessments of children occur in clinical settings rather than natural environments. Manuals of standardized instruments usually stipulate that the proper environment for test administration is a quiet room free from distractions. The administration guidelines typically have the examiner note certain behaviors that occur during the assessment, such as ease of separation from parent, distractibility during test administration, motivation to perform well, and cooperativeness. Early interventionists seeking to determine whether a child can perform a skill when removed from the distractions and chaos of a preschool room might even explore conducting informal observations under "clinical" conditions. The teacher can work with the child in a separate room that offers a quiet, distraction-free setting. Such clinical observations might be particularly useful when child performance is erratic or seems below expectations.

Even though such clinical observations can be of great value, particularly in monitoring how a child responds to a new environment or the effort he expends to cooperate with a new adult, they do not necessarily represent behaviors typical of that child in the natural environment. We can make comparisons between clinical observations and those done in natural environments to further our understanding of a child's functioning. The child who never speaks in her natural environments, including child care, around the neighborhood, at the park, but who will demonstrate age-appropriate speech and language skills in the clinical setting likely has a socialization problem rather than a communication-based problem. Observational data from the natural environment alone could have resulted in a misdiagnosis. If we relied solely on the clinical assessment, we would have missed the significant dysfunction that characterizes this child's ability to communicate with peers. We need both clinical and natural observations to complete our task.

Closing Thoughts

Theoretical perspectives influence our decisions about what and how to assess children. The most influential perspectives related to the assessment of young children with special needs are the maturational/developmental, behavioral, constructivist, and transactional. These perspectives are evident in the wide array of techniques used in assessment. In this chapter these techniques were organized into continuous strands that can be overlapped and used simultaneously to achieve the goal of context-based assessments.

Best practices do not necessarily dictate that we adopt one method or perspective to the exclusion of all others. It is the responsibility of the examiner to

be familiar with all of them and use them as tools to increase her effectiveness. The more tools an examiner has available, the better she can be in conducting accurate meaningful assessments.

We need to relax and forget ourselves as we focus on and interact with infants and young children. We need to be comfortable handling infants, displaying affection and communicating with them while other adults are observing us. We need to be sensitive to the child's cues that she is or is not ready to interact, change activities, separate from a parent, or return to a parent. We need to maintain an appropriate balance of physical closeness with distance, structure with freedom, and assistance with independent performance.

◼◼ For Your Consideration

1. What theoretical perspective seems to be most similar to your beliefs about child development? How will this theoretical perspective influence your practices in assessment?

2. What are the advantages and disadvantages of multidisciplinary, interdisciplinary, and transdisciplinary approaches to assessment?

3. What types of information about a child can be gathered through an arena assessment? What types of information could not be obtained through arena assessment?

4. When a child's disability seems to interfere with her performance on a standardized test, what accommodations can the examiner make and when would she make them?

CYBERSOURCES

Check out the following Web sites for more information related to the ideas presented in this chapter.

Council for Educational Diagnostic Services, Council for Exceptional Children

http://www.unr.edu/educ/ceds/indexceds.html

Transdisciplinary Play-Based Assessment and Intervention

http://www.pbrookes.com/store/books/linder-tpbai/

Special Education—Dynamic Assessment of Preschool Children

http://www.alliance.brown.edu/eac/sped_dynass.shtml

Observing Children's Social Communication

http://www.sasked.gov.sk.ca/docs/ela/e_literacy/observing.html

Observing Children

http://www.divine-design.biz/childcareinfo/observing_children.htm

 For additional resources on assessment, visit us on-line at www.earlychilded.delmar.com

CHAPTER 6

Norm-Referenced Standardized Assessment

Key Terms and Concepts

Norm group
Item difficulty
Normal curve
Measures of central tendency
- Mean
- Median
- Mode

Measures of variability
- Range
- Interquartile range
- Variance
- Standard deviation

Correlation coefficients
Standard error of measurement

Basal
Ceiling
Standard scores
Percentiles
Normal curve equivalents
Stanines
z-scores
T-scores
Age equivalents
Reliability
Validity
Confidence intervals
Reactivity

Chapter Objectives

After reading this chapter, you should be able to:

1. Analyze descriptions of norm groups in test manuals to determine the extent to which the norm group represents any child who may be given a particular test.
2. Identify ways to determine measures of central tendency and variability.
3. Identify and evaluate technical aspects of standardized tests, such as reliability and validity.
4. Compare different standardized scales used to provide scores for tests.
5. Discuss issues associated with test results derived from observational data.

Chapter Overview

The practice of giving infants, toddlers, and young children norm-referenced standardized tests is common. However, the meaningfulness of all this testing is subject to debate. The fact that these assessments can be "high stakes" is without question. A child's eligibility for early intervention, opportunity for special medical procedures, placement in inclusive preschool programs, and access to enrichment opportunities or private schooling can hinge on standardized test scores. Assessment results can cause children to receive diagnostic labels that may be with them the rest of their educational lives, even in light of contradictory evidence.

In spite of widespread criticism of the overreliance on norm-referenced standardized tests, particularly with infants and young children and children from cultural minorities, they remain a well-entrenched component of our assessment practices. We have eligibility standards for early intervention and special education services that seem to require the use of standardized tests. We rely on norm-referenced standardized test performance as a common means of communication regarding the development of children.

Standardized tests are not instruments that we can criticize and simply dismiss as no longer needed in our repertoire of assessment techniques. Rather, we must understand what they can do, what their limitations are, when they can be harmful and unfair to the children being tested, when to adapt them to better understand a child's abilities, how they fit into a comprehensive system of assessment, and how to interpret them within a context-based framework. Therefore, it is critical that we understand how they are constructed; the technical standards to which test developers should be held; and how to read, interpret, and critique statistical data reported in test manuals, particularly the standard error of measurement, reliability, and validity. Additionally, we must understand the process of test administration and have skills in the administering and scoring of these tests.

The chapter covers norm groups as a representative sample and other issues in test construction such as establishing item difficulty; the normal curve and patterns of distribution, including measures of central tendency and measures of dispersion; test administration and scoring procedures; derived scores; reliability, validity, and statistical factors for screening instruments; and issues of bias.

The Norm Group: A Representative Sample

The development of a standardized test requires the selection of a *norm group* or standardization sample. Each child in the norm group is given the test under designated standardized procedures. These procedures then dictate how the test will be given, including the order of test items, time allotments, wording of directions, where to begin testing and when to stop testing based on the child's performance, and so forth. Performance of the norm group on the test is then used to set the scoring standards, determine its consistency, and analyze its accuracy and meaningfulness. When selecting a norm-referenced test to administer or interpreting the results from previously administered tests of this nature, we must consider three factors: (1) the representativeness of the norm group, (2) the number of cases in the norm group, and (3) the relevance of the norm group (Sattler, 1992).

Representativeness is the extent to which the characteristics of the norm group correspond to those of the child being tested. Many tests that are used primarily to assess children with disabilities have norm groups that exclude such children. Although it might be of some value to know how a child compares to typically developing children of a similar age, the consideration of such scores outside of the child's context can lead to erroneous judgments. For example, a child with cerebral palsy may be unable to stack three one-inch blocks to form a tower, although she has the cognitive understanding required for the task. However, she will get no points for her failed tower building on a norm-referenced test that includes this physical task in the cognitive domain. As a result of the child's physical limitation, her score in cognitive development is diminished. Similarly, the determination of a child's intelligence based on an instrument normed on a hearing population will set the child with a severe hearing loss at a disadvantage. Fuchs, Fuchs, Benowitz, and Barringer (1987) have argued that many of the norm-referenced tests used in special education were not valid because of the lack of representativeness of the norm group. Some tests developed or renormed since 1987 have attempted to address this problem, with greater inclusion of children from diverse backgrounds and differing developmental levels.

The **size of the norm group** influences the stability and accuracy of scores. Scores increase in stability with the size of the norm group. Sattler (1992) recommends that a norm group include at least one hundred subjects for each age or grade level. However, this standard is intended for school-age children. Developmental measures for infants and toddlers require smaller age increments, and, therefore, need far more children per year of age in a standardization group.

Norm-referenced tests vary widely in the size of their norming groups and the age spans for the tests. The sizes of standardization groups often vary based on the resources available to authors and publishers. A test such as the Wechsler Preschool and Primary Scales of Intelligence-Revised (WPPSI-R; Wechsler, 1989b) for children ages three years zero months to seven years three months had a standardization group of 1,700 children, including 400 children who represented minorities. The test developers were willing to invest heavily for a widely used product that had already proven itself on the market.

The norm group size and age span covered by the Battelle Developmental Inventory (Newborg et al., 1984) and that of the Bayley Infant Neurodevel-

opmental Screener (Aylward, 1995) are shown in Table 6–1. The Battelle meets the standard set by Sattler, but does not adjust the sample size to take into consideration rapid development during infancy. The Bayley Screener covers one-fourth of the age span and has more infants in the standardization sample. An additional feature of the Bayley Screener norming process is that we can compare an infant's development to a clinical group (infants who were considered to be at medical risk, graduates of neonatal intensive care units, and infants previously diagnosed as developmentally delayed) and/or to a nonclinical group (infants with normal length of gestation and no prenatal, perinatal, or neonatal complications).

The size and representativeness of the norm group are critical components for marketing the test. Advertisements emphasize the size and representativeness in order to appeal to the widest market possible. The intention of the norm group is to provide a representative sample of the characteristics of the population for whom it is intended (e.g., all two-year-olds living in the United States). The characteristics most commonly used to achieve representativeness are age, gender, geographic region, ethnicity, and socioeconomic status.

The Bracken Basic Concept Scale-Revised (Bracken, 1999) has a standardization sample of 1,100 children who were representative of the general U.S. population. The group included fifty children, for every three months between two years and six months and five-years eleven months, and one hundred children for six-month intervals from six years up to eight years. Each child understood and spoke English, and was able to attend to and take the test in English in the standard fashion without modification. The sample was stratified by age, gender, race/ethnicity, region, and parent education level

TABLE 6–1 Norm Group Size Comparisons

Assessment Instrument	Age Span Covered	Norm Group Size
Battelle Developmental Inventory (Newborg et al., 1984)	0 to 8 years	800
Bayley Infant Neurodevelopmental Screener (Aylward, 1995)	3 months to 24 months	clinical sample of 303 nonclinical sample of 600 Total of 903

following demographic percentages that were based on the 1995 U.S. Census update for children ages two years six months up to eight years zero months. The manual depicts each of these stratifications individually, so it is not possible to determine how many children fall in any category that includes more than one factor, such as three-year-old African-American children with a parent education level of 13–15 years. A Spanish Edition of the Bracken has also been developed, using a research sample of 193 Spanish-speaking children between the ages of two years six months and seven years 11 months. Separate data regarding the reliability and validity of the Spanish Edition are provided in the manual. Table 6–2 provides examples of the types of information available about the Bracken norm group.

The Test of Early Language Development-3 (TELD-3; Hresko, Reid, Hammill, 1999) included 2,217 children from two separate testing periods. In 1990–1991, 1,309 children were tested using the TELD-2, and an additional 908 were tested in 1996–1997 with the TELD-3. Characteristics of the sample are provided by geographic region, gender, race, residence, ethnicity, family income, educational

attainment of parents, and disabling condition. The percentages for each of these characteristics within the sample are compared to the data provided by the U.S. Bureau of the Census for the school-age population for 1996 and that projected for the U.S. population for the year 2000 where available. Although the manual does not indicate from which sample children were derived, it does provide stratification percentages for the total population on all characteristics, as well as stratification by age for selected sample characteristics. Sample data are presented in Tables 6–3 and 6–4.

These data indicate that the TELD-3 standardization sample has an overrepresentation of European American children and an underrepresentation of Hispanic children. Both discrepancies become greater with the projected 2000 figures. The underrepresentation of Hispanic children is at its worst at the three-year-old level where the percentage of Hispanic American children in the sample drops to 9 percent. There are minor inconsistencies in the charts as they report percentages of the school-age population for Hispanic American children. In one table, which includes 1996 data and projected data for 2000, the percentage of Hispanic American children in the

TABLE 6–2 Norm Group Representativeness Data from Bracken Basic Concept Scale-Revised

Characteristics Gender	Number in Norm Group	Percentage of Norm Group	Percentage of U.S. Population
Males	550	50	
Females	550	50	
Race/Ethnicity			
African-American	181	16.5	16.2
Hispanic	172	15.6	14.9
Other	35	3.2	3.6
White	712	64.7	65.3
Parent Education Level			
11 years or less	149	13.5	
12 years	335	30.5	
13–15 years	355	32.3	
16 or more years	261	23.7	

Source: Bracken, B. A. (1984). *Examiner's Manual: Bracken Basic Concept Scale.* New York: The Psychological Corporation, pp. 20–21.

TABLE 6–3 Sample Data from TELD-3 Normative Sample

Characteristics	Percentage of Sample	Percentage of School-Age Population for 1996	Projected Percentage of School-Age Population for 2000
Race			
White	81	79	78
Black	13	16	16
Other	6	5	6
Ethnicity			
Native American	1	1	1
Hispanic	10	13	15
Asian	3	4	4
African-American	17	15	15
European American	69	67	65
Disability Status			
No disability	89	89	
Learning disability	3	5	
Speech-language disorder	5	3	
Mental retardation	1	1	
Other	2	2	

Source: Hresko, W. P., Reid, D. K., & Hammill, D. D. (1999). *Test of Early Language Development-3*. Austin, TX: Pro-Ed.

U.S. school-age population is reported at 13 percent and 15 percent, respectively. In another, shown in Table 6–5, the percentage is reported as 12 percent, with no explanation as to this inconsistency available in the manual. A possible explanation is that the 12 percent reflects older census data that were used during the norming of the TELD-2. Early interventionists who work with Hispanic American children need to understand that a total of 229 children ranging in age from two to seven years participated in the norming of the TELD-3. It is evident from the data in Table 6–4 that the distribution of urban/rural children is consistent across all age ranges. However, these percentages are slightly overrepresentative of the urban population, with increased discrepancy between newer census data from 1996 that drops the urban percentage from 78 to 75 percent.

There is not a uniform manner in which data descriptive of the norm group must be presented in examiner manuals. Therefore, test publishers will present the data in a manner that highlights the strengths or positive attributes of their norming techniques and the characteristics of the norm group itself.

In the case of the Bracken, the large numbers of children at relatively low age levels is a real strength. This information is presented in both narrative form and in a relatively prominent table. However, there is no indication of how well other characteristics are distributed across age or gender. We might legitimately wonder about this issue since the manual avoids it altogether. In the case of the TELD-3, there appears to be a large sample. However, reading the description of this sample, we learn that well over half of the group is from a previous standardization sample from 1990–1991 when the TELD-2 was developed. Unlike the Bracken manual, the TELD-3 manual includes numerous tables that document the equity of distribution of characteristics across age and gender. Additionally, the inclusion of a small number of children with known disabilities in the TELD-3 norm group is documented in table format. We must not only evaluate the information included in the manuals, but also remember that the absence of information could be hiding some of the weaknesses of the sample.

The final factor, **relevance,** is particularly critical to the context-based perspective of assessment. A

TABLE 6-4 Sample Data from TELD-3 Normative Sample Stratified by Ages

Residence and Age	Urban		Rural	
Age	n	%	n	%
2	179	79	47	21
3	207	78	59	22
4	330	78	93	22
5	385	78	109	22
6	344	80	86	20
7	299	79	79	21
Total		79	473	21
U.S. School Population		78		22

Ethnicity and Age	African-American		Hispanic American		Asian American		Native American		European American	
Age	n	%	n	%	n	%	n	%	n	%
2	38	17	23	10	6	3	3	1	156	69
3	38	14	24	9	9	3	5	2	190	71
4	62	15	42	10	12	3	8	2	299	71
5	72	15	49	10	14	3	14	3	345	70
6	97	23	51	12	9	2	8	2	265	62
7	58	15	40	11	12	3	7	2	261	69
Total	365	15	229	10	62	3	45	2	1,516	70
U.S. School Population		15		12		3		1		69

Source: Hresko, W. P., Reid, D. K., & Hammill, D. D. (1999). *Test of Early Language Development-3.* Austin, TX: Pro-Ed.

child may have never been exposed to nursery rhymes and, therefore, perform poorly on tests that require some familiarity to them. If the child is developing alternate evidence of appropriate language development, the absence of nursery rhymes in his or her experience is particularly irrelevant. Does it matter that a child cannot find a path through a maze with his pencil in a limited time if he can create beautiful artwork that shows spatial awareness and ability to plan ahead? The limitation of his ability to trace through the maze could be as related to his lack of exposure to such types of tasks as it might indicate a delayed or diminished ability to acquire the skill.

Item Difficulty, Discrimination, and Bias

During the norming process test developers determine the difficulty level and discriminatory power of test items. In some instances they use a tryout group

for this task to eliminate poor items and order those that remain in a hierarchical fashion prior to administering the test to the standardization sample. For example, 399 children participated in a tryout group for the Bracken, which resulted in the deletion of 11 items and the revision of many others. The Bayley Infant Neurodevelopmental Screener Manual (BINS; Aylward, 1995) provides detailed information about item selection with a tryout group consisting of 595 infants. Their tryout group included both infants who were developing at a normal rate and others with known developmental problems. Items were analyzed for their ability to discriminate between these two groups of infants, and those items with poor discriminatory power were deleted or improved. The proportion of individuals passing each item is used to determine its difficulty in comparison to other items on the test.

Test developers can establish their own standard of difficulty that is assigned to each item, based on the proportion of children in the sample who pass the

Know The Facts

The Learning Accomplishment Profile-Diagnostic Standardized Assessment (LAP-D; Nehring, Nehring, Bruni, & Randolph, 1992) can be used for children between the ages of 30 and 72 months. It had a total norming sample of 792 children who offer a close correspondence to the U.S. population according to the 1990 census for gender and race. A norm group distribution close to census data is desirable and appropriate. Nevertheless, when LAP-D figures are broken down into age levels, we can see exactly how many children like the ones we are testing were in the sample. There were a total of 253 children included between 36 and 47 months. Eight of these children were Asian, 41 were Hispanic, and 38 were African-American. The remaining 166 children were white. The inclusion of a small number of children with various characteristics does not eliminate the discrepancy between the norm group and children with specific conditions or backgrounds that influence their performance on the test.

item. For example, one test developer might set the criteria for inclusion of an item at a particular age level at 70 percent, meaning that any item correctly responded to by at least 70 percent of the children in the group remains on the test at that age level. Another test developer might select 40 percent as the standard. Such tests could have identical items, but result in dramatically different scores for the same child. In the first instance, items that were not passed by 70 percent of the group would be discarded, leaving the items that remained "easier" than the ones that would stay on the second test with a 40 percent standard. The first test will produce scores higher than the second one. Obviously, this makes the selection of tests more complicated than it might appear, as practitioners come to understand that some tests "test high" whereas others seem to produce consistently low scores.

A test should contain a variety of items that can discriminate between children who have the skill or understanding that the test is striving to measure from those who do not have that skill or understanding. However, items that are too easy or too hard for

the target group should be removed from the test. Anastasi and Urbina (1997) note that an average item difficulty of 50 percent, with a range from 15 to 85 percent, is an accepted standard. For example, if there were 50 three-year-old items on a test and a try-out group that included 100 three-year-olds, items missed by fewer than 15 children or more than 85 of them would be discarded, and the average proportion of children missing the items would be around 50 percent. Table 6–5 depicts how a test with 10 items could comply with this standard.

Although test items should be able to discriminate between children who have particular skills and those who do not possess the target skills, they should not be biased regarding gender, race, ethnicity, and other irrelevant factors. Hresko and colleagues (1999) provide comparisons of item performance between four dichotomous groups: male versus female, European Americans versus non-European Americans, African Americans versus non-African Americans, and Hispanic Americans versus non-Hispanic Americans. They combined statistical analysis with content analysis in this process, identifying a small number of items that produced a statistically significant indication that the item was potentially biased. The highest incidence of potential bias was with the African American versus all others on the Expressive Language (Form B) portion of the test with four out of 37 items being so identified. Hresko et al. argue that no item identified as potentially biased was judged to be overtly biased, therefore, no changes to the test

TABLE 6–5 Hypothetical Achievement of Standard for Item Difficulty

Item Number	Percentage of Children Passing Item
1	25
2	30
3	65
4	82
5	28
6	78
7	24
8	75
9	73
10	20
Average	50

were made. However, it does seem that the use of Form A for the Expressive Language portion of the test might be preferable to use when the child is African American since there were only 2 out of 37 items that were identified as potentially biased on it. The bias review of the Bracken was exclusively through content analysis conducted by an eight-member panel. Although no details are provided, it is noted in the manual that numerous changes were made based upon the feedback provided by panel members.

Distribution Patterns

The performance of a norming sample on a test under development must be used to establish standardized scores before the test can be put on the market. To create standardized scores, test developers must assume that the distribution of scores earned by the norm group should resemble that of a theoretical normal distribution as represented by the bell-shaped curve also known as the normal curve, illustrated in Figure 6–1.

Since the performance of the norm group does not likely precisely match that of the theoretical normal distribution, test developers must smooth the scores into such a distribution and use statistical procedures to complete the standardization process. When the norm group includes a few extreme scores or when the incidence of low scores is greater than the number in that range that would be predicted

from the normal distribution, test developers make adjustments accordingly. Minor scoring inconsistencies might also necessitate smoothing of the distribution. For example, a developmental quotient of 90 might be equated to percentile ranks of 43, 42, 44, and 43 for three-, four-, five-, and six-year-olds, respectively. The test developer could average these percentile ranks so that a developmental quotient of 90 was given a percentile ranking of 43 for each of these ages to avoid having slight deviations in the percentiles across these ages. The fewer adjustments that are required to bring the norm group's actual performance to conform with the normal distribution, the more confidence we can have in the quality of the norming process. Unfortunately, test manuals can leave us guessing how much adjusting might have been involved in the smoothing process, as evidenced from following the Bracken manual.

> Across age groups, score distributions were smoothed to account for irregularities associated with sampling error. . . . These distributions were smoothed to account for the irregularities in scores associated with sampling error and the distribution of standard scores were extrapolated to extend the distributions further than was permitted by the actual obtained scores. . . . Finally, smoothing was applied to eliminate any unusual fluctuations dues to sampling variation. (Bracken, 1999, p. 24)

The test must be standardized to conform to specific criteria, so that the distribution of scores fits into the normal curve. The test can then be used to compare a child's performance on that test to his own performance on the same test over time, the performance

FIGURE 6–1 The Normal Curve

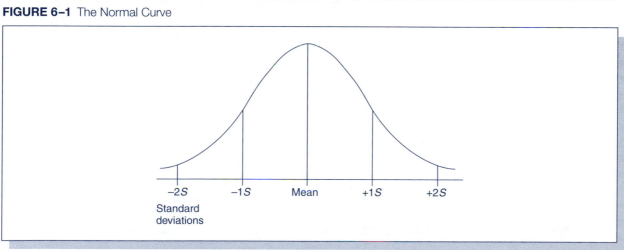

−2S   −1S   Mean   +1S   +2S

Standard
deviations

of other children, or his performance on other standardized tests with similar or different content. In order to follow this process, we must begin with an understanding of the basic numerical properties of the normal curve, including measures of central tendency and measures of dispersion. With this foundation, we can then begin to comprehend the measurement concepts of variance, standard deviation, correlation coefficients, and the standard error of measurement critical to the reliability and validity of standardized tests.

Measures of Central Tendency

There are three measures of central tendency that produce a single value that is characteristic or descriptive of a set of scores. The most common and reliable measure of central tendency is the **mean** or the arithmetic average of a set of scores. It is calculated by totaling the scores and dividing the sum by the total number of scores. There are two other types of averages that are more representative for some distributions—the **median** and the **mode.** The median is the middle score in a distribution or the number representing a point between the two middle scores. It is a representative measure of central tendency for distributions with extreme scores. The median is the value above which 50 percent of the cases fall and below which 50 percent of the cases fall. If a distribution has an odd number of cases, the median is calculated by putting the scores in order (either ascending or descending) and finding the middle score. The mode is the score that occurs most frequently in a distribution. On a normal curve it is the highest point on the curve. Table 6–6 shows a distribution of 12 three-year-old children and the age equivalent in months they earned on the eight subscales of the Learning Accomplishment Profile-Diagnostic (Nehring, et al., 1992). The mean, median, and mode for each subscale are presented at the bottom of the table.

In a theoretical normal distribution the three measures of central tendency are identical and any one of them can be appropriately used. In actuality, however, no distribution is perfectly normal. Measures of central tendency within a distribution are a foundation of data interpretation that can be misleading when children with disabilities are being assessed. For example, the assumption that the distribution of children's cognitive ability follows a normal curve does not take into account genetic disorders, birth trauma, and disease and accidents, all of which can result in severe cognitive impairments.

Therefore, the actual distribution of cognitive ability has an unexpected frequency increase at the lower end of the curve. However, the standardization process does not include this increase that we know occurs at the lower end of actual test scores.

When children who are not experiencing any disabilities are given tests on motor skills and perception, they will probably score within the average range. A mean score for such a child probably represents a fairly accurate picture of the child's functioning in these areas. However, a child with disabilities may have widely varying skills, depending on the nature of the disabilities. A child who has an orthopedic impairment might score well below the mean on a test of motor skills, but within the average range on a test of perception. If the scores for motor skills and perceptual skills are averaged and the mean reported, the child will appear below average in both areas (motor and perception).

Measures of Variability

Another type of index that describes a distribution is its **variability.** Variability indicates the degree to which scores differ from one another. If all children earned the same score on a test, and did so repeatedly, it would have no variability. A measure of variability indicates how spread out or scattered the scores are. Scores that are similar have little variability and scores that are widely dispersed have greater variability. Measures of variability include the **range, interquartile range,** the **variance,** and **standard deviation.** These measures are used in conjunction with measures of central tendency to provide more information about a large number of scores than measures of central tendency provide alone.

The simplest measure of variability is the *range,* the difference between the highest and the lowest scores in a distribution. This type of information makes a difference to a preschool teacher, who might want to know the range of communication skills in her class. Consider the difference between a class with a developmental range from two years to four years to that of a class with a range from one year to five years. Even though the mean of each distribution could be the same, the second class will require a greater diversification of activities than the first.

However, the range is based on only two scores and does not tell anything about the relationships of all the scores between the two extremes. This limitation is apparent in a distribution of scores based on

TABLE 6–6 Hypothetical Age Equivalency Scores from the LAP-D

Name	Fine Motor: Manipulation	Fine Motor: Writing	Cognitive: Matching	Cognitive: Counting	Language: Naming	Language: Comprehension	Gross Motor: Body Movement	Gross Motor: Object Movement
Dan	32	24	18	14	12	12	28	26
Rachel	28	22	16	12	15	14	26	24
Andrea	26	18	14	16	16	14	18	12
Amos	16	12	28	16	18	22	12	9
Marian	18	16	22	18	20	22	24	22
Sharon	24	18	26	20	22	24	24	22
Lynn	26	24	30	28	24	24	28	30
Tom	18	20	28	22	22	24	30	30
Glen	24	20	30	24	26	24	32	28
Charlotte	30	28	36	32	28	24	32	30
Rob	36	30	32	36	30	32	38	36
Terrance	30	34	30	32	32	30	36	32
Total	308	266	310	270	265	266	328	301
Mean	25.09	22.00	26.55	23.27	23.00	23.09	27.27	25.00
Median	26	20	28	22	22	24	28	28
Mode	26	18	30	16	22	24	24	30
Range	20	22	22	24	20	20	26	27
Interquartile Range	4	4	4	6	4	2	4	6
Variance	33.89	35.64	42.97	57.42	35.41	34.31	48.89	58.24
Standard Deviation	5.82	5.97	6.56	7.58	5.95	5.86	6.99	7.63

developmental age equivalents that range from two and one-half years to four and one-half years, where the second highest score may be only 3.1.

The *interquartile range* (IR) is the measure of variability that is most often used when the median is the preferred measure of central tendency. It provides a means for measuring skewed distributions or describing distributions that include extreme scores. This range is based on quartiles of the distribution. Just as the median divides a distribution in half, quartiles divide a distribution into four equal parts. Using the formula IR = $Q_3 - Q_1$, the range of the middle 50 percent of cases is identified and called the interquartile range, as shown in Figure 6–2. Q_1 is the point below which 25 percent of the cases fall and Q_3, the point below which 75 percent of the cases fall. Table 6–7 shows the range, interquartile range, variance, and standard deviation for 12 three-year-olds' hypothetical scores on each subscale of the LAP-D.

Two other measures of variability, the *variance* and the *standard deviation,* are more sophisticated measures. The variance is used in the calculation of

FIGURE 6–2 Interquartile Range

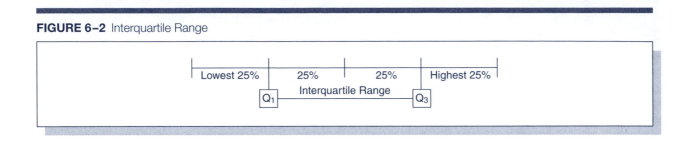

TABLE 6–7 Calculating the Variance and Standard Deviation

Name	Score	Mean	Score − Mean	Square of Difference
Dan	18	25.83	−7.83	61.31
Rachel	16	25.83	−9.83	96.63
Andrea	14	25.83	−11.83	139.95
Amos	28	25.83	2.17	4.71
Marian	22	25.83	−3.83	14.67
Sharon	26	25.83	0.17	0.03
Lynn	30	25.83	4.17	17.39
Tom	28	25.83	2.17	4.71
Glen	30	25.83	4.17	17.39
Charlotte	36	25.83	10.17	103.43
Rob	32	25.83	6.17	38.07
Terrance	30	25.83	4.17	17.39
Total	310	25.83	0.04	515.67
Mean	25.83			
Variance				42.97
SD				6.56

the standard deviation, an average of individual score deviations from the mean of all the scores. It is the most representative measure of variability, because it is not unduly influenced by extreme scores. To calculate the variance (S^2) the following formula is used:

$$S^2 = \sum \frac{(X-\overline{X})^2}{N}$$

Table 6–7 shows the steps in computing the variance and the standard deviation with data from the Cognition: Matching subscale presented in Table 6–6. The first step in the process is to calculate the mean of the distribution by adding the scores and dividing by the number of cases. The mean is then subtracted from each score resulting in a deviation score for each person. The scores that fall below the mean produce a negative number and the scores above the mean will produce positive numbers. The positive/negative element will be eliminated in the next step when these numbers are squared (multiplied by themselves). The important consideration here is how far away the deviation score is from the average of all of the other scores, not the direction of that difference. The sum of all the deviation scores is calculated, and the mean is calculated by dividing by the number of scores. This number is the variance. The square root of the variance is the standard deviation.

The *standard deviation* represents a set distance on the normal curve. The standard deviation lines are indicated by the Greek letter sigma (σ). These lines are always a standard distance from the mean ($\overline{X}$). In a normal distribution of scores, 34.13 percent of the scores will be plotted on the curve within 1 SD of the mean in each direction. This means that 34.13 percent of the scores fall within 1 SD to the right of the mean or 1 SD to the left of the mean.

Measures of Relationship

Measures of central tendency and variability provide information about a single variable. In test construction and the assessment of children, there are many situations where it is important to be able to answer questions such as the following:

- How do scores on a new test compare to scores on established tests?
- To what extent did a child who did well in one area also do well in another?
- How consistently does a test measure what it is measuring?
- What is the relationship between two different tests of a certain skill?

We answer questions such as these in part by determining the nature of the relationship between two sets of scores. Comparisons can be made between how children in the norming sample perform on one variable as compared to a second variable. When these comparisons are made for hundreds of children, we can have confidence in patterns evident in the relationship.

Data from Table 6–6 are used to illustrate the relationship between the gross motor body movement subscale and cognitive matching subscale in Figure 6–3.

FIGURE 6–3 Visual Comparison of Two Subscales

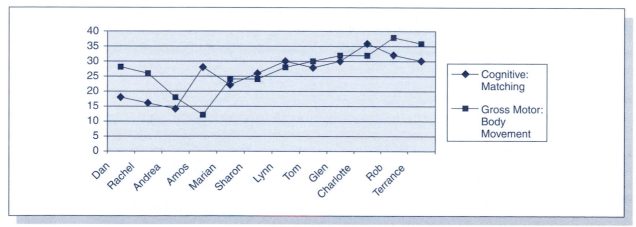

Although the scores are not the same on the two tests, there is a fairly consistent relationship between the two. Eight of the 12 children scored higher on the gross motor body movement subscale than on the cognitive matching subscale. Five of the children have scores on both subscales close to the same score.

Test developers are expected to provide quantitative analyses of relationships between their tests and other tests already on the market. They also often report relationships between test scores and child functioning related to their test. They conduct analyses of internal consistency of their test items. The primary statistic used to document these relationships is the correlation coefficient.

Correlation Coefficient

It is possible to calculate the degree of relationship between two variables using numerical indexes known as **correlation coefficients.** Correlation coefficients provide information about both the strength and the direction of the relationship. They help determine both the reliability and validity of tests. There are a number of different correlation coefficients that are matched to particular types of data. The data common to most standardized assessments of infants and young children meet the requirements for the **Pearson product-moment correlation coefficient (r)** that both variables be continuous on interval or ratio scales. If both variables are rank-ordered scales (first second, third), the **Spearman r** can be used. The **point biserial correlation coefficient (r_{pb})** is used if one variable is continuous and the other dichotomous (such as 0 = male, 1 = female).

Pearson product-moment correlation coefficients range from -1.00 and $+1.00$. The negative or positive value reflects the direction of the relationship, and the size of the number reflects the strength of the relationship. A positive relationship indicates that individuals who score high on one variable tend to score high on the other variable, and those scoring low on one, score low on the other. We would expect a strong positive relationship between the scores children make on two tests both designed to measure gross motor skills. Such correlations have positive values.

A negative relationship means that individuals scoring low on one variable tend to score high on a second variable, and conversely, those scoring high on one tend to score low on the second variable. A test that measures the number of articulation errors made by preschool children in their speech should have a negative relationship with scores from a test designed to measure a child's ability to speak and be understood by unfamiliar adults. Likewise, the number of minutes a child spends actively engaged in appropriate play would have a negative relationship to the number of minutes the child was off-task or disruptive. These correlations have negative values.

Strength of the relationship, either positive or negative, is represented by the numerical value of a correlation coefficient. Both extremes, -1.0 and $+1.0$, represent perfect relationships. As the coefficient goes from ± 1.00 toward zero (0.00), the relationship between the two variables weakens. Coefficients between $\pm .20$ are almost negligible. Those with strengths of $\pm .20$ to $\pm .40$ are considered small. Correlations of $\pm .40$ to $\pm .70$ are indicative of moderate relationships and $\pm .70$ to $\pm .90$ are strong relationships. Those with correlations greater than $\pm .90$ are very dependable relationships.

A correlation coefficient represents the direction and strength of a relationship, but does not address the reasons for the relationship. A strong relationship does not imply that variable A caused variable B or vice versa. For example, good performance on a readiness test does not *cause* a child to do well in school. However, the skills that enabled the child to perform well on the readiness test should also enable him to perform well in school. A strong correlation is a necessary feature of causality, but is not sufficient proof that a causal relationship exists between two variables.

Test Administration and Scoring Procedures

Norm-referenced standardized tests are established with the requirement that testing conditions, procedures, and scoring be the same for every child who takes the test. This requirement is based upon the notion that every child will then have an equal chance on the test. If we allow a child more time than others, give him hints, or let him try items more times than permitted in the standardization procedure, we have altered the test and the scoring no longer holds the same meaning. We must follow directions in examiner manuals on how to present each item, the order in which to present items, how to determine if an item has been passed, and where to start and stop testing. Presentation specifics can include exact words for the examiner to use, diagrams of how to present puzzle pieces, time allotments, and guidelines for when we can repeat or rephrase a question or ask for more information from the child. Scoring criteria to help us determine if an item has been answered correctly include answer keys with the correct choices, examples of correct and incorrect child drawings, and sample correct and incorrect oral responses.

Basals and Ceilings

Proper administration of a standardized test requires examiners to start and stop in a manner that gives children an opportunity to attempt items within the range of their ability without undue boredom or frustration. In order to meet this standard for tests that cover developmental skills from a fairly wide age range, the tests include specific rules about where to start and stop testing. Generally, the examiner is directed to begin testing at a point slightly below where we suspect the child is functioning developmentally to avoid wasting time on items that are easy for the child while beginning with items the child can perform correctly. For example, the TELD directs us to start at item 5 for two-year-olds on the receptive language subtests, but we can begin at item 20 with a five-year-old. We assume that the five-year-old can easily perform items below this point. Sometimes the examiner relies the child's performance on one portion of the test to determine starting points for later portions. In the case of the Bracken Basic Concept Scale, the examiner begins with the first item on the first six subtests for all children. Based on the child's performance on these six subtests, the examiner calculates the School Readiness Composite to determine where to start on subtests 7–11.

Starting points that do not begin with the first item on a test are based on the assumption that the child can successfully perform all of the items that fall below the starting point. In order to give us confidence in this assumption, we must follow the guidelines required to establish a **basal.** The basal requirement usually involves correct responses to a set number of items in a row or to all of the items at a particular age level. In the case of the TELD the basal requirement is three correct answers in a row. If we start testing a child and he fails one before getting

three correct, we move backward on the test until the basal has been achieved before moving forward.

It is possible for a child to achieve more than one basal. Different tests have specific guidelines about scoring when this happens. In many cases, the directions have us use the higher basal when we calculate the raw score, giving the child the benefit of the doubt for items missed beneath the highest basal.

Ending a test at a point that gives children an opportunity to demonstrate their best skills without putting them through repeated frustration and failure is the goal in the establishment of test **ceilings.** The goal in this instance is to find the point where it is safe to assume that a child is unable to perform items beyond the point we stop testing. Both the Bracken and the TELD use three incorrect responses in a row as the ceiling. Tests that require a set number of incorrect items in a row can become frustrating for both the child and the examiner, so the criteria for some test ceilings allows for more flexibility, such as missing three out of five items in a row. The accuracy of the assumption that we have in reaching the ceiling of the child's ability is somewhat sacrificed for the sake of reducing the child's exposure to failure.

Once the administration of a standardized test is complete, it is necessary to determine the child's scores on subtests and composite scores. The scoring begins with the calculation of the raw score, usually found by counting the correct number of responses or points earned between the basal and the ceiling. These raw scores are unique to the particular test and have no practical meaning until they are converted into standardized or derived scores. Raw scores generally reflect the number of items passed, but hold little meaning until they are converted to a derived score that is standardized. To illustrate, a 30-month-old has a raw score of 21 on the Bracken School Readiness Composite (comprised of six subtests from the BBCS), and a 48-month-old obtained a raw score of 47 points. What these scores mean and how they relate to scores on other tests is unknown until they are converted to standard scores.

Derived Scores

A child's score on a norm-referenced standardized test is determined by comparing that child's performance to the performance of the normative sample. Both the 30-month-old's raw score of 21 and the 48-month-old's 47 on the Bracken School Readiness

Composite equate to a standard score of 112 on a scale with a mean of 100 and a standard deviation of 15. Both children are in the upper range of average performance despite the difference of 26 points in their raw scores.

Converting raw scores into derived scores allows the examiner to make meaningful interpretations of test results and to compare test results across tests and/or across children. Many tests provide users the choice of several different types of derived scores. The derived scores can be converted to scores reflecting the relative standing of a child, including standard scores and percentiles. Derived scores based on developmental levels are age and grade equivalents, ratio IQs, and mental age. Figure 6–4 depicts commonly used derived scores and their relationship to the normal curve.

Scores Based on Relative Standing

Derived scores that are based on relative standing are expressed in terms of the individual's score as a position in relation to the normal distribution. These types of scores include **standard scores, percentiles, normal-curve equivalents (NCE), and stanines.** Several types of interchangeable standard scores are in use today, including *z*-scores, T-scores, and **deviation IQs.** Because *z*-scores are reported in positive or negative numbers and decimals, they can become confusing. Parents might not enjoy being told their child earned a −.5 and still falls within the average range. Additionally, *z*-scores are more difficult to use in statistical formulas. An alternative standard score is the *T*-score. Many tests developed for use with infants and young children use the Deviation IQs as the

FIGURE 6–4 Normal Curve with Standard Deviations and Standard Test Scores

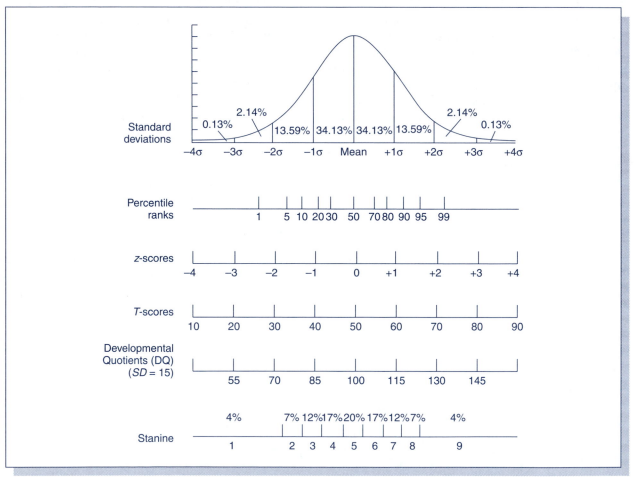

standard score, but label it simply standard score, or something related to the content of the test (e.g., language quotient). Table 6–8 depicts the formulas, means, and standard deviations for these commonly used standard scores.

Stanines are nine standard bands dividing the normal distribution. The lowest (first) and highest (ninth) stanines include all scores at or more than 1.75 standard deviations from the mean. The second through eighth stanines are .5 standard deviations wide, with the fifth stanine including ±.25 standard deviation from the mean. Normal-curve equivalents (NCE) have a mean of 50 and standard deviation of 21.06, dividing the normal curve into 100 equal parts.

Percentile ranks are standard scores of relative standing that indicate a person's performance as compared to the standardization sample. They indicate the percentage of children in the norming sample with scores at or below a given raw score. The 50th percentile corresponds to the median; children who score above the 50th percentile scored above average on that test. Those who score below the 50th percentile score below average. Percentile ranks should not be confused with percentage of items passed. Percentile ranks express the accumulating percentage of children achieving at or below specific scores, and do not reflect the number of items answered correctly on the test. If a child scores in the 75th percentile, that child scored as well as 75 percent of the children in the normative sample who match him in chronological age. Percentile ranks do have the drawback that points along the percentile distribution do not represent equal units. Near the mean of the distribution percentile points are closer together than they are at the outer edges of the distribution. Percentile ranks must be converted to another standard score for statistical analysis.

Scores Based on Developmental Levels

Derived scores based on developmental levels include **age** and **grade equivalents,** and **ratio IQs.** Age-equivalent scores are based on the average performance of a certain age group. Similar in concept are grade-equivalent scores, although not as relevant to the age range covered by this text. Expressed in grades and tenths of grades, these scores represent a level of performance similar to the level of average performance of children at a specific grade level. Cautions related to the interpretation of age- and/or grade-equivalent scores—based on Anastasi and Urbina (1997), Petersen, Kolen, and Hoover (1989), Sattler (1992) and Salvia and Ysseldyke (1995)—are presented in Figure 6–5.

Confidence in the tests we use and the scores they produce is at the foundation of standardized testing. As Hresko et al. (1999) note, because of the many concerns about age- and grade-equivalent scores, the American Psychological Association has gone so far as to advocate discontinuing the use of age and grade equivalents. Nevertheless, the authors "*very reluctantly*" provide age equivalents for the TELD based on the rationale that such scores are mandated by many school systems. Hesko et al argue effectively against the use of age equivalents, but justify their inclusion of them in the manual for the sake of marketing. Test developers and publishers do not have the individual responsibility to children and their families to which test users must adhere. The responsibility falls on the test user to understand the principles of sound testing, and to select those scoring procedures appropriate to the child being tested and that meet high standards of technical soundness. Although these types of scores have some suitability for group comparisons, their usefulness for individual assessment is limited.

TABLE 6–8 Standard Score Formulas, Means, and Standard Deviations

Standard Score	Formula	Mean	Standard Deviation
z-score	$z = (x - \bar{x})/s$	0	1
T-score	$T = 10z + 50$	50	10
Deviation IQ	$DIQ = 15z + 100$	100	15

FIGURE 6–5 Cautions When Using Age and Grade Equivalents

1. The distance between a one-year-old and a two-year-old age score is not equivalent to the difference between a seven-year-old and an eight-year-old score. The difference is one year in each case, but does not reflect equal distance in development.

2. Scores obtained by interpolation or extrapolation are questionable.
   a. Interpolated scores are scores that fall within the range of the norm group tested, but at a precise point where there were no specific individuals represented in the norm group. A child might earn a grade equivalent of three years six months, when in fact, no children three years six months of age were tested.
   b. Extrapolated scores are scores falling outside the range (higher or lower) than the norm group. If an age equivalent score of 12 months is obtained for a four-year-old and the norm group had no four-year-olds who fell below an age equivalent of three years three months in it, then the score has been extrapolated. That is, no four-year-old children in the norm group were tested who performed on the test to earn a score of 12 months.

3. Developmental age-equivalent scores encourage us to think that an average two-year-old or average five-year-old will perform a certain way. In fact, the average five-year-old or average two-year-old does not exist. Averages are created from children who represent a range of performances.

4. Grade-equivalent scores do not mean that a child is functioning at that particular grade level. For example, a first grader who has scored at the grade equivalent of 4.0 in reading is not necessarily functioning like a fourth grader. The first-grade student shares with the average fourth grader the number of items right on a specific reading test, not all other attributes associated with fourth-grade reading skills.

5. The age equivalents on one test may not be the same as the age equivalents on another. Item placement varies depending on the difficulty level set by the test developers. This influences how "easy" or "hard" the test will be. Tests with lower criteria for item placement will produce lower scores, and tests that required a higher percentage of the norm group to pass the item before placing at a specific age level will produce higher scores.

6. Grade equivalents assume that curricula are standard throughout school systems. Local variation of curricula influences grade-equivalent scores. Grade equivalents do not indicate where a child should be placed in a particular local school system.

7. Age and grade equivalents assume that a child's growth throughout a year is constant and linear. In actuality, development follows a sporadic pattern with spurts and plateaus, varying across developmental domains and areas of the curriculum.

8. Small differences in performance on a test between two children may result in one child obtaining an age equivalent of a six months above the other student.

9. Age- and grade-equivalent scores are based on ordinal scales. Since ordinal data are not continuous, there are limitations on the types of statistical analysis that can be calculated on these scores.

Technical Soundness

Tests can include only a sample of the skills we expect children to master. The extent to which the sample of items put on a test accurately reflects the entire pool of skills will influence the meaningfulness of our results. Additionally, we can reduce the degree of error that occurs when a child fails to get credit on items that he has mastered (possibly due to carelessness, inattention, lack of motivation, or examiner error) or gets credit for unmastered skills (possibly due to lucky guesses or inadvertent hints from the examiner). This contributes to determining the quality and meaningfulness of child assessments. We use measures of **reliability** and **validity** to enable us to evaluate the technical quality and soundness of norm-referenced standardized instruments.

Reliability indicates how much a test score is attributable to the true abilities of a child and the extent to which the score is attributable to chance errors. The closer the test represents a child's true score, the more consistently it will produce the same results for the same child. Validity is the extent to which the inferences drawn from test results are appropriate, meaningful, and useful. A test must be reliable if it is to be valid.

Although an instrument can be reliable without being valid, it would be of no value. The test would consistently measure something, but not what the test publisher claims that it measures.

Reliability

Classical test theory assumes that a person's score has two components. The first component is the true score, a score that represents a person's real ability. The second is error, randomly influencing the outcome of assessments. Error comes into a score for many different reasons, including content sampling error, time sampling error, and scorer differences. Since tests are generally representative samples of domains of skills rather than inclusive of all possible skills within a domain, they will never be perfectly representative of an entire domain. The number of items that would need to be included to measure all skills, even under a single domain, is far too unwieldy for testing purposes.

The performance of the child on the sample of items is generalized to assume competence or incompetence for a broader array of skills. For example, we might have items that sample skills, such as recognition of shapes, colors, or letters, counting ability, the correct use of syntax, or the ability to recall nursery rhymes. The items selected to comprise the sample of any one of these skills will influence the level of difficulty of the test both collectively and individually. What shapes belong on a test for three-year-olds to recognize? Which shapes should we expect four-year-olds to produce from memory? What letters constitute a representative sample of the entire alphabet? The recognition of the numerals 1, 2, and 3 would not be as challenging as the recognition of 5, 6, and 9, but both could serve as a sample of "recognizes numerals between 1 and 10." However, these samples are not of equal difficulty. If we used a test that relied on the first sample, many children's

scores might include an error because they were given credit for being able to recognize all the numerals between 1 and 10, when the truth was that they could only recognize 1, 2, and 3.

For each child's score, an estimate is needed that indicates what part of the score is true variance and what part of the score is variance due to error. It is possible to estimate the amount of error in any score. Two statistics, the reliability coefficient and the standard deviation, assist us in estimating the amount of error associated with a particular test. We can also calculate a range in which we can have confidence that the individual's true score falls. The reliability coefficient itself is an indication of how cautious we should be in accepting a score on a test. Correlation coefficients are used to calculate the reliability coefficient. The formulas used to obtain a reliability coefficient differ according to which of several types of reliability is being calculated, as summarized in Table 6–9.

Reliability coefficients are estimates of a test's dependability. Several factors can influence reliability coefficients. Guessing and conditions unique to the testing situation can influence test performance as well. In addition to the physical health of the child, other sources of error variance, not included in any of the common estimates of reliability, are the motivation and the stamina of the child. The examiner can influence test scores by giving extra help, pointing out errors, and allowing additional time. Situation-induced factors such as ventilation, noise level, lighting, and overcrowding can also influence reliability. Higher reliability coefficients are usually found with longer tests, and with norming groups that are heterogeneous in ability. With test-retest reliability, shorter times between testings yield higher reliability coefficients. Finally, the type of reliability estimate used will produce coefficients that differ. For example, equivalent forms testing tends to result in a lower estimate than either test-retest or split-half approaches. A reliability of .90 based on equivalent forms is harder to achieve than .90 using test-retest methods.

With these differences in mind, the lower the reliability coefficient for a particular test, the more caution we need to exercise in interpreting the scores. If test scores are used for administrative purposes and are reported for groups, .60 is the minimum acceptable reliability coefficient (Salvia & Ysseldyke, 1995). When test scores are used in relation to decisions for individual children, a much higher standard of .90 is needed (Salvia & Ysseldyke). For screening instruments, a standard of .80 is recommended.

TABLE 6–9 Reliability Coefficients

Reliability Type	How Derived	Uses
Internal consistency	Derived from scores obtained during one administration of the test to the standardization sample.	Not suitable for timed tests or tests that are not completed by the entire group taking the test. Does not provide any estimate of a test's stability over time, but shows homogeneity of test.
Split-half	Division of the test into two equivalent parts and comparison of performance between the two parts.	Appropriate for long tests that have items all intended to measure the same trait.
Intercorrelations	Estimated by determining how all the items on a test relate to all other items and to all comparable parts of the test.	Provides a measure of the extent to which items measure the same characteristic.
Test-retest	Determined by administering a test to the same group of individuals on two separate occasions within a short period (two weeks to one month) and correlating the scores. Periods of time between tests should be kept to a minimum to avoid allowing time for the development of new skills. This time factor is particularly critical for infants, toddlers, and preschool children.	Yields a stability coefficient that indicates the consistency of a test over time. Good for tests that are not subject to practice effect.
Equivalent forms Alternate forms Parallel forms	Correlates the results of two equivalent forms of a test that are administered to the same individuals and reflects variation in performance from one set of items to another. The two forms of the test should contain the same number of items, which should be expressed in the same form, covering the same information.	Measure of stability and equivalence obtained when the same children are tested with one form on one occasion and with another form on the second occasion, providing scores on two forms correlated over time.

Standard Error of Measurement

A reliability coefficient gives an estimate of the accuracy of a group of scores. The reliability coefficient also helps to determine the reliability of an individual score. Theoretically, if an individual takes the same test one hundred times, the scores would fall within a normal distribution around the individual's true score. The true score would be the mean of the distribution and approximately 68 percent of the scores would be within ±1 standard deviation of the mean. If the mean true score is 50 and the standard deviation is 5 points, then 68 percent of the time the individual's true score would be between 45 and 55.

The **standard error of measurement (SE$_m$)** shows the reliability of an individual score. It is an estimate of the amount of error that is part of an obtained score. The SE$_m$ is not affected by the variability of the group scores. If we know the reliability coefficient of a test, it is possible to compute the SE$_m$, which is equal to the standard deviation of the test divided into the square root of 1 minus the correlation coefficient of the test. This procedure is represented by the following formula:

$$SE_m = SD \sqrt{1-r}$$

Most test manuals today provide information about the standard error of measurement, so it is not necessary to perform these calculations.

Because an individual's true score is not known, SE$_m$ assists us in determining the probability that the obtained score reflects the true score. Using the SE$_m$, we can calculate **confidence intervals.** These provide a range of scores where a high probability exists that the true score is included. A 90 percent confidence interval represents the range in which an individual's true score will be found 90 percent of the time. The probability that the true score is outside this range is 10 times in 100. The range of a confidence interval is calculated by multiplying the z-score associated with the desired percentage of confidence by the SE$_m$ as shown in Table 6–10. This figure is then added to and subtracted from the obtained score to form the confidence interval.

Validity

Validity refers to the extent to which a test actually measures what the test developers claim it measures. Validity is the most important consideration in the construction and use of tests. Its importance is based on the need to understand exactly what a test measures in order for us to give meaning to a test score. Unless there is a clear picture of what a test measures, it is possible for us to make wrong assumptions about a child. It is better to err in the direction of unfair bias against the validity of standardized tests than it is to honor the results of any and all standardized tests simply because they are not "subjective." Validity has as much to do with how we use tests as it does the quality of individual tests. Technically, it is our inferences about test results that hold or fail to hold validity. However, in practice we discuss the validity of tests as a property of the test itself.

The validation of what a test measures and how well it is measured is a complex process. In the past, defining what a test intended to measure and then collecting data to show how well it did the job was sufficient. Validation was accomplished by correlating scores on the test with a criterion measure obtained in a real situation. For example, a measure of shyness

TABLE 6–10 Calculating Confidence Intervals Using Standard Error of Measurement

Percentage of Confidence Level	z-score	Example from Form A of the Receptive Language Quotient of the TELD for four-year-old with Score of 98 (SE$_m$ = 5)	
68	1.00	98 ± 5 (1.00)	93 − 103
85	1.44	98 ± 5 (1.44)	91 − 105
90	1.65	98 ± 5 (1.65)	90 − 106
95	1.96	98 ± 5 (1.96)	88 − 108
99	2.58	98 ± 5 (2.58)	87 − 109

Finding A Better Way

Imagine we give a child a test that has three items. During the test she is required to stack one-inch blocks, repeat lists of paired words, and select the correct picture when we say a word. The developers of this hypothetical test chose to name their test the Cognitive Abilities Test, and were able to obtain an excellent reliability coefficient using test-retest methods. We certainly would not like to think that such a test could then become the standard to determine children who were deficient in their cognitive ability. Unfortunately, in the history of assessment practices in special education, we have come all too close to making this seemingly absurd example a reality.

tablished tests, theories of child development, and developmental scales. Using different sources, Bracken, author of the Bracken Basic Concept Scale (BBCS), established content validity for the first version by surveying "five preschool and primary aged tests of general cognitive ability to determine the frequency of BBCS concepts in the directions of these commonly used instruments" (Bracken, 1984, p. 62). He concludes that the BBCS basic concepts contain a complete listing of the 11 conceptual areas assessed, and, therefore, content validity is established. He added 50 concepts in the Bracken Basic Concept Scale-Revised (BBCS-R) and states that these additions further strengthen the content validity of the instrument. He argues that the foundational nature of the concepts covered on the BBCS-R and their widespread presence in early childhood tests of cognitive and academic ability further demonstrate the test's content validity.

Construct validity is concerned with the relationship between test scores and a theoretical construct or trait that underlies test performance. Usually established for tests of intelligence and cognitive functioning, this type of validity provides a check on the theory underlying the test in three ways. First, the nature of the trait or construct being measured is logically expected to be related to certain other measures. For example, new tests designed to measure intelligence are frequently correlated with earlier, well-established intelligence tests. Hresko and colleagues (1999) present six testable constructs upon which the TELD is based, including the premise that since it measures language, children with typically developing language can be distinguished from those with language

might be correlated with the number of peer interactions in a 30-minute period. It is important to assess actual test content, constructs upon which the test is based, and correlations with a variety of criterion measures in order to explore a test's validity. The types of validity are summarized in Table 6–11 and described below.

Content validity involves the subjective analysis of test content. It is concerned with how well the items on a test represent the universe of items that could be covered in that particular domain. Usually test content is drawn from what children are expected to do or learn by a certain age. Sources of information to evaluate the universe of items are textbooks, child development experts, previously es-

TABLE 6–11 Types of Validity

Validity Type	Description
Content	How well the items on a test represent the universe of items that could be covered in that particular domain
Construct	Relationship between test scores and a theoretical construct or trait that underlies test performance

Criterion-related
    Concurrent
    Predictive
	Relationship between test scores and measures of some related criterion that is obtained at the same time
	Extent to which a test can predict future performance

disabilities (e.g., learning disability) and those with disabilities that can influence language development. In their efforts to validate this construct, they compare test scores of children in the norm group who were known to have learning disabilities (N = 108), delayed language (N = 104), and mental retardation (N = 36). The means for these three groups were well below the mean of 100 for all three scores that can be determined by the TELD-3—receptive language, expressive language, and spoken language composite. The patterns and trends in these means were consistent with the construct as well, with the children with mental retardation having the lowest mean (65) on the spoken language composite.

However, their proof of another construct is less convincing. The construct holds that the TELD-3 should correlate significantly with child performance on measures of academic abilities because of the strong relationship between oral language and school abilities. In order to validate this construct, they correlated TELD-3 to the Woodcock-Johnson Psycho-Educational Battery-Revised (Woodcock & Johnson, 1989). With results ranging from .33 to .59 and a median coefficient of .42, they were able to achieve a statistical significance at the .01 confidence level and conclude that the TELD-3 "assesses abilities that are somewhat related to academic abilities" (p. 108). Their descriptive words have changed from "highly related" in the construct to "somewhat related" in the results without any articulation by the test authors, who defend the relatively weak correlations with somewhat meaningless statistical significance. The statistical significance seems of less value than the interpretation of relatively weak coefficients.

Factor analysis is another statistical procedure that can be used to establish construct validity. Its purpose is to analyze the intercorrelations of a group of tests or subtests to determine the number of factors or clusters that suggest common traits. This procedure allows for the simplification of behavior descriptions by reducing multiple categories of variables to a few common factors or traits.

The third type of validity, **criterion-related validity,** is established by comparing test scores with an external variable that is a direct measure of the characteristic or behavior that the test claims to measure. It is usually documented through the validity coefficient, which is a correlation coefficient based on the relationship between the test scores and another criterion (e.g., scores on another test that measures

the same behaviors or skills). There are two types of criterion-related validity: concurrent and predictive.

Concurrent validity procedures are used to investigate the relationship between test scores and measures of some related criterion that can be obtained at the same time. This type of validity is useful for instruments designed to assess a child's current functioning. For example, the correlation between scores on a self-concept scale with teacher ratings of self-assurance displayed during peer interactions should be high.

Predictive validity refers to the extent to which a test can predict future performance and is expressed as the correlation between test scores and measures of an external criterion where there is a time interval between testing and performance on the related criterion. Readiness tests need to have strong correlations with future achievement test scores because they are intended to predict which children are ready to move into kindergarten or first grade. Screening instruments also need to have high predictive validity.

Validity coefficients are correlation coefficients that give information about the strength and direction of relationships between a test and other related tests or measures of relevant criteria. As correlation coefficients, validity coefficients are influenced by factors such as the length of time between test administrations, the range of the trait being measured, and the children taking the tests. These coefficients should not be automatically accepted at face value. Confounding factors to consider when evaluating the validity coefficient include the size of the sample, existing group differences, and the nature of the external criteria that are used to establish criterion-related validity.

Observational Data

A number of standardized assessment instruments rely on child observations as a primary source of data. Observations are particularly common in instruments focused on behavior and social development. Observation done well can provide an objective method of assessment because it allows us to reduce the assumptions we have to make when using clinical testing. However, observational data has its own limitations and required assumptions.

Direct observational processes may influence the accuracy of observational data we obtain. Observations may cause various types of reactivity to occur on the part of persons being observed. In collecting and using observational data, it is critical that we collect data in a systematic and meaningful way, and that the data constitute a representative sample of the behavior of interest as much as possible.

Reactivity

Direct observations can be obtrusive, meaning that the person or persons being observed are aware of the observation. Obtrusive observation may be **reactive,** resulting in the child's behavior changing because she knows that she is being observed. Obtrusive measures are not always reactive, but until an observer knows whether or not reactivity is occurring, the validity of the observational data is in question. Three types of reactivity relevant to the observation of young children with disabilities and their environments (Kazdin, 1982) are shown in Table 6–12.

There are two types of variables that contribute to reactivity: (1) valence, or the social value associated with a specific behavior, and (2) how the characteristics of the children and observers interact (Kazdin). The **valence** of a specific behavior may alter the frequency of that behavior. If a behavior is viewed as positive, such as offering assistance to a peer, there is a likelihood that the frequency of a positive valence behavior will increase when a person is being observed. On the other hand, a behavior with a negative valence will decrease in frequency during an observation.

Characteristics of children and observers also contribute to reactivity. For example, a female observer is charting the aggressive behavior of a boy and a girl. The behavior has been operationally defined, a time limit set for the observation to begin and end, and the observation is unobtrusive. Theoretically, because of the operational definition, a male child and a female child exhibiting exactly the same behaviors should have identical behavior charts. The

TABLE 6–12 Types of Reactivity to Observations

Reactivity	Description	Example
Type One	Observing others thereby changing others	A child has been described to an evaluator as overly aggressive during play situations. After operationalizing the term "overly aggressive" (i.e., identifying exactly what behaviors—hitting, yelling, etc.—are to be counted as overly aggressive), the observer enters the playroom to observe the child who realizes she is being watched. Because an adult is present watching the group, the frequency of her aggressive behaviors decreases. In essence, the observation of "aggressive behaviors" does not provide a representative sample of her actual play behavior.
Type Two	Observing oneself and changing oneself	James, a kindergarten teacher, has been asked to count the number of times he corrects behavior during the first 15 minutes of class time. "Offering correction" is operationalized (i.e., all requests to stop a behavior are considered a correction), and James keeps a record. It is possible, and even likely, that he may reduce the number of times he corrects the children because correcting may be seen as a negative strategy by others and James does not want to be viewed negatively. It is almost impossible not to change the frequency with which we do something when we observe ourselves. Making ourselves conscious of our own behavior alters our behavior.
Type Three	Being observed and changing oneself	If a teacher is being observed by his supervisor, the teacher is likely to be more patient with his students than he would be ordinarily, so that his supervisor will note this positive quality on the teacher's evaluation.

charts, however, may not be identical because the observer perceives male children to be more aggressive in general, transfers this unconscious perception to the child being observed, and charts behavior that merely approaches the operational definition of aggression. On the other hand, the same observer charts only those behaviors exhibited by the female that are clearly defined as aggressive. Similar perceived biases can influence interracial observations, observations across socioeconomic levels, between religious or cultural groups, and so on.

Reliability of Observational Data

Before assessing the reliability of observational data, we need to consider the quality of the data. Were the data gathered in such a way as to be able to answer the questions we had in mind? Were observers trained prior to making observations and how is their level of expertise described? Was the coding system and operationalization of terms used relevant to the assessment? For example, coding "staring into space" as off-task behavior may not be appropriate. "Staring into space" could be the behavior a specific child exhibits when thinking about the task at hand. Were behaviors coded at appropriate times? That is, if we want to know how a child functions socially at the beginning of the day, then data collected after lunch are not helpful. Finally, note the settings in which data were collected. Observations made and charted while a child is in school may not reflect the way a child behaves in other settings.

After the quality of data is established, procedures for assessing the reliability of the data may be carried out. Two important measures of observational data are **observer agreement** and **observer reliability.** Two or more observers simultaneously watching the same situation who independently chart the frequency of behavior the same way are said to have reached **interobserver agreement. Interobserver reliability** is reached when two or more observers chart behaviors independently over two or more observation sessions and are in agreement from the first session to the last session. One can have interobserver agreement on session A and interobserver agreement on session B, but fail to establish reliability across sessions. For example, during the first observation of a three-year-old child, both observers coded the three categories of behavior: attention seeking, aggression, and anger. During the second observation, the child behaves in exactly

the same manner; however, both observers code the behaviors as initiating social interaction, on-task behavior, and regard for self. Although the observers agreed among themselves in both instances, they were inconsistent in their interpretation of child behavior, and, therefore, failed to establish observer reliability.

Interobserver reliability estimates involve the comparison of scores of two or more observers on one or more observation sessions. The data may be nominal or interval scale ratings. For example, observers may code numbers of aggressive or withdrawn behaviors (nominal scale ratings) or degree of aggressive behavior ($0 = $ no aggression to $4 = $ very aggressive). When coding degree of behavior, the observer is using an interval scale rating. Generally, reliability estimates are calculated using correlation coefficients or percentage agreement indices.

If the data are interval and patterns of agreement between or among observers are desired, a Pearson product-moment correlation coefficient may be used. The product-moment coefficient will determine if the observers' measures are linearly related, that is, over time do the observational *patterns* match (e.g., observer A charts a high-low-high pattern and observer B charts a high-low-high pattern). An intraclass correlation coefficient is used on interval scale data when patterns and levels of agreement are measured. It shows the extent to which all observers share the same meaning in their judgments.

Often an uncorrected percentage agreement is used when it is not important to correct for chance agreements. Uncorrected percentage agreement, usually referred to simply as percentage agreement, is the percentage of agreement of two or more observers. The most often used percentage agreement methods with interval recording are (1) overall agreement, (2) agreement on the occurrence of the behavior, and (3) agreement on the nonoccurrence of the behavior. The Kappa statistic (k) may be used with nominal scale data when correcting estimates for chance agreements. Kappa's upper limit is 1.00, and the lower limit is between zero and -1.00. It is a measure of precision, not validity.

If target behaviors are sampled in more than one setting and on more than one occasion, then test-retest reliability methods will yield a measure of the consistency of behavior across time and settings. To determine an estimate of the internal consistency of an observational instrument, the split-half reliability method is appropriate.

Validity of Observational Data

Validity, as it applies to direct observational assessment, is a complex issue. It can be argued, however, that direct observational procedures are obviously valid if the behavior of interest has been observed, charted, and the data have been subjected to interobserver reliability estimates. It can also be argued that because observations are direct and have not been processed through the filter of sampling and generalization used in other test formats, validity can be assumed. This is incorrect. This characteristic of observational data might be thought of as accuracy rather than validity (Cone, 1982).

Validity is always a matter of degree. Tests and observational instruments cannot be separated from the social context in which they are used. The three types of validity—content, construct, and criterion-related—also apply to observational data and standardized instruments based on observational ratings.

Content validity can flow in two directions: from categories to specific behaviors or from specific behaviors to categories. Categories provide the label used to characterize a group of behaviors, such as withdrawn behavior, social interactions with peers, aggression, or cooperative play. Instruments based on data from direct observation have some degree of content validity if the category is represented by behaviors included on the instrument implied or listed under a specific category. To establish content validity (from category to behaviors), an instrument is judged by persons expert in the theory as to its validity.

The other direction of flow is from a set of behaviors to creation of a category. For example, a teacher may request that the troublesome behaviors of a particular student be charted and a frequency count recorded. The group of troublesome behaviors may not have a label as yet. The content validity is still an issue even though there is no specific label for this set of behaviors. To establish content validity for an unlabeled set of behaviors, the observational instrument is judged by persons to whom the behavior is important (e.g., teachers, parents, researchers, etc.).

Construct validity refers to the extent to which an instrument based on observed behaviors relates to a targeted construct or theory. Construct validity for direct observational assessment systems is established using the same methods appropriate for other types of assessment.

It must be shown that scores on an observation-based instrument relate to relevant factors. There are two ways to establish criterion-related validity of an observational instrument. The first way is to show that a correlation exists between the instrument in question and an instrument that has already been shown to have criterion-related validity. The second way is for the creators of the instrument to validate their categories against the judgment of people in the situation in which the behaviors occur (parents, teachers, peers, etc.). A simple method might be for an observer to chart a child's aggressive behavior over several days, and compare the observer's frequency count with the teacher's overall rating of how aggressive the child was at particular times on particular days. If the observer's and teacher's ratings agree, then the instrument can be said to have criterion-related validity for that specific teacher.

Closing Thoughts

One of the underlying premises of this book is that assessment of any type is a socially embedded activity. If one accepts this point of view, then ultimately there is realization that assessment is not a neutral activity, producing pure facts about a person's abilities or traits. Assessment is influenced and changed by the people doing the assessment, by the people being assessed, and by the social context in which these individuals operate. Even the testing industry itself reciprocally influences and is influenced by the politics of American education. Assessment is not a neutral business, and political decisions, not just educational decisions, influence the testing industry. Political decisions even influence the creation of knowledge because much research in America is funded through the government or private foundations. The policies of the funding agencies dictate who gets research funds, thereby influencing the creation of knowledge. Research scholars, in turn, have a major influence on state and federal government educational policies, and these policies influence funding decisions. And so the cycle continues.

Test publishers are sensitive to the marketplace like any industry. Therefore, they strive to produce tests that will be bought and used. Many school districts rely on standardized tests to make decisions about students' educational futures. Since standardized tests carry great weight in American culture and are often used as measures of teacher effectiveness, teachers, their supervisors, and school boards will adjust curricula accordingly. Teachers adjust their instruction to match the focus of tests that their students must take.

Overall, the testing industry is one of the participants in the monolithic conflicts of interest in American education (Spring, 1988). We are engaged in external conflict, struggling with many outside forces over the place of testing in education. We also find ourselves in internal conflict over many assessment-related issues, such as the suitableness of assessment results to be used to determine merit pay for teachers, the elimination of social promotions for children falling behind in school, and the transformation of federally funded preschool programs into prereading programs. The conflicts of interest surrounding assessment issues are both inside and outside the educational system.

If, in fact, the testing industry influences curricula, thereby influencing educational goals and values, what effect might this have on the assessment and education of young children with disabilities? What does it mean to "transform testing programs, ideally servants of educational programs, into masters of the educational process" (Meisels, 1989b, p. 17)?

The assessment of young children with disabilities often has as its intended outcome the gathering of data that will help us decide on appropriate educational objectives and appropriate teaching strategies for individual children. Following our initial testing of the child, we begin the never-ending circle of test-teach-test. If our interventions become "measurement-driven" (Madaus, 1988), then educational objectives, teaching strategies, and placement are all affected. Just as the need to show a profit sometimes drives the business industry without regard to the cost to the environment or the lives of persons comprising the labor force, educators can become driven by the need to demonstrate progress. We can target splinter skills or other isolated behaviors far removed from the day-to-day functioning of a young child, begin programming, and measure progress. However, the long-term benefits of such isolated progress should not be blindly assumed simply because progress can be measured.

Ideally, teaching strategies are influenced by the individual needs of children and the priorities the families have set for their children. In intervention with young children with disabilities it is almost an article of faith that interventionists constantly adapt strategies to the child. However, if interventionists are constrained in their decision making regarding teaching strategies because testing requires that children be able to demonstrate their knowledge in one way (i.e., on a standardized test), there is a danger that interventionists will proceed in a lock-step fashion in order to prepare their children to take tests or adopt ready-made test-curriculum packages that are not necessarily the most appropriate for every child.

It is difficult to assess precisely the impact that the testing industry has on education, but few would argue that there is no impact at all. If the testing industry can have a negative impact on children, then it is an educator's professional obligation to be aware of that impact and to reduce or eliminate, if possible, anything that lessens the probability that children will reach their highest potential.

■■ For Your Consideration

1. Why do some tests seem harder than others, even when they have similar test items?

2. Which of the following Pearson product-moment correlation coefficients shows the strongest relationship $+.35$, $-.79$, or $+.90$? Describe the type of relationship depicted by each of these correlation coefficients.

3. Does high correlation between two sets of scores imply any causal relationship?

4. How do you know where to start and when to stop when using a test designed for a wide age range?

5. If you wish to have 90 percent confidence that a test score accurately reflects a child's true score what must you do to that score?

CYBERSOURCES

Check out the following Web sites for more information related to the ideas presented in this chapter.

National Council on Measurement in Education

http://www.ncme.org/

ERIC digest on standardized testing

http://ericeece.org/pubs/digests/1991/perron91.html

ERIC digest on norm-referenced testing

http://www.ed.gov/databases/ERIC_Digests/ed410316.html

 For additional resources on assessment, visit us on-line at www.earlychilded.delmar.com

CHAPTER 7

Criterion-Referenced and Play-Based Assessment

Intelligence
Psychological processes
- **Attention**
- **Perception**
- **Memory**

Communication
- **Language**
- **Speech**

Attachment
Temperament
Coping
Reflexive movement
- **Primitive reflexes**

Chapter Objectives

After reading this chapter, you should be able to:

1. Describe multiple perspectives toward defining intelligence.
2. Describe the sequence of language development, including the match between receptive and expressive skills.
3. Link cognitive and emotional developmental sequences through Piaget's stages.
4. Understand when criterion-referenced assessment offers the best assessment option for young children.
5. Identify criterion-referenced assessments suitable for young children.
6. Participate as a team member in play-based assessments.

Chapter Overview

Standardized testing has two fundamental limitations, requiring that we also use other methods of assessment. First, it often does not provide the information we need to plan effective interventions. The tests document delays as conveyed by numerical scores. They do not tell us what skills a child has mastered under what conditions, what new things the child is just beginning to learn, or specific behaviors to expect of the child in particular settings. Second, it is rarely an appropriate or informative method of assessment for some children, such as those with severe physical impairments. No child is "untestable" when we expand our techniques to include the alternatives. Two such alternatives explored in this chapter are criterion-referenced and play-based assessment.

There is little, if any, value in administering standardized tests to children who will perform dramatically below the mean for the group. It serves little purpose to determine that a young child has an IQ of 35. If the child performed that poorly on an IQ test, it is likely that his cognitive delays were already apparent. It seems of no use to quantify just how far removed from the mean of his peers he is functioning with a test score from which he is unlikely to derive any benefit. Likewise, we do not need a test score to understand the extent of delay a three-year-old child is experiencing who has an expressive vocabulary of three words. It benefits the child far more if we put our efforts into understanding why the child has such a limited vocabulary, how the child communicates his wants and needs, how the child behaves in settings that include peers, and the nature of the child's interaction with toys and other objects, and how we can best expand his ability to communicate.

The move toward inclusion of young children with special needs into mainstream preschool settings during the 1980s and 1990s triggered debates about the suitableness of developmentally appropriate practices as defined by the National Association for the Education of Young Children for all children. When the debates ensued within the special education ranks and between special educators and early childhood educators, a revised guide to developmentally appropriate practices offered compromise and acknowledgment of the individual nature of appropriateness (Bredekamp & Copple, 1997). Best practices in early childhood special education broadened from an almost exclusive reliance on didactic teaching driven by goals and objectives to incorporate an activity-based intervention model. In this model, the goals and objectives are embedded into child-initiated play.

The development of nonstandardized approaches to assessment has accompanied the changes in intervention. Criterion-referenced assessment became a part of mainstream assessment options in the late 1970s, and continued to increase in popularity. It is now well established as an approach to assessment that can be linked to curricular goals and objectives. Play-based assessment of infants appeared in the literature on a limited scale for many years (e.g., Belsky & Most, 1981; Rubenstein & Howes, 1976; Watson & Fischer, 1977). Over the past three decades it has become far more popular, as it offers an assessment approach that is consistent with developmentally appropriate practices, and other principles of assessment reflective of best practices.

Persons using criterion-referenced and play-based assessment rely on developmental sequences to frame the assessment process. Therefore, the chapter begins with an overview of developmental progression related to cognition, communication, social and emotional behavior, and motor functioning. Sections on criterion-referenced assessment and play-based assessment follow.

Developmental Progression

For infants, toddlers, and young children, cognitive development is typically acquired through active play, including the manipulation of body parts and objects, and experimentation with words and language. Motor play is accompanied by play with sounds, communicative efforts that begin with crying and other sounds, and the development of language symbols associated with new knowledge. Social and emotional development surround the development of knowledge and communication in a similar fashion, as some children experience nurturing and caring environments whereas others face abuse and neglect.

The most common approach for describing and analyzing child development is via developmental domains. However, these domains develop interdependently as infants mature into socially competent children with effective communication skills and sufficient knowledge and impulse control to understand and relate to the world.

Knowledge and Knowing

Cognitive development, intelligence, and the ability to learn are all related concepts. Three basic components that definitions of intelligence have in common are (1) the capacity to learn, (2) the sum total of knowledge an individual has acquired, and (3) the ability to adjust to various environments, particularly new situations. Some have defined intelligence as a global capacity (Wechsler, 1991), whereas others speak of multiple types of intelligence (Guilford, 1967; Gardner, 1983, 1993, 1999). Still others theorize a general ability operating in conjunction with other more specialized skills (Vernon, 1950). Hunt (1975) speaks of intelligence as hierarchical learning sets, with multiple systems and skills, including information processing and motivation. Cattell and Horn (Cattell, 1963; Horn, 1985) developed the concepts of fluid (nonverbal mental efficiency) and crystallized ability (acquired skills and knowledge dependent on environmental influences). Watson (1976) speculated on three possible relationships between intelligence and learning: intelligence-determines-learning, learning-determines-intelligence, and learning-exposes-intelligence.

Cognitive development, as defined by Meier (1976), includes the ability to think about past, present, and future events or thoughts, to problem solve and to achieve a greater understanding about oneself and the world. A definition proposed by Glick (1975) has a similar theme of knowledge about the world. To understand cognitive development as related to knowledge requires an understanding of knowledge and knowing. Glick includes four overlapping categories of skills in his definition of knowledge that are presented in Table 7–1. Although these categories are not mutually exclusive, each represents a critical component of knowledge, which is the basic element of cognition.

The notion that cognition cannot be simply narrowed to a single set of behaviors is behind the idea

of multiple intelligences (Gardner, 1993). Gardner introduced his ideas regarding multiple intelligences with seven areas of intellectual competence: Linguistic, Logical-Mathematical, Spatial, Bodily-Kinesthetic, Musical, Interpersonal, and Intrapersonal. Since then, others have proposed other intelligences to be added to the list (Armstrong, 1999). Gardner has identified Naturalistic intelligence as one probably suitable to add to the list (Gardner, 1999). Using this orientation as the basis for assessing intelligence, the task of assessing a child's cognitive ability is significantly altered. A child's abilities as diverse as self-understanding, ability to interact effectively with peers, and musical abilities would become a critical part of understanding a child's intelligence.

Basic Psychological Processes

The attainment of cognitive skills requires that the child take advantage of basic sensory input as she explores her environment. In order for the child to do so, three basic psychological processes need to be operating—attention, perception, and memory. Before the infant can detect salient features of the environment, she simply must attend to them, that is, become aware of them. After becoming aware of features within the environment, the child must perceive those features, that is, translate them into meaningful information. Interpreting sensory information sent to the brain by the sense organs for seeing, hearing, smelling, touching, tasting, and moving is perception. Although dependent upon it, perception differs from acuity. Damage to a sense organ or nerves connecting an organ to the brain can impair acuity and/or perception. Perception refers to the process that occurs within the brain, involving the recall of past experiences, comparing those experiences to present ones, analyzing the information available, and finally interpreting present stimuli.

If a child is to obtain any long-term knowledge about features of the environment, she must store them in her memory so they are available as needed. Memory is the most complex psychological process involved in cognitive development. It includes the encoding, storage, and retrieval of information in the central nervous system. It has both short- and long-term components, which are related in a sometimes puzzling manner with the ability to retrieve needed information. Ellis's multiprocess memory model (1970), based on other theoretical models (e.g., Atkinson & Shiffrin, 1968; Bower, 1967; Hebb,

TABLE 7-1 Categories of Knowledge

Category	Explanation
Ability to detect environmental features	The acuteness with which a human can gain and ascertain the significance of information in the environment is basic to his ability to develop cognitively. Learning to distinguish the significant features between a square and a circle is less challenging than those of a square and a triangle, which is easier than distinguishing between a square and a rectangle. At first the differences between all of the shapes go unnoticed, but the child gradually comes to see the greatest distinctions. Eventually, the child comes to detect the difference between the square and the rectangle, something that was simply too fine a distinction originally.
Ability to organize diversity into categories	The ability to devise multiple categories, cross-categorize, or shift from one categorization system to another is evidence of cognitive development. For example, a young child might begin playing with blocks by organizing all the blocks into similar sizes or shapes so she can find what she needs as construction begins.
Formation of plans of behavior and/or theories about the world	An infant's actions are not characterized by planning and forethought as she moves about a room, stopping to put whatever she encounters into her mouth, distracted by anything in her immediate path of interest to her. As the child grows, behaviors clearly indicating advance planning begin to emerge. During imaginary play children are observed "setting the stage," assigning parts to themselves and others, and changing the script as needed to suit their purposes. Young children engaged in creative art activities often stop to ponder before beginning to work. The development of theories about the world may be less easily observed in young children, and yet the foundational thinking surely begins during this period. Some theories may be quite simple—temper tantrums are an effective method of obtaining my desires; death is only a temporary condition; play dough of two colors when mixed together can be separated; and so on. Experiences that contradict such theories will require the child to challenge their cognitive validity, and replace them with ones more consistent with their experiences.
Organization of thoughts	Systems—such as logic, mathematics, religion, and other advanced forms of thinking in which we organize our thoughts—are not necessarily based on the world of empirical knowledge. We use such organized thought processes to come to an understanding of both real and theoretical aspects of our world.

Source: Adapted from "Cognitive Development in Cross-Cultural Perspective," by J. Glick, in *Review of Child Development Resource* (Vol. 4), by F. D. Horowitz (Ed.), 1975, Chicago: University of Chicago Press.

1949) includes three levels of memory. As input is attended to and rehearsed, it cycles through the primary memory into the secondary and tertiary memories. Material that is not attended to or rehearsed can be forgotten at any one of these memory levels.

Development of Skills in Communication

The relationship between communication, language, and speech production is hierarchical in nature. **Communication** is the broadest term, including many types of interactions. It is characterized by an exchange of information or ideas. Communication can occur with or without language, through gestures, touch, facial expressions, and sounds, as well as through speech. Meaningful communication begins between infants and their caretakers long before they use formal language structures.

Language involves the use of signs or symbols to which meaning is attributed. It includes much more than the use of written and spoken language. Body language sometimes conveys more information than verbal exchanges. Persons with hearing impairments can communicate effectively using a number of different systems of sign language or develop oral/aural techniques of communication.

Speech is one means of language expression for the purpose of communication. It does require the precise coordination of the central nervous system and muscles used in the speech act. Other means of expression, using standard language systems (e.g., writing, typing, synthesized speech) as well as alternative systems (e.g., American Sign Language, picture exchange systems, computerized voicing), also achieve the purpose of effective communication.

Language development is complex, requiring the interactive use of the basic psychological processes of attention, perception, and memory in both visual and auditory modalities. It is also dependent on cognitive development. Unless a child understands the conceptual meaning of *in, out, under, over, big,* and *little,* it is very unlikely he can incorporate these words into his basic receptive or expressive language.

Language has traditionally been understood as consisting of five basic parameters: **phonology, morphology, syntax, semantics,** and **pragmatics,** summarized in Table 7–2. Bloom and Lahey (1978) have further conceptualized language as comprised of the three major components: **form, content,** and **use,** presented in Table 7–3. Form, content, and use involve both production (expression) and comprehension (reception).

Four broad perspectives that are used in the study of language development are (1) **behavioral theory,** (2) the **syntactic model of psycholinguistic theory,** (3) the **semantic/cognitive model of psycholinguistic theory,** and (4) the **sociolinguistic theory** (Owens, 1989). These perspectives, summarized in Table 7–4, vary in the way language is seen as developing and in the importance given to the language components of syntax and semantics, and pragmatics. Although none adequately explains all aspects of linguistic development, each offers an understanding of some parts of language development.

Early Language Development

Early language development involves the development of many skills, including audition and auditory perception of both environmental and speech sounds,

TABLE 7–2 Parameters of Language

Parameter	Description
Phonology	The sound system of a language.
Morphology	The rules used to build words, including bound and free morphemes. Words such as *hope, sad,* and *car* are considered to be free morphemes. Bound morphemes are units that can be attached to free morphemes to alter meanings (e.g., *hopeful, saddest, cars*).
Syntax	The grammatical rules used in determining acceptable sequencing, combining, and functional use of words in a sentence.
Semantics	The meanings of words and word relations.
Pragmatics	The use of language in social contexts (e.g., communication).

TABLE 7–3 Components of Language

Form	■ The structure of language ■ Consists of rules about phonology, morphology, and syntax ■ Comprises the system of symbols used in a language ■ Morphology and syntax combined form the grammatical rules of a language ■ Phonological and grammatical rules guide us in the pronunciation of words and the formation of sentences ■ Includes the gestures and verbalizations characteristic of the preverbal child ■ As a child develops verbal skills, recognizable speech sounds are used as words and word combinations in an increasing compliance with grammatical rules
Content	■ Parallel to semantics ■ Defined as knowledge about objects and events in the environment ■ Contingent upon cognitive development, achieved through sensorimotor means for infants/toddlers who are preverbal ■ Content increases in complexity and abstraction as the child develops cognitively and linguistically
Use	■ Similar to pragmatics ■ Referring to the communicative or functional properties of language development ■ A newborn infant's behaviors, such as crying or smiling, which typically result in social interaction, do not represent intentional efforts to communicate with another person; however, they soon become intentional and are expanded to include gestures and specific vocalizations, and eventually the child uses words and word combinations to communicate ■ The organizing principle in functionalist models of language development ■ Based on the logic that a desire to communicate must precede the application of form and content to the communication process

communication through sound and gesture, speech production, comprehension of meanings, understanding and application of grammatical and syntactical rules, and beginning an understanding of semantics and pragmatics. A summary of the developmental milestones of early language acquisition is presented in Table 7–5.

The accurate articulation of specific phonemes follows a developmental sequence. Although there is some discrepancy in the literature as to the specific ages certain sounds are acquired, there is relative agreement as to the sequence in which sounds are produced accurately, and that by eight years of age children should be correctly producing all sounds. Owens analyzed the findings of several studies on phoneme production and reached the several conclusions displayed in Figure 7–1.

Language development proceeds through four levels: prespeech, first words, first sentences, and grammaticization (Bates, O'Connell, & Shore, 1987). These levels are based on the construct that there is continuity between and within levels of development. Bates and colleagues also emphasize that language development is characterized by **individual differences**—individual variations in development at all levels, in contradiction with the view that language always develops in a universal sequential manner. The skills associated with each of these levels are summarized in Table 7–6.

In the past, psycholinguistic theory has been predicated on the assumption that significant language development milestones follow a universal sequence, developing in a common sequence and manner in every natural language. Cross-cultural studies conducted in the late 1970s and throughout the 1980s provide evidence to contradict this assumption of universal sequence (e.g., Slobin, 1986). The syntactical and morphological features of the language being learned do seem to influence the patterns and age of skill acquisition. Contributing even further to a child's individuality in his language development is his own language-learning environment (e.g., ratio of adults to children in the home, grammatical patterns used by parents).

TABLE 7–4 Theoretical Perspectives toward Language Development

Theoretical Perspectives	Description
Behavioral theory	■ Language is a learned or conditioned behavior, developing through a stimulus-response association ■ Emphasis is placed on reinforcement (either positive or negative) toward skill development ■ Positively reinforced efforts of imitation of speech sounds are repeated and eventually are learned ■ Fails to account for many aspects of language development such as production of immature word patterns never heard in adult speech (e.g., "me go")
Syntactic model of psycholinguistic theory	■ Emphasis on mental processes involved in language form ■ Chomsky (1959, 1965), the predominate syntactic psycholinguistic theorist, defined and described sentence structures across languages: **phrase structural rules** that are universal regardless of the language being used, and **transformational rules,** that control such things as word order ■ Knowledge of these rules enables us to produce a limitless number of grammatically correct sentences ■ We acquire ability to follow rules in a highly predictable sequential fashion, grounded upon an innate understanding of universal phrase structure rules ■ Phrase structure rules precede transformational rules ■ Limited by its focus on syntax, with no inclusion of phonetics or semantics in the language acquisition process ■ Relies on adult language patterns to explain and understand the language used by children
Semantic/cognitive model of psycholinguistic theory	■ Incorporates semantics, or meanings into psycholinguistic theory ■ Bloom (1970, 1975) initiated and Schlesinger (1971, 1974) contributed to what became known as the semantic revolution, by emphasizing the importance of semantics in language development over syntactic structure ■ The language of children reflects an understanding of word meanings, so that words are combined in a sensible fashion, not just as strings of noun-verb combinations ■ Refutes the innateness concept, by integrating language development with cognition in an inseparable relationship
Sociolinguistic theory	■ Focuses on the communication function of language rather than the structural emphasis evident in the previous theories ■ Language has no meaning outside the context in which it is spoken ■ Quality of linguistic utterances cannot be judged based upon grammatical rules, but on the speaker's meaning (Bruner, 1975) ■ Communicative context in which a person speaks includes features such as assumptions about the listener's knowledge and interest in the topic of discussion, previous history of listeners, and the roles and status of participants in the communicative act (Owens, 1989) ■ **Speech act** incorporates both grammatical and pragmatic rules as a speaker attempts to communicate his propositions and intentions and the listener is responsible for interpreting what was meant (Austin, 1962; Searle, 1965) ■ Children use **primitive speech acts,** which occur before the child has the ability to speak in sentences (Dore, 1974) ■ Rules of dialogue and communication precede the development of syntax or semantics (Owens, 1989)

TABLE 7–5 Milestones of Early Language Acquisition

Age	Receptive	Expressive
1 month	Reflexive smile	
2 months	Attends to speech	Cry for hunger; initiation of babbling
3 months	Locates speaker visually and looks into speaker's face	Expanding vocal noises; vocalizes pleasure; strings together 2 syllables
4 months	Turns to locate noise and voice	Self-initiated sound play; repeats 4–5 syllables in chain
5 months	Cries in response to angry tones; smiles at pleasant speech	Imitates self
6 months	Has understanding of some key words (e.g., *mama*)	Uses intonations and jargon; attempts to produce sound sequences
7 months	Attends to speech of known persons; responds to "bye-bye" and "up"	Expresses satisfaction and dissatisfaction vocally
8 months	Listens to common expressions, such as greetings	Communicates recognition and uses interjections
9 months	Responds to verbal requests (e.g., "open mouth") and information (e.g., "no-no," "hot," own name)	Experiments with pitch, sounds made with lips; repeats patterns in common phrases
10 months	Waves to bye-bye; responds to more verbal requests (e.g., "where is the dog?") and uses gestures to show understanding of simple yes/no questions	Starts naming familiar objects
11 months	Distinguishes family from strangers; shows understanding of many action words	First real word; communicates some needs (e.g., hunger; vocal play with self in mirror
12 months	Enjoys simple rhymes and songs	Vocabulary expands (5–6 words)
18 months	Understands emotional tone; enjoys looking at pictures while another names them; will retrieve objects from another room; recognizes body parts; can complete 2-step commands; selects pictures of familiar objects	Says 1-word sentences; repeats words heard
24 months	Identifies body parts in pictures; recognizes names of many familiar objects, persons, and pets	Speaking vocabulary up to 50–75 words (75% nouns); combines words into 2- and 3-word sentences; imitates animal sounds; begins using prepositions; pulls person and shows as means of communication
30 months	Can identify more body parts; listens attentively to simple stories	Speaking vocabulary over 270 words, with additions of many verbs, adverbs, pronouns; asks simple questions; names 1 color
36 months	Points to familiar verbs in action pictures; understands opposites such as yes/no, come/go, up/down; listens to longer stories	Speaking vocabulary close to 450 words; recites nursery rhymes; beginning to use *me* and *I*; pronunciation improving

FIGURE 7–1 Research-Based Phoneme Production Conclusions

1. As a group, vowels are acquired before consonants. English vowels are acquired by age three.
2. As a group, the nasals are acquired first, followed by the glides, plosives, liquids, fricatives, and affricatives.
3. As a group, the glottals are acquired first, followed by labials, velars, alveolars, dentals, and palatals.
4. Sounds are first acquired in the initial position in words.
5. Consonant clusters and blends are not acquired until age seven or eight, though some clusters appear as early as age four. These early clusters include /s/ + nasal, /s/ + liquid, /s/ + stop, and stop + liquid in the initial position and nasal + stop in the final.
6. There are great individual differences, and the age of acquisition for some sounds may vary by as much as three years.

Source: From *Language Development: An Introduction* (pp. 91–92), by R. E. Owens, 1989, Columbus, OH: Merrill.

Social Aspects of Development

The range of behaviors encompassed in the social-emotional domain of development is wide. A survey of multidomain assessment instruments that purport to measure social skills and/or emotional development provides evidence of this range. Some instruments focus on the child's interactions with other children and adults, some look at the child's ability to play, some look at self-esteem, and others contain items related to the child's skills in self-care. Broadly defined, the social-emotional domain involves the development of attachment, individuation (growth of self), emergence of emotions, and development of adaptive and coping behaviors, including self-care skills.

Attachment, the Self, and Emotions

Attachment, as defined by Sroufe (1979), is "an enduring affective tie between infant and caregiver" (p. 495). As a newborn, the infant displays indiscriminate attachment because she enjoys being handled by many people, although there is evidence that she can differentiate her primary caregiver as early as five weeks of age (Lewis, 1987). Around five months of age, however, the infant shows a strong preference for her primary caregiver and a rejection of others. The primary caregiver is visually tracked, receives more smiles, causes more distress when absent, and creates more pleasure when she or he picks up the child than do others.

Attachments become established with secondary caregivers and family members, followed by attachments to others with whom the child has contact. The failure of an infant to develop an attachment results in substantial affective impairments. Variations in child-rearing practices across differing cultures (e.g., communal care of all infants) do raise some questions as to the universality of this attachment sequence, but do not negate the need for enduring stable affective bonds as a precursor to healthy emotional development, as well as cognitive functioning (Lewis).

A child's future social and emotional development does not rest solely on his secure attachment to a single caregiver. A child raised in isolation who is securely attached to his mother will have difficulty in peer relations, whereas peer relations can be helpful in offsetting inadequate primary caregiver attachment relationships. However, maternal attachment problems may interfere with the development of compensating peer relationships for two reasons. First, mothers who fail to encourage secure infant attachments may also prevent the child from having peer experiences. Second, poor mothering that results in poor attachment relationships can produce a general fearfulness, influencing the child's ability to relate to his peers.

Child characteristics can influence relationships as well. Infants and children exhibit differential patterns of behavior in temperament, readability, and behavior (Huntington, 1988), which affect caregiver behavior. **Temperament** is the behavioral style of the individual child, with emphasis placed on how he behaves rather than what he is doing or why he is doing it. It refers to a cluster of characteristics including activity level, rhythmicity, approach/withdrawal, adaptability, intensity of reaction, quality of mood, distractibility, sensory threshold of responsiveness, attention span, and persistence (Thomas & Chess,

TABLE 7-6 Four Levels of Language Development

Level	Age Range	Associated Skills
Prespeech	Birth to 10 months	Development of sound (perception and production) Development of gestures Concomitant changes in nonlinguistic development Rapid development of sound perception; infant a few weeks old can distinguish phonological contrasts in human speech; speech production rooted in infant's crying and vegetative noises; play with speech sounds including reciprocal speech sounds with others begins after three months; between 6 and 10 months consonant and consonant-vowel imitations are evident in babbling
First Words: Emergence of naming	10 to 13 months	Single-word comprehension Single-word production Individual differences in single-word use Gestures that function as words Attention can be directed with object names ("see the dog," "Amy, dog"); by 13 months receptive vocabulary from 17 to 97 words; as speech production increases, gestures decrease
Word combinations	18 to 24 months	Transition between production of single words with complex meanings to multiword phrases Nature of word combinations and individual differences Parallel developments in other developmental domains Use of word combinations initiate shift into sentence use; size of spoken vocabulary undergoing rapid acceleration and expansion of types of words, especially verbs; parallel development includes gestural imitation, classification of objects, and multigesture strings in play indicating the need for accompanying cognitive development to allow language development
Grammaticization	20 to 30 months (fundamentals of grammar) 36 months (competent speaker)	Acquisition of rules of morphology and syntax Speed of morphemic acquisition Nature and sequence of grammatical development Uniqueness of language development for this age Application of rules Mastery of irregular patterns and rules Requires a baseline of cognitive and language development

Know The Facts

The studies of language customs in a small southeastern city conducted by Heath (1989) illustrate how culture influences language development. The African American children in this community attended integrated public schools and had white teachers. The white teachers found these children to be uncommunicative, unable to answer basic questions. Although these children had developed complex verbal skills that included storytelling and witty remarks to one another, they were puzzled by the questioning techniques used in school. Heath studied the interactions of both the white teachers and the African American children in their home settings. She discovered that the white teachers began questioning their own children early, reading stories and asking questions about the story and pictures in the books. The questioning techniques were designed to determine what the children knew and help them extend that knowledge. However, she discovered a dramatically different pattern of language interaction in the African American homes. The children were not asked these sorts of questions, but did participate in different language experiences, particularly oral storytelling traditions.

The teaching techniques used by the white teachers were consistent with their own rearing styles, with over 50 percent of their utterances being in the form of interrogatives. Had these teachers referred the poorly performing African American children for testing, it is likely that the children would have done poorly on norm-referenced tests. A norm-referenced test designed to assess language skills based on a series of pictures about which the examiner asked questions would lack connection to their life experiences. When teachers adjusted their teaching styles to match better the language experiences of these children, they transformed from uncommunicative to engaged and eager.

1977; Thomas, Chess, & Birch, 1968). Through a longitudinal study, Thomas and Chess identified three clusters of temperament characteristics related to the presence or absence of behavior disorders in later childhood shown in Table 7–7.

A few studies have produced results indicating that children with cognitive impairments and difficult temperaments are at particularly high risk of developing behavioral disturbances (Chess & Korn, 1970; Chess, Korn, & Fernandez, 1971). Other studies have correlated temperament with the type of disability a child has, and environmental context in which assessment of temperament characteristics was conducted (McDevitt, 1988). Infants with disabilities may be at a higher risk for demonstrating the characteristics of the "difficult" child. The child may have an impaired ability to respond to the environment, and, therefore, the disability influences characteristics such as activity level, distractibility, persistence, and sensory threshold. Even though the child's temperament might not be that of a "difficult" child, she may function as one due to her physical limitations.

Readability relates to the child's ability to provide caregivers with distinct signals and cues through overt behaviors. The difficulty that parents of infants with disabilities experience in understanding and responding to unclear cues can result in parental feelings of incompetence (McCollum & Stayton, 1985; McLean, Bailey, & Wolery, 1996; Yoder, 1987). On the other hand, lack of appropriate parental response can reduce the infant's understanding of cause and effect or his ability to interact with his environment effectively. Both parental feelings of incompetence and infant feelings of helplessness influence the others' behavior reciprocally.

Although the elements of **behavior** overlap with temperament and readability, and move into the realm of child functioning, it does include some child characteristics that might otherwise be overlooked. Certain characteristics, such as unusual caregiving demands caused by the disability, can increase parental stress and, therefore, affect the relationship. All new parents experience some stress as they begin feeding their infant solid foods; what to feed the child, how thick to mix the cereal, how much to give her, what to do if she spits it out, and how to be certain she is getting enough to eat. Add to this normal situation an abnormal gag reflex; an inability to control muscles in the oral cavity; and a persistent primitive reflex that makes feeding from the midline a greater challenge, and the stress is likely to increase.

The **development of self** for an infant involves knowledge of where he begins and ends. The first indication of the development of a self-concept is the social smile, which appears by two months of age. The awareness of self as a separate being is an essential

TABLE 7–7 Clusters of Temperament Characteristics

Cluster	Description
The difficult child	Arrhythmic, withdrawing, nonadaptable, intense, and negative (more likely to develop psychiatric problems)
The slow-to-warm-up child	Inactive, withdrawing, nonadaptable, mild, and negative (more likely to exhibit reactive disorders)
The easy child	Regular, approaching, adaptable, mild, and positive (not likely to develop behavioral problems)

TABLE 7–8 Periods of Growth of Self

Age Level	Characteristics
Birth to 3 months	■ Primarily controlled by biological needs and reflexes ■ Infant's responses and reflexive actions stimulate interactions with his caregivers ■ Through the infant's social and object interactions self-differentiation may begin toward the end of the period
3 to 8 months	■ Active learning replaces reflex patterns as cause-effect relationships are developing ■ Reflected images of the infant are interesting to himself because of the mirrored actions when he moves
8 to 12 months	■ Infant can stop and think before acting on a stimulus (response inhibition) ■ Self-other differentiation is established, resulting in the understanding of self across different situations (conservation of self) ■ Infant's ability to maintain his identity independent of the setting, persons, or interactions emerges between eight and nine months of age ■ Awareness of the permanence of self leads the way to object permanence and more complex means-end relationships
12 to 18 months	■ Child becomes self-conscious, showing embarrassment in front of a mirror if self-recognition is shown ■ Fear of loss of the mother intensifies as self-other differentiation increases ■ Child points himself out in a picture or in a mirror, using feature analysis rather than mirrored actions as the cue
18 to 30 months	■ Infant has self-knowledge, such as his gender, age, and goodness or badness ■ Responds to own name and can use own name to refer to self

prerequisite to social development and the establishment of relationships. There are two components in the process of individuation (Lewis, 1987). First, the infant becomes aware of his existential self, which involves an understanding of self-permanence similar to the conceptual development of object permanence. Second, the infant establishes a categorical self, that is,

the way he understands himself (e.g., gender, age, competence, value). Between birth and three years of age there are five periods in the growth of the self, as shown in Table 7–8.

The **development of emotions** must be inferred from an infant's behavioral responses to social and object interactions. However, there is a basic assumption

TABLE 7–9 Stages of Emotional Development

Stage	Age Range	Description
Stage One	0–1 month	There is an **absolute stimulus barrier** during the first month, which provides built-in protection for the newborn. Infants are generally safe from external stimulation.
Stage Two	1–3 months	The infant becomes vulnerable as he begins **turning toward** stimulation and becomes oriented to the outside world. It is during this stage that the exogenous (social) smile appears.
Stage Three	3–6 months	Positive affect becomes possible since the infant now has the capacity for awareness and anticipation. This ability can also cause frustration and negative emotions, such as rage and wariness. The infant can actively attempt to avoid noxious stimulation, and can laugh when vigorously stimulated.
Stage Four	7–9 months	This stage involves **active participation,** engagement, and mastery by the infant. She is aware of her emotions, including joy, fear, anger, and surprise. She will initiate interactions with her caregiver, and intentionally act on objects in the environment to create her own pleasure.
Stage Five	9–12 months	**Attachment** to the primary caregiver is the preoccupation of the infant during this stage, as she is the predominate source of security. Emotional reactions are further differentiated and refined, and some coping functions emerge.
Stage Six	12–18 months	During this **practicing phase** the infant establishes a balance between attachment and exploration. The child is busy actively exploring and mastering her environment, which creates a sense of confidence and well-being. However, it is accompanied by an awareness of separateness from the caregiver.
Stage Seven	18–36 months	**Formation of self-concept** is the task of the infant during this stage. Balancing a sense of self-awareness with the anxiety felt toward separation and the increasing awareness of limited power is the task of two-year-olds.
Stage Eight	preschool years	The resolution of self-identity is achieved through **play** and **fantasy.**

that no true emotions exist until self-differentiation has begun. Based on Bridges's (1932) classic work on the infant's differentiation of emotions and other more recent research, Sroufe (1979) has developed a theoretical view of affective development, involving an eight-stage sequence. These stages are similar to, but more specific than, a five-stage social development model described by Sander (1969) and are intentionally parallel to the cognitive stages of development defined by Piaget. The stages associated with specific emotional reactions, as shown in Table 7–9, represent an approximate age at which the emotion is a common behavior, not necessarily when it first appears, or when it is at its peak occurrence. The emotional reactions associated with each stage are presented in Table 7–10.

Adaptive Behavior and Self-Care Skills

Adaptive behavior is required in the physical, social, and emotional adjustment of a child to the environment. Physically, it involves basic functions of eating, keeping warm, and avoiding danger. Socially

TABLE 7–10 Development of Emotions

Emotional Reaction	Stages of Affective Development							
	One	Two	Three	Four	Five	Six	Seven	Eight
Pleasure-Joy								
endogenous smile	X							
turning toward		X						
pleasure			X					
delight			X					
active laughter			X					
joy				X				
elation						X		
positive valuation of self-affection							X	
pride, love								X
Wariness-Fear								
startle/pain	X							
obligatory attention								
wariness			X					
fear (stranger aversion)					X			
anxiety						X		
immediate fear						X		
shame							X	
Rage-Anger								
distress (due to covering the face, physical restraint, extreme discomfort)	X							
rage (disappointment)			X					
anger				X				
angry mood, petulance						X		
defiance							X	
intentional hurting							X	
guilt								X

related adaptive behaviors include communication of basic needs, cooperative play skills, and appropriate use of toys. Emotional adaptive behaviors involve the formation of relationships in a manner designed to preserve self-esteem and self-identity. Adaptive behaviors range from the primitive sucking reflex of the newborn to the complex skills involved in maintaining a home, having a job, paying bills, raising a family, and other behavioral expectations of adults.

Coping is the process of learning to use adaptive behaviors to function in the world. For the young child, coping behaviors center on nutrition, security, and a combination of activity and rest, coupled with an opportunity to pursue individual interests and mo-

tivations, and to satisfy the drive to achieve mastery (Zeitlin, Williamson, & Szczepanski, 1988). Children can develop **maladaptive** or **adaptive coping styles,** which influence their effectiveness in meeting their physical, social, and emotional needs. For example, a child when initially placed in a car seat begins to cry. The caregiver soothes the child and offers her a few toys, and the child is soon distracted from crying. After a few trips in the car seat, the child no longer cries, but does reach out and gesture to indicate her desire for the usual car seat toys. This child has adjusted to the expectation that she remain in the car seat and is using an adaptive coping style. Another child who screams upon being placed in the car seat, refusing all efforts to be comforted, throwing away all of the toys that are offered, is demonstrating a maladaptive coping style. His maladaptive behavior could result in his being removed from the car seat, thus increasing his risk of injury during a wreck and breaking the law in many states. If he remains in the car seat, he will, at the least, increase the stress of the driver and all others present in the car. Eventually this maladaptive behavior could result in his never being taken on any unnecessary trips in the car, thus reducing his life experiences.

A significant component of adaptive behavior is the development of **self-care skills.** For the young child these involve the skills of eating, dressing, and toileting, and the basic grooming skills (e.g., hand-washing, face-washing, tooth-brushing, and nasal hygiene). The general developmental sequence of eating, toileting, and dressing skills for the typical child can be used in developmental assessments.

The social or emotional status of a child is often evident through observations of the child at play. The interaction of the child's growing self-awareness, cognitive understanding of objects in the environment, and attachment to and investment in caregivers enables the child to begin playing. Parten's (1932) classic six developmental sequences of social play are shown in Table 7–11. Since her work is dated and based on a small number of children, these descriptions may not accurately represent the characteristics of social play of preschoolers today. A child might choose to engage in constructive, self-directed solitary play seen after he is capable of other more "advanced" stages of social play. The solitary play would indicate a lack of development only if it were the sole form of play in which a child engaged at an age where interactive play would be expected. Researchers have also noted that the parallel play of preschool children does not diminish as they mature, casting additional doubt over the sequential nature of Parten's classifications (Rogers, 1982). The classification system is more useful when considered as a description of various types of social participation in which young children engage, rather than as a cumulative developmental continuum.

Others have classified play in a variety of categorical systems based upon their descriptive studies of young children (e.g., Belsky & Most, 1981; Lifter & Bloom, 1989; Ruff & Lawson, 1990). Smilansky (1968), who identified four categories of play presented in Table 7–12, determined that children's communication skills could be improved through training in sociodramatic play. Specifically, children spoke a greater number of words, used longer sentences, engaged in more play-related speech, and developed a larger vocabulary. Wehman (1977) and Bailey and Wolery (1984) identified hierarchies of exploratory and toy play appropriate for assessment of and intervention with young children who have severe cognitive impairments that are shown in Figure 7–2.

TABLE 7–11 Parten's Classifications of Play

Type of Play	Description
Unoccupied behavior	No interpersonal interaction; child attends to anything that attracts her attention; includes engagement in self-stimulating behavior
Solitary play	No interpersonal interaction; child plays alone with toys different from those being used by other children who are nearby
Onlooker behavior	Child observes other children who are playing nearby; remains close and may speak to the children being observed
Parallel activity	Independent play in the vicinity of other children with toys that connect the child to the others
Associative play	Interactive play with other children that involves borrowing from one another, exchange of materials, and communication, but each child plays as she chooses
Cooperative or organized play	Organized group play in which 1–2 children direct the play and organize the group to accomplish common goals and divide the tasks of the group among the participating children

TABLE 7-12 Four Categories of Play Identified by Smilansky

Category	Description	Example
Functional play	Sensorimotor practice games that consist of repetitive movements with or without objects	Spinning a top; swinging arms
Constructive play	Goal directed; includes some representational play with the primary focus on the materials	Building a spaceship; using blocks to create a city
Symbolic play		
■ Dramatic play	Child pretends to be another person, emphasizing roles and themes rather than materials	Individual child becomes Tarzan and creates other characters through objects
■ Sociodramatic play	Two or more children cooperate together in dramatic play as they act out their roles	Firefighters work together to put out a fire; friends are coming over for dinner
Games with rules	Rule-bound group games	Duck, duck, goose

FIGURE 7-2 Hierarchies of Exploratory and Toy Play Useful in Assessment of Children with Severe Cognitive Impairments

Levels of exploratory play (Wehman, 1977):
1. Orientational responses
2. Locomotor exploration
3. Perceptual investigation and manipulation (examination of an object)
4. Searching (seeking new stimuli for exploration)

Levels of toy play (Bailey & Wolery, 1984):
1. Repetitive manual manipulations and oral contacts
2. Pounding, throwing, pushing, or pulling
3. Personalized toy use
4. Manipulation of movable parts of toys
5. Separation of parts of toys
6. Combinational use of toys

Motor Functioning

The difficulty in trying to separate child functioning into distinct domains is readily apparent when we consider the motor domain. Controlled movements serve as the expression of brain functioning. Sperry, as quoted by Wolff (1982), emphasizes the point:

To the neurologist, regarding the brain from an objective, analytical standpoint, it is readily apparent that the sole product of brain function is motor coordination. To repeat: *the entire output of our thinking machine consists of nothing but patterns of motor coordination.* (p. 130)

Through controlled movements, such as the simple reaching movements of an infant, the utterance of first words, the achievement of bowel and bladder control, coloring activities of the preschool child, young children demonstrate their overall development. The only concrete knowledge available about what children are doing, thinking, or feeling is based on our perceptions of their controlled movements (Wolff). Intact motor functioning affords the child the opportunity to explore and experiment with the environment, obtain an understanding of concepts such as cause and effect, and take full advantage of sensory stimulation.

Development of motor skills involves changes in motor behavior and motor control as children grow from infancy into adulthood. Motor functioning is influenced by underlying biological and mechanical factors. Related terms and concepts include psychomotor, perceptual-motor, sensorimotor, and motor learning. **Motor development** and **psychomotor development,** used synonymously throughout the literature, refer to change and stabilization evident in a child's physical structure and neuromuscular function (Gallahue, 1982). **Perceptual-motor skill** is based upon the integration of perceived sensations in a decision-making process, resulting in observable movement. **Sensorimotor** is a term most often associated with the developmental integration of the senses particularly prevalent during the first two years of life. **Motor learning** involves a change in behavior linked primarily to body movement, which is a result of the interaction of experience and maturation.

Reflexive and Volitional Movement

Motor development involves the acquisition of volitional muscle control used to accomplish gross and fine motor tasks. **Reflexive movement,** predominate in a typically developing newborn child, is that which spontaneously occurs in response to stimuli. There are **primitive reflexes,** present in the typically developing infant, and **postural reactions,** which emerge as infants integrate primitive reflexes and develop motor skills. If we slip and fall, our arms automatically reach out into a protective extension as a reflexive motion. Children with motor impairments may exhibit **pathological reflexes,** never present in the typically developing infant, and/or atypically persistent primitive reflexes. Table 7–13 describes some of the reflexes and postural reactions seen in infants and young children.

Volitional movements differ from reflexive movements in that they are under our control and are consciously and intentionally made. We feed ourselves, engage in sports activities, form letters and words through fine adjustments of our fingers while holding a pen, and speak through volitional muscle control. A child follows specific developmental patterns to accomplish motor control and engage in volitional movements, presented in Table 7–14.

Typical motor development requires adequate muscle strength and tone. **Strength** refers to the properties of the muscles, nerves that control muscle contraction, and motor control centers in the brain. Severed nerves, lack of exercise, or chemical changes (e.g., muscular dystrophy) can all adversely affect muscle strength. **Muscle tone** is the amount of tension present in the muscles, ranging from low tone (hypotonia) to high tone (hypertonia). An examiner can assess muscle tone using a range of passive movements, noting the amount of resistance the child shows. Observation of body parts at rest and in motion can also be helpful (Fetters, 1996). Abnormally high or low tone can be present in only those muscles used in flexion (flexors), those used in extension (extensors), or in both. Tone is influenced by environmental factors such as fatigue, temperature, speed of movement, positioning, and task difficulty (Fetters). The infant placed in a prone position (lying on the stomach) assumes a predominately flexed posture, whereas the supine position (lying on the back) increases extension. For a child whose flexor muscles are hypertonic, the prone position restricts his ability to move freely.

Theories of Motor Development

Some theories of motor development focus more on the influence of psychomotor factors on cognitive and emotional development than on how motor skills develop. The importance of the motor domain in the cognitive development of the child varies among the theories. Kephart (1971) views motor learning as the root of all higher forms of behavior, whereas Cratty (1979) considers movement important in the opportunities it creates for learning, rather than the basis of the intellect. Theories vary as to factors such as the role primitive reflexes play in the development of volitional movement, how speed and accuracy are increased, the importance of the knowledge of results on performance, the role of practice and correction of errors, and how extraneous movements are inhibited (Wolff, 1982). Presented in Table 7–15 are three models of motor development, including a basic theoretical model, and two models linked to therapeutic intervention for young children with motor impairments—neurodevelopmental and sensorimotor integration.

TABLE 7-13 Reflexes and Postural Reactions

Reflex	Description	Normal Age Span	Movement Limitations
Asymmetrical tonic neck reflex (ATNR)	When infant's head is turned to side, arm (and sometimes leg) on face side extend, and arm (and sometimes leg) on skull side flex	Birth to 4 months, then gradually fades, completely disappearing by 6 months	Interferes with rolling over, bringing hands to midline and to mouth, grasping objects while visually exploring them, coordinating hands and eyes; causes hip dislocation and scoliosis if persists
Symmetrical tonic neck reflex (STNR)	When head is in extension, arms extend and hips and legs flex; when head is flexed, arms flex and hips and legs extend	2 to 4 months, then gradually fades	Interferes with creeping and crawling and all functional ambulation; child cannot maintain a four-point kneel or normal sitting posture
Tonic labyrinthine reflex (TLR)	Supine: predominant posture is extension—neck extends, shoulders retrace, trunk and legs straighten	Birth to 4 months	Interferes with all volitional movements, including movements such as raising head, extending limbs in prone position and flexing limbs from supine position, sitting, side-lying, and rolling over
	Prone: predominant posture is flexion—arms flex in under chest, hips and legs are tucked in under tummy		
Moro reflex	Where there is a rapid change in head position or a sudden loud noise, the head falls back and arms and fingers extend and go out and up from the trunk	Birth to 4 months, then gradually diminishes, completely disappearing by 6 months	Interferes with sitting equilibrium reactions and protection reaction (absence in the newborn denotes central nervous system dysfunction
Palmar grasp	Hand stays in fisted position; when hand is touched near the little finger (ulnar side), object is immediately grasped	Birth to 4 months; still present in sleep at 6 months	Interferes with finger extension, volitional grasp and release, weight-bearing on palms, sitting, and pincer grasp

(continued)

149

TABLE 7–13 Reflexes and Postural Reactions (Continued)

Postural Reaction	Description	Age of Appearance
Neck-righting reaction	When head is turned to one side in supine position, the body turns in segments (shoulder girdle follows head, then pelvis) toward the same side	Birth to 4 months, then diminishes
Body-righting reaction: Acting on the body	When head is turned to one side in supine position, the body turns in segments (shoulder girdle follows head, then pelvis) toward the same side	Appears 6 to 8 months and inhibited by 3 years
Body-righting reaction: Acting on the head	When feet are placed on the ground or child is lying down, the head comes into alignment with the trunk	Appears at 4 to 6 months and inhibited 1 to 5 years
Equilibrium reaction: Prone and supine	When placed on a tilt board, head bends and body arches toward raised side with arms and legs extended, going out from midline	Prone: 4 to 6 months and persists Supine: 7 to 10 months and persists
Quadrapedal	When positioned on hands and knees and gently tipped to one side, the arm and leg on raised side straighten and extend out from midline while the opposite arm reaches out in a protective extension	10 to 12 months and persists
Equilibrium reaction: Sitting	When in a sitting position and gently pushed to one side, head moves toward raised side, arm and leg of raised side straighten out from the midline and opposite arm and straighten in protection extension; when pushed forward, the legs flex, spine and neck extend, and arms move backward; when pushed backward, the head, shoulders, and arms move forward and the legs straighten	12 to 14 months and persists
Standing	When in a standing position and one arm is pulled outward, the opposite arm and leg straighten outward and head is adjusted to maintain normal position	12 to 18 months and persists
Landau reaction	When child is suspended in prone position, head is raised up with symmetrical extension of spine and hips (shows integration of symmetrical tonic neck reflex and tonic labyrinthine reflex)	9 months

TABLE 7–14 Patterns of Motor Development

Pattern	Description
Cephalocaudal	Development progresses from head to toe, so the first volitional muscle control involves the head and neck and progresses downward
Proximal-distal	Pattern of development from the trunk outward to the extremities, thus sitting precedes throwing a ball
Gross to fine motor	Pattern of large muscle control preceding small muscle control, so children can throw and catch a big ball before they can draw a picture
Mass to specific	Gradually developing ability to isolate muscles for movement; initially, when a child rolls over she does so as a single unit, but soon gains adequate control over specific parts of her body so that the roll becomes more controlled, occurring in a smooth sequence of head and shoulders followed by trunk and hips and completed with the legs

Although Gallahue acknowledges the influence cognitive and emotional development can have on motor development, psychomotor and mechanical factors affecting progression through the stages are emphasized in the Phases of Motor Development model. **Physical fitness** (muscular strength, muscular endurance, circulatory-respiratory endurance, and muscular flexibility) and **motor fitness** (performance ability of a specific skill as influenced by movement, speed, agility, balance, coordination, and power) together make up the psychomotor factors. The mechanical factors influencing motor development are stability, giving force, and receiving force.

Developmental Progression

The developing child follows a sequence of motor development that serves to verify his physical and mental well-being. This sequence and the skills associated with chronological age of the child become the framework for assessment. Although knowledge of motor development sequences and expected age of performance is critical to the early interventionist, the context of performance must never be forgotten. Progression through motor milestones is a continuous, gradual development of skills—not a sudden burst of skill. The infant struggles to pull herself to standing, only to find herself right where she started hundreds of times before she finally remains standing for a few seconds. The excitement of the event immediately causes her to fall again. The level of perseverance and determination that a young child displays in

achieving "pulls to standing" cannot be justly represented in a checkmark on an assessment form. The developmental sequence presented in Table 7–16 is based upon material by Bobath (1970), Zelle (1983), Finnie (1975), and Bailey and Wolery (1984).

Early Sensory and Motor Development

As an infant matures physically and has opportunities to explore her environment, sensory and motor skills develop. As sensory skills develop, they become integrated and are coordinated with motor skills. We can observe this progression in an infant whose initial attempt to reach for and secure an object two feet out of her reach changes in time to a successful pattern, involving movement of her body within reaching distance of the object, and accurate eye-hand coordination as contact is made with the object on the first attempt to secure it.

Development of the senses enables the infant and young child to explore the environment, providing the opportunity for learning. When **tactile sensory development** progresses typically, the infant accepts touch. Normal caregiving routines (wrapping child in blanket, cuddling, patting, stroking) help increase tolerance for tactile stimulation, leading the way to the development of tactile discrimination skills. The child can distinguish tactile stimuli by features such as temperature or texture. Tactile reflexes (e.g., rooting reflex, Babkin reflex—squeezing palm causes mouth to open without a cry) demonstrate the tactile sensitivity of newborns. The tactile sense is

Finding A Better Way

In an effort to develop alternative approaches to the assessment of motor-disabled infants, Zelazo (1979, 1982a, 1982b) has explored infants' capacity to process information using sequential visual and auditory events. The procedure he developed from clinical study includes five events (two visual and three auditory) and is appropriate for infants between the ages of 3 1/2 and 36 months. The basic paradigm involves the presentation of an engaging visual or auditory event that is repeated until the child begins to expect it. Before the child loses all interest, the event is presented with some modifications three times. The original is then reintroduced for three additional presentations. The child's ability to create an expectation, and his recognition of the return to the original event, are noted.

An example of a visual event is the car-doll sequence. A small toy car is placed at the top of a wooden ramp approximately 22 inches long. A presenter, who is hidden behind a black curtain, holds the car there for four seconds and releases it to roll down the ramp and knock down a Styrofoam object. After a wait of four seconds, the presenter returns the Styrofoam object to an upright position and pushes the car back to the top of the ramp. The event is repeated six times, followed by three repetitions of a discrepant variation (the Styrofoam object is not knocked over). The original event is then repeated three additional times. The auditory events follow a similar pattern. For example, in one of them, the phrase ("Hello baby. How are you today?" is the first event. "Are today. How baby you hello?", spoken with the same rhythm and intonation, is the discrepant variation.

Observers record selected behaviors of the infant during each of the events, including (1) duration of visual fixation to stimulus, (2) smiling, (3) vocalization, (4) fretting for both auditory and visual events, (5) pointing to the speaker and baffle, (6) clapping, (7) waving of the arms through arc greater than 60 degrees, (8) twisting or extreme bending, (9) visual searching, (10) anticipatory fixation (darting of the eyes shed of the action in sequence, rather than searching), and (11) pointing to the visual stimuli. The infant's heart rate and electrocardiogram are recorded. The information recorded from both observers, the heart rate, and EKG can be combined into behavioral clusters, which begin to appear after the first year of life. For example, a typical 20-month-old during the third presentation of the car-doll sequence has a 12-beat cardiac deceleration, smiles, vocalizes, and points when the car taps the Styrofoam object. The cluster of behaviors fades out during subsequent presentations, and stops abruptly when the discrepant presentation is made. However, the behavior cluster reappears during the first reappearance of the standard event. This perceptual-cognitive processing assessment procedure is based upon three basic assumptions (Zelazo, 1979):

1. Infants have the capacity to form a memory for a perceptual event without the necessity for gross-motor involvement.
2. The capacity to form a memory for a perceptual experience begins almost from birth.
3. Infants form schemata for events in both visual and auditory modalities and presumable code information on a central level. (pp. 54–55)

used extensively as the young child explores his environment. The child with neurological impairments may display an intolerance to tactile stimulation.

Visual sensory development follows a pattern of sensation to light, visual fixation (present in two-week-old infants), visual tracking, convergence (using both eyes together), eye contact, reaching and grasping, and eye-hand and eye-foot coordination activities. At birth the infant's eye differs from an adult's eye on several significant dimensions: the optic nerve is not fully myelinated, retinal cellular structures are undifferentiated, the diameter of the eye is smaller, the pupillary opening is smaller, pigmentation of the macular area is incomplete, and there is a tendency toward hyperopia (farsightedness). Cellular changes and maturation enable the infant by four months of age to approximate adult ability to focus. By one year the child has a range of visual capabilities that enable him to explore the environment at many levels, including social aspects.

The **auditory senses** also develop in a sequential pattern, beginning with auditory attention (i.e., attending to sounds in the environment), and localization (i.e., the ability to identify where the sound

TABLE 7-15 Theories of Motor Development

Model	Source	Description
Phases of Motor Development	Gallahue, 1982	A child's observable movement behavior is the window through which motor development can be viewed. Movement is classified in one of four categories: nonlocomotor (stabilizing or balancing movements), locomotor (e.g., creeping, crawling, walking), manipulative (e.g., throwing, catching, cutting, drawing), or combination movements. The model is based on an overlapping progression through four phases from birth through the early teen years:
		reflexive movement — information encoding stage (birth to four months) and an information decoding stage (from four months to one year of age) is dominated by reflexive, involuntary, subcortically controlled movements
		rudimentary movement — involves stability movements (e.g., head and neck control), manipulative movements (e.g., reach, grasp, release), and locomotor movements (e.g., creeping, crawling, and walking). It contains a reflex inhibition stage (from birth to one year) followed by a precontrol stage (from one year to two years) when the infant learns to gain and maintain equilibrium, manipulate objects, and move about in the environment
		fundamental movement — ranges from age two up to seven years of age. The two- to three-year-old is in the initial stage, four- to five-year-old in the elementary stage, and the six- to seven-year-old in the mature stage of this phase. The child in the fundamental movement phase is learning how to perform a variety of basic observable patterns of behavior, such as running, jumping, throwing, catching, and balance beam walking. As the skill develops, increased control by the child results in the increased fluidity of movement
		sport-related movement — associated with children seven years and older

(continued)

TABLE 7-15 Theories of Motor Development (Continued)

Model	Source	Description
Neurodevelopmental treatment	Bobath & Bobath, 1975	Based upon two basic factors: 1. Damage to the central nervous system interferes with the normal maturation of the brain, leading to retardation or arrest of motor development. 2. A release of abnormal postural reflex activity results in the presence of abnormal patterns of posture and movement. The goal of neurodevelopmental treatment (NDT) is to inhibit patterns of abnormal reflex activity and facilitate normal motor patterns. Specialized techniques of handling the child incorporate guiding the child's movements through normal developmental patterns. Such treatment might require the temporary loss of functioning if a child has developed abnormal patterns of movement that will eventually impede his functioning (e.g., abnormal sitting posture that will encourage curvature of the spine and joint fixation). Abnormal movement patterns and excessive effort are replaced as the therapist controls the child aiming to establish a normal postural tone and a normal pattern of movement.
Sensory integration	Ayres, 1973; 1987	Functioning of the brain stem and early sensory integration processes are important influences on higher levels of the brain and, therefore, later cognitive development. From this theory sensorimotor integration therapy was developed for intervention with children with learning disabilities. It has come to be used in early intervention as well. Improving a child's functioning at the lower, less complex levels of sensorimotor skill development enables the child to become competent at higher, more complex levels (e.g., reading). The tactile, proprioceptive, and vestibular systems are viewed as important because of their contribution to generalized neurological integration and to enhanced perception in other sensory systems. Treatment based on sensory integration incorporates both perceptual motor theory and neurodevelopmental theory.

TABLE 7–16 Developmental Sequence of Motor Skills

Age	Description
Birth to 4 months	The newborn in the prone position maintains a flexed posture, with his head turned to one side, the pelvis tilted up high and knees tucked up under the abdomen. He can raise his head to a 45-degree angle and holds the head mostly in midline by eight weeks. By four months he can lift up his head and chest, with the plane of his face at 90 degrees to the surface. Limbs can be stretched out into full extension. In the supine position, the tonic labyrinthine reflex reduces the flexor posture by stimulating the extensor muscles. Gravitational forces pull the head to one side asymmetrically and the flexed arms down to the surface. The infant at this age will display an asymmetrical tonic neck reflex, which gradually diminishes. By the end of four months the infant has a symmetrical posture, with the head in midline and hands capable of moving to the midline.
	When the newborn is pulled to sitting, her head lags. When supported in a sitting position the head falls forward and the back is completely rounded. The four-month-old pulled to sitting displays only a slight head lag, and the back is not completely rounded. If the body is swayed during sitting, the head will wobble some. The arms remain flexed and forward, and when extended can result in a fall backwards.
	When held up with feet lightly touching a surface, the newborn displays a primitive walking reflex, which disappears by two months. The two-month-old will bear no weight, but the three- and four-month-old will bear a small amount of weight. The four-month-old may rise up on her toes and claw with them. The newborn's hands are tightly fisted, with a strong resistance to being opened. By two months, however, the hands are often open. The grasp reflex present in the newborn fades by four months, and pulling at others' clothing, and clutching emerges. The four-month-old can oppose gravity and clasp objects between both hands at the point of midline.
5 through 8 months	The five-month-old bears weight on her forearms, and can move her legs flexed up under her trunk to move forward short distances. Soon she bears weight on her hands and begins reaching for toys while supporting herself on one forearm. The five-month-old can roll from prone to supine. During this phase, the infant begins a modified combat (belly) crawl. When the infant spots something of interest to her, she waves her arms and rocks, providing vestibular stimulation. In a supine position the five-month-old can lift his legs to his mouth and play with his toes. He will hold out his arms to be picked up. At six months the infant can roll from supine to prone, and lifts his head spontaneously. He begins reaching for toys from a side-lying position, bearing weight in a supine position. During this period the infant begins raising his hips off the surface, arching his back.
	The five-month-old shows no head lag when pulled to sitting, holding the back straight in a sitting position. The head does not wobble when the body is swayed. During this period the child develops the ability to sit on the floor unsupported with her hands out forward for support. When given the opportunity, the five-month-old will bear almost all of her weight. By six months the infant may begin bouncing while held in a standing position. Soon she can stand, holding on to furniture and begins pulling herself up to stand. The five-month-old enjoys putting objects in his mouth. He now has volitional grasp, can hold his own bottle, and grasp his own feet. During this period he begins transferring objects from hand to hand, feeding himself biscuits, banging objects on the table, and patting his image in the mirror.

(continued)

TABLE 7–16 Developmental Sequence of Motor Skills (Continued)

Age	Description
9 through 12 months	The infant is free to move from prone to a sitting position and back to prone. He can creep on the abdomen backwards, and soon in a forward direction with a pulling motion of the arms. Around ten months, the infant begins rocking and creeping on his hands and knees. During this period he does not enjoy remaining in a supine position and most often rolls over or sits up. He can sit steadily with little overbalancing, has a protective extension forward, sideways, and finally backwards, and can pull himself to sitting. He pivots, rotating the head, shoulders, and trunk around to pick up objects and crosses the midline in his reaching. Finger-thumb opposition develops during this period, and the infant is able to pick up very small objects using pincer grasp. The index finger is used to explore and poke at objects. Initially, during this period, the infant holds objects to give to an adult, but does not release them. Soon, however, volitional release begins developing and the infant can release a toy when giving it to an adult.
13 through 18 months	The infant begins this period able to pull to standing and cruise about the room holding on. She soon accomplishes the feat of taking her first independent steps, and cannot be stopped. She develops the ability to rise to standing without objects to pull up on and can sit in a chair on her own. Toward the end of this period stiff running will begin. She can grasp very small items with a precise pincer movement, release objects one at a time, and move her hand to wave bye-bye. She will transfer even a speck of dust from one hand to the other, and can clap hands and bang objects together. She grasps crayons in a palmar orientation of her hand.
19 through 24 months	During this period of motor development the child attempts to jump and kick a ball, increases walking ability and starts running, and is able to rise to standing more efficiently. He can throw a ball in an overhand or underhand pattern. He catches a ball by trapping it against his chest with flexed elbows. He can release objects onto another object (stacking). He grasps crayons with a beginning radial-palmar orientation.
2 to 5 years	Between two and three years of age a toddler spends a great deal of time running and jumping. She is able to turn the pages of books carefully. The three-year-old rides a trike, climbs stairs in a reciprocal pattern, can stand on one foot for two seconds, and hops. She cuts with scissors, imitates circular and horizontal strokes, and copies a circle. By her fifth birthday, the preschool child can walk backward heel-to-toe and jumps over objects as high as ten inches. She starts holding a pencil in an adult manner, copies a cross, and can lace shoes.

was coming from). Soon auditory discrimination and association also develop. The infant can first distinguish the sounds of Mother's voice from the doorbell or phone ringing, and shortly thereafter from other voices. Human and environmental sounds become associated with certain events or conditions, so that parents resort to spelling certain words in the presence of even very young children. The auditory system anatomy is completely developed prior to birth. Myelinatization of the auditory nerve is complete at birth; however, the cortex is immature and may be limited in the ability to integrate sounds from both ears. An infant between the ages of four and six months can localize to environmental sounds, show differential smiling to Mother's voice, are more soothed by a female voice than a male voice, and able to discriminate many speech sounds.

The development of **gustatory** and **olfactory sensory systems** has received less attention than that of tactile, visual, and auditory development. It is known that the infant has a large number of taste buds, and that newborns do show a preference for sugar over water solutions. It is also known that infants vary in their responses to differing odors. A preference for specific odors has been noted in infants as young as 72 hours (Hanson & Hanline, 1996). Although a clear pattern of development in gustation and olfaction development is not available, there is adequate evidence to suggest that even a newborn is able to use her taste and smell senses to explore and learn about her world.

The **vestibular system** substantially influences sensory development and is sometimes considered a sixth sense. The vestibular receptors located in the inner ear detect degree of balance, muscle tone, and eye movement. Alertness level is also influenced by the vestibular system. As primitive reflexes are inhibited and postural righting and equilibrium reactions emerge, the vestibular system enables the body to maintain an upright head position, and keep body parts in alignment for normal movement (Fetters, 1996).

Effects of Sensory Impairments

The impact of sensory impairments can be observed even during the first four months of a child's life, influencing tolerance for weight bearing in a prone position, recognition and response to caregivers, and integration of reflexive responses (Zelle, 1983). The infant with a visual impairment has no opportunity to participate in mutual gaze, gaze aversion, or eye

brightening with his caregivers. He does not see the caregiver's smile, and therefore, his own smile is not as distinct and less frequent than the infant with intact vision. He has no visual lure to raise his head while in the prone position, to reach out toward objects and people, and would prefer to remain in a supine position. There may be a delay in the recognition and preference for caregivers. Even when provided with auditory stimulation, the infant with a visual impairment will not reach out because he does not associate the sound with objects available for exploration and play. The infant is not able to begin creeping about, distancing himself from a caregiver while keeping her in sight. However, once he has achieved the ability to reach toward sound cues, the sound of a caregiver's voice or desired objects can help stimulate self-initiated movements and position changes.

The infant with an auditory deficit does not hear the caregiver's voice and the cues available from voice and tone changes. Thus, she is deprived of information critical to both structural and emotional patterns with the language system. The opportunity to move in rhythm to sound is also impaired. When the infant is ready to move about, caregivers cannot restrict the child's movements or actions from a distance with a verbal warning. This inability to warn the child can result in greater than normal physical restrictions on the child, interfering with motor development as well as the separation/individualization process.

If the impairment involves the vestibular system, ocular control, visual, and auditory processing can be affected. Severe impairment can result in the infant curling up in the corner of his crib, keeping his head down. Righting and equilibrium responses will be delayed because the child is afraid of gravitational shifts and rapid movements. Tactile impairments can make the infant stiffen and withdraw when caregivers attempt to cuddle, feed, or dress her. The protective response against tactile stimulation interferes with her ability to tolerate weight bearing in all positions. It is also possible for the infant to crave tactile stimulation to the point of banging her head, pinching, biting, and hitting herself.

Criterion-Referenced Assessment

When using criterion-referenced assessment, we focus on identifying specific skills that a child has mastered and those she may be ready to learn in the immediate future. The emphasis shifts from the child's deficits or age level of development to what skills she has and where to begin instruction. When given too frequently, standardized tests become invalid. We can use criterion-referenced tests as often as needed to monitor a child's progress. If administering a criterion-referenced assessment frequently means that the child picks up the skill, that is of no concern. How the child developed the skill does not alter the fact that the child now has the skill.

Many criterion-referenced systems grew out of a need to document the efficacy of federally funded early intervention programs initiated in the 1970s. Project administrators throughout the country were unable to identify appropriate standardized instruments that would accurately reflect the progress of participating infants and toddlers. Therefore, they created their own developmental checklists and curriculum guides to accompany them. Two of the most successful of these that have revised and updated their content and remain in wide use today are the Hawaii Early Learning Profile (HELP; VORT Corporation, 1995, 1997; Parks, 1996), including assessment, curriculum materials, and home-based activity sheets for birth to three-year-olds and preschoolers; and the Carolina Curriculum for Infants and Toddlers with Special Needs (Johnson-Martin et al., 1991) and companion volume, Carolina Curriculum for Preschoolers with Special Needs (Johnson-Martin et al., 1990). The Assessment, Evaluation, and Programming System for Infants and Children Vol. 1–4 (AEPS; Bricker, 1993; Cripe et al., 1993; Bricker & Pretti-Frontczak, 1996; Bricker & Waddell, 1996) is another comprehensive assessment and curriculum system that originated in the mid-seventies as we began educating young children with severe to profound disabilities. Other criterion-referenced screening instruments useful with both infants and toddlers, and preschool- and primary-age children are the Brigance screens, including the Brigance Early Preschool Screen (Brigance, 1998a); Brigance Preschool Screen (Brigance, 1998b); and the Brigance K & 1 Screen-Revised (Brigance, 1997). The Learning Accomplishment Profile-Revised (LAP-R; Glover, Preminger, & Sanford, 1995b) and the Early Learning Accomplishment Profile (E-LAP; Glover et al., 1995a) are also criterion-referenced developmental checklists. Table 7–17 provides a synopsis of selected criterion-referenced assessment options.

Play-Based Assessment

Play-based assessment offers us an avenue to explore how a child thinks, communicates, moves about his environment, manipulates toys, and interacts with friends and adults, from a holistic perspective. It is a technique that is particularly suited for infants, toddlers, and preschool-age children because it allows the assessment process to move with the child's interests, rather than being dictated by the sequence of a test. The examiner is not faced with the task of putting away an object before the child is finished playing with it. Flagler (1996) identifies six reasons for using play-based alternatives to assessment in early childhood, summarized in Figure 7–3.

Children, who do not "perform" under routine standardized testing conditions, will participate in play-based assessments. The technique demands more from the examiner and those observing the assessment because it is an open, fluid process. The adults facilitating and observing the process must recognize when a child is exhibiting understanding of cause-effect relationships, engaging in symbolic play, using turn-taking in communicative efforts, and so forth. Concurrently, the facilitator must be actively playing with the child, thinking about his or her next moves in response to the child's direction, and how to create appealing opportunities to explore additional skills with this child. Play-based assessment is not simpler, faster, or more efficient than standardized testing; however, it can be more meaningful and offer far more insight into the child.

Play offers the ideal context to explore and determine a child's established and emerging developmental skills. Infants and children rarely resist play. It is unlikely that we would need to report that a child was "untestable" or uncooperative during a play-based assessment. The very nature of the assessment makes it appealing to the child. By definition, play is spontaneous and voluntary, enjoyable, valuable to the participants, intrinsically motivating, and involves active engagement. Children develop and mature through their play.

If a child is unable to play spontaneously, she misses the opportunity to interact with her environment, and, therefore, will likely experience developmental lags. Reasons why a child might be unable to engage in spontaneous play include extreme physical

TABLE 7-17 Selected Criterion-Referenced Assessment Options

Hawaii Early Learning Profile
HELP Strands: Curriculum-Based Developmental Assessment Birth to Three Years (Parks, 1996)
HELP For Preschoolers: Assessment Strands: Ages 3–6 Years (VORT Corporation, 1995)

General Description	Scoring	Links to Curriculum
Continuum of 1,300 skills grouped into 60 concept-based strands organized into 6 areas of development: ■ cognitive ■ language (receptive and expressive) ■ gross motor ■ fine motor ■ social ■ self-help Birth to Three also includes: ■ regulatory/sensory organization Infants and toddlers: use information available from caregivers, as well as observations during play-based and structured facilitation periods, a period of movement and motor activities, and a snack or feeding time. Preschool-age children: use information observations, and information from parents and other caregivers combined with results of a structured assessment of skills.	Skills are noted as: ■ observed or reported ■ not observed or reported ■ emerging ■ atypical or dysfunctional ■ not applicable due to disability, family preference, culture ■ appropriately not present ■ physical environment or caregiver interactions compromise child's development in this area, or if caregivers request help with specific behaviors, even when appropriately present	Form has the skills organized chronologically within each developmental area with the typical age at which the skill emerges indicated Each skill is identified by a number linking it to activities found in the curriculum materials and the home activity guides

(continued)

159

TABLE 7-17 Selected Criterion-Referenced Assessment Options (Continued)

Assessment, Evaluation, and Programming System for Infants and Children, Vol. 1–4 (AEPS; Bricker, 1993; Cripe et al., 1993; Bricker & Pretti-Frontczak, 1996; Bricker & Waddell, 1996)

General Description			Scoring	Links to Curriculum
Comprehensive assessment/curriculum system, includes developmental test, family report, child progress record, and family interest survey Six-phase process includes initial assessment, formulation of IEPs or IFSPs, intervention, ongoing monitoring for immediate feedback, quarterly evaluation, and annual or semiannual progress			Each strand is divided into goals and objectives, with specific criterion for passing the item, materials needed, and procedures involved in the presentation of the item Scoring points system: 2 = pass consistently 1 = inconsistent performance 0 = does not pass May also provide qualifying notes: A = assistance provided B = behavior interfered R = reported assessment M = modification/adaptation D = direct test Examiner records the total points the child earns in each domain and compares it to total points available in domain, calculating a domain percentage score Progress during intervention monitored using domain percentages	Results to provide interventions that are highly individualized in nature based on AEPS curriculum

Domain	Birth to 3 months	3 to 6 months
Fine motor	Reach, grasp, and release Functional use of fine motor skills	Manipulation of objects Prewriting
Gross motor	Movement and locomotion in supine and prone position Balance in sitting Balance and mobility Play skills	Balance and mobility in standing and walking Play skills
Adaptive	Feeding Personal hygiene Undressing	Dining personal hygiene Dressing and undressing
Cognitive	Sensory stimuli Object permanence Causality Imitation Problem solving Preacademic skills Interaction with objects	Participation Demonstrates understanding of concepts Categorizing Sequencing Recalling events Problem solving Play Premath and prereading
Social communication	Prelinguistic communicative interactions Transition to words Comprehension of words and sentences Production of social-communicative signals, words, and sentences	Social-communicative interactions Production of words, phrases, and sentences
Social	Interactions with adults Interactions with environment Interactions with peers	Interaction with others Interaction with environment Knowledge of self and others

TABLE 7–17 (Continued)

Carolina Curriculum for Infants and Toddlers with Special Needs (Johnson-Martin et al., 1991)
Carolina Curriculum for Preschoolers with Special Needs (Johnson-Martin et al., 1990)

General Description	Scoring	Links to Curriculum

Organized around five developmental domains (cognition, communication, social adaptation, fine motor skills, and gross motor skills) in 26 curriculum sequences	Items are scored:
	1. passed
	2. failed
	3. emerging (used under four conditions):
	  a. item passed after repeated tries
	  b. parent reports that child does behavior at home, but it has not been generalized to other settings
	  c. child needs additional practice for mastery
	  d. child performs motor behaviors in a functional, but abnormal manner
		Assessment is a means of determining where in the curriculum to begin working with a child, and to monitor the progress of the child in the curriculum
		
		Curriculum guide provides:
		■ description of materials needed
		■ procedures to follow
		■ instructions on how to use the procedure in daily routines
		■ adaptations needed for specific disabilities
		■ criterion used to determine mastery

FIGURE 7–3 Reasons to Use Play-Based Alternatives

1. Comprehensive nature permits use of multiple strategies to measure the same skill. Flexibility and substitutions of items that measure the same skill are possible.
2. Interplay between developmental areas possible. We can witness how language development influences emotions and behavior, or how motor skills influence the types of play a child chooses.
3. Multiple domains observed through the medium of play. We observe strengths and needs across all domains simultaneously, avoiding artificial compartmentalization.
4. Family focus and participation. Parents are not only permitted in the assessment arena, but they also are encouraged to participate actively. Instead of sitting on the sidelines prohibited from helping their child display their recently acquired skills, they can play with the child specifically to allow the child to show off his newest accomplishments. It allows for a natural observation of parent-child interactions that can provide additional information for an assessment team.
5. Eliminates the overreliance on sensorimotor skills, language abilities, and socialization evident in standardized testing, permitting us to observe and credit the child for perceptual skills, memory, or problem-solving skills.
6. Play setting frees the child and examiner from strict adherence to sequence, verbatim directions, and time factors. The child's attention can wander, she may continue to play with toys even after she has demonstrated the skills of interest, and she can even practice skills or receive a demonstration from us as part of our interactive play. The shift is away from giving the child no help, to seeing what the child can do in a relaxed play context that can include clues, assistance, and repetitions.

limitations due to an orthopedic disability, severe cognitive disabilities, a history of severe abuse and neglect, and disability-related behavioral characteristics. In such cases, play can serve as both the context through which we assess development and a target of assessment and intervention.

Play Shapes Development

Play both influences and is influenced by a growing child's cognitive skills, social-emotional development, communicative skills, and physical and motor development. As a child explores her world, making choices about what to touch, how to touch objects, when to bring them to her mouth, and when to throw them across the room, through repetition and choice making the child achieves new understandings. With these new understandings in hand, the child moves forward to make countless more decisions regarding engagement with objects, people, and the world. Much of an infant's initial play behavior seems to be characterized by trial and error. When success is achieved, the child is driven to persist at the task until it is mastered. Successes can provide for the child a continuing motivation to master more and more challenging tasks.

Structures for Play-Based Assessment

A popular play-based assessment system for young children with special needs in use today is the Transdisciplinary Play-Based Assessment (TPBA; Linder, 1993a). Linder's TPBA includes an adjustable six-phase process summarized in Table 7–18. Linder provides observational guidelines for cognitive, social-emotional, communication and language, and sensorimotor development. These guidelines allow observers to go beyond a traditional checklist format by focusing on both what the child did and how he did it. The TPBA manual provides a detailed description of behaviors for each area of development. These descriptive sections are accompanied by observation guidelines that are organized into outline formats, with questions provided to draw the observer's attention to specific skills displayed by the child. A parallel outline of skills for each developmental area provides approximate age ranges associated with these skills. The outline appears again on observation worksheets for use during the assessment, with space provided for observational notes. Information for each developmental area can be presented on a summary sheet for that area including areas of strength, an overall rating and justification for the rating, and a description of things that the child is ready to learn.

TABLE 7–18 Phases of Linder's Transdisciplinary Play-Based Assessment

Phase	Description	Role of Facilitator	Observations
Phase I: Unstructured Facilitation 20–25 minutes	Child moves about the defined play area, interacting with toys and materials as they interest him	Follows child, imitates child's behavior/vocalizations, talks to child, interacts with toys sequentially in parallel, associative, or cooperative play at appropriate developmental level, models higher levels of skill encouraging child to explore new skills; keeps directive "teaching" to minimum unless child appears highly motivated to accomplish task	Cues from the child regarding toy preferences, patterns of interaction, learning style; spontaneous behaviors and those that are imitation only; responses to prompting and reinforcement
Phase II: Structured Facilitation 10–15 minutes	Child asked to perform cognitive and language activities that were not explored during Phase I such as puzzles, or activities that require problem-solving skills	Takes more directive role while maintaining child-initiated play quality, selecting tasks and presenting them in a game format; keeps length of phase appropriate to developmental level and behavioral attitude of child	Reactions of the child to the new tasks (e.g., interest and cooperation, resistance); skills demonstrated and skills that emerge through prompting
Phase III: Child-Child Interaction 5–10 minutes	Another child joins the child in an unstructured play setting; playmate is preferred to be slightly older, of the same gender, and who has no disability, without wide range in developmental levels of the two children	Determines most appropriate time to bring in playmate following the completion of Phase I; offers diversity of play options to maximize social play opportunities: dramatic play produces social interactions and language; block area allows associative or cooperative play if trucks, dolls, and other representational toys are available	Play interactions and social patterns; cognitive, language, and motor behavior; differences in child behavior between child-facilitator and child-child
Phase IV: Parent-Child Interaction 5 + 5 minutes (unstructured, separation, structured)	Parent (one at a time when both are participating) plays with the child as they normally do at home, leaves briefly, returns to engage the child in structured activity that is slightly challenging to the child	Observes the parent-child interactions; prompts the parent to leave the setting; observes child behavior during separation from parent, and child's response to the parent's return; when the parent returns, prompts parent to engage in structured activity with the child	Language and interactive patterns with the parent; developmental skills demonstrated by the child during play with the parent; techniques used by parent to teach the child
Phase V: Motor Play 10–20 minutes	Begins unstructured and moves to structured to cover activities not chosen by the child	Initially follows child's lead, encouraging motor play, initiating play if necessary, can be joined by physical or occupational therapist as appropriate for child (considering child's familiarity with individual or reactions of child to additional person joining in play setting); introduces directed activities to cover skills not occurring unstructured	Muscle tone, equilibrium and other motor skills, anxiety or eagerness to engage in motor activities
Phase VI: Snack 5–10 minutes	Playmate from Phase II can rejoin child for snack	Presents age-appropriate snack for child and playmate to eat (snack can vary to demonstrate finger feeding skills, use of cup, etc.)	Social interactions, self-help skills, adaptive behavior, oral motor skills

Source: Adapted from *Transdisciplinary Play-Based Assessment: A Functional Approach to Working with Young Children* (Rev. ed.), by T. W. Linder, 1993, Baltimore: Paul H. Brookes.

A simple plus/minus (+/−) rating system is used to indicate those skills that the child clearly has mastered or has not yet mastered. The + rating indicates that the child demonstrated the skill at an appropriate age range, using typical behavioral patterns, and good quality of performance. The − is used to rate skills in which the child demonstrates delays in development, deviations from normal behavior patterns, or poor quality of performance. The quality and meaning of these ratings is only as good as the assessor's knowledge of and familiarity with the observation guidelines and expected performance in each area for specific ages. Other options in the rating system allow the examiners to indicate if insufficient information was obtained and further assessment needed; items were not applicable due to age, disability, or other factors; and there was no opportunity to observe, but no further evaluation is recommended.

A cumulative summary sheet can be used to summarize the child's areas of strength in each of four developmental areas, primary and secondary tasks for which the child is ready, and documentation of the participating members of the assessment team. Brief illustrative samples of the observation guidelines are presented in Table 7–19. Linder (1993b) has developed a companion volume to guide in the formation of a transdisciplinary intervention plan based on results of assessment.

The Infant/Preschool Play Assessment Scale (I-PAS; Flagler, 1995) is a play-based system that is available for use with all children. In addition to authoring the I-PAS, Flagler (1996) has developed guidelines for independent play-based assessments. These guidelines include assessment of general play repertoire, developmental and cognitive functioning, communication skills, sensorimotor abilities, social/emotional/affective development, preacademic skills, behavioral competence, family relations, and specific structures for the assessment of children with low-incidence disabilities and autism. For the general play repertoire, she refers to the play taxonomies of Parten, Piaget, Smilansky, Copeland and Golden, Wehman, and Linder. Additionally, she offers a series of guiding questions to consider related to the child's exploratory or concrete level of play, social levels of play, sensorimotor responses and preferences, distractibility and attention, the need for reinforcers, turn-taking abilities, concept-formation skills, seriation and sequencing abilities, memory skills (long and short term, visual and auditory), problem solving, motivation, manipulative and fine motor skills,

levels of communication, and gross motor abilities. In the area of cognition, she suggests guiding questions under the categories of distinct strategies of problem solving, short- and long-term memory skills, organization schemes for long-term memory storage, and completion of analogies, classifications, series patterns, and metaphors. Communication includes considerations at the prelinguistic level (e.g., cooing and babbling, sensitivity to touch in the face and mouth area, variation of facial expression, respiratory patterns, and evidence of turn taking) as well as expressive and receptive language. There are guiding questions specific for pragmatics, including three primary elements: use of language for multiple purposes (e.g., greeting, informing, requesting); adaptation of language according to listener needs and expectations; and application of rules for conversation and the telling of stories. The sensorimotor area includes consideration of sensory processing, motor processing, and processing skills. Samples of these areas are presented in Table 7–20. The social/emotional/affective area has an initial emphasis on attachment, accompanied by the development of a sense of self and self-concept.

Mastery Motivation

The motivation that a young child exhibits as she plays directly influences her opportunities for development. For the child who lacks the motivation to engage in an activity, there will be few chances for her to gain new skills. Therefore, knowledge about a child's motivation to master tasks is a critical component of assessment for planning intervention. Motivation may be influenced by physical factors, such as motor impairments that increase the difficulty of even simple tasks, social factors, such as peer accomplishments, and emotional factors, including the interactive patterns of primary caregivers with the child. For example, evidence suggests that the free play of abused or neglected infants is less persistent and of a poorer quality than that of infants raised in nonabusive homes (Gaensbauer, Mrazek, & Harmon, 1981). Specifically, neglected children demonstrate disinterest in the toys, whereas abused infants explore the room and the toys in a disorganized and destructive manner.

Research involving the comparison of the mastery motivation of preschool children with physical disabilities (cerebral palsy and spina bifida) to that of children without physical disabilities incorporated structured tasks, free play, and mothers' perceptions (Jennings,

TABLE 7–19 Examples from Linder's TPBA Observation Guidelines

Developmental Area	Sample Observation Guidelines
Cognitive	IV. Symbolic and Representational Play
	A. Symbolic object use
	1. To what degree is the child capable of abstracting a concept—or using one object to represent another?
	a. Real objects needed for activity
	b. Realistic object may substitute for real object
	c. Unrealistic item may be substituted for real object
	d. Can pretend an object exists without a prop
	B. Symbolic play roles
	1. What roles is the child capable of assuming in representational play?
	2. Toward whom or what are the child's present actions directed?
	a. Self
	b. Object or toy
	c. Another adult
	3. How does the child demonstrate understanding behaviors important to specific roles that he or she assumes?
	4. To what degree can the child direct the play scenario without being a player or role taker?
	5. When the child is directing actors in scenarios, how does he or she indicate understanding of the behaviors of the actors?
	6. What level of role interaction is demonstrated in the child's play?
Social-emotional	VI. Humor and social conventions
	A. Does the child demonstrate a sense of humor with smiling or laughter directed at appropriate events in the environment?
	1. Physical events in the environment involving self and others
	2. Physical events in the environment involving objects
	3. Physical events in the environment involving others
	4. Verbal jokes from self, parent, adult, child
	a. Involving labeling ambiguities
	b. Involving conceptual ambiguities
	B. Does the child show awareness of socially acceptable behaviors in specific contexts?
	1. Greetings
	2. Sharing, helping, and so forth
	3. Behaviors around eating, toileting
	4. Respect for adult authority
	C. Does the child exhibit maladaptive or socially inappropriate behaviors?
	1. Self-stimulating or self-abusive behaviors
	2. Eccentric habits or rituals
	3. Unacceptable behaviors directed toward others

(continued)

TABLE 7–19 Examples from Linder's TPBA Observation Guidelines (Continued)

Developmental Area	Sample Observation Guidelines

Communication and language	I. Modalities of Communication
	  A. What is the primary method of communication used by the child?
	    1. Eye gaze
	    2. Gesture
	    3. Physical manipulation
	    4. Vocalization (nonspeech, e.g., grunts)
	    5. Sign language
	      a. Idiosyncratic
	      b. Formal
	    6. Verbalization
	    7. Augmentation (e.g., symbol board)
	  B. What supplemental forms are used in communication?
	  C. What is the frequency of communication acts?

Sensorimotor	IV. Stationary Positions Used for Play
	  A. Prone
	    1. Is the child able to raise the head in prone?
	    2. Can the child prop on the forearms?
	    3. Can the child bring the hands together and look at them while propped on the forearms?
	    4. Can the child reach for a toy and play with it while lying on the stomach?
	    5. Are the legs widely spread apart or close together?
	  B. Supine
	    1. Can the child maintain the head in midline and turn it to both sides?
	    2. Does the child bring the hands together on the chest?
	    3. Does the child reach above the chest for objects? (with one or both hands?)
	    4. Are the legs together or apart?
	    5. Can the child play with the feet (e.g., put the hands on the knees, play with the feet, bring the feet to the mouth?)
	  C. Sitting
	    1. Does the child need to be held in sitting?
	    2. How much support does the child need when held in sitting?
	    3. Is the child able to hold the head up?
	    4. Is the child able to freely turn the head? (to both sides, up and down?)
	    5. Is the back rounded or straight?
	    6. Is the child able to sit by propping on the arms?
	    7. Does the child sit independently without support?
	    8. Can the child bring the hands together in front of the body?
	    9. Can the child use the arms and hands to play with toys in sitting?

TABLE 7-19 (Continued)

Developmental Area	Sample Observation Guidelines
	10. Does the child turn the upper body to reach for or watch objects, keeping the lower body stationary?
	11. Is the child able to cross the center of the body with the arms when reaching for a toy?
	12. Does the child use the arms to catch him- or herself when falling (forward, sideways, backward)?
	13. Are the legs spread widely apart or maintained more closely together?
	14. How many different sitting positions are used?
	15. When sitting in a chair, does the child's body droop forward?
	16. Does the child's bottom slide forward in a chair?
	D. Hands and Knees
	1. Can the child hold the head up when playing on hands and knees?
	2. Can the child reach for a toy while on hands and knees?
	E. Standing
	1. Does the child need to be held to stand?
	2. How much support is needed when held in standing?
	3. Can the child hold the head up in standing?
	4. Does the child stand alone at a low table or support, steadying by leaning against the table?
	5. Can the child stand without support, and for how long?
	6. How far apart are the legs when standing?
	7. Are the arms in "high guard"?
	8. Do both sides of the body appear to function equally well?

Source: Adapted from Linder, T. W. (1993). *Transdisciplinary Play-Based Assessment: A Functional Approach to Working with Young Children*, (Revised Edition) (pp. 100, 148, 191, 248–249). Baltimore: Paul H. Brookes Publishing Co., adapted by permission.

TABLE 7–20 Samples of Sensorimotor Play-Based Assessment from Flagler

Area	Systems	Sample Tasks
Sensory Processing	Tactile	Find small object in "feely" box Identify where (s)he is touched on the body
	Proprioception	Assume and maintain postures against gravity "Wheelbarrow-walk" for 10 feet
	Vestibular	React to being tipped backward Climb on playground equipment with balance
	Sensory defensiveness	React to being hugged, touched, or washed React to temperature, pain, and environmental changes
Motor Processing	Gross motor	Does (s)he roll, crawl, and climb at age-appropriate levels? Can the child somersault?
	Fine motor	Prehension patterns of grasp and release (e.g., do all the fingers open and close when child is cutting with scissors) Eye-hand coordination (e.g., behavior at sand and water table, use of toy hammer) Bilateral skills (e.g., playing a musical instrument, building towers or block structures)
	Body scheme	Know body parts Move in space without awkwardness or clumsiness
Processing Skills	Visual perception	Describe object that is shown and removed Orient to specific toy (e.g., turn to the stuffed bear beside you)
	Visual motor integration	Bead stringing Use pencil (observe prehension grip, wrist stability, efficiency, and accuracy)
	Auditory perception	Localize to sounds in both ears Discriminate nonspeech and speech sounds

Source: Adapted from *Infant/Preschool Play Assessment Scale*, by S. L. Flagler, 1995, Lewisville, NC: Kaplan.

Connors, Stegman, Sankaranarayan, & Mendelsohn, 1985). Structured tasks were used to assess persistence at difficult tasks and curiosity. Free play was observed to assess attention span, complexity of play, degree of involvement, and level of social participation. Mothers' perceptions included measurement of (1) general mastery motivation; (2) preference for easy and familiar tasks; (3) need for adult help or approval; (4) need for adult structure; and (5) resistance to adult direction. The children with physical disabilities demonstrated less motivation, particularly in the free playtime, when the children were expected to structure their own activities. Even during the adult-structured activities, they showed less persistence on difficult tasks. Likewise, the mothers of the children with physical disabilities reported that their children were more dependent, frequently seeking adult help and approval. However, the presence of a disability did not alter curiosity. These findings are consistent with the theoretical assumption that children with orthopedic impairments have been faced with more failure in their attempts to perform tasks independently, and have to rely on adults to direct their play.

There is a body of literature on the techniques used in research on the assessment of children's mastery motivation. Although these techniques have been used predominately in clinical research studies, they can be used to provide important information about the nature of a child's play and the implications of that play for planning intervention strategies. Four forms of mastery motivation assessment (Brockman et al., 1988) are described in Table 7–21. The process

---

TABLE 7–21 Assessment Strategies for Mastery Motivation

Strategy	Description
Structured mastery-task situation	The objective is to create opportunities for the child to master challenging tasks and to observe the child's efforts toward the task. Task-directed behavior is behavior related to trying to complete part of the task with no assistance. Whether or not the task is completed successfully is not particularly relevant. An observer should look for two types of behavior: • mastery pleasure—related the amount of positive affect the child displays while engaged in task-directed behavior or upon completion of the task • persistence—indicator of the amount of time the child works toward task solution
Parental reports of observed mastery behavior	The Dimensions of Mastery Questionnaire (DMQ; Morgan, Maslin, Jennings, & Busch-Rossnagel, 1988) can be used to assess parents' perceptions of the mastery behaviors a child displays, including: • general persistence • mastery pleasure • independent mastery during challenging play • competence The DMQ also elicits ratings of a child's persistence at five specific types of play: • gross motor • combinatorial • means-end • symbolic • social
Global ratings of goal-directedness	Use of a rubric to summarize child's motivation and persistence
Free-play situation	Scoring systems that are used during nonstructured free-play times for research purposes (Glicken, Couchman, & Harmon, 1981; Harmon, Glicken, & Couchman, 1981) can be used by an interventionist attempting to design appropriately challenging activities for children, avoiding frustrating the child who shows little, if any, persistence with a challenging task

TABLE 7-22 Developmental Hierarchy of Mastery Motivation Tasks

Exploration and curiosity (5 months & older)	• Is the child motivated to explore all parts of the object and will he maintain interest until exploration is completed? • Measures of both the duration or persistence and the variety of behaviors should be recorded. • Object should be complex enough to promote sustained exploration.

Persistence tasks	• Practicing an emerging skill—9 months (3 overlapping categories)
	  • Effect Production Tasks (cause-effect toys—busy box)
	  • Combinatorial Tasks (putting pegs in holes)
	  • Means-ends Tasks (getting toy from behind barrier)
	• Completing multipart task—15 months (2 overlapping categories, 90 seconds)
	  • Combinatorial Tasks (shape sorter, formboard)
	  • Means-end Task (appropriate use of all parts of cash register)

Preference for challenging tasks (3 years)	• Child is presented with a choice of a relatively hard and an easy task (build 6-block tower or 2-block tower) and is asked which he wants to work on.

Source: Adapted from "Mastery Motivation and Developmental Delay," by L. M. Brockman, G. A. Morgan, and R. J. Harmon, in *Assessment of Young Developmentally Disabled Children,* by T. D. Wachs and R. Sheehan (Eds.), 1988, New York: Plenum Press.

involves the use of tasks to determine an individual child's desire to master a given task. A developmental hierarchy of the tasks used in the structured mastery task situation is presented in Table 7–22.

Closing Thoughts

Criterion-referenced and play-based assessments offer alternatives that are fair to the child and should lead us to getting to know the child in a way that can benefit the child. These techniques are based upon a solid foundation of child development and the developmental sequences that we can expect to see over time. Test scores are replaced with descriptive accounts of what the child is able to do across develop-mental domains. The snapshot view is replaced by a progressive understanding of the child, her interests, and her response to challenging tasks. The parents are not shunned from the examining room, but welcomed in to help the others in the room see how much their child has accomplished.

These approaches are not compatible with the increased emphasis on documentation of child outcomes through standardized test scores. It is likely that both approaches to assessment will continue to coexist, as one offers the greatest instructional value to the teacher and parents, and the other is mandated by funding sources.

For Your Consideration

1. What impact do your beliefs about intelligence have on the way you approach assessment of a young child's cognitive development?

2. What comparisons are being made when we use criterion-referenced testing?

3. What benefits are there to play-based assessment?

4. What is the relationship between a child's motivation to master new skills and developmental progress?

5. How can these approaches to assessment complement the current emphasis on documentation of child outcomes?

CYBERSOURCES

Check out the following Web sites for more information related to the ideas presented in this chapter.

VORT Corporation, HELP

http://www.vort.com/

National Center for Early Development & Learning

http://www.fpg.unc.edu/~ncedl/

Paul Brookes, Linder, Transdisciplinary Play-Based Intervention

http://www.pbrookes.com/store/books/linder-tpbai/tpbi.htm

For additional resources on assessment, visit us on-line at www.earlychilded.delmar.com

Assessing Individual Progress through Portfolio and Work Sampling Assessments, Goal Attainment Scaling, and General Outcome Measurement

Key Terms and Concepts

Portfolio
Work sampling
Goal attainment scaling
General outcome measurement (GOM)

■ Individual Growth and Development Indicator (IGDI)
■ Exploring Solutions Assessment (ESA)
Galileo

Chapter Objectives

After reading this chapter, you should be able to:

1. Identify the process, contents, and uses of portfolios.
2. Describe the Work Sampling System developed by Meisels and colleagues.
3. Develop goal attainment scales based on individual objectives.
4. Discuss the differences in skill-specific assessment and general outcomes measurement.
5. Identify options for computer-based management of assessment data.

Chapter Overview

When we are interested in a child's progress during intervention, portfolio and work sampling systems, goal attainment scaling, and general outcome measurement offer particularly useful approaches. Through portfolio and work sampling systems we create visual documentation of a child's skills and her development over time. Portfolio assessment can be used independently or in conjunction with a work sampling system. The ability of interventionists to plan and deliver richer models of education is the reward for their efforts to maintain these assessment systems. Child-centered learning becomes the foundation, rather than progression through a predefined curriculum.

Goal attainment scaling can help us monitor a child's achievement of particular objectives. These objectives can be completely personalized. For children who might not make sufficient progress to show any change on developmental checklists or standardized tests, goal attainment scaling can offer a quantitative means of documenting progress. Parents and professionals can use the scaling process as a means of understanding what both think the stated objectives mean and what their expectations are for the child over a defined time frame.

General outcome measurement (Deno, 1997) offers a means of monitoring a child's progress toward achieving general standards. It differs from assessment focused on mastery of specific developmental skills. The approach provides evidence of a child's progress toward universal goals, such as "all children will start school ready to learn" set forth by the National Education Goals Panel (1999).

The chapter includes specific information and resources for portfolio and work sampling, goal attainment scaling, and general outcome measurement. The chapter concludes with a discussion of the need for data management systems that are useful in program planning and documentation of child progress toward general outcomes as required for new accountability standards facing publicly funded early intervention, and early childhood education programs.

Portfolio and Work Sampling Systems

Portfolio and work sampling approaches to assessment erase the false dichotomy between assessment and intervention, drawing both into a fully integrated process. By their very nature, these authentic assessments occur over time, whereas traditional assessment methods are based upon the assumption that a child can be "assessed" in a few hours. When fully integrated into an intervention program, they guide teachers into providing a qualitatively richer educational experience for individual children. Portfolios alone, or combined with a work sampling system of assessment, give a teacher a means of focusing on the individual child, getting to know that child in ways that have no preset boundaries. Portfolios and work sampling systems can become a central reference point for parents, teachers, and children when they form the basis for program planning.

Portfolios

Portfolio assessment involves the systematic accumulation of a child's work combined with a structured system of maintaining written records of a child's performance over time. The collection of a child's works found in her portfolio represents the child's interests, attitudes, ranges of skills, and ongoing development (Gelfer & Perkins, 1996). In addition to documenting a child's progress through the selection of work samples, photographs, and videotapes, the teacher maintains records such as notes from interviews with the child, anecdotal notes, records of observations, and learning logs. The process of portfolio development enables teachers, parents, and children to reflect on progress as they continually set goals for the children (Shores & Grace, 1998). Parents become engaged in assessment through communication regarding their child's portfolio. Seven goals of portfolio assessment are identified in Figure 8–1.

FIGURE 8–1 Seven Goals of Portfolio Assessment

1. Portfolios help student examine growth and development over time.
2. Portfolios help student and teachers establish and set student goals.
3. Portfolios provide a process for self-evaluation.
4. Portfolios provide hands-on and concrete experiences.
5. Portfolios help evaluate and revise curriculum.
6. Portfolios help evaluate teaching and effectiveness.
7. Portfolios can motivate parents and school personnel to become involved in each child's evaluation plan.

Source: From "A Model for Portfolio Assessment in Early Childhood Education Programs," by J. I. Gelfer and P. G. Perkins, 1996, *Early Childhood Education Journal, 24,* p. 6.

Portfolio assessment offers a structure or system for a personal, one-on-one, child-centered orientation. Although some portfolio systems include standardizing the process and rubrics for scoring portfolios, portfolio assessment does not naturally produce measurable data. The process does not fulfill the same purposes as traditional forms of assessment, and, therefore, should remain free from the drawbacks and disadvantages those approaches to assessment carry. There are already ample methods of determining how one child compares to other children. There is nothing more telling than samples of a young child's work over the course of an entire year to document the progress that the child is making. The portfolio of a child who stacks up as having made the least amount of progress in a group of children may reveal that even he made meaningful gains over the course of a year's time in spite of lagging behind all the others.

Portfolio assessment offers an integrated look at the child. Although the portfolio can be organized to highlight or emphasize particular developmental areas, child work samples and photographs naturally reveal information across developmental areas. For example, written work depicts fine motor skills as well as cognitive processing and social understanding. The approach permits a wide array of abilities to be documented, such as multiple intelligences (Gardner, 1999). One child's portfolio might include pictures of a structure he built with the classroom blocks demonstrating his spatial and logical-mathematical skills, whereas another child's portfolio contains a drawing documenting the same area of development. Language samples recorded on tape during dramatic play might reveal a child's linguistic abilities as well as her interpersonal abilities to organize a small group, encourage participation from peers, and settle disputes between peers equitably.

Shores and Grace (1998) recommend maintaining three types of portfolios: the private portfolio, the learning portfolio, and the pass-along portfolio. Each has a distinct function while overlapping with the others in content. The use of all three types allows a teacher to maintain records that require confidentiality and sensitivity, give children constant access to their portfolios, and can protect critical work samples from being misplaced. A description of each type is presented in Table 8–1.

Contents of the Portfolio

Portfolios contain a variety of work samples, learning logs, photographs, written records, and audio and video recordings. Samples of work are the foundation of the portfolio system. They are primary sources of evidence of a child's abilities. For young children work samples include artwork, pieces of dictation, and writing samples. These samples should be accompanied by brief teacher comments that include the date, the child's name, and descriptive information such as "good example of Carol's artwork; she enjoys scribbling with markers." Children's dictation offers a fun way for children to explore and demonstrate their emerging skills in the use of language and the telling of stories. Dictations can be recorded on audio or videotape or written down by the teacher. Writing samples from preschool children can reveal their emerging fine motor skills and eye-hand coordination as they use crayons, markers, or pencils to "write" stories, copy things of interest to them, draft letters to friends and parents, or make a picture-diary about things on their minds.

TABLE 8–1 Types of Portfolios

Portfolio Type	Description
Private	Use to retain and organize anecdotal and observational records, notes from interviews with parents, and other similar materials that require confidentiality; a resource from which the teacher can draw information as she studies and reflects on the nature of a child's progress
Learning	Collection of the child's work, containing recent work samples, the child's learning log, notes, and ideas for projects and interests expressed by the child
Pass-along	Selected work samples that represent major advances or persistent problems that the child is experiencing; should include selections made by the child and parents as well as some identified by the teacher; selected photographs, recordings, and copies of some narrative reports should be added; portfolio is passed along to teachers and/or therapists who will be working with the child in the future

Source: Adapted from "The Portfolio Book: A Step-by-Step Guide for Teachers," by E.F. Shores and C. Grace, 1998. Beltsville, MD: Gryphon House.

Photographs can record the types of activities in which a child is engaging at school, in the home, or in the community. They can capture works in progress, candid classroom scenes that reveal the nature of social engagements between children within a group, and offer physical evidence of a child's growth over the year. Photographs can also provide evidence of skills such as walking up stairs, kicking a ball, stacking blocks, feeding oneself, or going down a slide independently.

A learning log provides a record for individual children of their experiences, people they meet, activities they participate in or observe, books they look at, stories they listen to, and anything else of significance to them. Logs can be drawn, written, or dictated. Written records should include anecdotal records, portfolio conference summaries, and narrative reports in addition to the written comments that accompany work samples and other entries.

Gelfer and Perkins (1998) suggest organizing portfolios into six sections with measures of (1) social-emotional growth; (2) academic and literacy growth; (3) cognitive strategies, self-regulation, and independence, including problem solving and decision making; (4) cultural and language factors; (5) motoric competence, including fine and gross motor skills; and (6) teacher and family communications.

Children should be able to participate in the development of the portfolio and item selection (Benson, 1995). The child's perspective toward his work might not always be the same as that of the teacher or parent.

He should get the opportunity to identify work samples of which he is particularly proud, plan the photographing of work that cannot be placed inside a box or folder (e.g., block construction, events taking place outside), or request the recording of him performing a skill (e.g., reading a book, counting, saying the alphabet).

Portfolios enable children and adults to recall the entire period that they cover. Children enjoy critiquing their own work as they compare early work to those representing their most recently acquired skills. It may be as simple as a child's efforts to write her own name that begin as a few stray marks, transformed into products that show the correct letters out of sequence, and finally the letters lined up in the correct order. Such a progression can be shown indirectly through student artwork and other papers upon which the child has attempted to identify ownership of the work. Portfolios can be a natural component of a larger, comprehensive work sampling system.

Work Sampling Systems

Assessments based on the actual performance of a child in a natural setting reduce the dichotomy between teaching and assessment that can exist in traditional assessment formats. Work sampling or performance-based assessment can actually extend the child's opportunities to engage in complex tasks. Figure 8–2 lists four features common to authentic performance-based assessments (Meisels, Liaw, Dorfman, & Nelson, 1995).

FIGURE 8–2 Features Common to Authentic Performance-Based Assessments

1. Draws on the child's continuous daily activities, not a restricted "snapshot" approach
2. Integrates a broad range of curricular areas and actually engages the child in the process of reviewing and evaluating his own work
3. Individualizes the assessment process to accommodate the needs of different classroom settings as well as individual children within a setting
4. Can be used to explore higher order thinking skills, such as analysis, synthesis, evaluation, and interpretation that are often absent from standardized tests

Source: Adapted from "The Work Sampling System: Reliability and Validity of a Performance Assessment for Young Children," by S. J. Meisels, F. Liaw, A. Dorfman, and R. F. Nelson, 1995. [*Early Childhood Research Quarterly, 10*], p. 277–296.

The Work Sampling System (Meisels, Jablon, Marsden, Dichtelmiller, & Dorfman, 1994) is a curriculum-embedded ongoing assessment system for use with three-year-olds through fifth grade. It consists of three components: (1) teacher observations with supporting developmental guidelines and checklists, (2) collections of work organized into portfolios, and (3) teacher summaries. The purpose is assessment and documentation of children's knowledge, skills, behavior, and accomplishments over numerous occasions across a variety of classroom settings. Teachers need to be constantly recording observations, collecting materials for portfolios, and maintaining personal notes. These data are then used to complete individual reports on each child three times per year—fall, winter, and spring. The system includes a series of developmental guidelines and checklists that teachers use to record their observations of child performance. The guidelines and checklists are based on various state and national standards, such as those offered by the National Council of Teachers of Mathematics and the Center for the Study of Reading.

Teachers using the Work Sampling System do not test children, but collect their notes and observations of a child to determine how well they are able to perform the tasks identified on the checklist. The system includes detailed descriptions and examples of each item to assist teachers as they assess a child's performance as "not yet," "in process," or "proficient." The developmental guidelines are organized into five areas listed in Figure 8–3.

The Work Sampling System portfolio guidelines call for the collection of two types of items: core items and individual items. The core items are standard pieces intended to demonstrate the child's growth over time, such as language samples from the begin-

FIGURE 8–3 Five Subscales of the Work Sampling System

1. Art and fine motor
2. Movement and gross motor
3. Concept and number
4. Language and literacy
5. Personal-social development

ning, middle, and end of the year. Core items are included in all children's portfolios. Individualized items represent the uniqueness of the child, incorporating products of activities that integrate multiple curricular domains. In the summary report, the teacher provides a brief summary of the child's performance in the classroom setting, including specific criteria for the evaluation of the child's progress.

Although the system is not intended to provide any quantitative analysis of child performance, Meisels and colleagues (1995) acknowledge the need to give the system credibility in correlation to established assessment methods. Therefore, they established a quantitative system of analysis to test the reliability and validity of the Work Sampling System and found that it is able to accurately predict performance on norm-referenced achievement tests. Results also indicate that the Work Sampling System is stable over time, and in some instances, was a better predictor of performance than an individual achievement test in the comparison of fall to spring assessment results.

Additionally, this performance-based system avoids the many drawbacks of both group and individually administered standardized tests. Traditional tests cannot be easily modified to adjust to differences in learning style, cultural heritage, or language that children display. Traditional tests do not have a means of encompassing and integrating all parts of the day and areas of the curriculum as is done in the Work Sampling System. Meisels et al. argue that by relying on high-stakes standardized group tests as the measure of our success, we set the stage for narrowing of the curriculum, focusing on priorities that lie outside of the classroom, and tolerating other abuses that accompany these tests.

Goal Attainment Scaling

The determination of a child's progress in his educational program can be directly linked to progress toward the achievement of specific goals and objectives defined on an IFSP or IEP. Goal attainment scaling (Kiresuk & Sherman, 1968; Kiresuk, Smith, & Cardillo, 1994) offers a strategy that can be used to put structure to assessment based on progress toward individual outcomes. This process is particularly useful for children with severe to profound disabilities who might not be able to achieve measurable progress on other scales. It offers utility, relevance, ease of communication with parents, and a well-defined focus for our intervention efforts.

Goal attainment scaling (GAS) begins with the identification of realistic measurable objectives and target completion dates. This process is built into special education services through the IFSP and IEP process. A goal attainment scale is then developed for each of the objectives. This is accomplished by specifying the expected level of outcome, the "somewhat more" and "somewhat less" than expected levels of outcome, and specifying "much more" and "much less" than expected levels of outcome. Each of these levels is valued on a scale from −2 to +2. Figure 8–4 provides an example of the scaling process with three outcome statements taken from the Head Start Child Outcomes Framework.

Several rules are necessary when developing the scales, or they will be impossible to score (Smith, 1994). First, completely fill out the scales. The omission of a description at any level for any objective immediately limits the usefulness of the scale. If a child's performance falls out of one of the completed cells, there is no way to assign a value to the child's progress.

Second, write precise descriptions. Vagueness in the outcome description will force the evaluator into a subjective decision. The descriptions should be comparable to well-written objectives that can easily be matched to a child's performance.

Third, avoid overlapping levels. If descriptions overlap, then it becomes unclear how to score the child's performance. For example, in Figure 8–4 if the expected level for the outcome "identifies at least 10 letters" was that the child could identify 8 to 12 letters, that level would overlap with both the level above and below. A child who could identify 9 letters could earn a −1 or a 0, whereas a child with 12 letters identified could receive a 0 or a +1.

Fourth, leave no gaps between levels. Again, using the example in Figure 8–4, notice that none of the levels for following instructions, length of spoken phrases, or letter recognition leave gaps. If there is a gap and a child performs at a level in the gap, there is no way to assign a value to her achievements.

Fifth, avoid two dimensions or variables being a part of the description. If the descriptions in the example about letter identification involved recognition and writing of the letters, it would be impossible to score a child who could recognize but not write the letters.

A limitation of the goal attainment scaling approach is the evaluation of the objectives themselves. Even if a child achieved 100 percent of the stated objectives on an IEP, he might have been capable of achieving far greater objectives. If the child failed to achieve any of his stated objectives, the problem might be inappropriate objectives, rather than poor instruction or inability of the child to master the task.

These limitations can be reduced through the ongoing use of a monitoring system (Shuster, Fitzgerald, Shelton, Barber, & Desch, 1984; Simeonsson, Huntington, & Short, 1982). Five objectives for a child are given values reflecting each one's relative importance. The most important objective is given a weight of five, and the lowest priority objective is given a weight of one. Goal attainment scales are then developed for each objective. The "much less than expected" scale should be the child's current functioning level (showing no gain made on the objective). Progress over the course of intervention can be plotted on a graph that depicts the level a child has achieved. Objectives that remain unachieved for an extended period and those that are achieved can easily be monitored. Programming adjustments could then be made accordingly. The numbers can be converted into T-scores, which would account for the weighted value of each objective.

FIGURE 8–4 Example of Goal Attainment Scaling

		Outcome Statements from Head Start Child Outcomes Framework		
	Understands an increasingly complex and varied vocabulary	**Uses an increasingly complex and varied spoken vocabulary**	**Recognizes a word as a unit of print**	**Identifies at least 10 letters of the alphabet, especially those in name**
−2 Significantly less than expected	Requires physical demonstration and modeling to follow routine 1-part instructions	Relies heavily on gestures and nonverbal expressions for communication, speaking in 1- to 2-word phrases	Recognizes familiar letter-based symbols in the community	Can identify 0–4 letters
−1 Somewhat less than expected	Needs visual cues to understand simple 1- or 2-part instructions	Speaks in 2- to 4-word phrases that are not complete sentences	Points to individual words in a book and asks, "What is this?"	Can identify 5–9 letters
0 Expected level	Listens to familiar tapes or stories and acts out instructions	Answers simple "wh" questions posed by familiar adult, using 3- to 5-word sentences	Points to words in a book with finger and "pretend" reads	Can identify 10 letters
+1 Somewhat more than expected	Listens to and follows instructions on unfamiliar tapes or stories	Speaks to adults and other children, using 5- to 7-word sentences, and turn taking in conversation	Recognizes own name and names of some classmates in print form	Can identify 11–15 letters
+2 Significantly more than expected	Completes multipart instructions that involve proper sequencing, use of specific materials, and new activities	Has conversation with unfamiliar adult in classroom setting, using 5- to 7-word sentences	Can recognize and read some words	Can identify 16 or more letters

General Outcome Measurement

The use of student outcomes has become a common practice in school from kindergarten through high school as the nation focuses attention on the impact publicly funded education is making on children's learning. This trend represents a shift away from an emphasis on the "inputs" or resources put into education, such as expenditures on instructional materials, teacher qualifications, access to technology in the classroom, and teacher-to-pupil ratios. Tools, such as Dynamic Indicators of Basic Early Literacy Skills (DIBELS; Kaminski & Good, 1998), designed to measure the early literacy skills of children in the primary grades, are appearing on the market to meet this demand. The downward extension of this emphasis on child outcomes is evident in early childhood education programs, such as Head Start's Child Outcomes Framework. This framework consists of 8 general domains, 27 domain elements, and 100 examples of specific indicators of children's skills, abilities, knowledge, and behaviors. Head Start programs are expected to document the progress of participating children toward these outcomes.

Researchers in the Early Childhood Research Institute on Measuring Growth and Development (ECRI-MGD; Priest et al., 2001) are developing a comprehensive set of Individual Growth and Development Indicators (IGDIs) and Exploring Solutions Assessments (ESAs; Greenwood, Luze, & Carta, 2002; Luze, Linebarger, Greenwood, Carta, Leitschuh, & Atwater, 2001; Walker, McConnell, Priest, Davis, & McEvoy, 2002; Priest et al., 2001). The IGDIs and ESAs are based upon general outcome measurement (GOM) principles for children from birth to age eight. The goal of these efforts is the creation of general growth charts across five developmental areas that would be comparable to height and weight growth charts used by pediatricians to monitor the physical growth of infants and young children. When height and weight readings fall outside predictable healthy patterns, a physician begins exploring the causes and possible treatments. Developmental growth charts would similarly serve as a warning system. Additionally, they could be used to determine the benefits of interventions through changing developmental trajectory. The advantages of using a GOM approach to assessment are listed in Figure 8–5. Priest et al. have developed 15 general growth

FIGURE 8–5 Advantages of General Outcome Measurement

- Can be repeated
- Occurs in a natural setting
- Provides graphical representations of the data that helps teams plan interventions
- Supports direct communication and understanding between parents and collaborating professionals
- Assesses immediate growth without detailed skill sequences

Finding A Better Way

A parent is worried about her eighteen-month-old's development. Perhaps the child is not yet walking, has unusual difficulties eating, is not using words, or seems unwilling to engage in social play. She fills out the developmental screenings each time she visits the pediatrician for a well-child checkup and talks with the doctor about her concerns, but he takes a "wait and see" attitude. No need to rush to conclusions—the child will likely grow out of these delays or troubling patterns. The child falls within expected readings for height and weight, and head circumference is normal as well. All other physical measures are normal.

It takes nearly a year to get the pediatrician to act on the parent's concerns. He finally suggests to the mother that she take her now 30-month-old in for developmental assessments and diagnostic testing. Perhaps the administration and charting of a few quick indicators of general growth in communication, adaptive behavior, motor movement, social interactions, and problem solving added to the height and weight checks at each well-child checkup would have prevented this all too familiar delay from occurring.

outcome statements organized around five broad outcome categories shown in Table 8–2.

One of the key principles in the development of these assessment materials is the identification of key skill elements that cut across the age span of birth to

TABLE 8–2 General Growth Outcomes for Children between Birth and Age Eight

Domain	Outcomes
The child uses languages to convey and comprehend communicative and social intent.	■ Uses gestures, sounds, words, or sentences (including sign language and augmentative and alternative communication) to convey wants and needs or to express meaning to others. ■ Responds to others' communication with appropriate gestures, sounds, words, or word combinations (including sign language and augmentative and alternative communication). ■ Uses gestures, sounds, words, or sentences (including sign language and augmentative and alternative communication) to initiate, respond to, or maintain reciprocal interactions with others.
The child takes responsibility for his/her behavior, health, and well-being, even in the face of challenge or adversity.	■ Engages in a range of basic self-help skills, including but not limited to skills in dressing, eating, toileting/hygiene, and safety/identification. ■ Meets behavioral expectations (such as following directions, rules, and routines) in home, school, and community settings. ■ Appropriately varies or continues behavior to achieve desired goals.
The child negotiates and manipulates the environment.	■ Moves in a fluent and coordinated manner to play and participate in home, school, and community settings. ■ Manipulates toys, materials, and objects in a fluent and coordinated manner to play and participate in home, school, and community settings.
The child initiates, responds to, and maintains positive social relationships.	■ Interacts with peers and adults, maintaining social interactions and participating socially in home, school, and community settings. ■ Appropriately solves problems in his/her interactions with others. ■ Shows effect appropriate to the social context.
The child uses cognitive skills to explore the environment, reason, and solve problems.	■ Demonstrates an understanding of age-appropriate information. ■ Demonstrates recall of verbal and nonverbal events. ■ Understands and uses concepts related to early literacy and math skills. ■ Solves problems that require reasoning about objects, concepts, situations, and people.

Source: Adapted from "General Growth Outcomes for Children between Birth and Age Eight: Where Do We Want Young Children to Go Today and Tomorrow?", by Priest et al. (2001), *Journal of Early Intervention 24,* 163–180.

eight years. Assessments based on this principle make it possible to measure a child's progress toward the same general outcome from infancy. For example, Luze et al. (2001) identified three key skill elements of communicative expression: gestures, vocalization, and single- and multiple-word utterances. These skill elements provide three single-point criteria to monitor a child's communicative expression from infancy through early childhood.

Indicators of growth and development for preschool children are intended to provide (1) comparative data about the child's current performance level; (2) projected rates of growth and development and the likelihood that a general outcome will be achieved by a target age; and (3) effects of intervention on the child's growth and development and likelihood the outcome will be reached as a result of intervention. McConnell and colleagues (2002) have developed a series of such IGDIs organized around developmental and educational outcomes in expressive language, early literacy, and social interaction as shown in Table 8–3. Additional work is under way for IGDIs in motor and adaptive behavior domains.

Assessments that indicate a child is not progressing toward the general outcome at an acceptable rate should be followed up with Exploring Solutions

TABLE 8–3 Individual Growth and Development Indicators for Preschool Children

Outcome	Indicator	Description
Expressive language Child uses gestures, sounds, words, or sentences (including sign language and augmentative or alternative communication) to convey wants and needs or to express meaning to others.	Picture naming	Child names as many photos and color line drawings of common objects as possible in 1 minute
	Semistructured play	Play between 2 peers for 10 minutes with preselected materials; children asked to work together to make something; examiner records in 10-second intervals the number of 3 or fewer and 4 or more utterances
Early literacy Initial efforts to tap early literacy are related to a child's phonemic awareness and analysis, measured by alliteration, rhyming, and phoneme blending tasks.	Alliteration	Child looks at pictures and finds ones that start with the same sound for a period of 2 minutes
	Rhyming	Examiner presents cards with drawings and child matches rhyming pictures for a period of 2 minutes
	Phoneme blending	Examiner gives oral presentation of stimulus words with .5-second pause between phonemes. After demonstration and training items, child is asked to say words correctly
Social interaction Child interacts with peers and adults, maintaining social interactions and participating socially in home, school, and community settings.	Play ideas	Examiner presents picture and verbal prompts and asks child to think of all the things she could do in the setting with a friend for 3 minutes in each format (visual and verbal)
	Joint play	Semistructured 5 minutes of play activity between peers with examiner recording duration of play

Source: Adapted from "Best Practices in Measuring Growth and Development for Preschool Children," by McConnell et al., in *Best Practices in School Psychology* (4th ed.), by A. Thomas and J. Grimes (Eds.; 2002), Washington, DC: National Association of School Psychologists, pp. 1231–1246.

Assessments (ESAs). These assessments involve exploration of three components: (1) setting features, (2) skills/competencies, and (3) problem behaviors and engagement (Greenwood et al., 2002). Assessment of setting features includes specific elements within the environment related to the outcome, such as adult responses to child verbalizations for communicative expressions. For example, if it is discovered that adults around the child are missing opportunities to respond to the child when he makes efforts to communicate through gestures or eye gaze, the adults can be made aware of these missed opportunities and trained to respond differently to the child. The result of such a change in the adult behavior can be seen by a repetition of the original IGDI assessment.

Assessment of skills/competencies involves the use of activity-based assessment of the child. Problem behaviors and engagement are assessed through

Know The Facts

The measurement of a child's growth and development of expressive language skills can be monitored with a procedure as simple as counting the total number of pictures named correctly in one minute with technical soundness. McConnell et al. (2002) report strong concurrent relationships between it and norm-referenced tests, including the Peabody Picture Vocabulary Test (3rd ed.; Dunn & Dunn, 1997), and the Preschool Language Scale-3 (Zimmerman, Steiner, & Pond, 1992). There is also evidence that the measure is sensitive to a child's growth over time, yields expressive language from young children without difficulty, is easy for examiners to administer, and can be repeated as often as desired.

observations. ESAs are conducted in a cyclical fashion to develop, implement, and assess solutions. Repetition of assessment using the indicators allows teachers, parents, and others to determine whether to continue current interventions or seek additional solutions.

Computer-Based Data Management Systems

Management of assessment data for an individual child can be challenging. When the task is increased to an entire class the challenge intensifies. However, when the task expands to all preschool special education children in an entire school system, all children served through Title One preschools, or all Head Start children in a multicounty cooperative, a state, a region, or the country, the task becomes overwhelming. Nevertheless, data about progress toward outcomes for individuals and aggregate groups are essential for programs to meet the needs of their children and to monitor effectiveness. A number of assessment instruments now come with comprehensive data management systems. The Learning Accomplishment Profile-Diagnostic (LAP-D; Nehring et al., 1992) is a good example. The computer resources available include individual and group reports, projected next skills, and IEP objectives.

However, the use of a data management system tied to a single instrument is obviously limited to that particular instrument. The content of instruments such as the LAP-D and the HELP, which also offers computer-based scoring and data management, do not offer any means to document child progress toward general developmental and educational outcomes. Rather, they remain directed toward skill-specific developmental sequences, do not use single-skill criteria across age ranges, and offer no means of recording data from other sources. A program that uses transdisciplinary play-based assessment, goal attainment scales, or work sampling systems for child assessment needs a data management system just as much as those that rely on a comprehensive developmental assessment tool.

Galileo is a computer-based data management system that is on the market to address this need. Offered by Assessment Technology, Inc., Galileo is a Web-based suite of tools that allows on-line collection and aggregation of child outcome data and report production. The software can be customized around any assessment system or list of outcomes. It provides dynamic links between assessment, lesson planning, activity planning, individualization, and parent communication. Current clients include some Head Start programs, public schools, researchers, proprietary child care centers, and national preschool companies.

This resource does not come cheaply, in terms of money and effort. Software can only manage data that have been entered into a computer. The only way to keep the system current and useful is for that data to be entered frequently, most likely at the classroom level. Teachers will need to understand how they and their children can directly benefit from the available generation of reports before they will learn how to enter the data, much less take the time to record it. Administrators will have to weigh the merits of the system with the high financial costs attached.

Closing Thoughts

Each of the assessment methods described in this chapter focuses on the documentation of progress toward child outcomes. Individualized portfolio and work sampling systems involve the gathering of actual work samples and other evidence of child performance. These approaches can be time consuming for the teacher, particularly in their initial development.

However, we must remember that there is little point in doing assessment in a way that proves to be of little value or even harmful to the child. These methods should produce payoffs to the classroom teacher, parents, and program administrators that make the efforts worthwhile.

Goal attainment scaling offers a means of quantifying the progress an individual is making toward outcomes. Scales can be custom developed for individual children based on their individual objectives and expected rate of development. The creation of goal attainment scales must follow guidelines. The development of goal attainment scales also takes some time and effort, but offers a reasonable means of monitoring the effectiveness of an intervention, particularly for children with severe and profound disabilities.

General outcome measurement is compatible with the national emphasis on documentation of child outcomes. The work of the ECRI-MGD is far from complete, but does offer an interesting new approach to monitoring child development. As more details about the IGDI and ESA approach and access to the actual indicators and scoring systems become available, their usefulness to the field will be determined.

The reality of a need for a computer-based data management system must not come at the cost of establishing good assessment policies. Documentation and accountability decisions must follow policy decisions that are based on best practices and sensitivity to parental concerns. Although necessary to run a quality program, the generation of reports is not sufficient to have a quality program.

▪ For Your Consideration

1. When does portfolio assessment occur and how does this differ from other approaches to assessment?

2. How would you organize a portfolio for a preschool child with developmental delays?

3. In what situations might goal attainment scaling be particularly helpful in monitoring the progress of an individual child toward a specific IEP objective?

4. What happens if there are gaps or overlapping descriptions in goal attainment scaling?

5. If you had 14 children and were responsible for collecting data on their progress for 15 outcomes, how would you manage your assessment data?

CYBERSOURCES

Check out the following Web sites for more information related to the ideas presented in this chapter.

National Center on Educational Outcomes

http://www.coled.umn.edu/nceo/

Early Childhood Research Institute on Measuring Growth and Development

http://ici2.umn.edu/ecri/

Dynamic Indicators of Basic Early Literacy Skills

http://dibels.uoregon.edu/

Galileo Assessment Tracking System

http://www.ati-online.com

For additional resources on assessment, visit us on-line at www.earlychilded.delmar.com

Functional Behavioral Assessment

Chapter Objectives

After reading this chapter, you should be able to:

1. Identify several different types of functional assessment.
2. Describe situations in which a functional behavioral assessment is needed.
3. Plan and implement a functional behavioral assessment.
4. Conduct a functional analysis.
5. Make specific recommendations about how to respond to problem behaviors based upon an individual child's motives.

Chapter Overview

Functional assessment has several different meanings involving young children with special needs. The term is used by speech and language therapists, occupational therapists, physical therapists, and special educators in reference to the identification of alternatives to enable children to accomplish physical tasks, activities of daily living, communication, and interactive manipulation of toys and equipment when they are unable to complete these tasks in traditional ways.

Assessment of a child's ability to benefit from assistive technology also falls in the arena of functional assessment. The functions a child needs to accomplish lead the structure of an assistive technology assessment. Does the child need a means of communication? Is the child able to read independently? Can the child play, using physical skills to manipulate toys, turn knobs, push buttons, open boxes, and explore? Assistive technology becomes a vehicle through which such functioning can be achieved. Experts determine what motor control the child does have, her cognitive abilities, motivations, developmental levels, and needs within her environment. From these investigations come recommendations for specific hardware, software, and adaptive devices to achieve the desired functions. In-depth information about conducting team-based assistive technology assessments is available from Hutinger, Johanson, Robinson, and Schneider (1995). Matching infants and young children is the focus of work by Scherer (1997).

Functional assessment also refers to evaluations of children with cognitive impairments to determine what functional skills they possess. Such assessments place the emphasis on the ability of a child to demonstrate competency in functional tasks rather than what scores are earned on an intelligence test. These assessments are typically done with students much older than those targeted in this text (e.g., ability to use public transportation to travel to work, following the steps needed to sign in on the computer at work). For young children, such assessment might include their ability to play independently, prepare for and clean up from snacks and meals, to manage personal possessions, or enter and exit groups of peers playing without adult assistance.

The focus of this chapter is on one specialized type of functional assessment that is useful when a child is exhibiting particularly persistent behavioral difficulties known as **functional behavioral assessment.** Through functional behavioral assessment, we explore the motives behind children's behavior and what benefits they derive from that behavior. Through the process, we observe and analyze problem behaviors to identify what purpose those behaviors achieve for the child and how to best intervene to reduce or eliminate undesirable behaviors. Functional behavioral assessments are now mandatory for children with disabilities who are experiencing serious problem behaviors in educational settings.

Rationale for Functional Behavioral Assessment

Problem behaviors are traditionally viewed as maladaptive. An alternative view is that they serve a function for the child who is engaging in the behavior, and are actually adaptive from that child's perspective. Maladaptive behavior "fails to provide the individual displaying any advantages" (Carr, Langdon, & Yarabrough, 1999, p. 10). Problem behavior can lead to a variety of benefits—including attention and comfort from others, escape from undesirable tasks, ac-

cess to desired objects or activities—or provide sensory reinforcement. These functions account for most problem behaviors associated with aggression and self-injury (Carr, et al., 1999).

Interventions for problem behaviors that are not based on an understanding of why the child is engaging in the behavior can actually increase the incidence of the behavior. For example, if a child's motive is to escape an undesired activity, removal from the activity upon the child's misbehavior will do nothing to reduce the frequency of the problem behavior. It will more likely cause the behavior to increase. A

FIGURE 9–1 Primary Outcomes of Functional Behavioral Assessment

1. A clear *description of the problem behaviors,* including classes or sequences of behaviors that frequently occur together
2. Identification of the events, times, and situations that *predict* when the problem behaviors *will* and *will not* occur across the full range of typical daily routines
3. Identification of the *consequences that maintain the problem behaviors* (that is, what functions of the behaviors appear to serve for the person)
4. Development of one or *more summary statements* or hypotheses that describe specific behaviors, a specific type of situation in which they occur, and the outcomes or reinforcers maintaining them in that situation
5. Collection of *direct observation data* that support the summary statements that have been developed

Source: From *Functional Assessment and Program Development for Problem Behavior: A Practical Handbook* (p. 3), by R. E. O'Neill et al., 1997, Pacific Grove, CA: Brooks/Cole.

teacher or parent may feel that the child should not be allowed to remain in an activity when the problem behavior is occurring. There seems to be no solution to the problem.

A functional assessment can identify what purposes the child is achieving through her behavior so a suitable intervention can be planned. The primary advantages of functional assessment are that it (1) enables teachers to use hypothesis-driven treatment, (2) diminishes the emphasis on punishment and emphasizes skill building, (3) increases the likelihood of a positive outcome, (4) increases the chances of having sustained treatment benefits, and (5) adds to the overall knowledge and understanding of treatment effects (Blakeslee, Sugai, & Gruba, 1994). The outcomes we can achieve are summarized in Figure 9–1.

Behavior and Communication

Behavior and communication are interwoven in multiple ways. A child who experiences frustration in her attempts to communicate may begin to express that frustration through misbehavior. A child who misbehaves frequently and consistently may very well be attempting to communicate something to those around him. Stevenson and Richman (1978) found a marked association between the problem behavior of three-year-old children and expressive language delays. Carr et al. (1994) summarize this and related research, noting that children who are experiencing impairments in communicative development are more likely to be considered aggressive, noncompliant, or hostile.

We can use functional assessments to explore both sides of this puzzle. We can carefully analyze the achieved outcomes of problem behaviors, efforts and patterns of communication, and the communicative intentions of behavior. We can explore both physiological and environmental factors that contribute to a child's behavior (O'Neill et al., 1997). Additionally, the process gives us the opportunity to explore if existing consequences or factors in the environment might be helping to maintain problem behaviors.

Data Gathering Techniques

The three approaches used to conduct a functional assessment are informant methods, direct observations of the child in natural settings for extended periods, and functional analysis, involving systematic manipulations of variables and observation of their effects on the problem behavior. The primary means of data gathering from informants involves the use of interviews of parents, teachers, therapists, and possibly the child. Rating forms, questionnaires, and other reports can also be used to gather information.

Observations involve watching the child in settings in which the problem behavior has been occurring. The job of the observer is to identify factors within the environment that might be indirectly contributing to the problem behavior, as well as to identify the events that immediately precede and follow the behavior. After multiple observations over extended periods, patterns of behavior become apparent and can be used to hypothesize why a child is engaging in particular problem behaviors. If data from the interviews and/or observations remain unclear, functional analysis provides an opportunity to test differing hypotheses. The variables that seem to trigger the problem behavior and the possible purposes the child has for engaging in the problem behavior can be explored through a format similar to single-subject research design.

Informant Methods

People who know the child can provide information that helps us understand the benefits a child may gain from engaging in particular behaviors. The people who have frequent direct contact with the child can describe the nature of the child's behavior, how they react to the troubling behaviors, and how the child responds to their reactions. They can help identify possible triggers for the problem behavior, when and where the behaviors occur, how long problem behaviors are maintained by the child, and what, if any, techniques can redirect the child into appropriate behavior.

Interviews can provide a key to identifying the particular factors in a child's environment that seem to be associated with the problem behaviors. Interviews should cover a description of the behavior, the apparent triggers for the behavior, and the responses to or outcomes of the behavior. Descriptions of daily routines can serve as a good beginning point for the interview. For parents, routines at home include meals, baths, bedtime, transitions, cleaning up toys,

and so forth. They might equally be interested in describing routines in the community such as grocery shopping, visits to fast-food restaurants, or trips to the neighborhood park as they involve preparing for the outing, riding in a car or catching a bus, departing from the activity, and returning home. In a preschool setting routines include arrivals and departures, meals and snacks, transitions between activities, cleanup, bathroom breaks, preparation for outdoor play, and so forth. The interview can be used to identify when the problem behaviors occur and what particular aspects of a routine seem to make the behaviors worse, such as proximity to another child, the choice of food for snack, or loud noises in the environment.

We can use the interview opportunity to gather as much context-based information as possible. Through informant sources we gather answers to the questions presented in Figure 9–2.

An example of a rating scale that relies on informants as the source of information is the Motivation Assessment Scale (MAS; Durand & Crimmins, 1992). This questionnaire is based on a child's specific behavior, such as "bites other children." It uses a rating scale from 0 (never) to 6 (always) with 16 questions, such as "Does the behavior occur after you ask the child to do something difficult," "Does this child seem to do the behavior to upset or annoy you when you are not paying attention to him or her." Each of the items represents one of four categories: sensory, escape, attention, and tangible. The scale produces a score for each of these categories.

FIGURE 9–2 Functional Behavioral Assessment Interview Questions

1. In what ways does the child communicate his basic wants and needs?
2. What does the child seem to like and not like (including, toys, activities, food, playmates, settings)?
3. Are there factors external to the setting that might be associated with the behavior (such as sleep patterns, medicines, diet)?
4. What do the problem behaviors look like?
5. What events are likely to make the behavior occur?
6. Are there events or conditions within the setting that seem to be associated with the problem behavior even though they may not immediately precede its occurrence?
7. Are there any events and situations that happen just before the problem behaviors that consistently predict that the problem behaviors will *not* occur?
8. What consequences appear to maintain the problem behavior?
9. Does the child exhibit any appropriate behaviors that would produce the same consequences that appear to be maintaining the problem behavior?
10. What have been the outcomes of previous interventions?

Functional Assessment Interview Form

The Functional Assessment Interview Form (O'Neill et al., 1997) contains 11 sections that direct the interviewer as she seeks to gather information about the child's problem behavior. It begins with an opportunity for the person being interviewed to describe the behavior(s) of concern, including the frequency, duration, and intensity of each problem behavior. For example, for a particular two-year-old child the behavior of tantruming might be described as screaming, banging her arms and hands, and shaking her head back and forth rapidly. The frequency is approximately six times per three-hour preschool session. The duration is about five minutes per tantrum, and the intensity could be described as loud and hard.

Following this descriptive information about the problem behaviors, the interviewee is asked to identify any possible connections between the listed behaviors, and if they occur simultaneously, in a predictable sequence, or in response to similar conditions. If our tantruming two-year-old also bites other children, we would explore the connection, if any, between the tantrums and biting.

The second section focuses on setting events that seem to predict or trigger the problem behaviors. Questions addressing medications, medical or physical conditions, sleep patterns, eating routines and diets, daily schedules, opportunities for choices, and the presence of others in the setting and their roles are included in this section.

The third section of the interview form moves into the identification of immediate antecedent events that are likely to trigger the occurrence of the problem behavior(s). Factors that are probed include time of day, settings, people, and activities. A portion of the questions involve asking the interviewee to predict how the child would perform under conditions such as an unexpected change in his routine, the interruption of a desired activity, when confronted with a difficult task, when desired items are unobtainable, or if the child is left alone.

Following this section, the interview moves to the identification of consequences of the problem behaviors, particularly focusing on how those consequences might be maintaining the problem behavior. The behavior and particular situations in which the behavior occurred are noted along with descriptions of exactly what the child gained, and exactly what the child avoided as a result of the behavior.

The array of consequences starts with two types of options: obtaining desired events or escaping/avoiding undesirable events. Examples of disruptive behavior a child seeking to obtain a desired event might exhibit include throwing sand in another child's face to get the toy she had, pushing another child to make room at the top of a slide, and grabbing materials from a teacher to be first to do an activity. Examples of behavior associated with avoidance of undesirable events include shoving materials off a table, and refusing to move to a designated area. Table 9–1 presents a chart adapted from O'Neill and colleagues depicting these common outcomes of problem behavior that can motivate a child to continue engaging in problem behavior.

The next section has the interviewee consider how efficient this problem behavior is for the child, considering the physical effort of the behavior, how often it must be performed before the desired consequence occurs, and how long that consequence is in coming. The interviewee then identifies what, if any, appropriate behaviors the child already has that can achieve this same outcome.

Communication skills and patterns of the child are addressed in the next portion of the interview. The form includes a chart that lists basic communicative functions and how the child achieves them. The functions include: request attention, request help, request preferred food/objects/activities, request break, show you something or some place, indicate physical pain, indicate confusion or unhappiness, and protest or reject a situation or activity. The interviewee describes what communicative efforts are associated with each of these functions, such as the child requests help through gestures, physical tugging, and sounds. The next three sections cover general descriptions of things to do and things to avoid while working with this child and a review of the history of the problem behavior(s) and what effects previous interventions have had. The final section is a summary of the patterns of behavior that the interviewee considers descriptive for the child. The summary includes distant setting events, immediate antecedents, the problem behavior, the maintaining consequence for each major predictor, and the consequence for the target behavior.

Direct Observations

Systematic observation of a child during typical daily activities and routines is the second component of functional assessment. Even when it seems that a reasonable hypothesis regarding a child's behavior

TABLE 9–1 Consequences That Maintain Problem Behaviors

Problem Behavior(s)

	Obtain Desired Events			Escape/Avoid Undesirable Events		
	Socially Mediated Events				**Socially Mediated Events**	
Label	Positive automatic reinforcement	Positive reinforcement: social	Positive reinforcement: tangible/activity	Negative automatic reinforcement	Negative reinforcement: escape motivated social	Negative reinforcement: escape motivated task
Consequence	Internal stimulation	Attention	Activities or objects	Internal stimulation	Attention	Tasks/Activities
Examples	Visual stimulation	Smiles and hugs	Food Toys	Itching Hunger	Corrections	Changes in routine Undesired activities

Source: Adapted from *Functional Assessment and Program Development for Problem Behavior: A Practical Handbook*, by R. E. O'Neill et al., 1997, Pacific Grove, CA: Brooks/Cole.

can be reached through informants, we must take the time to conduct in-depth observations. Information derived indirectly from informant sources can be limited in perspective, inaccurate, or incomplete. Parents or teachers may prefer to avoid admitting that their own reactions to a child's problem behavior constitute giving in to the child. In other instances they might not realize that their behaviors are different from what they believe them to be. For example, if a teacher announces that she will not speak to any child who does not behave properly, but proceeds to fuss at a misbehaving child for five minutes, she may give inaccurate information regarding the consequences of misbehavior during an interview.

The observer is focused particularly on what conditions or events occur just before and immediately after problem behaviors. However, the traditional behavioral analysis model of observation focused on antecedents, behaviors, and consequences is expanded to incorporate setting events and the momentary effects of setting events on the value of consequences along with antecedents, behaviors, and consequences (Sprague & Horner, 1999). The function, or benefit, a child gets from his behavior is far more complex than it appears on the surface. A child misbehaves and is removed from the group. Does that consequence represent a negative or a positive outcome for the child? Even if the activity seems to be one preferred and enjoyed by the child, the need for separation from others, attention from a teacher, or a host of other benefits could be a stronger motivation to the child than is the activity.

Setting events are variables that can alter the nature of events that trigger problem behavior, including physical, biological, and social elements. Physical elements include things such as temperature, noise levels, and comfort of seating or lighting. Biological includes elements such as illness, height and weight of children, and any limitations due to disabilities. Social elements include friendships between children, preferred adults, and aggressiveness of other children in the group.

Setting events can include elements within the immediate environment as well as ones associated with other environments. For example, the biological setting event of hunger caused by a child's failure to eat breakfast before he left for school will likely influence his behaviors prior to and during snack time. A teacher trying to use snack time as an opportunity to build language or social skills may find this hungry child less tolerant of delays in receiving food than she expected or she might be more motivated than ever. The incorporation of such distant setting events into a functional assessment is consistent with a systems approach to understanding children and their families as discussed in chapter 1.

The observer should also consider what function behavior appears to accomplish for the child in each instance of problem behavior. Repetitive patterns over multiple observations will likely begin to be apparent. The answers to three questions presented in Figure 9–3 can then be given consideration.

Direct observations can be recorded through narrative techniques or descriptive analysis, using frequency counts, time sampling, and rates of behavior. The Functional Assessment Observation Form (O'Neill et al., 1997) has the observer target specific behaviors. When these behaviors occur, the observer records the time and frequency of the behavior as well as the predictors, perceived functions of those behaviors, actual consequences, and comments. The form includes five common predictors as well as space for additional ones. Those on the form are: demand/request, difficult task, transitions, interruption, and alone (no attention). Other predictors might include the presence of a particular person, specific activities, noise levels, specific classmates, or unexpected changes.

The perceived functions include the same categories as those listed in Table 9–1. Others can be added as needed for specific children. The identification of functions for problem behaviors represents a significant departure from the simplified and useless explanations of children's behavior based on diagnoses or personality traits, such as "she behaves that way because she has autism" or "he always hits Jason because he is a mean child."

FIGURE 9–3 Analysis of Functional Behavioral Assessment Observations

1. What problem behaviors happen together?
2. When, where, and with whom are problem behaviors most likely?
3. What consequences appear to maintain occurrence of the problem behavior?

Source: From *Functional Assessment and Program Development for Problem Behavior: A Practical Handbook* (p. 6), by R. E. O'Neill et al., 1997, Pacific Grove, CA: Brooks/Cole.

Actual consequences are listed on an individual basis according to information provided from informants. In the process of recording information, the recorder assigns an incident a number and puts that number in the corresponding column for each of the sections on the form—behaviors, predictors, perceived functions, and actual consequences. Patterns of common predictors and functions can be identified by the columns that have the greatest number of entries. Other patterns associated with the time of day or specific predictors, such as the presence of a particular individual, can also be noted. An observation period of two to five days or a minimum of 15–20 occurrences of behaviors is necessary for meaningful interpretation of observational data. If patterns are still not clear, additional data gathering for another two to five days should occur. The results of the observation can be compared to the information obtained through informants for similarities and inconsistencies. When the informant methods and lengthy observations fail to produce consistent patterns that lead to reasonable conclusions regarding the functions of problem behaviors, functional analysis is necessary.

Functional Analysis

Functional analysis involves the manipulation of variables as in an experiment. It requires systematic control of conditions, and necessarily involves manipulating conditions to cause the problem behavior to occur. Information derived from informants and observations provide guidance in determining which variables to manipulate. We begin by formulating several hypotheses—what are some plausible functions that could be motivating this child to behave this way? We then experiment to determine which one seems to be correct. Finally, we confirm which hypothesis is most consistent with the child's behavior during experimental conditions. Was the child motivated because he wished to escape a particular situation or task, draw attention to himself, or communicate a basic need?

We test the hypotheses by comparing a child's level of problem behavior under controlled conditions, manipulating structural aspects of the activity in which the child is engaged and consequences of the problem behavior. Structural aspects that can be manipulated include difficulty of activity, length of activity, adult attention during activity, number of peers participating in the activity, and opportunities for the

---

Finding A Better Way

You have a class with 12 three- and four-year-old children. Four of them, including Terrance, have developmental disabilities. Terrance, who is four years old, has a habit of shoving the other children in the room. This shoving exceeds the usual level of physical play of preschool children, and often results in the other child being pushed to the floor. The shoving has been a problem during group times, transitions, and particularly when the class is lining up to change locations. Terrance is bigger than most of the others in the room, so they do not retaliate physically but complain to the teacher or teaching assistant or cry. Interventions have varied based on when the shoving occurred. If it occurred in the classroom during group times or transitions, Terrance has been placed in "sit and watch." If the shoving occurred when the class was lining up, interventions have included having to walk holding the teaching assistant's hand, and a consequence at the destination (e.g., recess—loss of playing time; lunch—eating in isolation; bus—last one to get on). The teacher has been collecting data on the frequency of Terrance's shoving and has not seen any improvement. In fact, there has actually been an increase over the past month. Terrance's language development is delayed, and his speech is somewhat difficult to understand due to articulation errors.

Functional behavioral assessment gives us an alternative way to approach planning an intervention. What is the target negative behavior? What conditions appear to predict the occurrence of Terrance's behavior? What possible functions does Terrance's behavior appear to serve? What recommendations do we have for the teacher?

---

child to make choices. Consequences to be manipulated are defined by our hypotheses. We might hypothesize that a child is motivated to disrupt circle time because she (1) hopes to avoid group activities, (2) seeks the attention or one adult in the room, or (3) finds the reactions of her peers stimulating. We experiment with a consequence that represents each hypothesis. Accordingly, we implement a solitary time-out consequence, removal from circle to work with the target adult, and retention of the child within the group setting. Our experiment can reveal the motives if we see increases in the behavior under one condition and decreases under the others.

We might hypothesize that a child flaps his finger against the end of his nose for visual and tactile stimulation whenever there is a reduction in stimulation for him in the room. To test this hypothesis we need to arrange conditions that we believe cause the behavior to occur and arrange conditions that we believe cause it to diminish or disappear. In this case, we have to leave the child unoccupied and monitor the frequency and duration of flapping his finger against the end of his nose. We also introduce conditions in which the child is appropriately stimulated through positive attention, fun activities, food or other positive events to monitor if the flapping does not occur or occurs at a reduced rate. If the finger flapping is reduced, experimental design would dictate that we then return to the unoccupied condition to see if the child returns to the behavior pattern recorded previously under that condition. If so, the hypothesis is confirmed and can be the foundation for planning an effective intervention.

Functional analysis can also be set up to include multielements, using an alternating treatment design to explore the relation of problem behavior to numerous conditions. For example, activity periods with undesired activities in which escape, social attention, or receipt of tangible rewards is the outcome of problem behavior would be interspersed with a control condition that is unlikely to trigger problem behavior. Each condition would need to be repeated several times to allow patterns of behavior to emerge to determine which outcome caused the greatest amount of problem behavior.

Another example illustrates how functional analysis can be conducted in natural settings by classroom teachers (Arndorfer & Miltenberger, 1993). The setting is a preschool class in which a three-year-old is exhibiting self-injurious behavior. Based on data from an interview with the teacher, it is known that demands trigger this behavior. When the child engages in the self-injurious behavior, the teacher intervenes by holding her on her lap for a few minutes, trying to calm her down. The problem behavior could be motivated by either positive reinforcement through attention and physical contact or negative reinforcement through escape from the undesirable activity.

During the functional analysis the consequences are controlled to identify which one seems to be the purpose for the child's behavior. In the first condi-

tion, when the child begins self-injurious behavior she is allowed to leave the activity and sit by herself to calm down for a few minutes. No attention from adults or peers should be given. In the second condition, the teacher joins the child in the activity, assisting the child and providing attention and physical contact, but not allowing the child to escape the task. The child's reactions to each of these conditions lead us to the proper intervention.

It is parents and teachers who must implement the results of any functional analysis, so it makes sense to include them in the assessment process. They might realize that our consequences that are intended to reduce a behavior might actually be what is causing the behavior to continue or even increase. Once the principles of the process are understood and hypotheses formed, implementation of functional analysis need not be complicated. It has been shown that parents can effectively apply functional analysis over brief intervals of time in home settings (Arndorfer, Miltenberger, Woster, Rortvedt, & Gaffaney, 1994).

Functional treatments can address problem behaviors in at least three ways: (1) elimination of the identified reinforcer, (2) encouragement of appropriate alternative behavior that achieves the same function, and (3) change of setting variables that are contributing to the challenging behavior (Arndorfer & Miltenberger, 1993). When adults understand the motivation behind disruptive behavior, they can control consequences, avoiding the child's intended outcome. They can direct the child to alternative means of achieving the same benefit he was getting from the old behavior. If undivided adult attention is the motivating factor for a child, opportunities for such attention come while the child is behaving appropriately and withdrawn when inappropriate behavior begins. Adjustments of setting variables can prove equally effective in reducing or eliminating problem behaviors. Behavior motivated by the need to escape from an undesired activity can be altered by adjusting the length of the activity, which adult leads it, opportunities children have to make decisions during the activity, time of day it occurs, what precedes and follows it, format (e.g., computer-based, workbook, three-dimensional materials), and so forth.

Accuracy of Functional Behavioral Assessments

Just as quality of standardized tests is judged by reliability and validity, we must consider the threats to validity in functional behavioral assessments. Do we limit our informants, thus getting an incomplete picture of the child? Perhaps a child behaves differently for each of the three adults present in a preschool setting. Do we limit the number of observations we make, conduct them all under the same conditions, or begin with predetermined answers? Sources of threats to validity are: (1) sampling, (2) test-retest reliability, (3) content validity, and (4) predictive validity (Repp & Munk, 1999).

The accuracy of information obtained through an interview is dependent on the nature and amount of time a person spends with the child, the ability of the interviewer to ask pertinent questions, and the quality of recollection the person has. Data from direct observations are merely samples of behavior. The more direct observations under varying conditions (e.g., time of day, activities, people present) occur, the greater confidence we can have that they are representative of how the child behaves.

The exploration of various hypotheses during functional analysis is constrained by the variables we target to manipulate and the conditions under which we conduct these manipulations. We may draw inaccurate conclusions because the samples of behavior we took were so limited, were averaged together to mask irregularities in the data that do not lend support to the conclusions we have drawn, or setting

Know The Facts

Suppose a child's inappropriate use of toys in a specific setting has been charted. The data included in the report may be accurate, but the validity of the data has not been addressed until there is agreement about how the inappropriate use of toys has been operationally defined. The observers of the child have operationally defined "banging on the table" as inappropriate use of toys, and as a result have charted and reported an accurate count of the child's inappropriate use of toys. The validity question is this: Does "banging on the table" constitute inappropriate use of toys? It is possible that a child is trying to separate two toys stuck together. If the behavior under study is operationally defined in a way that cannot be justified to your satisfaction, the validity of the observational data is in question.

events have influenced the outcomes in ways we did not predict. Do the procedures we follow support the premise that repeatedly evaluating a behavior's function will enable us to identify the same function consistently? The issue is whether we would repeatedly reach the same conclusions regarding the function of a behavior.

The greatest threat to validity is found in the effectiveness of interventions based upon functional assessments. The predictive validity of our assessments is measured by the changes seen in child behavior from recommended interventions. Ways to address these threats to validity of functional behavioral assessment include taking data samples from multiple points in a session, using a one-way mirror for observation, scheduling observations at same time of day and under same conditions, and comparing data from different sessions.

Closing Thoughts

Through functional assessment, we place our attention on how a child is able to function in his environment. That functioning can relate to physical performance, such as eating, dressing, toileting, walking; communication, problem solving, or social-emotional behavior. We put the importance on how a child is actually functioning in and across settings, not test scores and comparisons to the norm. Can the child feed herself? Is she able to communicate basic needs? Can we increase her functioning through assistive technology? Does she follow an intentional strategy when approaching a challenging task? Are there benefits she achieves through problem behavior?

When a parent, teacher, or therapist needs to understand the motivations a child has for behaving in certain ways a functional behavioral assessment is needed. A thorough functional behavioral assessment requires tapping multiple sources of information, continuing the process over time, and being open to a wide range of motives that lie behind a child's behavior. Through structured observational approaches and data gathering from informants we can explore how the child acts and reacts with objects, peers, and adults.

When sufficient information through informants and observations is not available to plan an effective intervention strategy, we continue the process using functional analysis. This hypothesis-testing technique should reveal much about the benefits of a problem behavior for a child that we might not ascertain from traditional observations.

■■ For Your Consideration

1. Why is an assessment for assistive technology considered a functional assessment?

2. When would you conduct a functional behavioral assessment?

3. What is the difference between a functional behavioral assessment and functional analysis?

4. What role do informants play in a functional behavioral assessment?

5. How does functional behavioral assessment differ from traditional behavioral analyses of antecedents-behaviors-consequences?

CYBERSOURCES

Check out the following Web sites for more information related to the ideas presented in this chapter.

Work Sampling System (Rebus, Inc.)

http://www.rebusinc.com/index2.html

Family Center on Technology and Disability

http://fctd.ucp.org/

Council for Exceptional Children Technology and Media Division

http://www.tamcec.org/

SuperKids Educational Software review

http://www.superkids.com/

National Head Start Association

http://www.nhsa.org/

For additional resources on assessment, visit us on-line at www.earlychilded.delmar.com

CHAPTER 10

Assessment of Environments

Key Terms and Concepts

Activity theory
- Internalization
- Externalization

Cohesion

Adaptability

Distancing strategies

Developmentally appropriate practices

Child-initiated play

Setting features

Chapter Objectives

After reading this chapter, you should be able to:

1. Discuss activity theory and the concepts of internalization and externalization.
2. Apply activity theory to analysis of environments.
3. Realize the complex and interactive nature of parent-child influences and variability in positive home settings.
4. Match family priorities with community opportunities.
5. Conduct environmental assessments of center-based early childhood settings.

Chapter Overview

The underlying premise of this text is that behavior and development cannot be separated from the context in which they occur. Both historical and current environmental factors contribute to a child's context. The simple everyday activities in which children and families engage play a substantial role in the development of cognitive and communicative functioning (Gallimore & Goldenberg, 1993). The cumulative effects of daily activities combine with larger events in the lives of young children to produce the developmental outcomes we see. Since earlier life events have an ongoing influence on a child's behavior, such historical data are part of the picture of the child that we are attempting to understand. The context includes the family's cultural identity, social and political influences upon them, and many other factors. Activity theory and the analysis of activity systems (or settings) can help us keep this contextual information integrated into our assessments, rather than unintegrated appendages added to traditional assessment reports.

Settings and events that are part of the child's present experiences further contribute to or negate that child's opportunities for growth and development. Unlike the child's history and other elements of the background that are unchangeable, current settings can be adjusted to increase the likelihood that they will support the child's development. Both parents and professionals want to offer the best possible opportunities for growth and development of young children and, therefore, seek to define the best possible settings and conditions for children. What are the best approaches to parenting? How can we arrange a preschool environment to maximize learning? How do we stimulate the thinking skills of two-year-olds through environmental arrangements? Can environments be adjusted to increase the level of independence for a four-year-old child with a motor impairment? These questions have no one true answer. Instead they have many answers, some of which may be in direct conflict with other equally valid answers.

Activity Theory

Activity theory has historical roots in several schools of thought, including (1) classical German philosophy; (2) writings of Marx and Engels; (3) theoretical and research contributions of Soviet thinkers, including Vygotsky, Leont'ev, and Luria; (4) behavior setting concepts of Whiting (Whiting, 1980; Whiting & Edwards, 1988); and (5) ecological cultural models (Super & Harkness, 1986). Although activity theory itself has been described as a "well kept secret" (Engeström & Miettinen, 1999), many of the concepts associated with it, such as Vygotsky's zone of proximal development, are familiar. Theorists and researchers interested in learning and teaching are continuing to explore and develop theoretical ideas that offer extensions of activity theory that can be applied to the assessment of environments of young children. Activity systems or settings are the unit of analysis for this work. (Contextual and culturally situated theorists who are closely aligned with activity

theory may define the unit of analysis differently, such as mediated action or community of practice.)

Within activity theory, there are two basic processes, **internalization** and **externalization,** continuously at work during activities. The reproduction of existing culture occurs through internalization, whereas the transformation of culture takes place through externalization. Although theorists debate the details of such processes, parents and educators can see the concepts come to life in young children. Parents foster internalization of the basics of social culture in acts as simple as urging their infant to "wave bye-bye" while physically manipulating the child's arm. When the child finds his own inventive means of adapting this social custom, the proud parents enjoy the child's externalization of the skills and may even adopt the child's wave as the new family way to wave. Both the reproduction and transformation of society are represented in this simple event.

Activity is defined as a unit of life that has historically determined social origins (Göncü, 1999). According to Leont'ev (1981), we operate within an activity at three levels. The first level is our motive for engaging in the activity. For example, a mother prepares dinner because she is motivated to feed her family. The second level within an activity involves our actions and goals. The mother preparing dinner for her family determines the menu for the evening and confirms that she has the needed ingredients and when it needs to be ready. The third level involves the conditions and operations associated with the goals of the activity. Operations are automatic routines that come with little thought—putting a pot of water on to boil for the pasta, or setting the table. Conditions refer to the features of the environment associated with the activity—the size of the kitchen, the availability of pots and pans, spoons, and so forth. It is through participation in such social activities that individuals become skilled in use of the tools of the culture, needed to accomplish an activity and to acquire the essential skills for functioning in society (Göncü, Tuermer, Jain, & Johnson, 1999).

Something as simple as the involvement of a toddler with her mother during the activity of dinner preparation will vary as a result of many factors, such as cultural practices, number of adults and siblings present in the home, and the types of preparation a specific dinner requires. The mother might choose to place the toddler in a playpen nearby during her dinner preparation. She might let the toddler remain in the kitchen with access to one cabinet with pots, bowls, and spoons that can be used by the child in pretend cooking. She might find ways for the child to be directly involved in the meal preparation. Or she might direct an older sibling to play with the child in a different room during the meal preparation. The approach she chooses defines the learning opportunities available to the child during the period of dinner preparation.

In an adaptation of activity theory used to study children's play, Göncü et al. established five principles of a cultural approach to the study of children's play. These principles, presented in Table 10–1, can be helpful in guiding our assessment of environments of young children as well. Activity settings occur at home, in the community, and in center-based programs, and can be analyzed through five variables (Gallimore & Goldenberg, 1993) presented in Table 10–2.

Home and Community Environments

Traditional nuclear families operate with four major subsystems (Turnbull & Turnbull, 1986): (1) the marital subsystem (husband and wife interactions); (2) the parental subsystem (parent and child interactions); (3) the sibling subsystem (child and child interactions), and; (4) the extrafamilial subsystem (whole family or individual member interactions with extended family, neighbors, and professionals). Every family presents a unique combination of subsystems operating within the family. For example, if a child has no brothers or sisters there would be no sibling subsystem. However, he might have cousins who live in the same household. They might interact much in the fashion as siblings. Divorce and remarriage also create different subsystems, as do extended families residing within the same household or nontraditional household compositions (e.g., foster care, cohabitation).

Beyond the general features of a positive home environment for any child, such as adequate food and clothing, safety from harm, and sufficient nurturing and affection, the definition of an ideal home environment varies across many contexts. Six psychosocial mechanisms within the family context that contribute to developmental changes in both children and adults are (1) opportunities to explore and gather new information, (2) experiences that involve being mentored in new skills, (3) celebrations of developmental achievements, (4) review and rehearsal of new skills and knowledge, (5) avoidance of inappropriate punishment and ridicule, and (6) use of language as a mechanism for learning (Ramey, Ramey, & Lanzi, 1998). These mechanisms take place in the simple everyday activities of family life, but hold substantial power in their potential cumulative benefits.

Know The Facts

Family experiences that foster reading in school-age children are:

- Promotion of verbal skills (through verbal interactions, encouragement of verbal expression, time spent with the child)
- Modeling positive reading habits
- Time spent reading to the child
- Availability of reading and writing materials in the home
- Exposure to a variety of activities
- Providing the child with help in reading
- Regulation and use of the television

TABLE 10–1 Principles of a Cultural Approach to the Study of Children's Play

Principles	Examples
1. The economical structure of children's communities determines the availability of play as one type of activity.	Economic resources influence the types of toys and places where a child can play, broader life experiences of the child (e.g., types of travel the child experiences, access to medical care, and recreational opportunities). The child with more economic resources is likely to have the opportunity to engage in more activity settings (and therefore participate in a greater variety of learning opportunities) than the child with limited economic resources.
2. Understanding children's play requires identification of the beliefs of children's communities about the value of play.	Cultural values regarding the benefits of play influence the extent to which children are given the opportunity to play. In some environments, children take on roles and responsibilities that in other settings are considered unsuitable for children. These children might not perform well on a standardized developmental scale, but can plan and prepare a meal, safeguard a younger sibling, or complete any number of other functional tasks. The competencies that children develop are specific to their environments.
3. Understanding children's play requires analysis of how community values about play are conveyed to children.	How a group values play is conveyed through words and investments of time, money, and space in play materials. When only certain play materials are available, children develop skills associated with what is available. A child without frequent easy access to a place to swim is not likely to become a confident swimmer. The absence of certain play behaviors or skills might reflect such limitations of access rather than inability on the part of the child.
4. Understanding children's play requires an examination of how children represent their worlds in play.	By studying the behavior of children in play, we can discover their perceptions of the adult world. They assume adult-like roles in their pretend play. Children's play represents far more than their ability to imitate adults. It reveals a means by which we can see the world through the child's eyes, how they understand adult roles, and the behaviors in which they have observed adults engaging.
5. Understanding children's play requires adoption of an interdisciplinary methodology involving multiple data-gathering and analysis techniques.	Play is not a simple activity easily interpreted through the perspective of a single discipline. We must draw from historical, anthropological, psychological, social, and educational disciplines to begin to understand the play behaviors of children within a meaningful context.

Source: Adapted from "Children's Play as Cultural Activity," by A. Göncü, U. Tuermer, J. Jain, and D. Johnson, in *Children's Engagement in the World: Sociocultural Perspectives* (pp. 148–172), by A. Göncü (Ed.), 1999, New York: Cambridge University Press.

TABLE 10-2 Analysis of Variables Found in Activity Settings

Variable	Meaning	Sample Questions to Consider
Personnel present	The numbers of people present and the nature of the relationships between them along with other pertinent background information, such as, if parents are employed, their levels of education, languages they speak, and so forth	Do Mom, Dad, and children all participate in trips to the grocery store, or does one parent complete this activity while the other remains at home with the children?
Salient cultural values present	Broad cultural differences seen in attitudes and beliefs regarding disability and reactions to children with disabilities, as well as variance within cultural groups	Is the mother's goal to achieve a spiritual peace regarding her child's disability or to enhance the child's development to the maximum extent possible? Do the parents value socialization and interaction among peer groups for their child over individualized cognitive or motor skill development? Is learning to walk more important than achieving a functional means of mobility?
Task operations and demands	Observation and behavioral description of child behaviors within the activity setting	What does the child actually do during the transition from free play in centers to story time at the preschool?
Scripts for conduct governing participants' actions	Behaviors and routines associated with particular activities	The young child might know that the script for reading is opening a book, saying words out loud and turning pages. Does the child engage in such a script well before he is able to decode the actual words of the text? As he turns pages in a book, he might retell a memorized story, make up a story to go with the pictures, or just speak nonsensically. Any of these behaviors indicate that the child has a notion of the script of reading.
Purposes and motives of the participants	Setting-specific motives for a particular event; within some cultures, this last scenario might be the most common	The motives of the mother fixing dinner influence how she includes or excludes a toddler. Is the motive to prepare dinner as fast as possible? Is it to provide growth and learning opportunities for her young child? Is it for the child to be a competent assistant in the kitchen as quickly as possible?

Source: Variable and meaning adapted from "Activity Settings of Early Literacy: Home and School Factors in Children's Emergent Literacy," by R. Gallimore, and C. Goldenberg, in *Contexts for Learning: Sociocultural Dynamics in Children's Development* (pp. 315–335), by E. A. Forman, N. Minick, & C. A. Stone (Eds.), 1993, New York: Oxford University Press.

Research supporting the concept of environmental specificity in terms of racial or cultural environments suggests that no universal "best" home environment exists (Gottfried, 1984). To account for the environmental specifics, and yet acknowledge the global aspects of environmental influences, Wachs (1998) explored the complexities of how family environments influence development. He identified six key principles of environmental actions that are summarized in Table 10–3.

Environmental needs can vary according to the disability of a child, his temperament, the community in which the family resides, cultural norms, and so on. An environment filled with sound-producing toys might be needed to motivate the toddler with a visual impairment to move, but would have no similar benefit to the toddler who is deaf. An infant with motor impairments who has difficulty moving or conveying her interest in a particular activity might do well in an environment hyperresponsive to her weak signals, whereas a less responsive environment might be more appropriate for the child who is easily overstimulated. Life on a farm might be particularly difficult for a child with severe allergic reactions to animals, hay, and so on. The family that includes a child who is unable to walk might need a house with few or no steps. The ecological congruity between the child's needs and the nature of the home environment can play a critical role in the developmental progress of the child.

The social climate found within the home can have an impact on the development of young children. The availability of both formal and informal support systems, as well as parents' willingness and ability to use support systems, will influence their parental functioning, such as managing stress or obtaining needed counseling to increase acceptance of a child with a disability. The home environment and the nature of parent-child interactions, in this context, cannot be separated from the larger exo-systems and macro-systems within which they exist.

Four family influences contribute substantially to a child's social competence (Guralnick & Neville, 1997). First, parental fostering of peer social networks influences social competence. Parents typically assume the responsibility for providing their child with ever expanding peer experiences by arranging and monitoring suitable activities or participating in opportunities in the community. There is evidence to indicate that children who experience large peer networks become more socially compe-

tent, whereas parents of children less socially skilled tend to monitor and direct their child's play.

The reciprocal nature of parent-child influences also contributes to the picture (Guralnick, 1999). Young children who experience positive social interactions with their peers are likely to urge their parents to continue arranging such events. The parents who find their child's peer interactions to be successful are probably more willing to make the effort to arrange additional activities, than those whose experience was less positive. To the extent that children with disabilities have fewer opportunities to interact with the same group of peers across settings (e.g., neighborhood, Mother's Day Out in neighborhood church), they risk falling behind their peers in the development of social competence (Guralnick).

The second family influence involves three elements: (1) parental attitudes, beliefs, and knowledge about their child's level of social competence; (2) parental beliefs regarding the significance of peer relations and their ability to be changed; and (3) the techniques parents use to modify their child's peer interactions. When parents believe that social skills are important and capable of being changed, they will make the effort to ensure their child has social experiences. When parents see their child's behavior as simply an inherent trait, they are less likely to create opportunities to change that behavior. For example, a mother might attribute withdrawn behavior to a family pattern of shyness. Parents of children with disabilities have indicated that they are more likely to attribute behaviors to the child's disposition and to believe that adult intervention will have only a limited impact (Guralnick). The likely outcome of such attitudes and beliefs is for the parent to limit her efforts to arrange social experiences for her child.

Third is the quality of parent-child interactions. It is through parent-child interactions that the child comes to have a shared understanding of social rules and social roles. Positive affective parenting styles are associated with social competence, whereas negative affect between parents and children can lead to emotional regulation difficulties. These difficulties will, in turn, negatively impact the child's peer relationships. The fourth family influence is all the risk factors to which the child is exposed through the family. In particular, factors such as availability of social supports and financial resources, quality of marital relationships, child temperament, and maternal mental health can influence a child's emotional regulation and the quality of his peer interactions.

TABLE 10–3 Key Principles of Environmental Actions

Principle	Principle in Action
1. Development is influenced by both extreme and nonextreme environmental influences.	No one argues the profound impact extreme conditions (e.g., severe malnutrition, homelessness) can have on a developing child, but when the conditions under study are less dramatic, they still influence development. Although extreme environments might seem to have a more powerful influence, the normal day-to-day family life that is not characterized by extreme conditions influences the child as well.
2. Family environments are nested within a complex multilevel structure and the influences of each level cannot be understood apart from the others.	This multilevel structure is based on Bronfenbrenner's ecological model that moves outward from the micro-system and meso-system to the exo-system and macro-system. Although the exo-system and macro-system are distant from the child's immediate environment and may not appear to impact the child, they do influence the life of that child's family and indirectly his individual development. For example, parents reflect culturally based beliefs when they make decisions to encourage some behaviors and eliminate others in their infants. Influences between the systems that are in close proximity to the child and those more distant also move outward.
3. Environmental influences operate across time.	Mother-infant bonding, attachment, and language development are three areas of research that offer evidence of the lasting impact of early experiences. However, the benefits of early intervention for children at risk for academic failure seem to dissipate without proper follow-up support.
4. Different aspects of the environment influence different aspects of cognitive development.	Maternal language influences the child's language, but does not appear to influence the level of the child's play. Specific aspects of the environment differ in the impact on development depending upon the child's age.
5. Risk and protection factors within the environment covary with risk and protective factors that are not a part of the environment.	Passive environmental covariance is evident as children receive biological and environmental influences from their parents. Children of bright parents may inherit genes predisposed to advanced cognitive development and live in a stimulating environment created by these parents. Reactive covariance is also at play when the child's disposition or other characteristics trigger responses from parents or others in their environment. The individual characteristics of the child will affect the environment as the environment influences the child's development. The need for a good match between a child's traits and the home environment extends to psychological factors. Child traits, such as temperament interact with the features of the home environment, such as caregiving styles of parents. When these factors are compatible ecological congruence is the result.

Source: Adapted from "Family Environmental Influences and Development: Illustrations from the Study of Undernourished Children," by T. D. Wachs, in *Families, Risk, and Competence* (pp. 245–268), by M. Lewis & C. Feiring (Eds.), 1998, Mahwah, NJ: Lawrence Erlbaum Associates.

Dukes (1976) identified five ecological variables of socialization. Extending beyond the home environment, each contributes to the internal nature of the home environment and thus, the quality of parenting and opportunities for positive child development. The variables are summarized in Table 10–4.

Dunst (1993) has compiled a list of 30 risk and opportunity factors related to the home environment that can influence a child's development and functioning. These risk and opportunity factors, presented in Table 10–5, are not dichotomous. Rather, they represent critical levels of factors, such as adequate or inadequate income, or points on a continuum, such as locus of control and temperament. Dunst notes that exposure to a single risk factor may not necessarily cause a child harm, but the child facing multiple risk factors is not likely to escape childhood without some negative effects on his development. On the other hand, the child who experiences multiple opportunity factors faces a far greater chance of experiencing positive developmental outcomes. Opportunity factors can offset the potential impact of risk factors.

Environmental influences from the home might be overlooked or misinterpreted if not directly assessed. Professionals might question the nature and quality of the home environment of a physically healthy three-year-old who has a speaking vocabulary limited to 50 words. Contrary to their expectations, they might learn that the child's home is full of love and affection, including quality language experiences. After having observers spend over two and one-half years recording the vocabulary development of infants and toddlers in homes of families from high SES, middle SES, and those in which the family was dependent on welfare, Hart and Risley (1995) found that the frequency of quality language-based experiences was the critical variable in differences found among the groups. All three groups of parents interacted with their children in the same manner, about the same things. They talked about people and things, relationships actions and feelings, and past and future events. The parents prompted their children, responded to them, prohibited them, and affirmed them.

However, the groups showed a consistent pattern in which the high SES families exceeded the middle SES families, who exceeded the families on welfare on all measures representing frequency of language-based interactions, including minutes interacting with the child and number of words addressed to the child. The high SES parents addressed their children with an average of 487 utterances per hour as compared to 301 utterances for the middle SES parents, and 178 utterances for the parents on welfare. Parents who were on welfare were willing to work hard to care for their children, taking long bus rides holding a sick child only to wait for hours in a public health clinic for medical care for the child. Affection and concern were not missing from these children's lives, even though the parents interacted with less frequency and used far fewer words than the others. The relatively lower frequency of language-based interactions between the parents on welfare and their children did not represent a lack of concern for the child's language development or preparation for school. It did not reflect that the children were "neglected" in any sense of the word. Rather, it was evidence of a cultural pattern that had no direct relationship to the affection parents had toward their children, or the hopes they held for their future academic success.

Often simple modifications of the environment can provide the least intrusive, most effective intervention strategy to offset the difficulties associated with a disability. For the mother who is having difficulty feeding her child with physical disabilities, an environmental analysis might reveal the need to alter positioning for feeding, change the sequencing of events to reduce activity level just prior to feeding, adjust the number of people present in the room during feeding, or turn off the television during feedings. Repeated training sessions on how to feed the child properly might never address the specific circumstances present in the home that are contributing to the difficulty, and therefore would fail to lead to any improvement in functioning.

An awareness of the home environment can influence how the interventionist presents lessons even in a center-based program. In planning for the child with feeding difficulties, it might be beneficial to create as similar as possible circumstances surrounding feeding times at the center and at home (e.g., use similar seating, similar adapted utensils, plates, and cups, and consistent verbal and nonverbal cues throughout the feeding period, and maintain a stable routine and daily sequence related to feeding). Modifications in both the home routine and the center routine would be needed to achieve the most effective match. The center should adjust to those elements of the home environment that are primary to the home environment (e.g., two siblings present

TABLE 10–4 Ecological Variables Affecting Socialization

Variable	Meaning
Household composition	Socializing agents within a family contribute to different childrearing techniques. The amount and quality of interactions may differ substantially. The assumption that the lack of one or both parents causes cognitive and affective deficits is a value-laden perspective. Only about one-fourth of the world's cultures utilize the nuclear family model, predominate in the United States. However, it is perceived as the ideal within this country, so households with differing compositions are viewed less favorably. An individual's self-concept and self-esteem can be affected by societal attitudes toward their household composition.
Role status	What makes a person influential in a family and in the life of a child varies across cultural groups. The role status of the persons with whom a child interacts most will affect the child's cognitive and social behavior. For example, in a culture that honors and shows reverence for the elderly, grandparents would be more significant than in one where strong links to previous generations are weak.
Community setting	Density of neighborhoods and types of households vary. These factors determine mobility of the child, available resources, opportunities for adult and peer interaction, freedom to have some privacy, and a child's leisure activities. Childrearing techniques will most likely be consistent with the demands of the community setting, so that the child is equipped with behaviors necessary for adapting to the environment. Thus, childrearing practices of upper-income parents could expect to be quite different from those of low-income parents with greater density in neighborhoods.
Climate and geographic location	The type of activities in which a family can engage, and types of clothing worn differ. Health and physical well-being of community residents and adaptive survival techniques utilized are also included. For example, a child with cystic fibrosis might be more restricted in a cold region than he would be in a warmer climate. The child born with respiratory problems in an area with high pollution would suffer more than if he were somewhere with less pollution.
Economic base of a given group	The global research that has resulted in high correlations between low socioeconomic status (SES) and low intelligence test scores and poor school achievement does not account for the low SES child who excels, or why such wide variability in performance throughout all SES levels can be observed.

Source: Adapted from "The Effects of Early Childrearing Practices on the Cognitive Development of Infants," by P. J. Dukes, in *Demythologizing the Inner-City Child*, by R. C. Granger and J. C. Young (Eds.), 1976, Washington, DC: National Association for the Education of Young Children.

TABLE 10–5 Risk and Opportunity Factors Influencing Human Development and Functioning

Variables	Risk Factors	Opportunity Factors
Mother's age	Younger or older than normal childbearing years	Within optimal childbearing years
Parent education	Low educational attainment	High educational attainment
Income	Inadequate income	Adequate income
Occupation status	Low occupation status of head of household	High occupation status for head of household
Socioeconomic status (SES)	Low SES	High SES
Job stability	Repeated job changes or unemployment	Stable job
Pregnancy	Unplanned	Planned
Number of siblings	More than 4 children	1 or 2 children
Residential stability	Repeated relocations	None or few relocations
Marital status	Absence of spouse or partner	Supportive spouse or partner present
Marital relationship	Conflictive	Harmonious
Marital stability	Repeated changes in conjugal relationship	Stable conjugal relationship
Child temperament	Avoidant, difficult	Warm, responsive
Infant separation	Prolonged separation in first year	Limited separation in first year
Parental health	Poor physical health	Excellent physical health
Parental mental health	Repeated occurrences of mental health related problem	Stable emotional well-being
Parental self-esteem	Low self-esteem	High self-esteem
Parental locus of control	External	Internal
Parental social skills	Poor	Good
Coping strategies	Reactive	Proactive
Quality of primary caregiver/ child interaction	Controlling and emotionally unavailable	Stimulating and warm
Parenting style	Authoritarian/directive	Responsive/facilitative
Toxic substances	High exposure	No exposure
Nutritional intake	Inadequate	Adequate
Accidents	Frequent	Infrequent
Infections/illnesses	Frequent	Infrequent
Alternative caregivers	None	One or more
Presence of extended family	None or few available	Many and supportive
Extrafamily support	Poor/unsupportive	Good/supportive
Life events	Negative life events	Positive life events

Source: From "Implications of Risk and Opportunity Factors for Assessment and Intervention Practices," by C. J. Dunst, 1993, *Topics in Early Childhood Special Education, 13,* pp. 143–153.

during a feeding session), and modifications at the home should be aimed toward maximizing the potential success (e.g., appropriate activity sequencing prior to feeding). Interventionists who plan lessons hoping the children will generalize the skills taught across environments must be cognizant of the nature of those environments.

It is the ordinary activities of life in which human interactions are embedded. As parents prepare a meal, work in the yard, dress for school or work, read a story, or play a game, they teach their children language, culture, values, social meanings, and so forth (Gallimore & Goldenberg, 1993). Dunst and Bruder (1999a, 1999b) have identified categories of family activity settings that provide learning opportunities for young children within their natural learning environments. These categories and examples of each are presented in Table 10–6. The categories are not mutually exclusive, so many activities can fall within multiple categories of settings.

Identification of the activities and routines within our homes and in the community in which young children have learning opportunities is a start. However, we must look further into what features of these settings influence child outcomes. We can use the five variables of activity settings in this process. A sample structure for analyzing activity settings using the five variables is illustrated in Table 10–7.

Parameters of the Home Environment

The home environment is comprised of both physical and nonphysical properties that interact to influence the behavior of everyone residing in the home. The interaction between and interdependence of the physical and nonphysical properties within the home jointly contribute to influence behavior. For example, overcrowding in the home can increase aggression, leading to physical violence and possible child abuse. With increased physical space in the home that

---

TABLE 10–6 Categories and Examples of Family Activity Settings

Family Routines ■ Preparing a meal ■ Getting loaded up in the car for an outing	**Parenting Routines** ■ Bathing an infant ■ Putting a child to bed
Child Routines ■ Dressing ■ Putting away toys	**Literacy Activities** ■ Writing letters to friends ■ Making a book with drawings
Physical Play ■ Chasing one another ■ Playing with water guns	**Play Activities** ■ Working with modeling clay ■ Building a city with blocks
Entertainment Activities ■ Participating in ballet classes	**Family Rituals** ■ Giving bedtime hugs and kisses ■ Piling in one bed for horseplay on Saturday mornings
Family Celebrations ■ Attending weddings ■ Having birthday parties	**Socialization Activities** ■ Cooking out with the neighbors ■ Participating in a Mother's Day Out cooperative play group
Gardening Activities ■ Working in the yard ■ Planting herbs	

Source: Adapted from "Family and Community Activity Settings, Natural Learning Environments, and Children's Learning Opportunities," by C. J. Dunst and M. B. Bruder, 1999, *Children's Learning Opportunities Report, 1*(1–2).

TABLE 10–7 Analysis of Home Activity Setting for Two-Year-Old across Five Variables

Variable	Activity Setting: Dressing
Personnel present	Mother, who is hurrying to get child to doctor's appointment on time; six-year-old sibling who is asking about stopping at a store while they are out
Salient cultural values	Mother wants child to develop independent dressing skills as soon as possible, but she also wants to be prompt for the doctor's appointment
Task operations and demands	Identifying and opening clothing drawer, reaching and grasping suitable outfit, recognizing front and back, and putting on (with necessary buttoning, zipping, pulling) outfit; selecting and putting on footwear (socks and shoes or sandals)
Scripts for conduct	Consider destination and outside weather, open clothing storage area and select one outfit, check for front and back, position body for dressing, make physical motions associated with assisting in dressing or self-dressing, check appearance in mirror
Purposes and motives	Mother has as highest priority to be fast in the dressing routine to avoid being late for appointment

would have provided a place for an angry spouse, parent, or sibling to retreat, the anger might never have lead to physical violence. A spouse, parent, or sibling with a less volatile temperament might never resort to physical violence in spite of the crowded conditions of the home.

Nonphysical features of the home environment include both psychological and social factors. The interactive nature of many of the physical and nonphysical features of the home environment limits the meaningfulness of researchers' attempts to determine the impact of specific aspects within the home. Nonphysical features that appear to influence cognitive development include child-parent interaction, parent stress and mental health status, and socioeconomic status (Pianta & Egeland, 1994). These same factors are equally likely to affect the physical variables within the household.

Physical Features of the Home

Physical features of the home environment that may be of interest to the early interventionist include basic architectural features, such as the presence of steps in the home, types and amount of furniture present, or size and configuration (e.g., number of rooms in the home). Available play materials, ease of access to and appropriateness of play materials for developmental levels of the children are also considered physical features. The number of persons living in the home and their relationships to one another constitute additional elements of the physical environment as do the presence of adequate food supplies, availability of heating and cooling to maintain body comfort, and adequate plumbing facilities.

Physical variables in the home environment that have been positively linked to cognitive development in children include organization, stimulation, and play materials (Pianta & Egeland, 1994). In contrast, negative influences on cognitive development result from (1) the presence of noise-confusion in the home, (2) overcrowding, (3) irregularity in scheduling events in the home, and (4) physical restrictions on the child's exploration (Wachs, 1979). Several classic studies of the effects of stimulus deprivation and stimulus enrichment have provided dramatic evidence of the role environmental influences play in the development of infants and young children.

Interactions

Within the home, the nature of interactions contributes to the social climate. The concepts of **cohesion** and **adaptability** are useful in describing how family members interact (Turnbull & Turnbull, 1986). Cohesion incorporates both the emotional bonding and the degree of independence for individual family members. It is best viewed as a continuum between high disengagement at one end and high enmeshment at the other. Families at the high enmeshment end of the continuum may be characterized as overinvolved and overprotective. All decisions and activities must be family-focused, with little or no tolerance for privacy. Such a family might be highly resistant to risk-taking, avoiding many opportunities for a young child with special needs to begin gaining independence. This family might need gradual opportunities for risk taking.

At the other end of the continuum, highly disengaged families may be characterized as underinvolved, with rigid separate roles for each family member. When a child with a disability is born into such a family, the needed support and encouragement of a family system might not be available for the child or the caregiver. A balance between enmeshment and disengagement is evidenced in well-functioning families. Cultural patterns and value systems can also influence family cohesion. Rotunno and McGoldrick (1982) stipulate that Italian American families value enmeshment to a greater extent than families from other ethnic backgrounds. Rural Appalachian families, although enmeshed within the family subsystem, highly value their independence from outsiders. Such values and attitudes must be considered if early interventionists hope to have collaborative relationships with families.

Parent-Child Interaction   It is well established that interactions between caregivers and children influence cognitive, linguistic, social, and emotional development (e.g., Bee et al., 1982; Belsky, Goode, & Most, 1980; Bornstein, 1985; Laosa, 1982). Theoretical assumptions that are relevant to the understanding of parent-infant relationships from a context-based perspective are summarized in Figure 10–1.

In the vision for assessment sponsored by the National Center for Clinical Infant Programs (NCCIP) as presented by Greenspan and Meisels (1994), parent-child interactions are specifically recommended to be included in the assessment process. The intended purposes of such interactive assessments are to compare the parents' interactions with their child to standards considered ideal for optimal child development, to identify where parents might benefit from assistance or support, or to determine if the parents are placing the child at risk for developmental or behavioral problems (Mahoney, Spiker, & Boyce, 1996).

Mahoney and colleagues raise a number of serious concerns regarding such assessments. They argue that the intent of the NCCIP recommendation was to encourage the development of new techniques to observe parent-child interactions suitable for use by a wide variety of professionals, including early interventionists. The intent was not to encourage the use of unsubstantiated clinical judgments or technically questionable research instruments that are based on highly subjective constructs by untrained or poorly trained, but well-intended early interventionists. Furthermore, the traditional orientation to parent-child interactions has been on the behavior of the parent, shifting the focus away from the child. Parenting characteristics that are assessed through the existing research-oriented instruments include responsiveness, enjoyment, inventiveness, praise, achievement orientation, physical involvement, play, and teaching. Typically the instruments are oriented to a dominant universal cultural orientation rather than giving consideration to the fact that beliefs and values regarding parenting characteristics and styles vary both between and within cultural groups (Gushue, 1993).

Whether the observer is using informed clinical judgment, informal observations of such global constructs, or following the standards of a specific protocol, the characteristics of observation-based data are equally subject to challenges of validity. With the exception of responsiveness as a parenting quality, these characteristics are unable to stand alone as meaningful predictors of child development (Mahoney et al., 1996). Although it is tempting to accept the intuitive logic that praise or any other of these behaviors is a suitable measure of parental competence, there is no evidence to support such beliefs. Furthermore, Boyce, Godfrey, and Casto, as cited in Mahoney et al., found poor intercorrelations ranging from .20 and .60 for measures of the constructs maternal responsivity, directiveness, and effect across three different parent-child interaction scales. These findings cast further doubt on our ability to define, observe, and evaluate these constructs of parent behaviors. The appropriateness of early interventionists assuming the task of evaluating parenting style can also be questioned.

When data gathering on interactions does occur, it should be designed to take into account four principles. First, the **reciprocal nature of interactions** means that both the parent and the child influence each other. Therefore, single exchanges cannot be

FIGURE 10–1 Theoretical Assumptions of Parent-Infant Interactions

1. There is an interdependence among the roles and functions of all family members—families are social systems. To understand the behavior of one member of a family, the complementary behaviors of other members must also be recognized and assessed.

2. All family members directly and indirectly influence each other.

3. Different units of analysis are needed to understand families. Recognition of relationships among family members—mother-infant, father-infant, sibling-infant, or mother-father—require separate analysis. The family as a unit also requires separate analysis.

4. The embeddedness of the family within a variety of social systems must also be recognized.

5. The developmental perspective which one takes toward the consideration of family relationships will influence the interpretation of findings. A life-span perspective would address the age at which parenthood began, while the more common focus on perceptual-cognitive or social-emotional capacities of the child would not be concerned with parental age.

6. The level of development of the family as a unit can have mutual impact on relationships within the family. Changes in structure, norms, rules and strategies can be observed as families grow.

7. Social changes within a culture have significant impact on families. Family size, timing of parenthood, women in the work force are just three examples of the sociological shifts that are occurring in American families today.

8. A related assumption involves the appreciation of the historical time period in which family interactions are taking place (e.g., the Vietnam War era, the Great Depression).

9. Parental perception, organization, and understanding of infants and their roles as parents influences parent-infant interaction.

Source: From "Family Interaction in Infancy," by R. D. Parke and B. J. Tinsley, in *Handbook of Infant Development,* by J. D. Osofsky (Ed.), 1987, New York: John Wiley & Sons.

removed from the context in which they occurred without risk of misinterpretation.

Second, the **situational context** of the interaction is critical for complete analysis. The situational context includes what activity is occurring, where it is occurring, whether it is naturalistic or clinical, who is participating, the length of the observation, and how the observation is being recorded (Comfort, 1988). For example, parents are more likely to be directive with their child when being observed during a specific task, such as feeding the child or reading a book to the child, than when asked simply to play with their child (Mahoney et al.). Therefore, directiveness is likely to fluctuate across settings and conditions rather than be a constant characteristic of an individual's parenting style. We all become directive when child safety is involved. Priority should be given to arranging observations that include the ac-

tivities of most interest to or concern for the parents. One parent might appreciate guidance on how to encourage the child during play whereas another parent might be seeking ways to shorten a mealtime that has become overly stressful.

The use of clinical settings versus home settings will certainly affect both the parent and the child during an observation. When conditions are as close to routine conditions as possible, the validity of observations is strengthened. Observations should last from 3 to 20 minutes. Going beyond 20 minutes is not appropriate for observations of infants or very young children (Comfort). It is not routine for parents to sustain interactions with an infant over five consecutive minutes, therefore, observations that exceed this length are probably triggering patterns of behavior that are not typical (Mahoney et al.).

The third principle is that there is a tendency on the part of both the parent and the child to strive for a **homeostatic relationship.** If either the parent or the child changes his behavior, the other will attempt to regain the pattern of interaction with which he is familiar. The fourth principle is that parents have the ability to behave with a **view toward the future functioning** of the child. For example, parents talk to and ask questions of newborn babies, even though they are perfectly aware that the child is not capable of responding. It is assumed that the baby will develop the skills necessary to respond appropriately in the future, therefore, the parents behave as if the child already has them. Such behavior, on the part of parents, should not be interpreted as a lack of understanding of the child's current abilities or disabilities.

Child characteristics can affect the nature of parent-child interactions. In an extensive review of the literature on research related to interaction patterns of parent-infant pairs at risk, Hanson (1996) identified many child and mother characteristics that seemed to be condition specific. For example, premature infants, who are biologically not ready to function in an extrauterine environment, demonstrate poor motoric processes and state modulation (Sostek, Quinn, & Davitt, 1979); demonstrate less frequent and acoustically different crying (Lester & Zeskind, 1979); require more stimulation to become attentive and socially responsive (Field, 1977a, Field, Dempsey, Hatch, Ting, & Clifton, 1979); and demonstrate a lower threshold for stimulation (Field, 1977a, 1979). Mothers of premature infants more actively stimulated their infants during feeding, showing less sensitivity to the infant's rhythms and signals (Brown & Bakeman, 1979; Field, 1977b).

The context for interactions between caregivers and premature low-birth-weight infants differs from those between full-term infants and caregivers in four ways (Eckerman & Oehler, 1992) as presented in Figure 10–2. These conditions appear to place these children at risk for having difficulties in adaptive behavior as they mature.

Research related to the interaction patterns of infants and young children with developmental delays provides evidence that the presence of a disability can alter the nature of parent-child interactions. Conditions such as cognitive delay, physical disabilities, hearing impairment, visual impairment, and affective disorders can affect both child and parent behavior. Selected studies are summarized in Table 10–8.

Certain behavioral characteristics that cut across disability types can have a direct impact on family functioning and, therefore, child development. Three domains in which infants and children exhibit differential patterns of behavior are **temperament, readability,** and **behavior** (Huntington, 1988). Each of these domains has a reciprocal influence on parent-child interactions and thus impacts on the nature of the home environment. How the child behaves influences how the parent behaves, which influences how the child behaves.

The ways in which parents elect to instruct their children and help them learn to function in the world can influence their social and cognitive development. Style of communication can set the stage for the child's behavior. For example, the manner in which we instruct a child can foster independent thinking or an insecure dependence on others for approval. Sigel (1982) uses the concept of **distancing strategies** to study the mental operational demands

---

FIGURE 10–2 Context of Caregiving for Premature Infants

1. Social interactions start while the infant is at a much earlier developmental level.

2. Neurological impairments may cause the infant to have different social behaviors.

3. Interactions begin while parents may not be emotionally ready, distracted by their concerns for the child's health and well-being, and unable to understand the infant's behavioral intentions.

4. Interactions take place under the constraints of hospital settings, often involving lengthy stays in neonatal intensive care units.

Source: Adapted from "Very-Low-Birthweight Newborns and Parents as Early Social Partners," C. O. Eckerman, and J. M. Oehler, in *The Psychological Development of Low Birthweight Children* (pp. 91–124), by S. L. Friedman & M. D. Sigman (Eds.) Norwood, NJ: Ablex.

TABLE 10–8 Selected Studies of Parent-Child Interactions

Authors	Findings
Thoman, Becker, & Freese (1978)	In observations of mother interactions with infants with developmental delays during the first five weeks of life they noted less social interaction (looking, noncaregiving, and stimulation activities) and more caregiving during holding or carrying; the infants presented mixed cues, with rapid behavioral state changes, making it difficult to respond appropriately.
Kogan, Wimberger, & Bobbitt (1969)	Children with cognitive disorders are less assertive and more submissive.
Shere & Kastenbaum (1966)	Parents of children with cerebral palsy focus on the physical disability, failing to express concern for other areas of development, such as psychological development.
Kogan, Tyler, & Turner (1974)	Through observations made over several years, noted a decrease in mothers' affection and positive acceptance over time, particularly for children unable to walk.
Schlesinger & Meadow (1972)	Mothers of preschool children with hearing impairments have been found to differ from mothers of hearing children, with the mothers of hearing children receiving higher ratings on permissiveness, nonintrusiveness, nondidactic behavior, creativity, flexibility, and approval of the child. The hearing children faired better in ratings of compliance versus resistance, creativity versus lack of imagination, enjoyment of interaction with mother versus absence of enjoyment, happiness versus unhappiness, and pride in mastery versus absence of pride.
Fraiberg (1975)	Children who were blind have been observed as following the same developmental milestones (smiling, discrimination of familiar persons, stranger avoidance, person permanence, and separation protest) as found in other children, although somewhat delayed.
Kekelis & Anderson (1982)	Parents of children who are blind differ in the manner in which they use language with their children. These parents generally demonstrated a more restrictive use of kinds of sentences, tended to emphasize labeling and function of objects rather than expansions and descriptions, and focused on child-centered rather than environment-related and abstract topics.

parents place upon their children. Distancing refers to the psychological separation a person has from immediate ongoing events. A parent's ability to separate himself from the child and her accomplishment of a task, while providing encouragement and support, is at issue. Distancing is considered an essential element in the development of representational thinking in children.

Parent Stress and Mental Health

Maternal life stress and the absence of social supports, such as a supportive partner present in the home, correlate with lower scores on intelligence tests (Sameroff, Seifer, Barocas, Zax, & Greenspan, 1987). Mothers who experience poor or negative social relationships have been found to be more likely to have children with low scores on intelligence tests (Galler & Ramsey, 1985). Mothers' experience of life stress, particularly stress associated with spouse or partner relationships, has been identified as significant predictors of academic achievement and teacher ratings of child performance on learning tasks for six-year-olds (Pianta, Egeland, & Sroufe, 1990). Although clear causal links were not established, correlations between the performance of 12-month-olds and their mothers' scores on measures of mothers' depressive mood have been observed (Lyons-Ruth, Zoll, Connell, & Grunebaum, 1986). Infants whose mothers had elevated depression scores had significantly lower test scores in both intelligence and motor skills. Likewise, correlations have been found between child intelligence at four years and the degree that a mother's personality is characterized by conforming and rigid attributes (Barocas, Seifer, & Sameroff, 1985). Maternal attitudes regarding family relations and child-rearing has also been related to the intelligence of three-year-olds (McGowan & Johnson, 1984).

Socioeconomic Factors

Poverty and educational levels of parents, particularly the primary caregiver, are two persistent factors influencing children's development. Using the Eyberg Child Behavior Inventory (Eyberg & Ross, 1978), Dawkins, Fullilove, and Dawkins (1995) identified five factors that significantly affected the number of behavior problems in three- and four-year-old children whose parents were living in high-risk environments. They were (1) length of residence in the city, (2) marital status, (3) family violence, (4) roughness of neighborhood, and (5) negative reaction to the problem behaviors of the child. The combined threat of violence in the family and in the community appears to be the greatest contributor to these children developing problem behaviors.

Educational levels as well as knowledge of child development are associated with child outcomes. What parents know and/or believe about child development can influence their perceptions of their children. A father who expected his baby to be toilet trained by 6 months of age will not have the same attitude toward diapering a 15-month-old as one who expected toilet training to come later. The mother who is unaware that on the average, babies begin walking around 12 months of age might be unconcerned that her 20-month-old is not yet walking. The

reciprocal nature of parent-child interactions further contributes to the importance of parental beliefs and knowledge in child development. The father who thought toilet training occurred at 6 months might assume that his 18-month-old is misbehaving every time a toileting accident occurs. Such an assumption would likely lead to disciplinary action and words said to the child that would, in turn, influence the child's self-perception, his relationship with his father, and his future behavior when toileting accidents occur. Research on adolescent parental knowledge of typical developmental norms does, in fact, reveal that teenage parents expected toilet training to be completed by 24 weeks of age. The teenage parents demonstrated a similar lack of familiarity with virtually all motor, language, and social developmental norms (Parke & Tinsley, 1987).

Although most children are raised in home environments, some have no traditional home. Staff working at institutions are typically unable to provide the stimulating and nurturing home environment children need to achieve their full potential. Provence and Lipton (1962) conducted a study of institutionalized infants in which development during the first year was compared to that of infants living in a family setting. At the initiation of the study the infants selected for both groups were free from congenital disabilities, neurological disorders, and acute or chronic illness. The infants were admitted to the institution under three weeks of age. At the end of the first year of life the institutionalized infants showed a discrepancy between maturation of the motor system and their ability to use it in adapting to the environment. As early as the second month fewer vocalizations were noted, and by the end of the first year, delays in all forms of communication were evident. The children had very little interest in all aspects of the environment, even themselves. At the end of the first year of life, the basic processes of learning as well as the mastery of developmental tasks were seriously disturbed and distorted in the institutionalized infants. Previous studies by Spitz (1947) and Skeels and Dye (1939) also showed the dramatic contrast between a nurturing environment and an institutional placement.

Infants with known disabilities are particularly at risk to suffer detrimental effects of institutionalization, whereas at the same time being more likely to be so placed. Stedman and Eichorn (1964) analyzed the performance of infants with Down syndrome raised in an institution as compared to a home-reared group. Those raised in the institution scored significantly lower on mental and social scales than the home-reared group.

Babies left in hospital nurseries in states that prohibit release of newborns to known drug addicts join the children in need of alternative care due to severe abuse or neglect at the hands of their own family. For some of these children foster care will offer a successful option, but for others it will offer no real solution to their need for a stable, nurturing home environment. Another alternative that some children experience is homelessness. Such an option might make institutions appear more acceptable; however, as devastating as the physical discomforts of living on the streets or in temporary shelters can be for young children, the benefits of having a parent who can provide love and affection even in the absence of shelter might outweigh the physical benefits of institutionalizing the child.

Data Gathering Procedures and Techniques

The systematic collection of data for the purpose of an analysis of the home environment is challenging and intrusive. Scheduling interviews, honoring a family's right to privacy, and identifying relevant variables on which to gather data all require sensitivity and flexibility. If the collection of such data is viewed as part of an ongoing intervention program rather than an essential prerequisite to service delivery, relationships can be established over time, reducing parents' understandable initial hesitancy to share information. Once such barriers have been reduced or eliminated, a variety of procedures can be used. Three alternative methods of measuring a child's psychosocial environment are clinical interviews with parents, questionnaires and attitude scales, and direct observation of parent-child interactions. In many instances a combination of these techniques is best.

Parent Interviews

Interviews provide a relatively quick method of obtaining information about the past or present, and can cover incidents and settings for which other procedures cannot be used. They are most effective when combined with additional data gathering procedures, since limitations do exist in the interview process. These limitations include reporting by parents that may be inconsistent with other findings, difficulty for parents in accurately recalling past events, and the lack of quantitative evidence to confirm or deny the accuracy of information obtained through interviews. Reducing the effects of these limitations by using multiple sources of data increases our ability to obtain meaningful data.

The lack of psychometric information can be reduced when we use semistructured interviews, with predetermined questions covering specific areas of concern (Wachs, 1988). Ragozin, Basham, Crnic, Greenberg, and Robinson (1982) developed such a technique in the Satisfaction with Family Scale. Another technique to increase psychometric information is a postinterview rating by the interviewer. Greenberg (1983) created such a scale for use with parents of young children with hearing impairments. It includes four components—parental overprotectiveness, quality of environment, child adaptation, and child attachment. Appropriate use of the clinical interview procedure and cautious interpretation of the information obtained can provide the early interventionist with new insights into a developing child.

An ecocultural model for conducting interviews based on 12 domains that influence the lives of children and families has been developed by Nihira, Weisner, and Bernheimer (1994). In association with each domain, the interviewer can discuss three topics: the available resources and constraints the family is facing, goals and values important to the family, and what efforts the family is making to construct an everyday routine. The 12 domains are listed in Figure 10–3.

The diagrammatic assessment of family relationships through the development of an **eco-map** (Hartman, 1978) provides a visual image of the family operating within a multiplicity of systems. The eco-map is a visual representation of the major systems of which the family is a part, and the nature of the relationships within and among the various systems and family members. Figure 10–4 depicts a sample eco-map, which is most effectively created through an interview. In the center, the members of the family are represented in a traditional family tree, with squares representing males and circles representing females. The age of the individual should be placed in the center of the representative shape. Connecting lines indicate connections between the family and other systems within the environment, such as recreational programs, social welfare systems, health care providers, religious affiliations, employment, and extended family. The characteristic nature of the connection (strong, conflicted, or tenuous relationships) can be described through notes.

FIGURE 10–3 Twelve Domains of Family Ecology

1. Family subsistence, the work cycle, and the economic and financial base

2. Public health, and demographic characteristics of family and community

3. Home and neighborhood safety

4. The division of labor by sex, age, and other characteristics, including domestic task and chore workload

5. Childcare tasks: who does childcare and how is it organized

6. Roles of fathers and others in childcare

7. Composition of children's peer and play groups: who participates and age and sex of groups

8. Structure and quality of marital role relationship

9. Networks, supports, and organizational involvement for women

10. Multiple sources of child cultural influence available in the community

11. Sources of parental information regarding children and family

12. Degree of community heterogeneity influencing family

Source: Adapted from "Ecocultural Assessment in Families of Children with Developmental Delays: Construct and Concurrent Validities," by K. Nihara, T. S. Weisner, and L. P. Bernheimer, 1994, *American Journal on Mental Retardation, 98,* pp. 551–566.

FIGURE 10–4 Sample Eco-Map

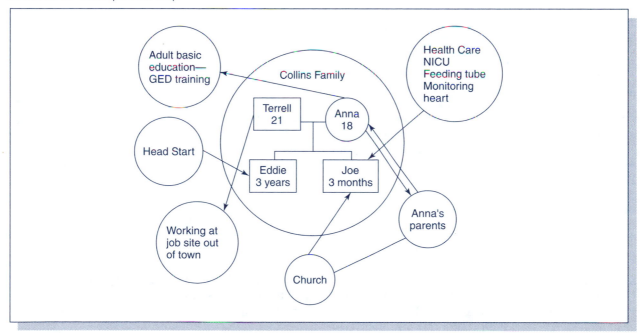

Hartman stresses the benefit of such a visual image on family members as the family picture emerges. The eco-map has been used effectively with natural parents whose children were in temporary foster care as a result of abuse or neglect, in the development of task-oriented contracts involving the identification of changes needed prior to family reunification. The ecological view of the family as provided by the eco-map helps professionals identify essential systems of nurturance, stimulation, and support. The social and functional skills that family members must have to cope with the demands of their lives also become apparent. As information is obtained to complete the eco-map, parents may naturally become aware of their successful coping strategies and positive sources of support or the dysfunctional patterns used by the family.

Questionnaires

Information about parental attitudes toward their child and parental perceptions about the family environment and/or other nonfamily environmental factors, such as social support networks, can be obtained through questionnaires. They are, however, subject to similar limitations as those related to interviews. Although psychometric information is more available regarding some questionnaires than interviews, the norming groups frequently represent a fairly narrow population (e.g., narrow age span of the children, parents of children with a specific disability or from a limited geographic area). If questionnaires that were intended for one population are used with parents who were not represented by the norming group, interpretations of results need to be considered with great caution.

A number of questionnaires have been developed that are intended to address parental perceptions of the family environments in which their children with disabilities live. The Questionnaire on Resources and Stress (Holroyd, 1974, 1986) has been used with families that include children with several different types of disabilities, including cognitive impairments (Holroyd & McArthur, 1976), motor impairments (Friedrich & Friedrich, 1981), and deafness and hearing impairments (Greenberg, 1983) and behavior disorders (Holroyd & Guthrie, 1979). Another instrument, designed to rate parental perceptions of the social climate of the family, is the Family Environment Scale (FES; Moos & Moos, 1986). The FES contains 90 true-false items that represent 10 dimensions of social climate, such as family conflict, family cohesion, and family achievement orientation. Questionnaires that address social support networks were presented in chapter 5.

Direct Observation

Observation techniques can be applied to gather data on both physical and nonphysical aspects of the home environment. Structured coding systems and/or predetermined categories can be used or running records can be analyzed for significant environmental factors affecting behaviors. Specific concerns can also be targeted for observation. For example, a parent might request an observation that would focus on her response to her child's tantrums, a child's refusal to speak when her siblings are present, or how well the home is arranged to meet the needs of a toddler with visual impairments. Such a request would require the development of an individual observation plan that would employ personalized categories of behavior. On other occasions, a general analysis of the home environment might be what is needed.

Rating systems available for use in assessing home environments should be used with a great deal of caution and cultural sensitivity. Such instruments might be of more value in identifying areas to consider than as actual rating tools. A brief summary of several of these instruments is presented in Table 10–9.

The best known of these instruments is the Home Observation for Measurement of the Environment (HOME; Caldwell & Bradley, 1984), which is divided into four scales based on age of the child. The one for families of infants and toddlers (birth to three), and the one for families of preschool-age children are described here. Data are obtained by a combination of observation and interview because some of the items require information that cannot be directly observed. For example, there are items that address trips out of the home and visits into the home, toys available to the child, ways the family arranges the daily routine, and discipline. The current version of the HOME Inventory designed for use with families of infants and toddlers has 45 items divided into six subscales. These subscales and descriptions are presented in Figure 10–5. The preschool version has a total of 55 items divided into eight subscales, presented in Figure 10–6. Items are rated on a yes/no basis. Reliability as measured by internal consistency estimates for the total scale and each subscale of both inventories was reported at acceptable levels. Stability of

TABLE 10–9 Home Environment Rating Instruments

Title	Source	Description
Home Quality Rating Scale	Meyers, Mink, & Nihira, 1990	Assesses child-rearing attitudes and family adjustment to a child with developmental disabilities based on an interviewer's observations and impressions; covers five qualities of home environments: harmony in the home, quality of parenting, concordance in support of child care, awareness of disability, and quality and safety of the physical environment.
Purdue Home Stimulation Inventory (PHSI)	Wachs, 1979; Wachs, Francis, & McQuiston, 1978	Involves both interview and observation, and provides guidance for an overall analysis of the home environment. The most recent version is divided into four sections. Inter-observer reliability checks, based on 45-minute observations scheduled twice a month over a one-year period, are satisfactory. Section I covers basics, such as the number of siblings living at home, the frequency the child is taken out of the neighborhood, whether the child has a regular naptime, and the number of adults who actively care for the child. Section II addresses specific characteristics of the physical environment, which can be easily noted during an observation. Items included in Section II cover features of the home environment, such as home has a place where the child can be away from people and noise (stimulus shelter); free and easy access to appropriate toys, papers, books, and magazines; decorations of pictures and/or objects within the child's room and whether those are periodically changed; and the rate of maternal speech. Section III covers a variety of physical features of the environment, such as the number of stimulus sources on, sound and activity levels, and the total number of people in the house. Section IV addresses the social environment within the home. Ratings include parental investment (ignoring the child, responsive to child-initiated acts, parental-initiated acts), parental affect toward the child, spontaneous vocalizations made by adults present to the child, and the number of times anyone names a definite object for the child.
Home Observation for Measurement of the Environment (HOME)	Caldwell & Bradley, 1984	Divided into four scales based on age of the child, including one for families of infants and toddlers (birth to three), and one for families of preschool-age children. Data are obtained by a combination of observation and interview. Content is presented in Figures 10–5 and 10–6.

items has also been studied across extended time periods. Although there appears to be some test-retest influence, scores are generally stable over time.

Observation instruments that have been used, primarily in a research context, to gather information about parent-child interactions are numerous. Yarrow, Rubenstein, and Pedersen (1975) developed several such observational systems, including one that focuses on mother-infant interactions. Within the context of interactions, the observer looks at the proximity

FIGURE 10–5 Subscales from HOME (Birth to Three Version)

I. Emotional and Verbal Responsivity of Mother

Includes items that note the types of affection the mother displays and verbal interactions she initiates; scolding and other negative exchanges are not counted in this section.

II. Avoidance of Restriction and Punishment

Includes items that cover whether the mother interfered in the child's play or restricted his movements and the mother's negative verbal interactions with the child.

III. Organization of Physical and Temporal Environment

Covers the breadth of a child's environment (e.g., frequency of trips out of the home), the use of appropriate caregivers, and the safety of the child's play environment.

IV. Provision of Appropriate Play Materials

Addresses the types of toys available (e.g., muscle activity equipment) and how the mother entertains the child during the interview (are toys provided?).

V. Maternal Involvement with Child

Covers mother's general supervision and awareness of the child (e.g., maintaining child within visual range, "talking" to the child while she is working).

VI. Opportunities for Variety in Daily Stimulation

Includes variety available in the child's daily experiences (e.g., opportunities for interaction with father, the frequency stories are read to the child).

Source: Adapted from *Home Observation for Measurement of the Environment* (rev. ed.), by B. M., Caldwell, and R. H. Bradley, 1984, Little Rock, AK: University of Arkansas.

of the caregiver, infant behavior, sources of stimulation, social stimulation provided for the infant, changes in location of the infant, and inanimate stimulation. A second instrument provides a maternal rating on two dimensions—expression of positive affect, and contingency of maternal responses to distress. Characteristics of the inanimate environment and infant problem-solving ability are addressed on two additional instruments. A selected sample of other observation systems that are designed primarily for research purposes is presented in Table 10–10. Additional instruments are summarized and reviewed in Munson and Odom (1996). However, it is not recommended that early interventionists attempt to use these instruments in a clinical context. Rather, we can move toward the development of more appropriate structures for parent-child observations within the context of early intervention by exploring the limitations and strengths of existing resources while becoming familiar with tools in use in the emerging field of infant mental health.

No single observation of parent-child interactions holds validity. Many observations in natural settings are needed when exploring the nature of parent-child interactions for children with disorders of attachment. The need for multiple sources of data, including parent reports and observations across time, settings, and activities, is a minimal standard for persons choosing to explore parent-child interactions as a part of the assessment process.

Parameters of Community

There is a push to ensure that early intervention services are provided in settings that are natural environments of young children and their families. As a result, efforts have been made to consider how community settings can be used effectively as a context for enhancing child development. Communities can be defined both geographically and psychologically (Magrab, 1999). Communities represent complex networks of people and institutions with shared in-

FIGURE 10–6 Subscales from HOME (Preschool Version)

I. Stimulation through Toys, Games, and Reading Materials

Covers the breadth and depth of materials present in the home (e.g., are puzzles, or blocks with letters or numbers available, is newspaper read in the home on a daily basis?).

II. Language Stimulation

Addresses the availability of toys and materials that encourage language development, parent requesting child to use appropriate speech (e.g., please and thank you), and permitting the child to make choices.

III. Physical Environment: Safe, Clean, and Conducive to Development

Reviews the characteristics of the environment (e.g., amount of living space per person, clutter, safe outside play area).

IV. Pride, Affection, and Warmth

Notes frequency of mother's positive interactions (both physical and verbal) with the child during the visit.

V. Stimulation of Academic Behavior

Notes the extent to which the mother encourages the child to learn (e.g., colors, letters, and simple reading words).

VI. Modeling and Encouragement of Social Maturity

Covers range of characteristics (e.g., use of television, reactions to child's expression of negative feelings).

VII. Variety of Stimulation

Addresses the child's exposure to variety in language, experience, and play (e.g., mother's use of complex sentence structure, trips of distances greater than 50 miles, availability of musical instruments for play).

VIII. Physical Punishment

Notes the mother's avoidance of physical punishment (restraint, shaking, grabbing, pinching) during the observation and over the past week as based on parent report.

Source: Adapted from *Home Observation for Measurement of the Environment* (rev. ed.), by B. M., Caldwell, and R. H. Bradley, 1984, Little Rock, AK: University of Arkansas.

terests, locality, and a sense of psychological belonging. Smaller communities exist within larger ones, offering people a sense of solidarity and significance. The five major functions associated with a community are production-distribution-consumption; socialization; social control; social participation; and mutual support. The move toward inclusion and early intervention in natural environments is creating opportunities for families with children who have disabilities to become participants in these functions to a far greater extent than in the past.

The features of organizational design of communities are similar whether the identified community is a neighborhood, a city block, or the entire city. These features can be thought of in terms of a continuum with extremes at each end (Magrab). The features and the extreme end points of the continua are presented in Figure 10–7.

Communities differ in the quality of life they offer, and particularly the extent to which all their resources are available to families with children who have special needs. Roberts (1999) has identified six basic principles within communities that can affect the outcomes families are able to achieve. The support system within the community should reflect these principles presented in Figure 10–8.

Communities play an important role in the process of child development as they exert influence over a child's family as well as the child himself. Communities convey their norms through peers in a process that has been compared to an epidemic of social contagion. They can provide resources and support

TABLE 10–10 Observation Instruments for Parent-Child Interactions

Title	Sources	Description
Dyadic Parent-Child Interaction Coding System	Robinson, E. A., & S. M. Eyberg. (1981). The dyadic parent-child interaction coding system: Standardization and validation. *Journal of Consulting and Clinical Psychology, 49,* 245–250.	Assesses degree to which parent's or child's behavior during play is deviant and can be used to evaluate effectiveness of treatment; parent's direct and indirect commands, labeled and unlabeled praise, positive and negative physical contact, descriptive statements or questions, child's compliance, whines, and yells; normed on children with and without behavior problems ages 2 to 7 years, mothers and fathers of low- and middle-class single and 2-parent families with +/− 2 children, parent age 28–32
Interaction Rating Scales	Clark, G. N., & Siefer, R. (1985). Assessment of parents' interactions with their developmentally delayed infants. *Infant Mental Health Journal, 6,* 214–225. Available from Ronald Seifer, Institute for the Study of Developmental Disabilities, University of Illinois at Chicago, 1640 West Roosevelt Road, Chicago, IL 60680	Assesses parental sensitivity to child behavior and reciprocity of interactions during free play; parent's imitating; affect; child's gaze aversion, social referencing; dyadic reciprocity; behaviors grouped as interaction style, social referencing, assessment of context; normed with heterogeneous group of infants with Down syndrome, neurological and multiple disabilities, and high risk and their mothers (maternal characteristics not reported)
Maternal Behavior Rating Scale-Revised	Mahoney, G., Powell, A., & Finger, I. (1986). The maternal behavior rating scale. *Topics in Early Childhood Special Education, 6,* 44–45. Available from G. Mahoney, Family Child Learning Center, 143 Northwest Ave. (Bldg. A), Tallmadge, OH 44278	Assesses quality of maternal interactive behavior during play with young children with mental retardation for use in program evaluation; parent's expressiveness, warmth, sensitivity to child state, achievement orientation, social stimulation, effectiveness, directiveness; child's activity level, attention span, enjoyment, expressiveness; normed on children with organic disabilities, mental retardation (primarily Down syndrome), 1–3 years; mid-class mothers, 60% white, mostly married, 68% unemployed

TABLE 10–10 (Continued)

Title	Sources	Description
Nursing Child Assessment Teaching and Feeding Scales	Barnard, K. E., Hammond, M. A., Booth, C. L., Bee, H. L., Mitchell, S. K., & Speiker, S. J. (1989). Measurement and meaning of parent-child interaction. In F. Morrison, C. Lord, & D. Keating (Eds.), *Applied developmental psychology* (Vol. 3). *Psychological Development in Infants* (pp. 39–80). New York: Academic Press. Scales available from NCAST Publications, University of Washington, WJ-10, Seattle, WA 98195	Assessment of parent and child behaviors during teaching and feeding as screening device and pre-/postintervention; parent's verbalizations, positioning, handling; child's gaze, verbal cues; factor analyzed into six subscales: parent's sensitivity to cues, response to distress, cognitive and socioemotional growth fostering; child's clarity of cues; responsiveness; normed with healthy, typically developing children 1–36 months, preterm infants, 4–8 months; mothers of full range of educational status, 1- and 2-parent families, mostly white, also black and Hispanic
Parent Behavior Progression	Bromwich, R. (1983). Parent behavior progression (PBP), manual and supplement (Rev. ed.). Available from The Center for Research, Development, and Services, Department of Educational Psychology, California State University, Northridge, CA 91330	Assesses infant-related maternal behaviors to develop short-term goals aimed at changing maternal attitudes and behavior for the purpose of enhancing maternal-infant interaction; six levels ranging from maternal enjoyment of infant to mother independently providing developmentally appropriate activities; behaviors such as parent's pleasure in watching infant, physical proximity, awareness of signs of distress, comfort, provides stable caregiver, provides variety of stimulation; used with parents of premature/low-birth-weight infants at risk for health or developmental problems, 9–24 months; heterogeneous SES, maternal age and family structure, black, white, Chicano
Parent-Child and Family Interaction Observation Schedule	Sigel, I. E., & Flaugher, J. (1987). Parent-child and family interaction observation schedule (PCI). Princeton, NJ: Educational Testing Service.	Designed to evaluate parent-child and family (mother, father, child) interactions. Interactions are coded as to the level of mental operational demands (low, medium, or high distancing demands), structuring, correction, and level of content of information. Additional characteristics of the interaction, such as verbal emotional support systems (approval, disapproval, information giving), nonverbal behaviors (helping, taking over, modeling, positive/negative affect), and behavioral responses (activity, initiative, resistance, parallel activity, no time)

(continued)

TABLE 10–10 Observation Instruments for Parent-Child Interactions (Continued)

Title	Sources	Description
Parent/Caregiver Involvement Scale	Comfort, M., & Farran, D. C. (1994). Parent-child interaction assessment in family-centered intervention. *Infants and Young Children, 6,* 33–45. Available from Dale Farran, Department of Child Development and Family Relations, Univ. of North Carolina, Greensboro, NC 27412	Description of parent's involvement in play interaction with special needs, high-risk, or typically developing children; adult's amount, quality, appropriateness of involvement via 11 behaviors (e.g., physical, verbal, responsiveness, control), overall impression of affective climate and learning environment; normed on children with mental retardation, medical or environmental high risk, or multiple handicaps, 2–57 months, typically developing children +/−3 years, mothers and fathers of heterogeneous SES, low SES, or mid SES, varied parental age and number of siblings, 1- and 2-parent families, Caucasian and black
Social Interaction Assessment/Intervention	McCollum, J. A., & Stayton V. D. (1985). Infant/parent interaction: Studies and intervention guidelines based on the SIAI model. *Journal of the Division for Early Childhood, 9*(2), 125–135.	Evaluation of parent-child interaction pre/postintervention to increase parent's ability to make independent adjustments to child's behavior during play; communicative social interaction, individualized target behaviors for parent and child (e.g., imitation, vocalization, turn taking) normed with severely motor- and cognitively delayed children, 2–34 months; mothers of lower mid-income families with 1 and 2 parents, 0–3 siblings, ages 20s to 30s
Teaching Skills Inventory	Rosenberg, S., Robinson, C., & Beckman, P. (1984). Teaching skills inventory: A measure of parent performance. *Journal of the Division for Early Childhood, 8,* 107–113. Available from Cordelia Robinson, JFK Center for Developmental Disabilities, Univ. of Colorado Health Sciences Center, Campus Box C234, 4200 East Ninth St., Denver, CO 80262	Assessment of parent's teaching skills with child pre-/postintervention; parent's clarity of verbal instruction, task modification, effectiveness of prompts; child's interest; normed with heterogeneous group of children with mental retardation with mixed and multiple handicaps, mild to severe disabilities, 2–36 months; mothers primarily Caucasian, mid-income, at least high school graduates

FIGURE 10–7 Features of Community Organizational Structure

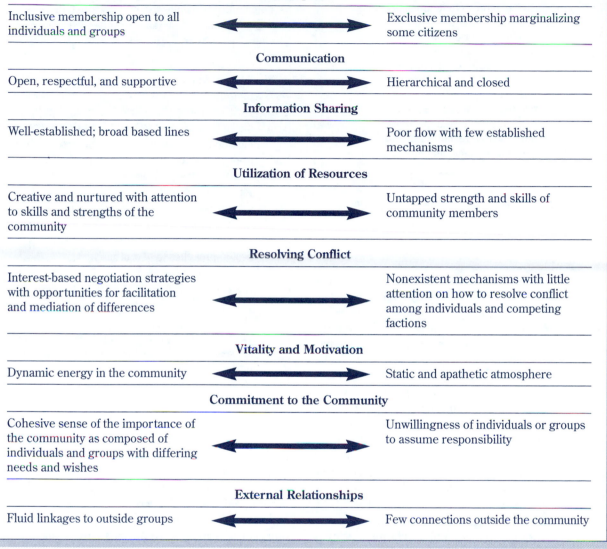

Source: Adapted from "The Meaning of Community," by P. R. Magrab, in *Where Children Live: Solutions for Serving Young Children and Their Families* (pp. 3–30), by R. N. Roberts (Ed.), 1999 Stamford, CT: Ablex.

or serve to restrict opportunities and hope. Communities with families from widely differing economic levels living within close proximity of one another can have a discouraging effect on the less advantaged children as they become aware of their status of disadvantage. It is most difficult for families with the fewest resources to invest in community building, leaving them without resident-initiated support systems that might be in place in more affluent settings.

Data Gathering and Techniques

Although there are many community variables that influence a child's development, it is typically beyond the scope of an early interventionist to evaluate an

FIGURE 10-8 Basic Principles within Communities
Affecting Family Outcomes

1. Responsive to family challenges, priorities,
   and strengths.
2. Developed in partnership with constituents.
3. Reflective and respectful of the cultural
   norms and practices of the families
   participating.
4. Accessible to everyone.
5. Affordable to those who need assistance.
6. Organized and coordinated through
   collaboration so that resources are equitably
   distributed in an efficient and effective manner.

Source: From "Supporting Families with Children in a
Community," by R. N. Roberts, in *Where Children Live: Solutions for Serving Young Children and Their Families*
(p. 32), by R. N. Roberts (Ed.), 1999 Stamford, CT: Ablex.

Finding A Better Way

Community principles can be seen in action as we observe community reaction to families who wish to include their children with disabilities in the everyday
world of community.

- When a family wants their child with physical
  limitations to have access to a neighborhood
  park, are there people willing to support the addition of some accessible play equipment, make
  modifications to existing equipment, and provide
  priority parking in adjacent parking lots?
- Do parents have an equal say in the development of
  services and models of delivery, as do professionals
  and representatives of government agencies?
- Can the professionals working in the support systems honor and accept differing views on the
  best approaches to parenting?
- Do the services offered to families reflect real ac-
  cessibility in terms of transportation issues, child
  care provisions, and time of day services are
  available?
- Parents living in communities that have already
  addressed these issues positively do not have to
  face the same battles faced by those living in
  more restrictive settings.

entire community in association with the identification of suitable activity settings and activities for a particular child. The professional does not have the
capacity to change the economic base of the community, the types of recreational opportunities available,
the quality of child care available, or any other similar
feature of communities. However, the early intervention community can engage in community mapping to
determine what activity settings are within the community that should offer learning opportunities to
young children. Dunst and Hamby (1999) have identified 11 categories of community activity settings that
provide learning opportunities for young children.
These settings and examples of specific activities that
might occur in them are presented in Table 10-11.
The categories can provide a structure for early interventionists attempting to complete community mapping to identify appropriate activity settings within the
natural environments of a community.

The analysis of specific activity settings for a particular child is needed as well. We can use the same
five variables applied to the analysis of home activity
settings to the analysis of community activity settings. An example of such an analysis is presented in
Table 10-12.

Matching individual family priorities in community-
based delivery of services is more likely when there
is a strong network of flexible service delivery models. Roberts (1999) illustrates this with two examples within the same community. One family was able

to schedule a physical therapist to attend a swim
class for moms and babies so the mother and child
could participate in a community activity open to
other families and concurrently receive needed physical therapy. The mother, swimming instructor, and
physical therapist were all participants in planning
and delivery of intervention within the activity setting. Over time, the physical therapist reduced her
attendance at the swim lesson, but maintained contact with the mother. Another family wanted physical
therapy to occur at a center-based early intervention
program. The mother particularly liked the supportive resources that were available to her when she
brought her child in to participate in therapy. Concurrently, the therapist taught the mother exercises
that she could do with the child at home. Both options were individually matched to family preferences and produced positive results. The expansion
of early intervention services into community-based

TABLE 10–11 Examples of Community Activity Settings

Family Excursions ■ Gathering at a relative's home or Sunday afternoons ■ Visiting the library	**Outdoor Activities** ■ Swimming at a community pool ■ Attending soccer games
Play Activities ■ Visiting the community park ■ Digging in the sandbox	**Family Outings** ■ Visiting the zoo ■ Camping
Community Activities ■ Attending an open-air band concert ■ Having faces painted at an art festival	**Recreation Activities** ■ Attending special sessions at the nature center ■ Spending the day at a water park
Children's Attractions ■ Attending a puppet show ■ Listening to children's stories at a bookstore	**Art/Entertainment** ■ Attending preschool art workshops at the museum
Church/Religious Activities ■ Attending vacation bible school ■ Participating in worship services	**Sports Activities** ■ Participating in T-ball ■ Going fishing
Groups/Organizations ■ Participating in swim lessons ■ Attending gymnastics classes for preschoolers	

Source: Adapted from "Family and Community Activity Settings, Natural Learning Environments, and Children's Learning Opportunities," by C. J. Dunst and M. B. Bruder, 1999, *Children's Learning Opportunities Report, 1*(2). "Community Life as Sources of Children's Learning Opportunities," by C. J. Dunst and D. W. Hamby, 1999, *Children's Learning Opportunities Report, 1*(4).

TABLE 10–12 Sample Analysis of Community Activity Setting

Variable	Activity Setting: Music Classes for Toddlers
Personnel present	Young, energetic African-American music teacher; five three- and four-year-old children (three white and two African-American); one parent for each child (four mothers and one father)
Salient cultural values	Music is a worthwhile part of our lives; participation in music activities will enhance that child's development across all domains
Task operations and demands	Listening; cooperating with teacher; participating in music and movement activities individually and in concert with the group
Scripts for conduct	Child separates from parent who remains in lobby area, enters room, and moves to circle area with small chairs; when "instrument box" is presented, child selects one instrument; taking turns and sharing are standards for the group
Purposes and motives	Provide a fun group activity for the children; introduce music concepts through musical experiences; enhance gross and fine motor movements in concert with music; provide opportunities for children to interact with peers and follow directions given by a teacher

natural environments, in concert with existing services, should increase the child's functional application of new skills.

Center-Based Environments for Infants, Toddlers, and Preschool Children

In addition to spending time in their homes and communities, infants, toddlers, and preschool-age children attend a variety of center-based programs. These settings include a diverse range of possibilities from speech and hearing clinics to infant and preschool child care linked with adult education and family literacy programs. The purposes of these programs also reflect their diversity, incorporating traditional domain-specific goals of early intervention as well as more recent emphases on the development of the child's more global social competence. Just as there are no definitive "best" home or community environments, there is no single set of criteria to define the "best" environment for center-based services.

Obviously, minimum standards regarding safety and the welfare of the child must be given due consideration. Center-based programs must adhere to legal standards regarding adult-to-child ratios, square footage, distance between cribs, fire safety, food preparation and storage, and so forth. In addition to these basics, there are principles and guidelines that define best practices associated with quality programs. For example, links between features of the environment and the number of children's social interactions (Odom, Peterson, McConnell, & Ostrosky, 1990) and language production (Hemmeter & Kaiser, 1990) have been demonstrated.

Four behavior patterns can be symptomatic of problems in the environment (Nordquist & Twardosz, 1990). Low levels of child engagement can indicate a poor match between child preferences and available toys and activities. When the nature and extent of behavior problems is broad, involving many children throughout the day, the cause is likely to be the environment rather than individual child-based problems. Poorly managed transition times that leave children waiting for extended periods will inevitably lead to behavior problems. Additionally, individual children might have environment-caused behavior problems specific to themselves.

The primary task for early interventionists is to approach the assessment of environments as a way to create the best possible match between an individual child and the environment. For a three-year-old who has recently been diagnosed with autism, does an inclusive preschool program offer a better option than an individualized program of discrete trial training offered in the child's home seven days a week? Maintaining a familiar routine and schedule within the preschool setting may not be enough to prevent this child from becoming highly agitated during every transition. Can the environment be adjusted to better accommodate the child's present functioning? Should we decide, instead, that the child is not yet ready for an inclusive placement? The introduction of a visual schedule to help this child anticipate transitions before they occur, combined with verbal supports from a teacher, might enable the child to make it through transitions with far less agitation. On the other hand, if the child is highly aggressive, biting other children and teachers, an alternative placement might be warranted until the aggression is controlled. Does a specialized early intervention program offer a suitable option as the child develops more of the skills needed for an inclusive setting, or will being placed in an inclusive setting stimulate development of appropriate behaviors?

Can an inclusive preschool program built around the concepts of developmentally appropriate practice as defined by the NAEYC (Bredekamp & Copple, 1997) meet the needs of a four-year-old who has recently been placed in foster care after being discovered severely neglected by his family, who had been living in an old school bus? This child may have no play skills whatsoever. The ideal atmosphere in which to introduce her to play might not be an open preschool setting, even if it is considered the best in the community. The pursuit of a placement that meets a child's special needs must be balanced against selecting a placement that can make reasonable accommodations to meet the child's needs. How much accommodation is reasonable? What types of accommodation challenge the underlying integrity of the program? When does the safety of other children take precedence over the need to accommodate a child within an inclusive setting?

In spite of these quandaries, environmental adjustment is a critical variable in reducing the practice of segregation by disability. When properly designed, environmental changes intended to meet the needs of individual children enable them to respond to the environment in new ways. Eventually, the need for environmental adjustments related to behaviors should be reduced, whereas accommodations needed for physical or sensory impairments will likely remain.

Parameters of Center-Based Environments

Center-based environments include physical, and social and programmatic variables that influence how a child behaves. Physical variables include room layout, equipment and furnishings, materials and activities available for play, and food service (type and manner of serving). Social and programmatic variables include theoretical perspectives upon which the program is based, stated program goals, schedules, roles of adults, curricular materials, and numbers and types of children served. Additionally, there is a reciprocal influence between physical and social/programmatic aspects of the environment. For example, children are more likely to run and chase one another in a room arranged with open spaces than one with dividers. They are more likely to engage in social interactions with peers in small spaces than in large spaces. Toys and equipment can foster social interactions (e.g., a ball), or be individual in nature (e.g., headsets used to listen to read-along stories). Use of carpet squares during story time to define individual space can reduce child-to-child contact.

Three relational aspects of the environment that influence the language of preschool children are child engagement with the environment, child and caregiver contingent interactions, and caregiver efforts to mediate the environment to encourage communication (Hemmeter & Kaiser, 1990). Evidence of engagement includes the child's directed visual attention, physical handling of objects, and verbal behavior. Contingent interactions involve two-way reactions to one another between child and caregiver, such as a morning greeting. The teacher may enthusiastically greet the child upon arrival, calling her by name, and asking her a question or two. Another teacher might approach the mother and child at the classroom doorway, take the child in her arms with a smile, and begin speaking to the mother. The first greeting style gave the child an opportunity to interact with the teacher, use communication skills, and expect more interaction from the teacher. In the second scenario there was no opportunity for the child to use any oral communication skills.

Mediation involves the adult's efforts to establish a meaningful connection between the child's attempts at communication and the environment. The adult can mediate by responding to the child's attempts at communication, initiate conversations with the child, and arrange the environment to encourage the child to communicate (e.g., allowing two children to play together at a computer station).

Since the move to include young children with disabilities in preschool programs began, there has been extensive discussion as to what the nature of an inclusive setting should be. The standard for early childhood programs throughout the 1980s and 1990s were the guidelines for developmentally appropriate practice as defined by the NAEYC (Bredekamp, 1987; Bredekamp & Copple, 1997). These guidelines emphasize child-initiated play, characterized by a teacher's role that is far less intrusive than typical of traditional special education practices. The integration of young children with disabilities into early childhood settings based on 1987 NAEYC guidelines triggered debates regarding the appropriateness of them for many children (e.g., Wolery & Bredekamp, 1994). The revised version of these guidelines reflects a shift toward individually developmentally appropriate guidelines, while continuing to endorse the appropriateness of child-initiated, center-based play.

Concurrently, special educators have redefined best practices in early intervention by transforming the role of the teacher from direct instructor to one who operates on a continuum, offering the least intrusion possible. The programs are now designed around child-initiated play-based activities to the maximum extent possible. The need for and potential benefits of peer interactions forced special educators to reconsider the segregated environments they had created for early intervention. However, early childhood educators who accepted children with disabilities into inclusive settings found themselves unable to manage these children unless they deviated from the guidelines. The extent to which early childhood environments should or can be altered to accommodate the needs of individual children and the extent to which such settings do offer effective interventions for them remains under scrutiny.

Today, early intervention services that combine early childhood education with the specialized services come in many varieties. Options include children with disabilities in Head Start classes, combining preschool special education classes with early childhood education programs for a time period on a regular basis, itinerant support for a child with special needs who attends a community-based program, or any other service model that involves having young children with special needs integrated with other children for shared experiences. Each of these models and numerous variations have proven to offer suitable environments for early intervention. However, any one of these options is only as good as it matches the individual needs of a specific child.

Center-based environments provide opportunities for children to experience and gain skills in a number of social tasks, including joining a group of peers already playing, resolving differences, and sustaining a play activity with a peer. Within social tasks, children employ social strategies to achieve their own goals (Guralnick, 1993). However, some children are unable to master these strategies, displaying instead a disorganization of social behavior or withdrawal from social interactions. They may be unable to attend selectively to the cues present in a social situation, leading to an inability to anticipate the consequences of the strategies they do use. Guralnick notes, "the experientially impoverished backgrounds of many young children create additional difficulties by limiting a shared understanding for peer interactions" (p. 356). Within the framework of the guidelines for developmentally appropriate practice, teachers are reluctant to intervene in social interactions between children, expecting them to develop an awareness of the consequences of their behaviors toward one another with as little direct intervention as possible. The preschool setting provides the necessary opportunities for the child to develop social competence. However, some children will be unable to benefit from these opportunities without guided support. Teachers must determine what modifications can be made to social settings within a preschool for children unable to decipher social cues or evaluate the consequences of their actions.

Data Gathering Procedures and Techniques

Environmental assessments can focus on general characteristics of a setting or an individual child's reactions to a particular environment. General environmental assessments typically include consideration of the room arrangement, staffing patterns, the availability and types of toys and play materials, the size and nature of peer groups, scheduling patterns, and accommodations to adult needs. Such assessments are often linked to program evaluation systems, including reviews associated with accreditation and program licensure, and monitoring by funding sources. Although it is useful for early interventionists to be familiar with these types of environmental assessments, how an individual child is interacting with specific elements of the environment is also needed. Ecobehavioral analysis involves consideration of how the child is influenced by and influences the environment.

General Environmental Assessments

Rating systems and checklists are often used for general environmental assessments. The Infant/Toddler Environment Rating Scale (ITERS; Harms, Cryer, & Clifford, 1990) and the Early Childhood Environment Rating Scale-Revised (ECERS; Harms & Clifford, 1998) have been used extensively in the evaluation of center-based settings. The ITERS can be used to evaluate programs serving infants and toddlers less than 30 months of age. Following several hours of observation and interviews with staff, evaluators using the ITERS or the ECERS rate items from inadequate to excellent on a seven-point scale. Environmental rating instruments are summarized in Table 10–13.

Another useful approach to environmental analysis is the creation of a classroom map. The map should include the entrance and permanent walls, child storage areas (cubbies), moveable room dividers as they are currently arranged, equipment and furniture, areas designated for specific activities, access to toilets, and storage and access to toys and other instructional materials. A separate map of outdoor play areas and any other common areas (e.g., cafeteria, gymnasium, music room) can give a more complete picture of the environmental setting. Classroom maps of this nature can be used to detect general problems, such as activity centers that disrupt the flow of traffic in the room, incompatible activities adjacent to one another, or art activities that require water too far from a water source.

Maps can also be helpful when analyzing how an individual child interacts with his environment. An observer records where a child goes in the room, how much time is spent there, and what behaviors were displayed at each location (e.g., engagement with toys, engagement with peers, random wandering). This mapping of an individual child's day can offer teachers guidance in making adjustments to the environmental arrangements that might increase task engagement, peer interactions, use of language, or motivation to complete an activity.

Ecobehavioral Analysis

Ecobehavioral analysis of a preschool setting involves the analysis of interactions between the environment and an individual child. Such an analysis of the interactions between the child and his environment provide information about (1) ways a child spends time, (2) how a child's behaviors in one set-

TABLE 10–13 Environmental Rating Scales

Instrument	Source	Description
Infant/Toddler Environment Rating Scale (ITERS)	Harms, Cryer, & Clifford, 1990	Thirty-five items organized into seven subscales: 1. Furnishings and displays for children 2. Personal care routines 3. Listening and talking 4. Learning activities 5. Interaction 6. Program structure 7. Adult needs
Early Childhood Environment Rating Scale-Revised (ECERS)	Harms & Clifford, 1998	Thirty-seven items organized into seven categories: 1. Personal care routines 2. Furnishings and displays for children 3. Language-reasoning experience 4. Fine and gross motor activities 5. Creative activities 6. Social development 7. Adult needs
Preschool Assessment of the Classroom Environment-Revised (PACE-R)	Raab, Dunst, Whaley, LeGrand, & Taylor, 1994	Thirty-five items arranged in seven categories: 1. Program foundation and philosophy 2. Management and training 3. Environmental organization 4. Staffing patterns 5. Instructional context 6. Instructional techniques 7. Program evaluation

ting compares with behaviors displayed in another, (3) environmental arrangements that foster child engagement in activities, (4) environmental arrangements that foster social interaction, and (5) behaviors that appear to be most closely related to developmental gains (Carta, Atwater, Schwartz, & Miller, 1990). One ecobehavioral system mentioned in research literature that can provide some guidance in this process is the Ecobehavioral System for the Complex Assessment of Preschool Environments (ESCAPE; Carta et al., 1990; Carta, Greenwood, & Atwater, 1985) described in Table 10–14.

Template matching offers a structured approach to the analysis of child behaviors and environmental variables found in activity settings (Le Ager & Shapiro, 1995). The ESCAPE combined with the Complex Assessment Code/Checklist for Evaluating Survival Skills (ACCESS; Atwater, Carta, & Schwartz as cited in Le Ager & Shapiro, 1995) and the School Survival Skills Rating Scale (SSSRS; Sainato & Lyon,

1989) are used for detailed observations of a child over an extended period of time (at least two hours). From the ESCAPE, information is available about the activity, materials, grouping, initiator of the activity, and group composition. It further provides information about the behavior of the teacher and the child. ACCESS is focused on child-teacher interactions during group instruction, independent times, and transitions. Data is gathered through a 10-second momentary and whole-interval time-sampling system. Observations include coding for the activity, the engagement of the child in the activity, and the interactions between child and teacher. Teacher arrangement, material location, and type of prompt are recorded for each 5-minute observation. The SSSRS is completed by teachers, rating a child's behavior in the classroom. The checklist includes 52 items that address 8 skill categories: instruction following, classroom behavior, work, large group responding, transition, independent work, social behaviors, and

TABLE 10–14 Ecobehavioral Analysis

Instrument	Source	Description
Ecobehavioral System for the Complex Assessment of Preschool Environments (ESCAPE)	Carta, Atwater, Schwartz, & Miller, 1990; Carta, Greenwood, & Atwater, 1985	Time sampling approach to analyze how an individual child behaves in regard to ecological, teacher, and child factors that are organized into 12 categories with 92 subcategories.
		Child is observed over an entire day, with recordings for each variable based on a 15-second time period occurring once per minute.
		Results can be analyzed in general terms, such as what the teacher actually engaged in over the day, or how the observed child spent the day (e.g., engaged or not engaged).
		Results can also be analyzed to determine if and how the child was likely to be participating during a particular type of activity, such as story time or playing in the block area.
		Ecological categories: ■ activities ■ activity initiator ■ materials ■ locations ■ groupings ■ composition / Teacher categories: ■ teacher definition ■ teacher behavior ■ teacher focus / Child categories: ■ target behaviors ■ competency behaviors ■ talk

self-care behaviors. Teachers can also use this checklist to indicate how important each item is within their particular setting. The ESCAPE and ACCESS together offer data on 12 variables. These are presented in Table 10–15.

The template approach to environmental analysis can be used when a child is about to transition to a new setting. The child's current setting can be analyzed and compared to possible placement options. Such comparisons can then be used by teachers in the current setting to plan interventions to assist the child in developing skills that will be needed in the future placement. The process can also be used to identify environmental variables that can be modified to improve learning opportunities for the child. For example, activities might be shifted from a table setting to the floor or vice versa. The size of groups in which a child is expected to participate can be adjusted to meet the child's current behavioral abilities. For the child who may be unable to select an activity and engage in it over several minutes, such analysis can guide the teacher in her efforts to provide a structure that encourages child-initiated play.

Haney and Cavallaro (1996) have devised the Ecologically Based Activity Plan (EBAP) model to use in daily planning for children in inclusive preschool settings. The model involves linking traditional child-focused assessment data with analyses of the skills needed to participate in common activities within the setting. First, broad goals and objectives are established based on developmental assessments of the child. A selected classroom activity is analyzed

TABLE 10–15 Systems and Definitions for Key Observation Variables

Variable	System	Definition
Active engagement	ACCESS	Engaged in gross or fine motor actions that are part of the instructional task or assigned for an activity
Art and writing materials	ESCAPE	Objects used for painting, drawing, and creating (markers, clay, pipe cleaners, scissors, paint)
At table	ESCAPE	Sitting or standing at a table
Attending	ESCAPE	Looking at teacher who is lecturing, giving directions, or leading discussion; observing another child
Competing behavior	ACCESS	Behaving in a manner that interferes with appropriate engagement
Engaged composite	ACCESS	Active engagement and attending combined
Fine motor activity	ESCAPE	Focus on the movements of fingers, wrists, and hands, usually involving grasp (cutting, painting, sewing)
Group prompts	ACCESS	Directions or cues for specific behaviors given to a group of children ("everyone line up")
Individual prompts	ACCESS	Directions or cues for specific behaviors given to an individual child ("Tamara, line up")
Large group	ESCAPE	An activity with 5 or more children
Solitary	ESCAPE	Child engaged in an activity by him- or herself
Teacher initiated	ESCAPE	Activity engaged in has been selected by an adult

Source: Adapted from "Applications of Ecobehavioral Analysis to the Study of Transitions across Early Education Settings," by J. J. Carta, J. B. Atwater, I. S. Schwartz, and P. A. Miller, 1990, *Education and Treatment of Children, 13,* pp. 298–315.

according to what the children do in the activity. A specific goal related to the activity is then developed for the child (e.g., respond verbally to initiations made by other children during a free-play activity).

The next step is the identification of skills needed to participate in the activity and the description of the target child's current ability to perform these skills based on test data and observations. Materials used in the activity are identified and needed modifications (if any) are noted. Children typically involved in the activity and special friends who might be targeted to participate are listed and their roles during the activity are described (e.g., natural play models; use prompting strategies). Finally, adult involvement in the activity is analyzed in terms of their typical proximity to the activity, the teaching approaches used, and the availability of adult(s) to support the child's engagement in the activity.

The Assessment of Peer Relations (APR; Guralnick, 1992) focuses on social strategies used by preschool children (ages three to five) within social tasks. Information is obtained through observations focused on the nature of the child's interactions with peers and used to develop a peer intervention program. The first of three major sections of the APR includes assessments of the general level of a child's peer-related social interactions, foundational processes, and developmental issues. In the general or overview portion, the observer rates the child using a four-point scale from rarely to almost always on items related to involvement and group play, purposes of initiations to peers and success of initiations. The focus is on the extent to which a child plays with others, and the duration and complexity of peer interactions. Foundational processes relate to the child's emotional regulation and shared understanding.

The same four-point scale is used to assess the child on emotional regulation and shared understanding. Sample items from the overview and foundational processes are presented in Figure 10–9. The third portion of the first section of the APR addresses developmental issues, including a brief summary of the child's status in language, cognitive, affective, and motor development, other relevant characteristics (e.g., sensory impairments), and the child's developmental strengths. The examiner then identifies any areas of concern or strength that warrant special consideration and uses the Peer Intervention Program (Guralnick, nd) to begin planning the involvement phase of intervention. This involves conducting an inventory of resources of preferred peers, preferred activities and materials, classroom organization factors, and adult-organized play strategies, including degree of initial structure, level of adult participation, and use of peers.

The second section of the APR looks at peer group entry, conflict resolution, and maintaining play. The observer analyzes a child's efforts to enter peer groups, observing the extent the child uses harmonious strategies initially to gain entry (e.g., waiting for an opportunity, gaining attention of a peer), possible reasons for failed attempts to enter a group (e.g., trying to redirect peers' activity), outcomes of attempts (e.g., accepted, ignored), and strategies used during second efforts. Conflict resolution includes identifying the reasons the child experiences conflict (e.g., possessions, space, social rules) and the role played by the child in the conflict (initiator/ recipient). The observer also notes reactions to and from the child, looking for patterns of behavior. For example, one child might consistently use hitting as a strategy to resolve conflicts while another withdraws from conflicts. The child's ability to maintain group play, the third element of this section, involves analyzing the role and activity structure strategies used by the child (e.g., remains within theme or role of play activity) and management strategies used by the child (e.g., tries to escalate play, making reasonable requests to increase its interest or complexity).

Throughout the observations, the observer also looks for elements of the child's higher order and social-cognitive processes, which comprises the third section of the APR. Higher order processes are indicated when a child can recognize the social task before him, then organize, integrate, and sequence his behaviors for the task. Social-cognitive processes involve attending to and correctly interpreting relevant social information, thinking of possible strategies to try, evaluating the specific circumstances of the social situation, and selecting and applying an appropriate strategy. Patterns of behavior are explored across the tasks of peer group entry, conflict resolution, and maintaining play.

Closing Thoughts

The potential influence of environments on a young child's growth and development within these settings

FIGURE 10-9 Sample Items from the Assessment of Peer Relations

Section I	
Overview	
Involvement	Plays near others using similar toys
	Engages in simple brief responses or exchanges
Purpose of Initiations	Gain attention of others
	Propose joint activities
Success of Initiations	Peers acknowledge or comply with requests for action
Foundation Processes	
Emotional Regulation	Plays with considerable enthusiasm and expressiveness
	Hovers around others in play, vacillating between approaching and withdrawing
Shared Understanding	
Social Rules	Appropriately varies style of interacting depending upon whether peer is unfamiliar or familiar
Pretend Play Complexity and Diversity	Engages in organized, coherent, and elaborated pretend play sequences
Everyday Events	Scripts of everyday events (e.g., lunch, circle time) have a well-developed sequential character

is the focus of our interest in this chapter. The complexity of environmental influences on child development is evident. The social and economic resources available to a child are set by family and community membership. The educational and employment opportunities of the parents are directly influenced by the nature of the community in which they live and broad government policies. The reciprocal relationships between the many direct and indirect components of a young child's environment force us to acknowledge the complicated context in which we strive to understand and positively influence a child's development. Just as we cannot assess a child meaningfully without acknowledging her context, we cannot assess environments without due consideration of the multiple layers of reciprocal influence from homes, communities, and schools as well as the environmental specificity needed by individual children.

Environments do influence behavior and the results of those influences are cumulative in nature. Most children are exposed to both risk and opportunity factors that directly and indirectly influence their development. When the balance of risk and opportunity factors tilts to the risk side for an individual child, professionals must keep these conditions as an integral part of conclusion drawn from an assessment. If the child is isolated from his context in the assessment process, the diagnostic label that he is likely to acquire can further separate us from understanding the individual before us.

For Your Consideration

1. How do parents and teachers foster both the internalization and externalization of culture?

2. In what ways does the social climate within the home impact the development of young children?

3. How should professionals in early childhood special education approach the assessment of parent-child interactions?

4. How can we facilitate positive community experiences for children with disabilities and their families?

5. What features of early childhood settings do we have control over and how do these features influence child behavior?

CYBERSOURCES

Check out the following Web sites for more information related to the ideas presented in this chapter.

Environment Rating Scales, Frank Porter Graham Child Development Center

http://www.fpg.unc.edu/~ecers/

National Center for Family Literacy

http://www.famlit.org/

National Institute for Urban School Improvement

http://www.edc.org/urban/

 For additional resources on assessment, visit us on-line at www.earlychilded.delmar.com

CHAPTER 11

Context-Based Assessment Cases: Infants and Toddlers

Chapter Overview

Stories of the assessment of three infants and toddlers and their families are told in this chapter. The characters described do not represent specific persons known to me, but rather represent a collage of many children and families. Where the families live is relevant to the extent that it defines part of the context for the child and family. The stories illustrate a cross-section of issues and concerns associated with assessment of birth to three-year-olds and their families. Factors such as socioeconomic level of the family, nature and severity of disability, resources within the community, patterns of family life, educational levels of parents, and age of the child vary across the cases. The combinations of these factors present in the stories just begin to show the individuality of each child and family; therefore, the need for assessment always must be context-based.

Ericca

Ericca is nine months old. She lives with her mother, grandmother, and two uncles in a government-subsidized apartment located on the east side of a large midwestern city. Ericca was born six weeks premature and stayed in the hospital neonatal intensive care unit for two months following her birth. When the hospital released Ericca, the staff gave her mother information about early intervention services and suggested that she contact a service coordination program in the city for developmental follow-ups.

Juliana, an enthusiastic young mother, immediately followed up on this suggestion. Gina Barton, a member of the staff, made a home visit to Ericca and Juliana. She completed a developmental screen of Ericca, who was then three and one-half months old, using the Early Learning Accomplishment Profile (E-LAP). Considering how young the child was chronologically, and that she had an adjusted age of only one and one-half months, it was not surprising that Ericca did not appear eligible for services as developmentally delayed. Although Juliana reported that she was having some difficulty feeding Ericca, there were not sufficient symptoms or specific motor behaviors to diagnose any motor impairment or brain injury resulting from the premature birth. Well-child checkups were already available to Ericca through the local health department. The service coordinator explained the results of her screening and the meaning of chronological age and adjusted age to Juliana, and indicated that she would like to reevaluate Ericca in six months, when the child would be nine months old. She also gave Juliana developmental questionnaires from the Ages and Stages Questionnaire for two months and four months and asked her to complete them over the next week and return them to her by mail. She gave her a stamped self-addressed envelope for the return.

Gina Barton, whose background is in early childhood special education, documented her visit to Ericca's home and the results of the developmental screening. She coded the file so she would be prompted to contact the family about the reassessment if she did not hear from them within the designated six months. She was currently carrying a caseload of 57 families, including 27 children who would turn three within the next six months and need transition planning during that time. It would be easy for her to forget Ericca without this reminder,

and she was not confident that Juliana would contact her again, even if the child were experiencing some developmental problems.

Juliana was 17 years old and had little knowledge of infant development. Her reading skills were limited and she seemed hesitant when given the developmental questionnaires to complete. Gina was wishing that she had taken the time to go over the questionnaires during the home visit. Although Juliana expressed a fierce determination to take care of Ericca, it seemed that her skills in child care had yet to be developed.

Six months later, when the prompt from Ericca's file appeared, Gina had to review the case before she could clearly recall the child or her mother. She was able to remember Ericca and Juliana, and gave the case high priority for follow-up. When she called the apartment, Juliana was not available. Gina explained to Ericca's grandmother, Sarah, who she was and why she was calling. Sarah said that Juliana and Ericca were still living with her and that she was providing child care for Ericca part time. Sarah explained that two weeks ago, Juliana and Ericca began participating in an Even Start program. In the mornings Ericca was attending an early childhood education program while Juliana took basic adult education and parenting classes through an Even Start program. Gina debated to herself quickly about whether to schedule the appointment for Ericca through Sarah, but decided to ask that Juliana return her call instead. Juliana was the child's mother, even if she had just turned 18, and Gina was afraid that the cost would be high in terms of her relationship with Juliana if she side-stepped her. The grandmother's tone as she took the message was not encouraging, but Gina knew that she had to give Ericca's mother proper courtesy even though the grandmother was probably serving as the mother figure for Ericca in their multigenerational household. As she returned the file to the "needs follow-up" pile on her desk, she realized that she had never received the developmental questionnaires that she had left with Juliana. Now she had to decide how long to wait to hear from Juliana before calling again.

A few days later Gina received a call from Sarah about scheduling an evaluation for Ericca. Sarah explained that she had spoken with Juliana about her follow-up call and her daughter had asked that she make the arrangements since she was in classes or at work all day. Gina had no way to confirm the grandmother's information, but agreed to schedule another evaluation of Ericca. The appointment was arranged for late morning so Juliana could join them for at least some of the visit on her lunch break between the Even Start program and work. By this time, Ericca was 10 months old. Gina began with the Ages and Stages Questionnaires for 6 and 9 months. She went over these checklists with Sarah and realized that Ericca seemed to be well below expected development. Using the context-based assessment model outlined in chapter 2, Gina, Sarah, and Juliana planned the assessment of Ericca. The results of this planning are shown in Figure 11–1.

The primary questions to be considered in this assessment of Ericca were:

1. How can we get Ericca to eat more and stop spitting up so much?
2. How can we get Ericca to sit up and start playing with toys more?
3. What are Ericca's current developmental levels and what skills are beginning to emerge in all developmental areas?

Sarah and Juliana agreed that Ericca was a happy child who smiled frequently and seemed to enjoy the attention of her young uncles who would play with her after school. Therefore, it was hard for them to believe that anything serious was wrong with her. However, Sarah realized that the infant's inability to gain weight or eat anything but formula was becoming a big problem. She realized that Ericca seemed to be falling behind in her development and was anxious to find out why. She had taken her to the health department for several well-baby checkups. Initially, the health department staff talked about Ericca's prematurity and how they would use her "adjusted age" to understand her development. They had explained to Sarah and Juliana that the eight weeks that Ericca did not have developing in the womb could be a possible explanation for some of her slowness in development. Recently, they became more concerned since Ericca was still more resistant than typical to eat semisolid foods. Sarah and Juliana were not particularly troubled by this behavior as other children they knew had relied primarily on bottle-feeding well past their first birthdays. However, they were concerned that Ericca was still spitting up and unable to gain weight. They had been told that the spitting up should improve after she began standing, but they were still waiting for her to begin standing. It was beginning to look like this might never happen—she was not even sitting yet.

The service coordinator assured Sarah and Juliana that the feeding issues would be the top priority for the evaluation. Ericca's poor weight gain, spitting up problems, and intolerance of any textured foods all seemed to indicate that she was having significant eating difficulties. She would arrange for a feeding evaluation by a speech pathologist. The service coordinator working with the Johns also wanted them to follow up on the health department recommendation that a neurological examination be completed. Ericca's prematurity, coupled with her eating problems and apparent delays in motor development and play behaviors were reasons for this recommendation.

Gina talked with Sarah and Juliana about how best to answer the other two questions regarding Ericca's development. She explained that the questions could be addressed somewhat through an arena transdisciplinary play-based assessment that would include a physical therapist, an early interventionist, and the same speech pathologist who would conduct the feeding evaluation. The physical therapist might also need to conduct a more thorough individual evaluation of Ericca, using a standardized assessment, such as the Peabody Motor Development Scales. However, they would need a doctor's referral before the therapist could provide any therapy recommended as a result of this evaluation. Once again Gina stressed their need to take Ericca to a neurologist. She also explained that additional standardized testing of her developmental levels would be needed to determine if Ericca was eligible for services due to a developmental delay.

Findings

The feeding evaluation included interviews with Sarah and Juliana and an observation of each of them feeding Ericca. The speech pathologist asked both Sarah and Juliana to describe Ericca's eating patterns and habits. Both essentially indicate the same behaviors during feeding time. Ericca is eager and almost too excited when presented with the bottle. She has difficulty getting started, but is able to suck with some success once she gets going. However, it seems to be exhausting for her and frequent breaks are needed. Each time she has to reestablish the sucking process. After feeding, they hold her upright on the shoulder and gently pat her back. They maintain her in this position while they either walk around or remain seated. They report that regardless of how much Ericca has eaten, she typically spits up large

FIGURE 11–1 Context-Based Assessment Identification Sheet

Ericca Johns

								Premature?
Today's date	Yr.	2003	Mo. 04	Day 01				Yes ☒ No ☐
Birth date	Yr.	2002	Mo. 05	Day 05				Number of weeks 8
	Age	Yrs. 0	Mo. 10	Days 27		Adjusted age	Yrs. 0	Mo. 08 Days 27

Child's name _Ericca_

Primary adult contact _Sarah_

Relationship to child _grandmother_

Work phone _____ Home phone _____

Street address _____

City, State, Zip _____

E-mail _NA_ FAX _NA_

Overall health of child:
Failing to gain weight; health department staff concerned about development and have suggested neurological exam, but it has not yet been scheduled

Mother:

Name _Juliana_

Street address _____

City, State, Zip Code _____

Phone _____

Living with child? ☒ Yes ☐ No

Father:

Name _Tennell_

Street address _____

City, State, Zip Code _____

Phone _____

Living with child? ☐ Yes ☒ No

Others in home:

Names	Ages	Relationship
Jamil	_15_	_uncle_
Terrance	_13_	_uncle_
Lloyd	_adult_	_Sarah's partner_
_____	_____	_____

Other relevant information:
Juliana is participating in Even Start program that involves classes 5 days a week, and grandmother is serving as primary contact with the mother's consent

FIGURE 11-1 (Continued)

Identifying Family Resources, Priorities, and Concerns

What are the priorities and primary areas of concern related to the child for the family?	What efforts have already been made to address these concerns?
Not yet sitting up	*Family plays with her and encourages her to sit up, but no improvement*
Has difficulty taking a bottle; spits up after taking bottle	*Seems hungry, cries frequently, changed formula, but still spitting up*
Has trouble holding and playing with toys	*Family tries to play with her, but she is not able to reach and grasp*

What resources are available to assist the family in addressing these priorities and concerns?

Family already has medical services through government-funded insurance, so neurological exam can be scheduled; Even Start program providing Juliana with education and parenting skills; early childhood education also available through Even Start

(continued)

237

FIGURE 11–1 Context-Based Assessment Identification Sheet (Continued)

Structuring the Assessment

Primary Questions	Assessment Techniques
1. *How can we get Ericca to eat more and stop spitting up so much?*	1. *Schedule neurological exam; arrange oral-motor feeding assessment by speech-language pathologist, including in-home observation of feeding*
2. *How can we get Ericca to sit up and start playing with toys?*	2. *Schedule motor evaluation by physical therapist; conduct play-based assessment to determine Ericca's interest in and reactions to play opportunities (e.g., visual tracking of toys and sounds, attempts to reach and grasp)*
3. *What are Ericca's current developmental levels and what skills are beginning to emerge in all developmental areas?*	3. *Use play-based assessment to determine developmental skills, emerging skills, interactive style between parent and child; use Bayley Scales of Infant Development to determine eligibility for services*
4.	4.
5.	5.
6.	6.

amounts of the formula she has just eaten. They described this "spitting up" as forceful, almost violent in nature. The pathologist explained to them that this is known as projectile vomiting. Several months ago, at the urging of health department staff, they tried to get Ericca to eat highly diluted baby cereals. Her resistance to this textured food was far more extreme than Sarah had seen with any other infant. Ericca gagged, seemed to pull away, and her mouth gripped the spoon and she appeared unable to release it. After several other efforts failed, they quit trying to entice her to eat cereal. They have also offered her finger foods, such as crackers and dry cereal, but she does not eat any of these things. Sarah did comment that the feedings seem to go best when the apartment is quiet, when just she and Ericca are at home.

A transdisciplinary play-based assessment was conducted. The session included Gina, the speech therapist, an early intervention specialist, a physical therapist, Sarah, and Juliana. The early intervention specialist served as the facilitator while others watched and prompted her during the process. Ericca was initially placed on the floor in a prone position. Although she could manage to lift her head, it seemed to take most of her energy to maintain this position. She did not have the freedom to shift her weight to one or the other elbow to free the other hand for reaching and exploring toys that were placed on the floor in front of her. She was able to roll from a prone position to a supine position. While Ericca was prone, the interventionist presented a variety of colorful toys, including some that made noise. Ericca would turn her head to the toys as they were presented. She would smile and laugh along with the interventionist as she reached for the toys. Her arm would fully extend and move in a jerky fashion toward the object. The quality of her reach prevented her from actually retrieving the desired object unless the interventionist placed it in her hand. Then she was not able to maintain a grasp of the toy. It would fall from her hands and Ericca seemed to forget about the toy rather than continuing to pursue it. When Juliana joined Ericca, she was asked to place Ericca in her lap as she sat cross-legged on the floor. Ericca's legs flexed easily over Juliana's crossed legs and her bottom tucked comfortably into a snug fit as she leaned back against her mother's trunk. In this position, the interventionist faced Ericca and played with a ring-stack toy while Ericca watched. Then the interventionist asked Juliana to take over the "playing" while she observed Ericca's interest in and attempts to in-

teract with the toy. Ericca watched and listened to her mother while she placed the rings on the base in the proper order. When she began reaching out to take one of the rings in her own hand, the quality of her arm control was far better than it had been in the prone position. The arm remained partially flexed as her mother assisted her by bringing the ring within easy reach. She held her hand over Ericca's to keep the ring from dropping and used her other hand to bring the base in close so Ericca could "place" the ring on the base. Ericca enjoyed "placing" several of the rings on the base in this fashion with her mother's assistance. Later in the assessment, an infant seat was used for positioning Ericca. In this seat, she was at a gentle angle. However, her arms and legs returned to a more extended posture and she lost some of the control that she had achieved while sitting with her mother in a flexed position.

Ericca's motor delays would interfere with her performance on a standardized developmental assessment of children within her age range, therefore, the play-based assessment was also used as an opportunity to explore her development in other areas. When properly positioned, Ericca established eye contact with the examiner and visually tracked a variety of rattles and small toys. She would turn her head to orient to sounds when they were made outside of her visual range. When a rattle or small toy was placed in her hand, she would show excitement and attempt to bring the object to her mouth. While seated in her mother's lap she grasped and banged objects that were put in her hands. She maintained visual contact with the object, occasionally looking up to her mother with a smile. Thus, it became evident that Ericca wanted to engage in exploratory and sensorimotor play, but has some physical limitations that restrict her. Her play skills correspond with the three- to six-month focus on actions performed on objects and the six- to nine-month exploration of object characteristics.

Throughout the play session and other times, Ericca did imitate vocalizations made by her mother, grandmother, and uncles. She smiled and imitated simple actions, such as waving, or patting a doll, but had difficulty reaching and grasping objects independently. These behaviors indicate that Ericca has achieved imitation skills associated with six- to nine-month levels. She did not attempt to imitate sounds, gestures, or behaviors that were new to her during the assessment. She demonstrated object permanence by attempting to remove a small cloth from a hidden toy, visually tracked objects, and showed the ability to anticipate where an object would appear from after it disappeared. These skills also represent a six- to nine-month level.

Ericca showed interest as adults made toys spin, make noise, or fit into holes. She would explore the objects and make some attempts to achieve the same results that she had seen demonstrated by the adult. However, she did not persist in her exploration when these initial efforts were unsuccessful; rather, she would seek adult help in getting the toy to perform the action again. There might be a link between her apparent physical limitations and the efforts she seems willing to put forth to explore a complex object. A child nine months and older would typically show more persistence in the pursuit of complex objects than was seen from Ericca.

Ericca clearly showed a distinction between her mother and others involved in the assessment. Because of her strong preference for her mother, Juliana remained in the assessment area with her throughout the session. Ericca was willing to draw her attention to others and play with them while her mother remained nearby. She would frequently look in her mother's direction, seeming to make sure her mother was watching, then return to her play. She also became more animated while playing directly with her mother. These behaviors indicate that she is progressing at age level in attachment and separation development.

Although no peer was used in the play-based assessment, Juliana was able to report on Ericca's behavior at the Even Start early childhood education program. The schedule includes a 30-minute period when the mothers who were taking classes join their children for some parent-child interactive time. For the infants and toddlers, these sessions were unstructured, allowing the mothers and children to interact spontaneously on the floor as the children played. Ericca noted that Juliana was not moving as much as the others, who are crawling and pulling to a stand. However, she does appear to be aware of the others, watching them as they move about the room. Although her physical delays put her at risk to fall behind socially, she appears to be within expectations for her age at the present time.

Ericca has been making sounds and babbling. She uses full-body movements and general excitement to express herself, when either distressed or happy. The result sometimes is a shift into reflexive patterns that interfere with her voluntary movement. She then ap-

pears to get distracted from her original communicative intention, as the reflexive pattern takes over. When "bebby" was spoken in reference to her favorite teddy bear, Ericca would turn in the direction it had been and look around for it, indicating that she understood that word represented her teddy bear. When she was not playing directly with her mother, she frequently "communicated" with her through eye contact, gestures, and sounds. The speech therapist will explore the specific sounds she is making as part of an ongoing monitoring of communication and language development as a part of the feeding program.

Answering the Assessment Questions

How can we get Ericca to eat more and stop spitting up so much?

The speech therapist explained that Ericca was showing signs that her prematurity might be causing her to have some long-term feeding difficulties. She pointed out the need to have Ericca prepared for feedings and the need to continue trying to keep the feeding times quiet and peaceful for Ericca. The therapist assured Sarah and Juliana that they were trying all the right ways to encourage Ericca to eat, but that she might need some additional approaches. She suggested some gentle rubbing away from the mouth, gradually approaching the mouth shortly before feeding times were to occur. She also described ways to introduce new nonfood textures to Ericca's mouth and oral cavity in a gradual, progressive way. However, these strategies would take time to learn and be modified to Ericca's particular reactions to them. This would mean that ongoing feeding therapy, provided by a speech pathologist, was likely to be needed several times a week.

Ericca's weight gain would also need to be closely monitored. If the problems persisted, it might be necessary to begin feeding Ericca with a gastrointestinal feeding tube (g-tube). This, too, would require training and practice, but Sarah and Juliana could be taught how to manage such a procedure. The speech therapist expressed the need for Ericca to have a neurological examination to determine if brain injury were the cause of the present feeding problems and how extensive and persistent the problems were likely to be. She also encouraged them to see a nutritionist for guidance and suggestions on suitable foods to introduce to her in what forms and to monitor Ericca's weight gain.

How can we get Ericca to sit up and start playing with toys more?

Throughout the play-based assessment Ericca attempted to interact with the adults who played with her. She showed interest in many of the toys that were presented during the assessment. The position in which she was placed contributed to her ability or inability to interact with toys. Her failure to play with toys independently did not appear attributable to a lack of interest in objects or desire to play. Her limited motor skills were interfering with her attempts at even the simplest interactions with objects. A prone position, without the use of a bolster, left her putting all of her energy into achieving and maintaining a position. A supine position or propping in an infant seat offered her a better visual view of the world, but caused her to have poor-quality voluntary muscle control. The best quality of motor control came while Ericca was placed securely in Juliana's lap.

Two recommendations should increase Ericca's ability to play independently. First, she needs to have proper positioning to achieve improved quality of her voluntary movements. Such positioning can include small bolsters or rolled towels for the prone position, soft padding around shoulders and hips for infant seats, and limited use of a wedge for supine positioning. Ericca needs adult assistance right now as she has a strong desire to interact with people and objects. If her caregivers work to bring interesting toys and objects to Ericca in the best possible positions, she will expand her interest in the toys and be more likely to improve her voluntary motor control. The ability of Ericca to achieve independent sitting will come with time. However, a thorough evaluation by the physical therapist is likely to lead to the conclusion that Ericca would achieve this motor skill sooner and in a more appropriate manner if she participates in ongoing physical therapy sessions.

What are Ericca's current developmental levels and what skills are beginning to emerge in all developmental areas?

Although this approach to assessment did not produce any norm-referenced test scores for Ericca, it has given the professionals and family members a clearer picture of Ericca's progress. The primary areas of concern are motor development and feeding. Ericca seems to be developing close to age level in cognition, social-emotional behavior, and communication/language ability. However, her motor and feeding problems make her vulnerable for delays in all of these areas. Generally, Ericca appears to be ready to face the cognitive, social, and communicative tasks before her, if her motor and feeding problems can be addressed. Developmental expectations will increase in both quality and quantity over the next six months. Her young age makes it difficult to define the extent of her vulnerability. Will she be able to persist and problem solve when faced with a complex toy, develop schemes in her play, speak her first words, show a desire to interact with peers, and so forth? We can confirm through this assessment that she is slightly behind, but progressing reasonably in these areas. The absence of independent play seems to be more a factor of the motor limitations than disinterest or cognitive delay. She will need the benefit of physical handling, proper positioning, and therapy to achieve developmental gains across the board.

Tyler

Tyler, a 21-month-old, lives with his aunt and uncle and their two children. Tyler and his parents were involved in an automobile accident that killed his mother and caused significant brain damage to his father. Tyler suffered a closed head injury in spite of having been properly restrained at the time of the wreck. Following the accident, his mother's sister, Anne, immediately agreed to assume responsibility for Tyler. Although his father had survived the crash, he was far too severely injured to care for the child. It was projected that his father would be facing a minimum of several years in rehabilitation and his ability to serve as a responsible parent for the child even at the end of this rehabilitation was unlikely. Both Tyler's maternal and paternal grandparents were available and willing to support Anne and her husband, Ronnie, as they worked to make Tyler a part of their household.

After the wreck, Tyler spent approximately two weeks in a pediatric intensive care unit. During this time Tyler experienced multiple seizures, so he began taking seizure medications that seem to have them under control. In a few weeks, he was transferred to an in-patient rehabilitation facility where he received daily physical, occupational, and speech/language therapy. After approximately two months, Tyler was able to go home with Anne and Ronnie. Their two sons, ages seven and five, made room for Tyler in the three-bedroom home by sharing a bedroom. A special room was set up for Tyler. Medical intervention has continued through weekly physical and occupational therapy sessions at a community rehabilitation center for children. However, Anne is also concerned about his developmental progress and speech development. The therapists referred her to the statewide early intervention system. Carol Jenkins, a service coordinator in her community, worked with Anne to plan the process of determining Tyler's eligibility for services. The beginning of this process is depicted in Figure 11–2.

The primary questions to be considered in Tyler's assessment were:

1. Based on his developmental levels, is Tyler eligible for early intervention services?
2. How can we help Tyler improve his communication and encourage appropriate behavior?
3. Is Tyler progressing in adaptive and functional skills?

Anne knew she had to make Tyler a part of the family, and yet she was afraid of disrupting the routines and schedules that were already established in her home. Although she wanted to do everything possible to help Tyler progress, she had to balance his needs with those of her two sons, who had been already keeping her on the go with their own after-school activities. They were already sacrificing their privacy by agreeing to share a bedroom, so a toddler could have his own room. Her husband Ronnie also understood the responsibility they had to accept Anne's deceased sister's child into their family. He would have expected nothing less if the circumstances had been reversed and his own sons needed a new family. The family was living well on his income and Anne enjoyed being active in school and after-school activities with the boys, and participating in arts-related activities within the community. Tyler's addition to the household would necessitate some changes, both financially and personally, for all of them. Both Anne and Ronnie hoped that Tyler's abilities would prove to be delayed rather than permanently impaired as a result of his head injury. His inability to play independently, almost unintelligible speech, and emotional outbursts were taking its toll on their patience. They approached this assessment with anxiety as well as anticipation.

Tyler was continuing to receive individual speech/language therapy from the rehabilitation center, but the family wanted to know more about day-to-day communicating with Tyler. Although they hoped his speech would become more easily understood, they needed to communicate with him now. The family needed to understand Tyler's communicative intentions and explore possible connections between his frustrations and the emotional outbursts. The outbursts were likely attributable to a combination of the brain injury that he had suffered, the trauma of a change in his life circumstances, his chronological age, and the frustrations he was experiencing in trying to communicate. Improved communication seemed the most likely to offer some immediate possibilities for positive change in his emotional development.

Tyler has been receiving physical and occupational therapy since the accident. Now Anne and Ronnie would like some sense of their responsibilities in helping him gain back functional skills. They are trying to avoid increasing his frustration, while wanting to encourage his independence and skill development. The therapists are doing a good job working with Tyler, and communicate with Anne before and after therapy sessions about the nature of their work with Tyler, yet she still feels uncertain about his physical progress. They agreed to explore this area in more depth as a part of the assessment.

Findings

Because a primary issue for this assessment was the determination of eligibility for early intervention services, the service coordinator recommended that Tyler be given the Bayley Scales of Development-II. A psychologist previously unknown to Tyler or his family administered this test. The mental portion of the scale can be used to compare Tyler's development in cognitive, language, and fine motor areas to other children his age. Although Anne Barlay remained with him during the assessment, his performance during the test administration seemed somewhat erratic. He was hesitant to try the tasks presented to him by the examiner, preferring to seek attention and comfort from Anne. The examiner drew her into the exam by presenting a task to Tyler, followed by guidance to Anne about getting him to attempt the task for her. Anne followed the examiner's lead in this way, enabling them to get an estimate of his current functioning. His cognitive development index was calculated to be 83, placing him at the 35th percentile.

Carol Jenkins observed Tyler in the home setting as he interacted with both his aunt and uncle and the

FIGURE 11–2 Context-Based Assessment Identification Sheet

Tyler Witt

Child's name _Tyler_

Today's date	Yr.	2003	Mo.	10	Day	11
Birth date	Yr.	2002	Mo.	01	Day	15
	Age	Yrs.	1	Mo.	8	Days 27

Premature? Yes ☐ No ☒

Number of weeks _____

Primary adult contact _Anne_

Relationship to child _aunt & legal guardian_

Work phone _____ Home phone _____

Street address _____

City, State, Zip _____

E-mail _abarlay**@***_ FAX _NA_

Adjusted age Yrs. _____ Mo. _____ Days _____

Overall health of child:
Medically stable and doing well since head injury resulting from car wreck; ongoing therapy for physical and behavioral symptoms; seizures controlled with medication; no additional health-related problems

Others in home:

Names	Ages	Relationship
Ronnie	_adult_	_uncle & legal guardian_
Rob	_7_	_cousin_
Terry	_5_	_cousin_
_____	_____	_____
_____	_____	_____

Mother:

Name _deceased_

Street address

_____

City, State, Zip Code

_____

Phone

_____

Living with child? ☐ Yes ☒ No

Father:

Name _Jeff_

Street address

Rehabilitation unit

City, State, Zip Code

_____

Phone

_____

Living with child? ☐ Yes ☒ No

Other relevant information:
Maternal grandparents are supportive and helpful with Tyler, and with Rob and Terry as the older boys adjust to their new "brother"; maternal grandparents trying to help with Tyler as well, but are putting most of their energy into supporting Tyler's father as he remains in rehabilitation

(continued)

FIGURE 11–2 Context-Based Assessment Identification Sheet (Continued)

Identifying Family Resources, Priorities, and Concerns

What are the priorities and primary areas of concern related to the child for the family?	What efforts have already been made to address these concerns?
Developmental progress for Tyler	Are just getting started and have scheduled this assessment
Maintaining family routines and fitting Tyler into them	Struggling to maintain activities and schedules that were in place, but adding a third child with many needed appointments hard
Communication and speech development for Tyler	Has been receiving speech therapy through rehabilitation unit; family working to become familiar with Tyler's speech, but still cannot understand most of what he is trying to say

What resources are available to assist the family in addressing these priorities and concerns?

Insurance coverage from accident will cover all therapy needs for Tyler; additional support for other related family needs, such as family counseling, transportation for Tyler's appointments, and so forth, are being negotiated with insurance company

FIGURE 11-2 (Continued)

Structuring the Assessment

Primary Questions	Assessment Techniques
1. Based on his developmental levels, is Tyler eligible for early intervention services?	1. Use of Bayley Developmental Scales
2. How can we help Tyler improve his speech skills and encourage appropriate behavior?	2. Observations and play-based assessment; analysis of functional outcomes of emotional outbursts and apparent communicative intentions with children and adults; interview Anne and Ronnie using the Vineland Social-Emotional Early Childhood Scales
3. Is Tyler progressing in gross and fine motor skills?	3. Use Pediatric Evaluation of Disability Inventory with assistance from physical and occupational therapists who are currently treating Tyler
4.	4.
5.	5.
6.	6.

two boys. She arranged these observations to cut across a variety of typical activities for toddlers in their homes, including unstructured indoor and outdoor play with adults and children, meals, dressing, and transitions to the car. She also interviewed Carol and Ronnie, using the Vineland Social-Emotional Early Childhood Scales (SEEC) to structure the interview.

Although much of his speech is unintelligible, Tyler is highly vocal. He is producing sounds and speech that he clearly intends to as communication. He is active, using gestures, sounds, shrieks, tugging, and animation in his efforts to communicate. These efforts at communication are present both during informal periods of play and during more structured routines and activities. Anne and Ronnie were particularly careful to respond as best as possible to Tyler's efforts at communication. When it was not critical that they understood the specific words, as in many casual play moments, they would respond with words and actions in ways that seemed consistent with his other signals (e.g., they might say "oh, you want to move the cow into the barn" after his actions seemed to indicate these intentions). The boys are not as skilled in reading his intentions and might be more tempted to play as they preferred than to struggle to understand and defer to their new brother. However, they certainly made some efforts and have learned to notice when Tyler's frustration level would be approaching explosion. If some brief efforts to redirect his attention away from the frustration were failing, both boys had learned to clear the area and warn the nearest parent that Tyler was upset. This could mean that objects would be thrown, book pages torn, toys scattered, and the approaching parent might have to take a few blows before getting a grip on Tyler's legs or arms.

Out of seven 30-minute observations of informal play between Rob, Terry, or both, outbursts of this intensity occurred three times. Anne or Ronnie would come as quickly as possible, secure Tyler as best he or she could in a cuddling position that prevented his further kicking or hitting, and hold him using soft words and a slight rocking motion until he calmed down. The calming could take up to 20 minutes, and sometimes was simply a matter of Tyler's falling into an exhausted sleep. When the parents' attentions were needed elsewhere (e.g., another child, food preparation, preparing to leave the house), they reported that these outbursts were particularly troublesome. Carol did not witness an outburst of this

strength when either Anne or Ronnie were included in the play, although both report that it does happen to them if they fail to notice the warning signs, such as increased shrieking coupled with fewer speech sounds, and eye gaze that shifts to a glare. Sometimes it also seems to them that once Tyler is headed toward such an outburst, nothing can stop it.

Tyler's behavior generally indicates that his receptive skills are developing typically. He heads to the bathroom and gets his favorite bath toys when Anne indicates that it is bath time. Similar anticipatory behaviors are seen for all the routines and activities that Tyler knows. He dislikes car travel and becomes wary when he sees signs that an outing might be coming. Tyler will cling to Anne and whine when he sees her getting ready for a trip in the car. She has learned to avoid saying anything about going out until the last possible minute. When Rob and Terry are in the car, they sit near Tyler's car seat and try to keep him reasonably tolerant of the car ride. When it is just Anne and Tyler, he is by himself in the back seat. He cries, but no longer throws the toys intended to distract him or kick and punch the air. On trips over 10 minutes without anyone else in the back seat, he often cries himself to sleep.

Based on the responses from Anne and Ronnie, Tyler's scores on the Social Emotional Early Childhood Scale are shown in Table 11–1. These scores are consistent with the behavioral observations of Tyler. The fact that he is able to score at the 1-1 age equivalency in interpersonal relationships after the trauma he has experienced over the past few months is a promising sign of his adaptability and potential to continue improving in his social-emotional adjustment.

This assessment was intended to give Anne and Ronnie a better sense of Tyler's functional abilities and how much assistance they should continue to offer him in activities of daily living. Carol Jenkins chose to use the Pediatric Evaluation of Disability Inventory in an interview format with Anne. They hoped that the interview process and inventory content would help answer some of the questions facing Anne and Ronnie. The inventory includes a measure of self-care, mobility, and social function according to functional skills and the degree of caregiver assistance required. The scores obtained for Tyler on these six scales are presented in Table 11–2. In the area of self-care, they explored eating, grooming, bathing, dressing, and toileting skills. Tyler is quickly regaining his interest in and tolerance of many food textures, and is able to eat finger foods

TABLE 11–1 Tyler's Scores on the Social Emotional Early Childhood Scale

	Standard Score	90% Confidence Interval	Percentile Rank	90% Confidence Interval Percentiles	Stanine	Age Equivalent
Interpersonal relationships	79	68–90	8	1–25	2	1–1
Play and leisure time	60	49–71	.4	0–3	1	0–9
Coping skills*						
Composite	63		1			

*Tyler was too young to be tested in this category.

TABLE 11–2 Pediatric Evaluation of Disability Inventory Scores for Tyler

Domain		Raw Score	Normative Standard Score	Standard Error	Scaled Score	Standard Error
Self-care	Functional skills	21	38.9	3.3	42.0	1.8
Mobility	Functional skills	18	18.9	3.2	40.3	2.3
Social function	Functional skills	24	44.2	3.3	45.0	1.2
Self-care	Caregiver assistance	8	52.3	5.2	39.3	4.6
Mobility	Caregiver assistance	11	34.7	4.7	44.3	4.1
Social function	Caregiver assistance	4	43.1	5.2	31.6	6.9

independently. He has some difficulty using a spoon and makes only the briefest attempts at using a fork before reverting back to his fingers. He enjoys using a knife with a character from TV on the handle, spreading soft textures such as jelly or butter after Anne has placed some on crackers or bread. He needs help holding the cracker, but they seem to be inventing a way to "catch" it in the corner of a little tray so he can do this with less help. His grooming skills seem to have been slowed as a result of the accident. Although he does not usually resist grooming efforts by Anne or Ronnie, Tyler is not participating in these activities as much as typically seen at his age. It is likely they hold less motivation for him than does the development of eating skills. Dressing is also an area in which Tyler has fallen behind. However, he can remove socks, shoes, and even short pants with an elastic waist. He is cooperative, and attempts to hold his arms in the proper positions for dressing, but has a hard time pushing his arms through sleeves or getting his legs into pants without Anne reaching through the sleeve or pant leg to retrieve the arm or leg.

Tyler is still working to regain the mobility skills he once had. He can sit without support and has reestablished creeping, crawling, and scooting movement. He does attempt to pull-to-stand, but has not yet been consistently successful. He has begun working his way up and down the stairs. Rather than discouraging this, the family is working to teach him safe ways to get up and down the stairs. When he needs to travel more than a few feet, he tries to get attention first by raising his arms and shouting. If this is not noticed quickly, the shouting changes to shrieks and distressed waving of the arms. When placed in a walker, he is able to push off and move greater distances with more independence. However, Anne is concerned that the availability and dependence on the walker might reduce his motivation to regain the ability to walk. She does use it outdoors on the patio area, so Tyler can have some independent movement and she can play with the older boys without having to carry him. The issues that arose on the social function scale were similar to those explored earlier regarding communication and behavioral concerns. His comprehension of words, efforts to communicate, quick frustrations, and inability to problem solve were patterns that were evident.

Answering the Assessment Questions

Based on his developmental levels, is Tyler eligible for early intervention services?

Based on Tyler's performance on the Bayley and the SEEC, he is eligible for early intervention services. He is well below the state eligibility criteria, set at a 40 percent delay in one developmental area or a 25 percent delay in two areas.

How can we help Tyler improve his communication and encourage appropriate behavior?

Tyler can recognize many objects and toys in the home, as evident during his play: he points to them and says the names. However, his speech would be almost impossible to understand without the actual objects to help a listener recognize his sounds. This ability to recognize objects, combined with the fact that Tyler is still working hard to produce speech, can

offer guidance in increasing his functional communication within the home setting. The family can hold up and point to objects when they are communicating with Tyler and encourage him to do the same when he is speaking. They can also begin matching photographs to common objects within the home so that these photographs gradually replace the objects themselves. Each family member can have a set of photos to use when speaking so that it becomes a routine within the household.

Although this intervention should lead to improvement in Tyler's functional communication, it will not eliminate developmentally appropriate tantrums or the possible behavioral outcomes of brain damage. The Barlays will likely want to have ongoing counseling available to explore the best approaches to reducing Tyler's tantrums, but their current efforts to calm him through holding, rocking, and soothing words seem appropriate while he is still recovering from multiple traumas in his life, including the death of his mother and loss of his father as a presence in his daily life. The time commitment to this process is a necessary part of bringing him into a new home with new relationships to establish. Gradually, the Barlays can make the transition to trying the parenting strategies they used when Rob and Terry were having toddler tantrums.

Is Tyler progressing in adaptive and functional skills?

It appears that Tyler is regaining functional skills that are associated with high motivations for him. Particularly skills in eating and mobility are reappearing, whereas progress in grooming skills seems less apparent. Anne and Ronnie can make decisions now with an understanding of Tyler's interests in mind. They can keep their expectations balanced so Tyler is not exposed to high levels of frustration, while being given the freedom to regain old skills that he is motivated to acquire. The area of grooming might be one in which they continue to provide him more assistance, while exploring ways to increase his motivation to progress in this area as well. For example, to increase his efforts in pushing his arm through a sleeve, a favorite toy might be waiting for his hand at the other end of the sleeve. The eating skill progression can continue along normal paths, although they might want to continue accepting his use of finger feeding until he has better hand and grasp control. The use of a spoon and fork need not be a top priority while Tyler works to regain motor control, mobility, and communication skills.

Matt

Due to medical complications associated with her blood pressure, it became necessary to induce labor for Melissa 10 days before she was due to have her second child. When Matt was born, she knew immediately that his blue color was not normal. For what seemed to her to be an extraordinarily long time, the doctors worked with the infant while she had no idea of what was happening. Eventually, they explained that the baby was having difficulty breathing and they needed to call in an ear, nose, and throat specialist. After this examination found no structural cause for the breathing problem, a heart specialist was called in, who quickly confirmed that there was a problem with Matt's heart. He recommended that the child be sent to the heart center at Premier Medical Center, over 200 miles away, to see if there was any hope for the child. The infant's departure was treated as a final good-bye for Clay and Melissa, who were told that might be the last time they would see the child alive. In the meantime, Melissa was having problems of her own. Difficulties during the delivery had necessitated a Caesarean section delivery. Further complications required that she have an immediate complete hysterectomy. Clay drove to Premier Medical Center while Matt was transported by plane. Clay arrived shortly after the plane and hoped for the best while his newborn son faced surgery and his wife remained back at the hospital recovering from her own surgeries. Clay, a police officer who worked hard and had received several promotions, had the flexibility to take time off from work to be with his new son without undue concern for his job, through which the family had excellent insurance benefits.

Melissa and Clay were fortunate to live close to their own hometown and have extended family members in the area. Clay's parents were caring for Alex, their five-year-old son, during the delivery. They and Melissa's sister provided the care for him over the next several days while Clay attended to Matt out of town and Melissa recovered from surgery in the local hospital. Melissa's physician had experienced his own personal trauma a few years previously when his daughter nearly died in a car accident. Because he had felt the pain of a parent whose child was near death, he released Melissa the second day following her surgeries to travel. Her father ran her by her house to prepare quickly for the trip to reunite her with her husband and new son. Within five minutes of being home, five different friends and family members had each given her $100. Although the costs associated with the treatment that Matt was and would be receiving had not really been on Melissa's mind, these financial gestures of support and goodwill overwhelmed her. She headed off to Premier Medical Center with her father and Alex, knowing that many people were supporting them and hoping for the best for their youngest child. Before their crisis ended, the police department alone gave Melissa and Clay $2,500 to help offset the costs of Matt's medical care.

Matt did survive. His heart problems are serious and will require numerous additional surgeries over the next two years. Genetic testing has revealed that the cause of his heart problems is the absence of a portion of the 22nd chromosome. Melissa and Clay declined to undergo genetic analysis primarily because of the motives of the physicians. They seemed eager to perform these tests for research-related rather than treatment-oriented reasons. However, their brothers and sisters, who might anticipate becoming parents in the future, and their other child will all likely have genetic screening as needed sometime in the future.

The family eventually returned home. Although there would be multiple additional surgeries needed in the future, they finally had their three-month-old home. They have survived well over another year and have settled into routines. Matt's medical problems are never far from Melissa's mind as she goes about the routines of getting Alex off to school, maintaining the household, returning to work as a part-time parent trainer in an early intervention program, and playing with Matt. Although she worries about his developmental progress, she is far more concerned about his ability to survive the major surgeries that she knows the child is still facing. However, she realizes that as an 18-month-old Matt is lagging in his language development as well as his motor skills. She has decided to contact the early intervention service coordinator and update the developmental assessment of Matt and consider the possibility of placing him in some type of group-based early intervention program. The initial planning is outlined in Figure 11–3.

The primary questions to be considered in this assessment of Matt are:

1. What can be done to increase Matt's communication and speech development?
2. What are Matt's current developmental levels of functioning?
3. What is the best approach to increase Matt's motor development?

FIGURE 11–3 Context-Based Assessment Identification Sheet

Matt Collier

Child's name _Matt_

Primary adult contact _Melissa_

Relationship to child _mother_

	Yr.	Mo.	Day
Today's date	2003	03	22
Birth date	2001	09	17

Age	Yrs.	Mo.	Days
	1	06	05

Adjusted age Yrs. _____ Mo. _____ Days _____

Premature? Yes ☐ No ☒

Number of weeks _____

Work phone _____ Home phone _____

Street address _____

City, State, Zip _____

E-mail _mcollierxx@***_ FAX _____

Overall health of child:
Has serious heart condition linked to genetic problem—Trisomy 22; had emergency heart surgery a few hours after birth and will likely need additional surgery several times in the next three years

Mother:

Name _Melissa_

Street address _____

City, State, Zip Code _____

Phone _____

Living with child? ☒ Yes ☐ No

Father:

Name _Clay_

Street address _____

City, State, Zip Code _____

Phone _____

Living with child? ☒ Yes ☐ No

Others in home:

Names	Ages	Relationship
Alex	_7_	_brother_

Other relevant information:
Mother was working part time as a parent trainer in an early intervention program with flexible hours and schedule when Matt was born; she has worked only limited evening hours since then

FIGURE 11–3 (Continued)

Identifying Family Resources, Priorities, and Concerns

What are the priorities and primary areas of concern related to the child for the family?	What efforts have already been made to address these concerns?
Matt is not yet talking	All family members, including grandparents and other extended family, speak to and encourage Matt to speak; he has very limited vocalizations, primarily using gestures, grunts and simple sounds, and crying as means to having needs met; he does laugh and enjoy playing with family members
Matt is not yet pulling to stand or walking	Family members also encourage Matt to move about, but he still relies on scooting on his bottom to move about or gestures to be carried

What resources are available to assist the family in addressing these priorities and concerns?

Melissa has worked in early intervention and knows the available services and resources available within the community; Clay holds family insurance plan through his job so medical needs for Tyler are currently secure

(continued)

FIGURE 11–3 Context-Based Assessment Identification Sheet (Continued)

Structuring the Assessment

Primary Questions	Assessment Techniques
1. *What can be done to increase Matt's communication and speech development?*	1. *Observations of communication efforts and current speech/sound production; administration of Preschool Language Scale-3; exploration of Matt's reaction to nonverbal approaches to communication such as a picture exchange system*
2. *What are Matt's current developmental levels of functioning?*	2. *Play-based assessment and/or HELP*
3. *What is the best approach to increase Matt's motor development?*	3. *Explore techniques that motivate Matt to increase movement and attempt new physical tasks*
4.	4.
5.	5.
6.	6.

Findings

The assessment of Matt's communication efforts and his speech development were focused on functional ways to increase his functional communication because the parents were particularly concerned about his ability to be understood by the family. The service coordinator, Ellen Thomas, arranged for a speech/language pathologist to do observations focused on the communicative skills of Matt in his home setting and to give him the Preschool Language Scale-3. During the observation, Elizabeth Fox, the speech pathologist, used a naturalistic play-based approach to observe Matt's communicative behaviors. The setting was arranged so that Matt and his mother and brother were playing. Elizabeth sat nearby observing and gradually eased her way into the play. Matt banged objects, attempted to build with blocks, and appeared to enjoy knocking down tower blocks constructed by the others. He got his mother's attention with sounds and poking at her. During the play, his mother spoke to him frequently and encouraged him to repeat sounds or respond to her questions. He consistently made eye contact with his mother or others who were speaking and repeated sounds in vocal play, but relied primarily on physical manipulation as a means of communication. He was particularly interested in interactive toys that made sounds. When he wanted an interactive toy to be started, he would put his hands on his mother's arm or hand and pull it to the object. She encouraged him to tell her what he wanted. However, if she did not provide the outcome he was seeking within a brief period, his frustration became apparent. Melissa indicated that when she has held out for more language before responding to his request, his frustration quickly turns to anger and crying. She prefers to maintain a positive interaction with Matt instead of demanding more language out of him at the cost of upsetting him.

Elizabeth Fox used the observations she had made of Matt to calculate both an auditory comprehension and expressive comprehension score on the PLS-3. These are presented in Table 11–3. Matt received credit for all of the items on both scales at the birth to 5 months level, including auditory skills such as the ability to look at a speaker during play, react to the sound of a cellophane wrapper, and expressive skills such as vocalizing a variety of pleasure and displeasure sounds, vocalizing in response to speech, and laughing. All items on both scales at the 6 to 11 months level were also demonstrated. He can anticipate an event and follow a line of action. He approximates sounds made by others, communicates through gestures, and produces at least four different consonant-like sounds. Matt had 2 of the 12 to 17 months level auditory skills, but none of the expressive skills. He was able to maintain attention for two minutes during play and could identify familiar objects, but was unable to identify pictures from the PLS picture manual.

Ellen Thomas, the service coordinator, chose to use the Hawaii Early Learning Profile (HELP) as a guide to identify Matt's current developmental functioning. The HELP checklist is organized into sections for cognitive, expressive language, gross motor, fine motor, social-emotional, and self-help. The lists are arranged in sequential order with an age range associated with each item that indicates the approximate age a typically developing child will acquire that skill. Ellen completed the checklist from her own observations of Matt playing at home with family members and parent interview. It appeared that Matt has

TABLE 11–3 Matt's Scores on the Preschool Language Scale-3

	Raw Score	Standard Score	90% Confidence Interval	Percentile Rank	90% Confidence Interval for PR	Age Equivalent	Age Equivalent Confidence Interval
Auditory comprehension	10	73	63–83	4	1–13	0–11	0–7 to 1–7
Expressive comprehension	8	69	60–78	2	1–7	0–10	0–5 to 1–5

demonstrated most of the skills listed below six months of age, so she started at the six-month point for each of the developmental areas. In the cognitive area, he could also perform all items that begin at the six-month level, such as, "looks for family members or pets when named," "plays 2–3 minutes with single toy," "retains two of three objects offered," and "smells different things." He has most of the items falling in the 7- to 10-month range, but is still missing a few, such as "looks at pictures one minute when named."

Matt's developmental skills become inconsistent for items that have developmental ages 8 months and older. However, he does have some skills in this range, such as "throws object," "knows what 'no-no' means," and "unwraps a toy." Yet, there were skills that he has demonstrated or are emerging that are identified as between the 12- to 18-month level. For example, he has consistently demonstrated "moves to rhythms," "places round piece of formboard," and "understanding pointing." Emerging skills at this level include "matches objects," "pats picture," and "helps turn pages." His expressive language skills include most of the skills associated with 8-month-olds and younger. Emerging skills are between 7 and 15 months, and include "shouts for attention," "shows understanding of words by appropriate behavior or gesture," and "babbles in response to human voice." He is also missing some skills at this approximate level, such as "says 'dada' or 'mama,' nonspecifically." Most items between the 12- and 18-month level are beyond his current skill development, such as "babbles intricate inflection," "uses single word sentences," and "names one or two familiar objects." He does vocalize or gesture spontaneously to indicate needs and greet with verbal cues, and attempts to sing sounds to music.

In the gross motor area, Matt has accomplished skills through the 6-month level, but has gaps beyond that point. Skills that typically appear starting at 6 months that he does have include "sitting without assistance," "bears large fraction of weight on legs," and "bounces." Pulling to a stand might be considered as an emerging skill because he has recently started attempting to pull to stand. Older skills that do not involve standing, such as "sits without hand support for ten minutes," "creeps on hands and knees," and "protective extension of arms to back," are established.

Fine motor skills are at approximately a 1-year level, according to the HELP checklist. Matt takes objects out of containers, releases objects voluntarily, marks paper with crayon, and bangs two cubes held in his hands. Examples of skills that are emerging include scribbling spontaneously, using both hands at midline, and building 3-cube towers.

The social-emotional skills that Matt currently has mastered are in the approximate range of 9- to 12-month-olds. Melissa indicated that he is currently in a phase of letting only her meet his needs, has been testing her during meals and bedtime routines, and enjoys simple imitative play. He also has a few of the skills at the 12- to 18-month level, such as "gives toy to familiar adult spontaneously and upon request," "acts impulsively, unable to recognize rules," and "needs and expects rituals and routines."

In the area of self-help, Matt has most skills up to the 12-month level. He can feed himself finger foods, sleep through the night, and cooperates for dressing. Skills that typically begin appearing between 12 and 18 months are spotty. Emerging skills at this level include holding and drinking from a cup and showing discomfort with a soiled diaper.

Answering the Assessment Questions

What can be done to increase Matt's communication and speech development?

The results of the observation and scoring of the PLS-3 do indicate that Matt has many communicative skills, even though he is not yet using words. Communicative intent is well established, as Elizabeth Fox quickly caught on to many of his intentions during the play. However, Melissa indicates that in other contexts it can be a real challenge to try to comprehend what he is trying to communicate through grunts, gestures, and frustrated crying. Receptive skills seem to be far less of a problem, especially when many clues are provided (e.g., when Melissa says "time for bath" she also holds up his favorite bath toy). Even though the PLS-3 scores did not indicate a big difference between auditory and expressive comprehension, functionally there is a considerable gap in his communicative skills. Matt's efforts at communication should be as pleasant and relaxed as possible. He should continue to have rich language models to listen to and learn from. Now that his health is currently stable, he should have the opportunity to increase his expressive skills rapidly over the next several months. It would be premature to attempt using any picture communication system, as he lacks the necessary prerequisite skills, shows many positive signs of oral language development (although delayed), and enjoys making speech sounds when he is not in a frustrating situation.

What are Matt's current developmental levels of functioning?

Matt appears to have consistently mastered most developmental skills in cognition, fine motor, social-emotional, and self-help areas under 12-month levels. Language and motor skills are more consistent at approximately a 9-month level. He does have emerging skills across all areas that exceed the 12-month level. The delays in his developmental progress are likely, in part, attributable to the number of times he has been hospitalized and had surgery. He is a good candidate for early intervention.

What is the best approach to increase Matt's motor development?

Matt has successfully mastered creeping on his hands and knees throughout the house, and can bear weight when placed in a standing position by an adult. He has attempted pulling to stand, but does not show the persistence Melissa saw from Alex when he was first learning to stand. One or two attempts that end in failure result in Matt either looking for adult assistance to achieve his goal or giving up on it. Melissa and Ellen experimented with various ways to increase his motivation to pull to standing. They use two independent strategies and three interactive play-based strategies. These attempted interventions and their outcomes are presented in Table 11–4. Neither of the independent strategies was effective. The

most effective interactive play-based strategy included some physical assistance, close physical contact with an adult, and a play scenario that was not directly related to the skill. It and similar strategies should be used while Matt works to master the skill of pulling to stand. As he gains skill and confidence, the independent strategy of placing preferred toys within sight, but out of reach, should be reintroduced. Similar "experiments" can be conducted if he hits other similar snags in his motor development and motivation to advance seems weak.

Closing Thoughts

These cases and the approaches to assessment used in them vary in many ways. Family structure, cause of disability, resources available to the family, and reasons assessments were needed were different in each case. Although the socioeconomic levels of the families differ, as does the level of knowledge of child development and experience in parenting, the level of love and concern for each child was high. It is impossible to predict the future for them, but the opportunity to have family-focused early intervention services should make a significant impact on each of their lives. The quality of the intervention will be controlled by the extent to which professionals and family members continually assess the effectiveness of their efforts and the developmental progress of the child. The recommendations outlined for the children will last only a brief period as they grow and mature and respond to new efforts to help them develop to their fullest.

TABLE 11–4 Attempted Interventions to Increase Pull to Stand for Matt

	Intervention	Outcome
Independent strategies	When he attempts to stand and calls out and gestures for adult assistance, gradually increase the time he needs to wait while offering verbal encouragement.	Even a short increase of 30 seconds seemed to make him lose interest in pulling to stand; when adult did arrive he expected to be picked up rather than helped to pull to stand.
	When Matt is playing independently, place preferred toys within sight, but at a level that requires pulling to stand, such as the seat of a chair or sofa.	This strategy seemed to have no effect; he simply did not attend to the toys placed out of reach even when they were known favorites.
Interactive play with adult strategies	During a play session between Matt and adult, place preferred toys within sight, but at a level that requires pulling to stand, such as the seat of a chair or sofa.	This strategy offered some improvement in effort from Matt, but he communicated through shouts and gestures for adult assistance that he expected help retrieving these toys.
	During a play session between Matt and adult, pretend that the adult is a horse; the adult assumes a position on hands and knees and encourages Matt to climb on for a ride, adjusting the height to require some movement toward pulling to stand, while providing some physical assistance in the process.	This strategy was the most successful. He enjoyed the activity and always wanted to continue it beyond the physical stamina of the adult involved; it did require providing a high level of assistance, but appears to be a positive approach to build this skill over time.
	During a play session between Matt and adult, secure a grocery cart toy that is designed to be a push toy so it does not move; place items in the basket of the cart; pretend that it is time to unload the cart and Matt needs to help; he must pull to stand to reach these items.	Matt enjoyed the interactive play with the adult and the grocery cart, but was primarily interested in handing objects to the adult and having the adult hand those objects back to him to empty the cart; this strategy is probably a bit premature to use with him.

CHAPTER 12

Context-Based Assessment Cases: Preschool and Primary-Grade Children

Chapter Overview

The stories of two children and their families and their assessment through a process of getting to know them are presented in this chapter. In addition to having disabilities of differing origins, the children come from quite different social con-texts. Their circumstances vary widely in terms of family composition, educational levels of parents, economic stability of their families, and interaction styles between parents and children.

Karen

Janice and her husband, Daniel, both grew up and attended college in the same southern mid-sized city. Their casual friendship through high school and college developed into a serious relationship and marriage after college graduation. They settled into their new lives in the same community, both enjoying the start of their new marriage and careers. Twelve years later Janice spends her time primarily raising their two children, Karen, a four-and-one-half-year-old, and Bobby, an active two-year-old. She recently returned to work on a part-time basis, two days a week. Janice gave some thought to serving as a parent advisor for a home-based early intervention service, but decided that returning to her career in business had more appeal to her.

The couple had been married seven years when Janice became pregnant for the first time. She experienced a normal pregnancy and was not in any "high risk" category to cause her any particular concern about genetic disorders or other conditions that can be diagnosed prenatally. Throughout her pregnancy, she and her family were distracted by her 14-year-old nephew who was fighting a loosing battle with cancer. Her nephew, who lived in a distant state, died the day before Janice went into labor. Her parents and other extended family members had left town to attend his funeral and comfort the child's grieving parents and siblings, while her husband remained by her side. While she and her husband grieved for their nephew from a distance, Janice gave birth to her own child. They immediately learned that their daughter, Karen, had a heart defect and the genetic disorder Down syndrome.

Janice's supervisor from work was married to a nurse practitioner with a specialization in neonatalogy and early intervention. He offered to have his wife visit the family in the hospital. Although they were suffering grief for their nephew as well as experiencing their own shock with the medical problems facing their own child, Janice recalls the importance of her visit. The nurse practitioner was able to provide them with the information they needed to find appropriate early intervention when they were interested and Karen was ready. She also gave the couple the name of another couple with a child who has Down syndrome willing to speak with new parents.

Unfortunately, this couple was out of town over a week when the couple was back home from the hospital and extremely anxious to talk with them. Reaching the early intervention agencies was not so difficult, but proved to be painful in other ways. When Janice heard the voice on the other end of the phone answer, Oldham County Association for Retarded Citizens, she could only hang up. She was not prepared to hear or accept the significance of the phrase *mental retardation*. However, over the first few weeks of Karen's life, Daniel, first, and Janice, shortly thereafter, did accept Karen as their daughter for whom they would provide love, nurturance, understanding, and care. Soon they found many friends able to put them in touch with other families with children who had Down syndrome. Janice recalls one particularly helpful conversation she had with the father of a child who was about five at the time. The man bragged to her of his son's achievements, just like any father. Although she could express none of her emotions to this caller at the time, the love he clearly held for his own son gave Janice the strongest sense of hope she had had since her child's birth.

When confronted with multiple agencies and a separate service coordination system, Janice was initially confused and overwhelmed. Information such as "the state early intervention system provides service coordination, but no direct services" held no meaning for her at the time. She wondered what "direct services" were. However, by the time Karen was four-weeks-old and ready to begin early intervention, Janice did know that she preferred home-based services over center-based services. Karen needed heart surgery and Janice would not have been comfortable being distant from her. The surgery was performed four weeks later at an out-of-state facility recommended by their pediatrician. By choosing this facility, the family understood that their insurance coverage would not be comprehensive. Indeed, when the first insurance payment was made, it was very small. After an appeal, the insurance coverage improved slightly, but left a tremendous bill for them to pay. They then approached the surgeon about making an adjustment to the bill. To their great relief he agreed to waive the entire amount in exchange for a picture of Karen.

Eligibility assessments of Karen were not necessary to initiate early intervention since she was born with a specific condition known to cause developmental delays. However, an informal developmental assessment was arranged by a state early intervention service coordinator when Karen was four-weeks-old. Janice recalls this assessment only because the home visitor who conducted it noted that Karen was functioning at her chronological age level at the time and would not have been eligible for services had she not had Down syndrome. A physical therapist, an occupational therapist, and a speech/language pathologist conducted formal evaluations. Karen began receiving early intervention services on a regular basis through a rehabilitation agency and a speech and language clinic.

When Karen was approaching three years of age, the transition from these services to preschool special education services began. This transition meant a shift from Individualized Family Service Plans (IFSPs) to Individualized Education Programs (IEPs). The first school-based multidisciplinary team meeting lasted two hours and proved confrontational and unpleasant. Karen had been receiving private physical therapy from Early Rehabilitation Therapies for over two years. Janice arranged for Karen's therapist to attend the meeting, hoping to ensure a smooth transition between the two service providers. What happened instead, from her perspective, was that the therapist from the school and the one from the community agency could not communicate effectively with one another and appeared to be unwilling to attempt to do so. Nevertheless, the school team proceeded to plan and conduct a comprehensive assessment of Karen, including intelligence testing, speech and language assessment, adaptive behavior skills, and motor skills. As a 35-month-old, Karen had a developmental level of approximately 15 months as measured by the Bayley Scales of Infant Development-II. Overall adaptive functioning was measured at the first percentile on the Vineland Adaptive Behavior Scales. Communication skills and overall language functioning were observed in natural settings and appeared to correspond to her cognitive abilities as measured on the Bayley. She did have several signs and gestures that she was using consistently to communicate. The therapist, who had been serving Karen at the Early Rehabilitation Therapies, reported on her gross motor skills. On the Peabody Motor Development Test she achieved a basal age of 18 to 23 months and a ceiling age of 24 to 29 months.

Since this initial transition from early intervention into the school system, the couple has been through the assessment process with Karen a number of times. She has been attending preschool special education for three years, and her parents realize that it is time for another transition. Their big concern going into this assessment is the type of class and curriculum that will be deemed appropriate for Karen. They are starting to see the developmental differences between their two children, as Karen's younger brother's development surpasses hers on all counts. Yet, her parents are confident that Karen can benefit from and should have opportunities to develop to her fullest potential through interaction with typically developing children combined with special educational services. The plan for the assessment that will guide the team in making the transition decisions about Karen's education is outlined in Figure 12–1.

The primary questions to be considered in this assessment of Karen are:

1. What preacademic skills does Karen have now?
2. What is the most suitable curriculum to give Karen over the next year?
3. Can Karen function in a regular classroom setting, working independently, following directions, and completing activities?
4. What are Karen's communication skills and how effectively can she communicate with her peers and teachers?
5. Is Karen's hearing within normal limits?
6. What part do motor and visual motor skills play in Karen's speech production?

Findings

Karen's behavior and cooperativeness seems to vary across settings. The preschool special education teacher sees Karen as slow to acquire classroom skills, such as following directions, independent functioning, following rules, concentration, fine motor coordination, relations with peers and adults, self-help skills, and communication skills. She perceives the child to be strong-willed, often refusing to comply with her requests. However, Janice reports that Karen is willing to follow directions at home. She does not see the degree of behavioral resistance reported by the teacher. The after-school care provider also indicates that she has not experienced any extreme problems in regard to Karen's cooperation and following requests. She reports that Karen is animated and willing to interact with peers when encouraged to be a part of the group. However, she has observed that Karen will remain to herself if allowed to stay apart from the group. There are several possible explanations for these differences. It is possible that the preschool setting is the one in which Karen is challenged the most, naturally triggering some frustration-related behavior that could be interpreted as the necessary path to progress. It could be that the teacher is placing developmentally inappropriate expectations on Karen, causing her to

FIGURE 12–1 Context-Based Assessment Identification Sheet

Karen Dobbins

Child's name _Karen_	Today's date	Yr.	2003	Mo.	03	Day	07	Premature?
Primary adult contact _Janice_	Birth date	Yr.	1997	Mo.	01	Day	17	Yes ☐ No ☒
Relationship to child _mother_		Age	Yrs.	6	Mo.	01	Days	20	Number of weeks ____

Adjusted age ____ Yrs. ____ Mo. ____ Days ____

Overall health of child:
Chronic ear infections and repeated insertion of tubes in ears to reduce infections; possible temporary hearing loss during infections; no remaining heart-related problems since surgery as infant

Work phone ____ Home phone ____

Street address ____

City, State, Zip ____

E-mail *********.*** FAX _NA_

Others in home:

Names	Ages	Relationship
Bobby	_3.5 years_	_brother_
____	____	____
____	____	____
____	____	____

Mother:

Name _Janice_

Street address ____

City, State, Zip Code ____

Phone ____

Living with child? ☒ Yes ☐ No

Father:

Name _Daniel_

Street address ____

City, State, Zip Code ____

Phone ____

Living with child? ☒ Yes ☐ No

Other relevant information:
Mother returned to working part time a few months ago

FIGURE 12–1 (Continued)

Identifying Family Resources, Priorities, and Concerns

What are the priorities and primary areas of concern related to the child for the family?	**What efforts have already been made to address these concerns?**
Limited speech	*Have focused on speech production in the classroom—have seen improvement in turn taking and efforts to communicate*
Not fully toilet trained	*Will toilet when prompted, but has accidents without reminders*
Unwilling to participate in group activities	*Remains in structured group setting five minutes or less even with one-to-one adult physical contact*
Does not interact with peers	*Will engage in limited parallel play when adult is present and encouraging the behavior*

What resources are available to assist the family in addressing these priorities and concerns?

Continued special education, occupational therapy, and speech/language services through local school system; will continue after-school care and private physical therapy paid for through private insurance

(continued)

FIGURE 12–1 Context-Based Assessment Identification Sheet (Continued)

Structuring the Assessment

Primary Questions	Assessment Techniques
1. What preacademic skills does Karen have now?	1. Observations; administration of Bayley Developmental Scales (administered by school psychologist)
2. What are Karen's communication skills and how effectively can she communicate with her peers and teachers?	2. Observations; Vineland Adaptive Behavior Scales—Classroom Edition
3. Is Karen's hearing within normal limits?	3. Observations of Karen in her current preschool; analysis of regular classroom environment in which she would be placed; administration of Woodcock-Johnson Scales of Independent Behavior
4. What is the most suitable curriculum to give Karen over the next year?	4. Observations; language samples, and administration of Clinical Evaluation of Language Fundamentals-Preschool
5. Can Karen function in a regular classroom setting, working independently, following directions, and completing assignments?	5. Obtain results of hearing screen and observe her in the classroom setting

react to avoid tasks beyond her developmental level. There could be an underlying power struggle between the teacher and Karen that has not occurred in the other settings.

Based on observations within the preschool classroom and formal testing results, the school psychologist also notes that Karen is still developing basic academic readiness skills, social skills needed for group settings, communication skills needed to interact with peers and adults, and adaptive behavior, including toileting, feeding, and dressing skills. She has a speaking vocabulary of approximately 20 words. The teacher has been unable to get Karen to participate in group activities. Karen resists participating in teacher-led activities, and cannot complete any paper and pencil activities. Her performance on the Woodcock-Johnson Scales of Independent Behavior produced a developmental age of 3-0, a standard score of 51, with a percentile rank of 0.1. Scores on the Vineland Adaptive Behavior Scales-Classroom Edition were similar, as noted in Table 12–1.

The school psychologist chose to use the Bayley Scales of Infant Development-II as a standardized measure of cognitive functioning in spite of the upper age limit for the test being 42 months. The manual does indicate it can be used with older children when their developmental functioning is not suited to more structured standardized testing. Karen's limited language skills, delayed fine and visual-motor skills, and resistance to teacher-directed activities lead him to the conclusion that the Bayley would be more suitable than the Stanford-Binet or the Wechsler Preschool and Primary Scales of Intelligence. During the administration of the Bayley, Karen was easily distracted, resistant to engaging in many of the tasks, particularly those she found difficult, such as visual-motor activities, and reluctant to perform tasks on request. However, the psychologist felt that Karen's performance on the Bayley, indicating an approximate functioning level of 20 months, was a reasonably accurate measure of her current abilities. He pointed out that the results from the testing are consistent with the functional behaviors observed in the classroom and behavioral descriptions provided by the teacher. The report from the testing indicates that Karen is able to understand slightly more than she is able to express verbally, with most oral responses being single words. She could point to and name pictures and objects, identify body parts, attend to a story, and follow simple directions in play with a doll. Karen was inconsistent in matching pictures and could not match colors during the testing. However, the teacher has reported that Karen has successfully sorted colored bears into matching cups in the classroom setting. Karen was able to build a four-block tower, but unable to imitate other block designs. Again, her mother indicates that she has done better at home in play. Karen was uninterested in a form-board puzzle, but did accurately place pegs in a peg-board. Karen would not imitate written designs, but enjoyed coloring on a plain sheet of paper. A great deal of prompting was required to get Karen to try these visual motor activities.

Karen's parents were concerned about some aspects of this assessment. When they received the report, they realized that Karen's health might have played a significant part in how she performed that day. She had been suffering from an ear infection and had tubes inserted for the fourth time one week after the test. Karen's mother knew that she had seen Karen perform many of the tasks that she was unable to receive credit for during the formal examination. It disturbed the couple to think that decisions regarding Karen's placement and curricular content would be based on these suspect test scores.

TABLE 12–1 Karen's Scores on the Vineland Adaptive Behavior Scales-Classroom Edition

Domain	Standard Score	Percentile Rank	Age Equivalent
Communication	64	1	1–7
Daily living skills	60	0.4	1–11
Socialization	67	1	1–11
Motor skills	63	1	2–5
Composite	61	0.5	

The speech-language pathologist observed Karen in the preschool setting, gave her the Clinical Evaluation of Language Fundamentals-Preschool (CELF-Preschool), and reported that she passed a hearing screening administered by an audiologist. Karen's language skills were considered comparable to her cognitive skills. Scores from the CELF-Preschool are presented in Table 12–2.

During her observations and assessments, the speech-language pathologist heard Karen say only two words spontaneously, *Barney* and *no*. She was able to imitate other words, such as *bus, outside, baby, ball, mama,* and *bye-bye,* with some articulation errors. No significant problems were noted in her voice qualities, but there was not enough spontaneous speech to evaluate Karen's fluency. Physical characteristics of Karen's oral cavity do interfere with her speech production, including low tone, poor tongue

control, a small palate, and difficulty separating tongue and jaw movements.

An educational diagnostician observed Karen in the classroom setting and engaged her in some informal academic tasks rather than attempting to administer standardized achievement tests to her. Karen could point to common items, such as a fork, spoon, and a Jello box, but was unable to name any of these objects. She was able to imitate words, but understanding Karen was a problem for the examiner throughout the assessment. She is not yet able to pick out letters or numbers when asked, or hold up a correct number of fingers to represent an amount. The examiner found Karen to be cooperative for the most part, making reasonable efforts throughout these activities. The examiner also observed that Karen knew the names of all of her classmates and was able to engage in several activities within the preschool setting independently.

TABLE 12–2 Karen's Scores on the CELF-Preschool

	Raw Score	Standard Score	Points – or +	Confidence Interval 68% Level	Percentile Rank
Linguistic Concepts	12	4	1	3 to 5	2
Basic Concepts	10	3	2	1 to 5	1
Sentence Structure	9	3	2	1 to 5	1
Sum of 3 Standard Scores	10				
RECEPTIVE LANGUAGE SCORE	61	6	55 to 67		1
Recalling Sentences in Context	8	3	1	2 to 4	1
Formulating Labels	10	3	1	2 to 4	1
Word Structure	10	3	1	2 to 4	1
Sum of 3 Standard Scores	9				
EXPRESSIVE LANGUAGE SCORE	50	5	45 to 50		1
Sum of 6 Standard Scores	19				
TOTAL LANGUAGE SCORE	58	4	54 to 62		1
Sum of 6 Subtest Raw Scores	59				
AGE EQUIVALENT 2-11				2-8 to 3-2	

Sum of 6 Subtest Standard Scres 19/6 = 3.1 (mean)

Answering the Assessment Questions

What preacademic skills does Karen have now?

Karen has some readiness skills typically considered prerequisite to beginning reading and math instruction. Her current skills do not include letter or numeral recognition; however, she does recognize store signs in the community, pointing and showing interest and excitement for some of her favorite places. She has learned the names of her classmates and can point to each child when his or her name is called. She has sorted by colors in the past, although she did not demonstrate this skill during formal testing. She is currently learning to recognize color and shape names. She can mark with crayons, but is not yet able to copy shapes, form letters, cut with scissors, or perform other prewriting skills. She has been introduced to computers and is able to use a touch-screen to play cause-effect games independently. She is beginning to master the use of a mouse as a point-and-click tool on fairly large objects on the screen. Karen enjoys listening to short stories and can recognize her favorite books. She can point to some objects within pictures when asked.

What are Karen's communication skills and how effectively can she communicate with her peers and teachers?

She has a speaking vocabulary of approximately 20 words, but appears to have somewhat greater receptive understanding of what is said to her. She does not speak much spontaneously, but will imitate words. She uses gestures and signs spontaneously at school and in her home. At school she also uses communication picture cards when prompted. Articulation is impeded by the low muscle tone in and around her mouth, tongue protrusion, and poor jaw control. Persons who do not interact with her on a frequent basis have difficulty understanding her more than others who are with her daily. She participates to a limited extent in small group play and activities, but does not speak much to other children. She relies primarily on physical gestures with peers for communication. She does appear to understand when peers speak to her in play or during classroom activities and routines.

Is Karen's hearing within normal limits?

At the time of the hearing screening Karen was hearing within normal limits. However, her chronic middle ear infections seem to be causing intermittent hearing loss. Adults working with Karen should keep the possibility of temporary hearing difficulties in mind.

What is the most suitable curriculum to give Karen over the next year?

This is the primary issue for Janice and Daniel. They consider it premature to assume that Karen will not be able to develop academic skills. Although it might be necessary to reach this conclusion after more time has past, they see enough progress in Karen's development at home, in school, and at the child care setting to continue with an academic curriculum for her. School personnel fear that the discrepancy between the standards of an academic curriculum and Karen's current functioning is likely to increase her frustrations, causing an increase in the behavioral problems reported by the preschool special education teacher.

After these assessments, there is a mutual understanding between the school personnel and Karen's parents that a first-grade curriculum is beyond this six-year-old's reach. Janice and Daniel consider it critical to keep as many doors open for Karen as possible. They are uneasy about the decisions that might be made about a suitable curriculum for Karen if standardized test scores and the preschool teacher's negative opinions weigh heavily in the decision. They know that there are many adaptive behavioral skills that Karen needs to develop, but are still pushing for a curriculum that is primarily academically oriented. They believe that they can provide Karen opportunities to progress in adaptive behavior skills at home, in the child care, and through occupational therapy. They feel she needs continued exposure to letter and numeral recognition, shape recognition, sequencing, size and quantity concepts (e.g., more, less, big, little), and similar preacademic content. A compromise is reached that incorporates adaptive behavior goals to be achieved primarily outside of the classroom setting, preacademic skills that will be the focus of classroom instruction, and communication skills that will be provided through a combination of individual speech therapy and in-class language activities.

Can Karen function in a regular classroom setting, working independently, following directions, and completing activities?

The assessment has provided a great deal of information about Karen's current functioning through both formal and informal assessments. Karen has displayed at least some ability to work independently, follow directions, and complete activities in all three of her primary settings. However, it is difficult to predict with certainty how she would behave in a regular classroom setting, based on the inconsistent patterns that were evident during the assessment. Her parents feel that the evidence is there to support an academic special education program with opportunities for inclusion in a first grade. The inclusion experience, they argue, is something that Karen deserves. The after-school child care and summer sessions have been successful inclusion experiences for Karen, proving her suitability for partial inclusion. School personnel are concerned that Karen's limited communication skills and slow development in adaptive behavior, particularly toileting, will present serious limitations to the inclusion experience that the couple has in mind for their child. The couple questions how their child can develop social and self-care skills without age peers to show the way. The decision is reached to use a developmental kindergarten as an inclusion experience for Karen. The classroom environment is arranged in centers, where the teacher relies on child-initiated play for much of her teaching. A teaching assistant will accompany Karen to the kindergarten to be available and provide the encouragement and support Karen might need.

Todd

Todd is a 3-year-old who has already experienced many moves and caregivers in his life. His mother, Joycelle, is 20 and his father, Mart, is 25. Todd has four older half-brothers and sisters, including one who was killed in a house fire caused by a lit cigarette. These children live in a distant state under the care of various paternal relatives of each child. Todd also has a younger half-brother who lives with Joycelle and that child's father, Darrick. Joycelle is still legally married to Todd's father, whereas Darrick is married to a different woman who lives out of town. As a 2-year-old, Todd was enrolled in a state-sponsored insurance program for families living in poverty. Todd's medical records indicate that he has been taken to the emergency room on multiple occasions for a variety of accidents that are suspicious of abuse. Severe bruising, hair-line skull fractures, and a gash across the back are all part of Todd's past.

When seen by a pediatrician for a checkup, Todd's speech was observed to be completely unintelligible. The medical staff found it impossible to assess his communicative and developmental skills due to his extremely combative behavior. Todd already had a significant history of oppositional defiant behavior as seen in attacks toward others and himself, including head banging and biting. The pediatrician recommended that Joycelle contact the state early intervention system to explore the possibility of receiving services for these developmental concerns. She gave the pediatrician's staff permission to make this referral for her.

Since Todd was due to turn three in a few months, the early intervention system service coordinator arranged a number of diagnostic evaluations and contacted the local school system so they could participate in planning for the child. A developmental evaluation was arranged to rule out pervasive developmental disorder or any related syndromes. Shortly before the evaluation appointment, Todd, his younger half-brother, Joycelle, and her boyfriend were kicked out of the boyfriend's parent's home and moved into a homeless shelter. During their stay at the shelter, Joycelle contacted the Department of Human Services to report that she had hit Todd. When she punched him in the stomach trying to stop a tantrum, she knew that it was time to get help. She did not want to repeat the pattern of abuse that had been so much a part of her own childhood. She realized that she simply could not manage him. As requested by Joycelle, respite services were arranged that included housing for the child. Todd was placed in foster care. Joycelle was able to move out of the shelter, but had no telephone. Joycelle had indicated that she was interested receiving early intervention services for Todd, but the service coordinator never heard from her after a plan of care for the child was arranged through the Department of Human Services.

Currently, Todd remains in foster care with a family who have one seven-year-old adopted daughter. Todd has been living with them for approximately six months, during which time they have worked to give him a sense of stability and nurturance. Although he never had the developmental evaluation that had been scheduled, his foster parents have contacted the local school system for testing through their Child Find program. The plan for that evaluation is outlined in Figure 12–2.

FIGURE 12–2 Context-Based Assessment Identification Sheet

Todd Dunn

Child's name *Todd*

Primary adult contact *Sarah*

Relationship to child *foster mother*

Work phone _____ Home phone _____

Street address _____

City, State, Zip _____

E-mail *NA*   FAX *NA*

	Today's date	Yr.	2002	Mo.	07	Day	10	Premature?
	Birth date	Yr.	1999	Mo.	04	Day	06	Yes ☐ No ☒
		Age	Yrs.	3	Mo.	03	Days	04	Number of weeks _____

Adjusted age   Yrs. _____ Mo. _____ Days _____

Overall health of child:
*Malnourished when placed in foster care, since coming to the Bevins's eating habits have improved
and Todd has gained weight; chronic head congestion has improved*

Mother:

Name *Joycelle*

Street address _____

_____

City, State, Zip Code _____

Phone _____

_____

Living with child? ☐ Yes ☒ No

Father:

Name *Mart*

Street address _____

_____

City, State, Zip Code _____

Phone _____

Living with child? ☐ Yes ☒ No

Others in home:

Names	Ages	Relationship
Barbara	*7 years*	*foster-sister*
Eric	*adult*	*foster-father*
_____	_____	_____
_____	_____	_____

Other relevant information:
*Mother made self-referral to Human Services after hitting Todd because of tantruming; still married to Todd's father who is in prison in a remote state and
the mother is afraid of him due to physical abuse; mother wants to reunite with Todd, but has a baby and has recently been asked to leave the home of the grandparents of that baby; they are in a homeless shelter; the mother also has three older children that she no longer has custody of and one killed in a wreck*

(continued)

267

FIGURE 12-2 Context-Based Assessment Identification Sheet (Continued)

Identifying Family Resources, Priorities, and Concerns

What are the priorities and primary areas of concern related to the child for the family?	What efforts have already been made to address these concerns?
Increasing Todd's communication skills	*Speaking vocabulary limited to about 20 words; foster family has started encouraging speech before he receives desired outcomes*
Reducing severe tantruming	*Foster family has been focused on establishing his trust and sense of security rather than controlling bad behavior; the behavior not improving and the family is ready for some guidance on how best to proceed to reduce the tantrums with a minimum of harshness; they ignore tantrums as much as possible, restraining him when he begins hitting or kicking*
Improving eating habits	*Now on schedule with three meals and three snacks during the day; other times food is not available; even when tantruming is food related*
Increasing ability to play independently	*His attention span is gradually increasing so family members can engage him for brief (2–3 minute) play sessions; when left to play independently he tends to wander about without really engaging in any particular activity*

What resources are available to assist the family in addressing these priorities and concerns?

The local school system through the Child Find program will evaluate and provide needed special education services; Health Department will provide additional guidelines for nutrition and family will participate in counseling and support offered by social worker support through foster care program

FIGURE 12-2 (Continued)

Structuring the Assessment

Primary Questions	Assessment Techniques
1. What communication skills does Todd have and how can he increase these skills?	1. Observation of Todd's preferences and current communicative intentions—when and how does he attempt to communicate, how does he respond when others speak to him, and how does he react to adults and peers who speak to him?
2. What is the best approach to reducing Todd's severe tantruming?	2. Conduct functional behavioral assessment in the home setting and in foster parent-selected community-based settings; if mother wishes to participate, could also be arranged in a community-based setting
3. What developmental skills does Todd have and how can we increase his ability to play independently for increased amounts of time?	3. Administer Learning Accomplishment Profile-Diagnostic to explore his developmental levels and ability to sustain interest in play activities
4. Is Todd's hearing normal?	4. Audiological exam
5. How will Todd behave socially in a preschool setting?	5. Observations based on the Assessment of Peer Relations in a center-based preschool setting

The primary questions for Todd are:

1. What communication skills does Todd have and how best can he increase these skills?
2. What is the best approach to reducing Todd's severe tantruming?
3. What developmental skills does Todd have and how can we increase his ability to play independently for increased amounts of time?
4. Is Todd's hearing normal?
5. How will Todd behave socially in a preschool setting?

Findings

The assessment of Todd was designed to avoid triggering his resistance as much as possible, with most of it being conducted in the foster home. Although it is the custom for the school system to use a team of professionals to complete assessments of this nature, the team felt that it would be best to have one person work with Todd. It would reduce the challenges of scheduling multiple persons to make home visits, while concurrently lowering the number of strangers to whom Todd would be expected to adjust. Barbara Simpson, a speech-language pathologist with an early childhood special education background, was chosen to be the primary person administering assessments to Todd. She made home visits twice a week for six weeks for this assessment. Initially, these sessions were kept low key, primarily observation and natural interactions when Todd approached her or sought her attention. In the third week of visits, she began administering parts of the Learning Accomplishment Profile-Diagnostic (LAP-D). She completed the LAP-D and gave Todd the Preschool Language Scale-3 over a two-week period. Visits have also included trips to a community playground, and a fast-food location that has a play area. No observations that included Todd's mother were possible, because school system personnel were unable to locate her during the six-week assessment period.

Todd was also being introduced to a preschool setting with twice-a-week three-hour sessions where Barbara also visited. She observed Todd, gathered language samples, and participated in play-based interactions with him within this setting. The teacher also observed Todd, compiled samples of his work (e. g., artwork, photos of him engaged in activities such as completing puzzles) and recorded information regarding his social interactions to assist in the assessment process. The classroom includes seven other three- to four-year-old children who attend the program four days a week from 8:30 to 11:30 A.M. Monday through Thursday. The group includes two girls and five boys, each of whom has some type of developmental delay. The classroom is structured primarily around a play-based, child-initiated approach. The room layout permits children to engage in well-defined centers that include blocks, art, housekeeping, dramatic play, stories, and computer activities. Photographs of the children are used throughout the room to define personal space, such as cubbies for coats and bags; identify and manage numbers of children playing in one center at a time; and identify birthdays on a bulletin board within the room.

Answering the Assessment Questions

What communication skills does Todd have and can he increase these skills?

Sarah reports that Todd's expressive vocabulary has been increasing since he came to live with them. Initially, she was able to understand only three expressions, "mama," "no," and "stupid shit," when he was speaking. Even though he would attempt to say other things, his articulation was too garbled to be understood. Todd can now be understood saying approximately 20 to 25 words. He has begun putting words together into short phrases, such as "go out," and "here dog." Barbara Simpson also observed continued improvement in his speech during her six weeks of observation. The production was best at home, whereas at school he spoke far less and had trouble making himself understood. During play, both at home and in the school setting, Todd demonstrated communicative intention. He gestured, pulled at Barbara, brought her objects to look at, and shouted to get attention when he wanted to show off a skill he had. When he needed his words to be understood and adults or children could not understand him, he became frustrated, often throwing objects.

On the Auditory Comprehension subtest of the Preschool Language Scale-3, Todd received a standard score of 83 (Mean = 100, SD = 15), with a percentile rank of 13, and an age equivalent of two years six months (chronological age three years two months). He followed simple directions without gestural cues, identified pictures, and demonstrated understanding of verbs in context. He did not receive credit for understanding spatial concepts or several pronouns, or recognizing actions in pictures. On the Expressive Communication subtest of the Preschool Language Scale-3, Todd received a standard score of 83, with a percentile rank of 13, and an age equivalent of two years nine months. He named objects, used one pronoun, and used a question inflection. He did not combine three or four words in spontaneous speech, name pictures, or use plurals during the assessment. Articulation was not directly assessed due to his limited verbalizations.

What is the best approach to reducing Todd's severe tantruming?

Barbara was able to identify several warning signs that typically precede Todd's tantrums. These behaviors include an intense staring, legs bending at the knees in a slight walking-in-place motion (a prestomping motion), scrunching up of the shoulders, and self-abusive behavior, such as pinching. One or more of these signs would appear up to five minutes before a tantrum would strike. The tantrums often seemed linked to Todd's desires. The tantrums were most often a means by which he hoped to acquire his preferences, whether that be food on demand, watching television, or access to playground equipment free of all other children. He needs to become accustomed to household routines and patterns (e.g., set meal and snack times), community-based social rules (e.g., sharing community playground equipment), and preschool routines (e.g., clean-up times, transitions to new activities, moving from one location in the building to another as a group, numbers of children allowed in one play area at a time). Modifications in each of these areas coupled with awareness of the warning signs and on-the-spot adjustments should be structured to reduce the tantrums. For example, snacks and meals might initially be spaced fairly close together. Rather than eating on demand, Todd receives a small snack every hour. The length between snacks is gradually stretched into longer periods. A timer might be used to assist Todd in understanding that another opportunity for a snack would be coming up soon. Desirable events away from the food issue, such as watching a favorite video could be presented as a distraction if warning signs are noticed. Priorities should be set that establish which triggering factors the family and teacher will address first.

Tantrums also occurred when Todd was attempting to speak about something he wanted or needed and could not make an adult understand. Although the tantrum might not occur instantly, there was a pattern of tantrums occurring within a 20-minute period following particularly unsuccessful efforts at communication. Although he is in the process of improving his articulation and increasing his expressive vocabulary, Todd needs a functional means of communicating basic needs and wants. A picture exchange system can be explored as a means of giving him greater communicative success immediately.

Todd has a high level of anger and needs an acceptable means of expressing that anger without putting himself and others in danger. Access to play materials that allow a fair amount of aggression, such as building and tearing down block structures, should be provided under adult supervision. The adult's task would be to anticipate and redirect when Todd is escalating his behavior beyond a level that he can calm himself with some adult assistance.

What developmental skills does Todd have and how can we increase his ability to play independently for increased amounts of time?

During the assessment period, Barbara tried to observe Todd's play preferences and let him take the lead during play sessions. At home, the couple was just beginning to collect a variety of age-appropriate toys, but did already have some toys that their older daughter had used. They had an old kitchen set, blocks, several baby dolls, musical toys, balls, a car that could be ridden in the driveway, and many books. New toys included a farm set, toy cars and trucks, puzzles, and action figures from several recent popular children's movies. When Barbara played with Todd in the couple's home, blocks, cars and trucks appeared to be his favorite toys. He played best while Barbara or Sarah was actively engaged with him, playing up to 15 minutes at a time without becoming distracted or frustrated. He would build structures with the blocks and use the cars and trucks to drive in and around these structures. He would "crash" the vehicles into the structures and watch them tumble to the ground. Without adult redirection, he would repeat this process until he became agitated, and began throwing blocks or tossing vehicles high into the air. This pattern of play escalating into aggression was typical.

Barbara was able to administer the Learning Accomplishment Profile-Diagnostic over the six-week period of assessment. The test includes eight subscales that represent four developmental domains. Todd's scores are presented in Table 12–3.

TABLE 12–3 Todd's Scores on the Learning Accomplishment Profile-Diagnostic

Subscale	Percentile Rank	Age Equivalent (months)	z-Score
Fine motor: manipulation	3	30	−1.88
Fine motor: writing	27	32–37	− .61
Cognitive: matching	14	31–32	−1.08
Cognitive: counting	16	32–33	−1.00
Language: naming	3	<30	−1.88
Language: comprehension	3	<30	−1.88
Gross motor: body movement	10	31	−1.28
Gross motor: object movement	25	30–31	− .68

Under fine motor: manipulation, Todd could build a tower with 8 large blocks, construct a bridge using 3 large blocks, and build a tower of 10 small blocks. He was not willing to attempt stringing beads or placing pegs in a pegboard, but did enjoy manipulating play dough. His fine motor writing skills include the ability to hold a pencil by his fingers, imitation of circular, and straight horizontal and vertical lines. He was unable to imitate intersecting lines, an H stroke and a V stroke. At the outset of the six-week period, Todd was unable to perform matching activities. By the fifth week, he could place basic shapes into a form-board, and match simple geometric shapes and patterns. He was not yet able to match pictures of like objects or animals.

The highest skills Todd exhibited in the cognitive: counting subtest were "responds to prepositions of over and under," and distinguishing the little block from others. He was unable to point to the group with "more" blocks, place one block on request, or respond to empty or full. Todd was unable to demonstrate competence in any of the language/cognitive: naming subtest, including the imitation of simple names, and naming common objects and body parts. In the language/cognitive: comprehension subtest, he was able to give the examiner three common objects, and could point to three pictures of common objects. Todd has mastered the ability to walk up and down stairs without assistance, and jumping from a child's chair in the area of gross motor: body movement. In gross motor: object movement, Todd could catch a large ball with arms against body while standing, but was unable to catch a t-shirt with one hand or kick a large soccer ball.

Generally, he demonstrated mastery of developmental skills at and around the 30-month level.

In only a few instances did his unwillingness to attempt a task interfere with his test performance. However, this was partially due to the fact that the test was administered over a 5-week period. Barbara was cautious to avoid placing expectations of cooperation on Todd that would trigger resistance and tantruming. Over this extended testing period, Todd was rapidly progressing in his developmental skills and should continue closing the gap between his chronological age and developmental skills. Continued improvement in communication skills is the most critical and should result in improvements across other developmental areas as well.

Is Todd's hearing normal?

Todd responded appropriately to all sounds presented during a hearing screening. These results indicate that he does have the hearing acuity needed for speech reception.

How will Todd behave socially in a preschool setting?

Guralnick's Assessment of Peer Relations was used as a tool to explore Todd's behavior while in the preschool setting. His interactions with peers were considered in regard to his level of involvement, purpose of initiations of interactions with peers, and the success of those initiations. Initially, Todd would often remain unoccupied if no adult stepped in to play directly with him. Random wandering about the room has diminished as he can be seen watching the play of other children on occasion. After a group of children at play have moved on to another area, he will move into the abandoned space, but is still unable to initiate independent play with the available materials. During the first weeks, when playing with an adult, he would resist the efforts of another child who attempted to join them. If the other child did not back away quickly, Todd would push him and physically prevent him from approaching. He now sometimes accepts having Eric join him and the adult in block play. The adult can then slip out and Todd will continue in appropriate play for up to two minutes. However, when another child approaches him when he is by himself, he most often ignores that child or pushes the child away. During the six-week period of assessment, Todd rarely initiated an interaction with a peer. However, in the last two weeks, Barbara observed him seeking the attention of Eric, especially when Eric is engaged in play with another child.

When approached by others, Todd often would ignore them. However, sometimes he would reject the social overtures of peers, physically pushing the child away. If he remained in play with Eric beyond two minutes, Todd often increased the aggressiveness of the play (crashing blocks into one another, destroying the buildings under construction), which would then lead to hostility between the boys. Todd's behavior toward peers who approach him to distribute materials on behalf of the teacher changed over the six weeks. Initially, he ignored these approaches. Now he sometimes reaches his hand out to accept the materials being distributed, making eye contact with the other child. His reactions to the teacher's efforts to introduce him to large group time were disorganized. He would become upset, but seemingly uncertain how he could escape. He would stand in place, kicking his feet and throwing out his arms, preventing other children from taking a place in the group. This behavior might then be followed by his dashing about the room in a frenzy. Sometimes, Todd gets upset in this fashion and takes up to 30 minutes to regain his composure, even with the assistance of a nuturing adult. The teacher realized that Todd was not ready for any large group time. Barbara has gradually been introducing him to the types of activities done during group time (e.g., singing songs, doing finger plays, interactive listening to stories told and read). Todd has started observing the group time from the safety of the back of the room, occasionally quietly attempting to perform the current activity.

Todd does appear to understand the concept of ownership, as when he takes possession of play materials and guards his right to those materials. However, he rarely demonstrates an understanding of sharing and turn-taking. The family-style approach to snacks and meals has given Todd an opportunity to begin to accept turn taking. Sharing of blocks with Eric is also gradually giving him some understanding of these social rules. Todd has very rarely become involved in pretend play, and only then with Barbara or another adult. He seems unfamiliar with many everyday events on which the other children base their pretend play (e.g., grocery shopping, preparing a meal).

Closing Thoughts

These children and their needs for intervention are quite varied. Karen's disability has been evident since shortly after birth. She suffered from heart problems that required surgery and the necessary follow-up care from her family. She has a nurturing family who have actively sought appropriate educational interventions for her since her birth. Even though she has been slow to develop in some areas, they have pushed for her integration with typically developing children. Karen will enjoy the benefits of these involved parents throughout the remainder of her education.

Todd has had a far different start to his life, as did his own mother. She wanted to break the cycle of abuse and neglect of which she had been a victim, but was not able to do so for Todd. His unstable home life was confounded by poverty and homelessness. It is not surprising that Todd is an angry child, who has fallen behind in his development. His future is far less certain than Karen's. For the moment, he is safely placed in a foster home, showing many positive signs that he is adjusting and settling into a routine home and preschool social structure. However, this situation cannot be considered permanent. Although Todd's mother has disappeared for now, she could reappear at any time and seek to be reunited with her son. Whether or not she does actually reappear, the foster parents do not have the same long-term responsibility held by Karen's parents. Their concerns for Todd are going to be far more immediate. Debates over the nature of his curriculum are not likely, as everyone focuses on establishing Todd's ability to maintain self-control and establish a functional means of communication. A crisis-intervention model is likely to continue to be part of Todd's educational and personal experience for years to come.

References

Abidin, R. R. (1986). Parenting Stress Index (2nd ed.). Charlottesville, VA: Pediatric Psychology Press.

Als, H. (1997). Earliest intervention for preterm infants in the newborn intensive care unit. In M. J. Guralnick (Ed.), *The effectiveness of early intervention* (pp. 47–76). Baltimore, MD: Paul H. Brookes.

American Academy of Pediatrics. (2000). Recommendations for Preventive Pediatric Health Care. *Pediatrics, 105,* 645.

American Psychiatric Association. (1994). *Diagnostic and statistical manual of mental disorders* (4th ed.). Washington, DC: Author.

Anastasi, A., & Urbina, S. (1997). *Psychological testing* (7th ed.). New York: Macmillan.

Apgar, V. (1953). A proposal for a new method of evaluation of the newborn infant. *Current Researches in Anesthesia and Analgesia, 32,* 260–267.

Armstrong, T. (1999). *Seven kinds of smart: Identifying and developing your multiple intelligences.* New York: Plume.

Arndorfer, R. E., & Miltenberger, R. G. (1993). Functional assessment and treatment of challenging behavior: A review with implications for early childhood. *Topics in Early Childhood Special Education, 13,* 82–105.

Arndorfer, R. E., Miltenberger, R. G., Woster, S. H., Rortvedt, A. K., & Gaffaney, T. (1994). Home-based descriptive and experimental analysis of problem behaviors in children. *Topics in Early Childhood Special Education, 14,* 64–87.

Atkinson, R. C., & Shiffrin, R. M., (1968). Human memory: A proposed system and its control processes. In K. W. Spence & J. T. Spence (Eds.), *The psychology of learning and motivation: Advances in research and theory* (Vol. 2). New York: Academic Press.

Austin, J. (1962). *How to do things with words.* London: Oxford University Press.

Ayers, W. (1989). *The good preschool teacher: Six teachers reflect on their lives.* New York: Teachers College Press.

Aylward, G. P. (1995). Bayley Infant Neurodevelopmental Screener. San Antonio, TX: The Psychological Corporation.

Ayres, A. J. (1973). Sensory Integration and Learning Disorders. Los Angeles: Western Psychological Services.

Ayres, A. J. (1987). Sensory Integration and Praxis Tests. Los Angeles: Western Psychological Services.

Bagnato, S. J., Neisworth, J. T., & Munson, S. M. (1997). *Linking assessment and early intervention: An authentic curriculum-based approach.* Baltimore, MD: Paul H. Brookes.

Bailey, D. B., & Wolery, M. (1984). *Assessing infants and preschoolers with handicaps.* Columbus, OH: Merrill.

Bale, J. F. (1990). The neurologic complications of AIDS in infants and young children. *Infants and Young Children, 3,* 15–23.

Barocas, R., Seifer, R., & Sameroff, A. (1985). Defining environmental risk: Multiple dimensions of psychological vulnerability. *American Journal of Community Psychology, 13,* 433–447.

Bates, E., O'Connell, B., & Shore, C. (1987). Language and communication in infancy. In J. D. Osofsky (Ed.), *Handbook of infant development.* New York: John Wiley & Sons.

Bayley, N. (1969). Bayley Scales of Infant Development. New York: The Psychological Corporation.

Bayley, N. (1993). Bayley Scales of Infant Development-II. San Antonio, TX: The Psychological Corporation.

Bee, H. L., Barnard, K. E., Eyres, S. J., Gray, C. A., Hammond, M. A., Spietz, A., et al. (1982). Prediction of IQ and language skill from perinatal status, child performance, family characteristics, and mother-infant interaction. *Child Development, 53,* 1134–1156.

Belsky, J., & Most, R. K. (1981). From exploration to play: A cross-sectional study of infant free play behavior. *Developmental Psychology, 17,* 630–639.

Belsky, J. L., Goode, M. K., & Most, R. K. (1980). Maternal stimulation and infant exploratory competence: Cross-sectional, correlational and experimental analyses. *Child Development, 51,* 1168–1178.

Bennett, F. C. (1982). The pediatrician and the interdisciplinary process. *Exceptional Children, 48,* 306–314.

Benson, T. R. (1995). Portfolio-based assessment: Tips for a successful start. *Dimensions of Early Childhood, 23,* 21–23.

Bernheimer, L. P., Gallimore, R., & Kaufman, S. Z. (1993). Clinical child assessment in a family context: A four-group typology of family experiences with young children with developmental delays. *Journal of Early Intervention, 17,* 253–269.

Bernheimer, L. P., & Keogh, B. K. (1995). Weaving interventions into the fabric of everyday life: An approach to family assessment. *Topics in Early Childhood Special Education, 15,* 415–433.

Bertalanffy, L. V. (1968). *General systems theory.* New York: Braziller.

Bhavnagri, N. P., & Gonzalez-Mena, J. (1997). The cultural context of infant caregiving. *Childhood Education, 74,* 2–8.

Blakeslee, T., Sugai, G., & Gruba, J. A. (1994). Review of functional assessment used in data-based intervention studies. *Journal of Behavioral Education, 4,* 397–413.

Bloom, L. (1970). *Language development: Form and function of emerging grammars.* Cambridge, MA: MIT Press.

Bloom, L. (1975). Language development review. In F. D. Horowitz (Ed.), *Review of child development research (Vol. 4).* Chicago: University of Chicago Press.

Bloom, L., & Lahey, M. (1978). *Language development and language disorders.* New York: John Wiley & Sons.

Bobath, B. (1970). *The concept of "neurodevelopmental treatment."* London: Western Cerebral Palsy Centre.

Bobath, K., & Bobath, B. (1975). *Motor development in the different types of cerebral palsy.* London: Heinemann Medical Books.

Bornstein, M. H. (1985). How infant and mother jointly contribute to developing cognitive competence in the child. *Proceedings in the National Academy of Science, 82,* 7470–7473.

Bowen, M. (1985). *Family therapy in clinical practice* (3rd ed.). Northvale, NJ: Jason Aranson.

Bower, G. A. (1967). A multicomponent theory of memory trace. In K. W. Spence & J. T. Spence (Eds.), *The psychology of learning and motivation: Advances in research and theory.* New York: Academic Press.

Bracken, B. A. (1984). *Examiner's manual: Bracken basic concept scale.* New York: The Psychological Corporation.

Bracken, B. A. (1999). *Bracken basic concept scale-revised examiner's manual.* San Antonio, TX: The Psychological Corporation.

Bracken, B. A., & McCallum, R. S. (1998). Universal Nonverbal Intelligence Test. Itasca, IL: Riverside.

Brandt, R. M. (1975). An historical overview of systematic approaches to observation in school settings. In R. A. Weinberg & F. H. Wood (Eds.), *Observation of pupils and teachers in mainstream and special education settings: Alternative strategies.* Minneapolis: University of Minnesota.

Bray, J. H. (1995). Family assessment: Current issues in evaluating families. *Family Relations, 44,* 469–477.

Brayden, R. (1990, September). Medical, neurodevelopmental, and behavioral influence of cocaine on the fetus and infant. Cocaine use during pregnancy: Consequences for fetus, infant, and family conference. Sponsored by Tennessee Department of Human Services, John F. Kennedy Center, Peabody Vanderbilt University, Our Kids, Nashville Child Abuse Program, Johnson City, Tennessee.

Brazelton, T. B. (1973). Neonatal behavioral assessment scale. *National Spastics Society Monograph.* Philadelphia: Lippincott.

Brazelton, T. B. (1984). Neonatal Behavioral Assessment Scale. Philadelphia: Lippincott.

Bredekamp, S. (1987). *Developmentally appropriate practice in early childhood programs serving children from birth through age 8: Expanded edition.* Washington, DC: NAEYC.

Bredekamp, S., & Copple, C. (Eds.). (1997). *Developmentally appropriate practice in early childhood programs: Revised edition.* Washington, DC: NAEYC.

Bredekamp, S., & Rosegrant, T. (Eds.). (1992). *Reaching potentials: Appropriate curriculum and assessment for young children* (Vol. I). Washington, DC: NAEYC.

Bricker, D. (Ed.). (1993). Assessment, Evaluation, and Programming System for Infants and Children: AEPS Measurement for Birth to Three Years (Vol. 1). Baltimore, MD: Paul H. Brookes.

Bricker, D., & Pretti-Frontczak, K. (Eds.). (1996). Assessment, Evaluation, and Programming System for Infants and Children: AEPS Measurement for Three to Six Years (Vol. 3). Baltimore, MD: Paul H. Brookes.

Bricker, D., Squires, J., & Mounts, L. (1995). Ages and Stages Questionnaires: A Parent-Completed, Child-Monitoring System. Baltimore, MD: Paul H. Brookes.

Bricker, D., & Waddell, M. (Eds.). (1996). Assessment, Evaluation, and Programming System for Infants and

Children: AEPS Curriculum for Three to Six Years (Vol. 4). Baltimore, MD: Paul H. Brookes.

Bridges, K. (1932). Emotional development in early infancy. *Child Development, 3,* 324–341.

Brigance, A. H. (1997). Brigance K & 1 Screen-Revised. North Billercia, MA: Curriculum Associates.

Brigance, A. H. (1998a). Brigance Early Preschool Screen. North Billercia, MA: Curriculum Associates.

Brigance, A. H. (1998b). Brigance Preschool Screen. North Billercia, MA: Curriculum Associates.

Brockman, L. M., Morgan, G. A., & Harmon, R. J. (1988). Mastery motivation and developmental delay. In T. D. Wachs & R. Sheehan (Eds.), *Assessment of young developmentally disabled children.* New York: Plenum.

Bronfenbrenner, U. (1976). The experimental ecology of education. *Educational Research, 5,*(9), 5–15.

Bronfenbrenner, U. (1979). *The ecology of human development: Experiments by nature and design.* Cambridge: Harvard Univ. Press.

Bronfenbrenner, U. (1986). Ecology of the family as a context for human development research perspectives. *Developmental Psychology, 22,* 723–742.

Bronfenbrenner, U. (1999). Environments in developmental perspective: Theoretical and operational models. In S. L. Friedman & T. D. Wachs (Eds.), *Measuring environment across the life span: Emerging methods and concepts* (pp. 3–28). Washington, DC: American Psychological Association.

Brown, J. V., & Bakeman, R. (1979). Relationships of human mothers with their infants during the first year of life. In R. W. Bell & W. P. Smotherman (Eds.), *Maternal influences and early behavior.* New York: Spectrum.

Bruner, J. (1975). The ontogenesis of speech acts. *Journal of Child Language, 2,* 1–19.

Caldwell, B. M., & Bradley, R. H. (1984). *Home observation for measurement of the environment* (Rev. ed.). Little Rock: University of Arkansas.

Campione, J. C., & Brown, A. L. (1987). Linking dynamic assessment with school achievement. In C. S. Lidz (Ed.), *Dynamic assessment: An interactional approach to evaluating learning potential.* New York: Guilford Press.

Cantrell, M. L., & Cantrell, R. P. (1985). Assessment of the natural environment. *Education and Treatment of Children, 8,* 275–292.

Carr, E. G., Langdon, N. A., & Yarbrough, S. C. (1999). Hypothesis-based intervention for severe problem behavior. In A. C. Repp & R. H. Horner (Eds.), *Functional analysis of problem behavior: From effective assessment to effective support* (pp. 9–31). Belmont, CA: Wadsworth.

Carr, E. G., Levin, L., McConnachie, G., Carlson, J. I., Kemp, D. C., & Smith, C. E. (1994). *Communication-based intervention for problem behavior: A user's guide for producing positive change.* Baltimore, MD: Paul H. Brookes.

Carta, J. J., Atwater, J. B., Schwartz, I. S., & Miller, P. A. (1990). Applications of ecobehavioral analysis to the study of transitions across early education settings. *Education and Treatment of Children, 13,* 298–315.

Carta, J. J., Greenwood, C. R., & Atwater, J. B. (1985). Ecobehavioral System for the Complex Assessment of Preschool Environments: ESCAPE, Kansas City, KS. (ERIC Document Reproduction Service No. ED288268, EC200587).

Cattell, R. B. (1963). Theory of fluid and crystallized intelligence: A critical experiment. *Journal of Educational Psychology, 54,* 1–22.

Centers for Disease Control. (1984). U.S. Department of Health and Human Services. *Morbidity and Mortality Weekly Report.* Atlanta, GA: U.S. Department of Health and Human Services.

Centers for Disease Control and Prevention. (1998). *HIV/AIDS Surveillance Report, 10,* 1–40. Atlanta, GA: U.S. Department of Health and Human Services.

Chess, S., & Korn, S. (1970). Temperament and behavior disorders in mentally retarded children. *Archives of General Psychiatry, 23,* 122.

Chess, S., Korn, S., & Fernandez, P. (1971). *Psychiatric disorders of children with congenital rubella.* New York: Brunner/Mazel.

Children's Defense Fund. (1993). *Annual report: The state of America's children.* Washington, DC: Author.

Children's Defense Fund. (1994). *Annual report: The state of America's children.* Washington, DC: Author.

Chomsky, N. (1959). A review of Skinner's *Verbal Behavior. Language, 35,* 26–58.

Chomsky, N. (1965). *Aspects of the theory of syntax,* Cambridge, MA: MIT Press.

Clarren, S. K., & Smith, D. W. (1978). The fetal alcohol syndrome. *New England Journal of Medicine, 298,* 1063–1067.

Cohen, D. J., Allen, M. G., Pollin, N. W., Inoff, G., Werner, M., & Dibble, E. (1972). Personality development in twins. *Journal of the American Academy of Child Psychiatry, 11,* 625–644.

Cohen, M. J., Riccio, C. A., & Gonzalez, J. J. (1994). Methodological differences in the diagnosis of attention-deficit hyperactivity disorder: Impact on prevalence. *Journal of Emotional and Behavioral Disorders, 2,* 31–38.

Comfort, M. (1988). Assessing parent-child interaction. In D. B. Bailey & R. J. Simeonsson (Eds.), *Family assessment in early intervention.* Columbus, OH: Merrill.

Cone, J. D. (1982). Validity of direct observation assessments. In D. P. Hartmann (Ed.), *Using observers to study behavior.* San Francisco: Jossey-Bass.

Cratty, B. J. (1979). *Perceptual and motor development in infants and children.* Englewood Cliffs, NJ: Prentice Hall.

Cripe, J., Slentz, K., & Bricker, D. (Eds.). (1993). Assessment, Evaluation, and Programming System for Infants and Children: AEPS Curriculum for Birth to Three Years (Vol. 2). Baltimore, MD: Paul H. Brookes.

Dale, N. (1996). *Working with families of children with special needs.* London: Routledge.

Davis, S. K., & Gettinger, M. (1995). Family-focused assessment for identifying family resources and concerns: Parent preferences, assessment information, and evaluation across three methods. *Journal of School Psychology, 33,* 99–121.

Dawkins, M. P., Fullilove, C., & Dawkins, M. (1995). Early assessment of problem behavior among young children in high-risk environments. *Family Therapy, 22,* 133–141.

Deno, S. L. (1997). Whether thou goest . . . Perspectives on progress monitoring. In J. W. Lloyd, E. J. Kameenui, & D. Chard (Eds.), *Issues in educating students with disabilities* (pp. 77–99). Mahwah, NJ: Lawrence Erlbaum.

Dewey, J. (1916). *Democracy and education: An introduction to the philosophy of education.* New York: Macmillan.

Diamond, K. E., & Squires, J. (1993). The role of parental report in the screening and assessment of young children. *Journal of Early Intervention, 17,* 107–115.

Dokecki, P. R., Baumeister, A. A., & Kupstas, F. D. (1989). Biomedical and social aspects of pediatric AIDS. *Journal of Early Intervention, 13,* 99–113.

Dore, J. (1974). A pragmatic description of early language development. *Journal of Psycholinguistic Research, 3,* 343–350.

Dubowitz, L. M. S. (1985). Neurological assessment of the full-term and preterm newborn infant. In S. Harel & N. J. Anastasiow (Eds.), *The at-risk infant: Psycho/Socio/Medical aspects* (pp. 185–196). Baltimore, MD: Paul H. Brookes.

Dubowitz, L. M. S., & Dubowitz, V. (1981). The neurological assessment of the preterm and full-term newborn infant. *Clinics in Developmental Medicine, 79.* London: SIMP with Heinemann Medical.

Dukes, P. J. (1976). The effects of early childrearing practices on the cognitive development of infants. In R. C. Granger & J. C. Young (Eds.), *Demythologizing the inner-city child.* Washington, DC: NAEYC.

Dunn, L. M., & Dunn, L. M. (1997). Peabody Picture Vocabulary Test (3rd ed.). Circle Pines, MN: American Guidance Service.

Dunst, C. J. (1993). Implications of risk and opportunity factors for assessment and intervention practices. *Topics in Early Childhood Special Education, 13,* 143–153.

Dunst, C. J., & Bruder, M. B. (1999a). Family and community activity settings, natural learning environments, and children's learning opportunities. *Children's Learning Opportunities Report,* Vol. 1, No. 2.

Dunst, C. J., & Bruder, M. B. (1999b). Family and community activity settings, natural learning environments, and children's learning opportunities. *Children's Learning Opportunities Report,* Vol. 1, No. 1.

Dunst, C. J., & Hamby, D. W. (1999). Community life as sources of children's learning opportunities. *Children's Learning Opportunities Report,* Vol. 1, No. 4.

Dunst, C. J., & McWilliam, R. A. (1988). Cognitive assessment of multiply handicapped young children. In T. Wachs & R. Sheehan (Eds.), *Assessment of developmentally disabled children.* New York: Plenum.

Dunst, C. J., Trivette, C. M., & Deal, A. (1994). Enabling and empowering families. In C. J. Dunst, C. M. Trivette, & A. G. Deal (Eds.), *Supporting and strengthening families: Methods, Strategies and Practices* (Vol. 1; pp. 2–11). Cambridge, MA: Brookline.

Dunst, C. J., Trivette, C. M., & Mott, D. W. (1994). Strengths-based family-centered intervention practices. In C. J. Dunst, C. M. Trivette, & A. G. Deal (Eds.), *Supporting and strengthening families: Methods, Strategies and Practices* (Vol. 1; pp. 115–131). Cambridge, MA: Brookline.

Durand, V. M., Crimmins, D. B. (1992). The Motivation Assessment Scale. Topeka, KS: Monaco & Associates.

Dworkin, P. H. (1992). Developmental screening (still) expecting the impossible? *Pediatrics, 86,* 1253–1255.

Eckerman, C. O., & Oehler, J. M. (1992). Very-low-birth-weight newborns and parents as early social partners. In S. L. Friedman & M. D. Sigman (Eds.), *The psychological development of low birthweight children* (pp. 91–124). Norwood, NJ: Ablex.

Ellis, N. R. (1970). Memory processes in retardates and normals. In N. R. Ellis (Ed.), *International review of research in mental retardation* (Vol. 4). New York: Academic Press.

Engeström, Y., & Miettinen, R. (1999). Introduction. In Y. Engeström, R. Miettinen, & R. Punamäki (Eds.), *Perspectives on activity theory* (pp. 1–18). New York: Cambridge University Press.

English, D. J. (1998). The extent and consequences of child maltreatment. *The Future of Children, 8,* 39–53.

Ensher, G. L., & Clark, D. A. (1986). *Newborns at risk: Medical care and psychoeducational intervention,* Rockville, MD: Aspen.

Escalona, S. K., & Corman, H. H. (1966). Albert Einstein scales of sensorimotor development. Unpublished manuscript. New York: Albert Einstein College of Medicine.

Eyberg, S. M., & Ross, A. W. (1978). Assessment of child behavior problems: The validation of a new inventory. *Journal of Clinical Child Psychology, 7,* 113–116.

Fackelmann, K. (1988). Children who need technology—and parents. *Technology Review, 91,* 26–27.

Fantuzzo, J. W., & Mohr, W. K. (1999). Prevalence and effects of child exposure to domestic violence. *The Future of Children, 9,* 21–32.

Fetters, L. (1996). Motor development. In M. J. Hanson (Ed.), *Atypical Infant Development* (pp. 403–450). Baltimore, MD: University Park Press.

Feuerstein, R. (1979). The Dynamic Assessment of Retarded Performers: The Learning Potential Assessment Device. Baltimore, MD: University Park Press.

Feuerstein, R., Miller, R., Rand, Y., & Jensen, M. R. (1981). Can evolving techniques better measure cognitive change? *The Journal of Special Education, 15,* 201–219.

Fewell, R. R. (1983). Assessing handicapped infants. In S. G. Garwood & R. R. Fewell (Eds.), *Educating handicapped infants: Issues in development and intervention.* Rockville, MD: Aspen Systems.

Field, T. M. (1977a). Effects of early separation, interactive deficits, and experimental manipulations on infant-mother face-to-face interaction. *Child Development, 48,* 763–771.

Field, T. M., (1977b). Maternal stimulation during infant feeding. *Developmental Psychology, 13,* 539–540.

Field, T. M., Dempsey, J. R., Hatch, J., Ting, G., & Clifton, R. K. (1979). Cardiac and behavioral responses to repeated tactile and auditory stimulation by preterm and term neonates. *Developmental Psychology, 15,* 406–416.

Finnie, N. (1975). *Handling the young cerebral palsied child at home.* New York: E. P. Dutton.

Flagler, S. L. (1995). Infant/Preschool Play Assessment Scale. Lewisville, NC: Kaplan.

Flagler, S. L. (1996). Multidimensional Assessment of Young Children Through Play. Lewisville, NC: Kaplan.

Fraiberg, S. (1975). Intervention in infancy: A program for blind infants. In B. Z. Friedlander, G. M. Sterritt, & G. E. Kirk (Eds.), *Exceptional infant: Assessment and intervention* (Vol. 3). New York: Brunner/Mazel.

Francis, P. L., Self, P. A., & Horowitz, F. D. (1987). The behavioral assessment of the neonate: An overview. In J. D. Osofsky (Ed.), *Handbook of infant development,* New York: John Wiley & Sons.

Frankenburg, W. K., & Dodds, J. B. (1970). Denver Developmental Screening Test. Denver, CO: LADOCA Project and Publishing Foundation.

Frankenburg, W. K., & Dodds, J. B. (1990). *Denver II screening manual.* Denver, CO: Denver Developmental Materials.

Frankenburg, W. K., Dodds, J., Archer, P., Bresnick, B., Maschka, P., Edelan, N., et al. (1990). *Denver-II: Technical manual.* Denver, CO: Denver Developmental Materials.

Frankenburg, W. K., Dodds, J., Archer, P., Shapiro, H., & Bresnick, B. (1992). The Denver II: A major revision and restandardization of the Denver developmental screening test. *Pediatrics, 89,* 91–97.

Friedrich, W., & Friedrich, W. (1981). Psychosocial assets of parents of handicapped and non-handicapped children. *American Journal of Mental Deficiency, 85,* 551–552.

Fuchs, D., Fuchs, L. S., Benowitz, S., & Barringer, K. (1987). Norm-referenced tests: Are they valid for use with handicapped students? *Exceptional Children, 54,* 263–271.

Gaensbauer, T. J., Mrazek, D., & Harmon, R. J. (1981). Behavioral observations of abused and/or neglected infants. In N. Frude (Ed.), *Psychological approaches to the understanding and prevention of child abuse.* London: Batsford.

Gallahue, D. L. (1982). *Understanding motor development in children.* New York: John Wiley & Sons.

Galler, J., & Ramsey, F. (1985). The influences of early malnutrition on subsequent behavioral development: The role of the microenvironment of the household. *Nutrition and Behavior, 2,* 161–173.

Gallimore, R., & Goldenberg, C. (1993). Activity settings of early literacy: Home and school factors in children's emergent literacy. In E. A. Forman, N. Minick, & C. A. Stone (Eds.), *Contexts for learning: Sociocultural dynamics in children's development* (pp. 315–335). New York: Oxford University Press.

Gallimore, R., Weisner, T. S., Bernheimer, L. P., Guthrie, D., & Nihira, K. (1993). Family responses to young children with developmental delays: Accommodation activity in ecological and cultural context. *American Journal of Mental Retardation, 98,* 185–206.

Garbarino, J. (1990). The human ecology of early risk. In S. J. Meisels & J. P. Shonkoff (Eds.), *Handbook of early childhood intervention.* New York: Cambridge University Press.

Gardner, H. (1983). *Frames of mind.* New York: Basic.

Gardner, H. (1991). *The unschooled mind: How children think and how schools should teach.* New York: Basic.

Gardner, H. (1993). *Frames of mind* (Rev. ed.). New York: Basic.

Gardner, H. (1999). *Intelligence reframed: Multiple intelligences for the 21st century.* New York: Basic Books.

Gelfer, J. I., & Perkins, P. G. (1996). A model for portfolio assessment in early childhood education programs. *Early Childhood Education Journal, 24,* 5–10.

Gelfer, J. I., & Perkins, P. G. (1998). Portfolios: Focus on young children. *Teaching Exceptional Children, 31,* 44–47.

Gesell, A. (1925). *The mental growth of the preschool child.* New York: Macmillan.

Gesell, A., & Amatruda, C. S. (1947). *Developmental diagnosis.* New York: Paul B. Hoeber.

Giles-Sims, S. J. (1985). A longitudinal study of battered children of battered wives. *Family Relations, 34,* 205–210.

Glick, J. (1975). Cognitive development in cross-cultural perspective. In F. D. Horowitz (Ed.), *Review of child development research* (Vol. 4). Chicago: University of Chicago Press.

Glicken, A. D., Couchman, G., & Harmon, R. J. (1981). Free Play Social Scale. Denver: University of Colorado School of Medicine, Infant Development Laboratory.

Glover, E., Preminger, J., & Sanford, A. (1995a). Early Learning Accomplishment Profile. Lewisville, NC: Kaplan.

Glover, E., Preminger, J., & Sanford, A. (1995b). Learning Accomplishment Profile-Revised. Lewisville, NC: Kaplan.

Göncü, A. (1999). Children's and researchers' engagement in the world. In A. Göncü (Ed.), *Children's engagement in the world: Sociocultural perspectives* (pp. 3–22). New York: Cambridge University Press.

Göncü, A., Tuermer, U., Jain, J., & Johnson, D. (1999). Children's play as cultural activity. In A. Göncü (Ed.), *Children's engagement in the world: Sociocultural perspectives* (pp. 148–172). New York: Cambridge University Press.

Gorski, P. A., & VandenBerg, K. A. (1996). Infants born at risk. In M. J. Hanson (Ed.), *Atypical infant development* (pp. 85–114). Austin, TX: Pro-Ed.

Gottfried, A. W. (1984). Issues concerning the relationship between home environment and early cognitive development. In A. W. Gottfried (Ed.), *Home environment and early cognitive development.* Orlando, FL: Academic Press.

Graue, M. E., & Marsh, M. M. (1996). Genre and practice: Shaping possibilities for children. *Early Childhood Research Quarterly, 11,* 219–242.

Greenberg, M. (1983). Family stress and child competence: The effects of early intervention for families with deaf infants. *American Annals of the Deaf, 128,* 407–417.

Greenspan, S. I. (1992). *Infancy and early childhood: The practice of clinical assessment and intervention with emotional and developmental challenges.* Madison, CT: International Universities Press.

Greenspan, S. I., & Meisels, S. (1994). Toward a new vision for the developmental assessment of infants and young children. *Zero to Three, 14,* 1–8.

Greenwood, C. R., Luze, G. J., & Carta, J. J. (2002). Best practices in assessment of intervention results with infants and toddlers. In A. Thomas & J. Grimes (Eds.), *Best practices in school psychology* (4th ed., 1219–1230). Washington, DC: National Association of School Psychologists.

Groves, B. M. (1997). Growing up in a violent world: The impact of family and community violence on young children and their families. *Topics in Early Childhood Special Education, 17,* 74–102.

Groves, B. M., & Zuckerman, B. (1997). Interventions with parents and caregivers of children who are exposed to violence. In J. D. Osofsky (Ed.), *Children in a violent society.* New York: Guilford Press.

Guilford, J. P. (1967). *The nature of human intelligence.* New York: McGraw-Hill.

Guralnick, M. J. (nd). *Peer intervention program.* Seattle: Center on Human Development and Disability, University of Washington.

Guralnick, M. J. (1992). *Assessment of peer relations.* Seattle: University of Washington, Child Development and Mental Retardation Center.

Guralnick, M. J. (1993). Developmentally appropriate practice in the assessment and intervention of children's peer relations. *Topics in Early Childhood Special Education, 13,* 344–371.

Guralnick, M. J. (1999). Family and child influences on the peer-related social competence of young children with developmental delays. *Mental Retardation and Developmental Disabilities Research Reviews, 5,* 21–29.

Guralnick, M. J. (Ed.). (1997). *The effectiveness of early intervention.* Baltimore, MD: Paul H. Brookes.

Guralnick, M. J., & Neville, B. (1997). Designing early intervention programs to promote children's social competence. In M. J. Guralnick (Ed.), *The effectiveness of early intervention* (pp. 579–610). Baltimore, MD: Paul H. Brookes.

Gushue, G. V. (1993). Cultural-identity development and family assessment: An interaction model. *The Counseling Psychologist, 21,* 487–513.

Haney, M., & Cavallaro, C. C. (1996). Using ecological assessment in daily program planning for children with disabilities in typical preschool settings. *Topics in Early Childhood Special Education, 16,* 66–81.

Hanson, M. J., & Hanline, M. F. (1996). Behavioral competencies and outcomes: The effects of disabilities. In M. J. Hanson (Ed.), *Atypical infant development* (pp. 149–234). Baltimore, MD: University Park Press.

Harmon, R. J., Glicken, A. D., & Couchman, G. M. (1981). *Free play scoring manual.* Denver: University of Colorado School of Medicine, Infant Development Laboratory.

Harms, T., & Clifford, R. M. (1998). Early Childhood Environment Rating Scale-Revised. New York: Teachers College Press.

Harms, T., Cryer, D., & Clifford, R. M. (1990). Infant/Toddler Environment Rating Scale. New York: Teachers College Press.

Harrington, H. L., Meisels, S. J., McMahon, P., Dichtelmiller, M. L., & Jablon, J. R. (1997a). *Observing documenting and assessing learning: The work sampling system handbook for teacher educators.* Ann Arbor, MI: Rebus Planning Associates.

Harrington, H. L., Meisels, S. J., McMahon, P., Dichtelmiller, M. L., & Jablon, J. R. (1997b). *The work sampling system handbook for teacher educators: Observing documenting and assessing learning.* Ann Arbor, MI: Rebus Planning Associates.

Hart, B., & Risley, T. R. (1995). *Meaningful differences in the everyday experience of young American children.* Baltimore, MD: Paul H. Brookes.

Hartman, A. (1978). Diagrammatic assessment of family relationships. *Social Casework, 59,* 465–476.

Haywood, H. C. (1992). Interactive assessment as a research tool. *Journal of Special Education, 26,* 253–268.

Heath, S. B. (1983). *Ways with words: Language, life, and work in communities and classrooms.* Cambridge, NY: Cambridge University Press.

Heath, S. B. (1989). Oral and literate traditions among black Americans living in poverty. *American Psychologist, 44,* 367–373.

Hebb, D. O. (1949). *The organization of behavior.* New York: John Wiley & Sons.

Helms, J. E. (1984). Toward a theoretical explanation of the effects of race on counseling: A black and white model. *The Counseling Psychologist, 13,* 695–710.

Helms, J. E. (1990). Toward a model of white racial identity development. In J. E. Helms (Ed.), *Black and white racial identity: Theory, research and practice* (pp. 49–66). Westport, CT: Greenwood.

Hemmeter, M. L., & Kaiser, A. P. (1990). Environmental influences on children's language: A model and case study. *Education and Treatment of Children, 13,* 331–346.

Hill, H. M., Levermore, M., Twaite, J., & Jones, L. (1996). Exposure to community violence and social support as predictors of anxiety and social and emotional behavior among African-American children. *Journal of Child and Family Studies, 5,* 399–414.

Hines, P. M. (1988). The family life cycle of poor black families. In E. Carter & M. McGoldrick (Eds.). *The changing family life cycle,* pp. 513–544. New York: Gardner.

Hingson, R., Alpert, J. J., Day, N., Dooling, E., Kayne, H., Morelock, S., et al. (1982). Effects of maternal drinking and marijuana use on fetal growth and development. *Pediatrics, 70,* 539–546.

Hoffmeister, R. J. (1988). Cognitive assessment in deaf preschoolers. In T. D. Wachs & R. Sheehan (Eds.), *Assessment of young developmentally disabled children* (pp. 109–126). New York: Plenum.

Holroyd, J. (1974). The questionnaire on resources and stress: An instrument to measure family response to a handicapped member. *Journal of Community Psychology, 2,* 92–94.

Holroyd, J. (1986). *Questionnaire on resources and stress for families with a chronically ill or handicapped member: Manual.* Brandon, VT: Clinical Psychology Publishing.

Holroyd, J., & Guthrie, D. (1979). Stress in family of children with neuromuscular disease. *Journal of Clinical Psychology, 35,* 734–739.

Holroyd, J., & McArthur, D. (1976). Mental retardation and stress on the parents: A contrast between Down's syndrome and childhood autism. *American Journal of Mental Deficiency, 80,* 431–436.

Holtzman, N. A., Morales, D. R., Cunningham, G., & Wells, D. G. T. (1975). Phenylketonuria. In W. K. Frankenburg & B. W. Camp (Eds.), *Pediatric screening tests.* Springfield, IL: Charles C. Thomas.

Horn, J. L. (1985). Remodeling old models of intelligence. In B. Wolman (Ed.), *Handbook of intelligence.* New York: John Wiley & Sons.

Horowitz, F. D., Sullivan, J. W., & Linn, P. (1978). Stability and instability in the newborn infant: The quest for elusive threads. In A. J. Sameroff (Ed.), *Organization and stability of newborn behavior: A commentary on the Brazelton Neonatal Behavioral Assessment Scale. Mono-*

graphs of the Society for Research in Child Development, 43, (5–6 Serial No. 177).

Howard, J. (1982). The role of the pediatrician with young exceptional children and their families. *Exceptional Children, 48,* 296–304.

Hresko, W. P., Reid, D. K., & Hammill, D. D. (1999). Test of Early Language Development-3. Austin, TX: Pro-Ed.

Hunt, J. McV. (1975). Psychological assessment in education and social class. In B. Z. Friedlander, G. M. Sterritt, & G. E. Kirk (Eds.), *Exceptional infant: Assessment and intervention* (Vol. 3). New York: Brunner/Mazel.

Huntington, G. S. (1988). Assessing child characteristics that influence family functioning. In D. B. Bailey & R. J. Simeonsson (Eds.), *Family assessment in early intervention.* Columbus, OH: Merrill.

Hutchings, J. J. (1988). Pediatric AIDS: An overview. *Children Today, 17,* 9–14.

Hutinger, P., Johanson, J., Robinson, L., & Schneider, C. (1995). *The technology team assessment process.* Macomb, IL: Macomb Projects.

Jennings, D. K., Connors, R. E., Stegman, C. E., Sankaranarayan, P., & Mendelsohn, S. (1985). Mastery motivation in young preschoolers: Effect of a physical handicap and implications for educational programming. *Journal of the Division for Early Childhood, 9,* 162–169.

Johnson-Martin, N., Attermeier, S., & Hacker, B. (1990). *Carolina curriculum for preschoolers with special needs.* Baltimore, MD: Paul H. Brookes.

Johnson-Martin, N., Jens, K. Attermeier, S., & Hacker, B. (1991). *Carolina curriculum for infants and toddlers with special needs* (2nd ed.). Baltimore, MD: Paul H. Brookes.

Jones, K. L., & Smith, D. W. (1973). Recognition of the fetal alcohol syndrome in early infancy. *Lancet, 2,* 999–1001.

Kahn, R. J. (2000). Dynamic assessment of infants and toddlers. In C. S. Lidz & J. G. Elliott (Eds.), *Advances in cognition and educational practice: dynamic assessment: Prevailing models and applications* (Vol. 6; pp. 325–373). New York: Elsevier Science.

Kaminski, R. A., & Good, R. H. III. (1998). Assessing early literacy skills in a problem-solving model: Dynamic indicators of basic early literacy skills. In M. R. Shinn (Ed.), *Advanced applications of curriculum-based measurement* (pp. 113–142). New York: Guilford Press.

Kaufman, A. S., & Kaufman, N. L. (1993). Kaufman Survey of Early Academic and Language Skills. Circle Pines, MN: American Guidance Service.

Kazak, A. E., & Marvin, R. S. (1984). Differences, difficulties and adaptation: Stress and social networks in families with a handicapped child. *Family Relations, 33,* 67–77.

Kazak, A. E., & Wilcox, B. L. (1984). The structure and function of social support networks in families with handicapped children. *American Journal of Community Psychology, 12,* 645–661.

Kazdin, A. E. (1982). Observer effects: Reactivity of direct observation. In Donald P. Hartman (Ed.), *Using observers to study behavior.* San Francisco: Jossey-Bass.

Kearsley, R. (1979). Iatrogenic retardation: A syndrome of learned incompetence. In R. Kearsley & I. Sigel (Eds.), *Infants at risk: Assessment of cognitive functioning.* Hillsdale, NJ: Lawrence Erlbaum Associates.

Kekelis, L., & Andersen, E. (1982). Blind children's early input: Mother accommodations. Unpublished manuscript. Los Angeles: University of Southern California.

Keogh, B. K., Bernheimer, L. P., Gallimore, R., & Weisner, T. S. (1998). Child and family outcomes over time: A longitudinal perspective on developmental delays. In M. Lewis & C. Feiring (Eds.), *Families, Risk, and Competence* (pp. 269–287). Mahwah, NJ: Lawrence Erlbaum Associates.

Kephart, N. C. (1971). *The slow learner in the classroom.* Columbus, OH: Merrill.

Kienberger-Jaudes, R., Ekwo, E., & Van Voorhis, J. (1995). Association of drug abuse and child abuse. *Child Abuse & Neglect, 19,* 1065–1075.

Kiresuk, T. J., & Sherman, R. E. (1968). Goal attainment scaling: A general method for evaluating community mental health programs. *Community Mental Health Journal, 4,* 443–453.

Kiresuk, T. J., Smith, A., & Cardillo, J. E. (Eds.). (1994). *Goal attainment scaling: Applications, theory, and measurement.* Hillsdale, NJ: Lawrence Erlbaum Associates.

Kogan, K. L, Tyler, N., & Turner, P. (1974). The process of interpersonal adaptation between mothers and their cerebral palsied children. *Developmental Medicine and Child Neurology, 16,* 518–527.

Kogan, K. L., Wimberger, H. C., & Bobbitt, R. A. (1969). Analysis of mother-child interaction in young mental retardates. *Child Development, 40,* 799–812.

Kopp, C. B. (1987). Developmental risk: Historical reflections. In J. D. Osofsky (Ed.). *Handbook of infant development.* New York: John Wiley & Sons.

Krug, D. A., Arick, J. R., & Almond, P. J. (1993). *Autism Screening Instrument for Educational Planning* (2nd ed.). Austin, TX: Pro-Ed.

Lambie, R., & Daniels-Mohring, D. (1993). *Family systems within educational contexts: Understanding students with special needs.* Denver, CO: Love.

Landau-Stanton, J. (1990). Issues and methods of treatment for families in cultural transition. In M. P. Mirkin (Ed.), *The social and political contexts of family therapy* (pp. 251–275). Boston: Allyn & Bacon.

Laosa, L. M. (1982). Families as facilitators of children's intellectual development at 3 years of age: A causal analysis. In L. M. Laosa & I. E. Sigel (Eds.), *Families as learning environments for children.* New York: Plenum.

Le Ager, C., & Shapiro, E. S. (1995). Template matching as a strategy for assessment of and intervention for preschool students with disabilities. *Topics in Early Childhood Special Education, 15,* 187–218.

Leont'ev, A. N. (1981). *Activity, consciousness and personality.* Englewood Cliffs, NJ: Prentice Hall.

Lester, B. M., & Zeskind, P. S. (1979). The organization and assessment of crying in the infant at risk. In T. M. Field, A. M. Sosteck, S. Goldberg, & H. H. Shuman (Eds.), *Infants born at risk: Behavior and development.* New York: Spectrum.

Lewis, M. (1987). Social development in infancy and early childhood. In J. D. Osofsky (Ed.), *Handbook of infant development.* New York: John Wiley & Sons.

Lidz, C. S. (1991). *Practitioner's guide to dynamic assessment.* New York: Guilford Press.

Lidz, C. S., & Elliott, J. G. (Eds.). (2000). *Advances in cognition and educational practice, dynamic assessment: Prevailing models and applications (Vol. 6).* New York: Elsevier Science.

Lidz, C. S., & Thomas, C. (1987). The preschool learning assessment device: Extension of a static approach. In C. S. Lidz (Ed.), *Dynamic assessment: An interactional approach to evaluating learning potential.* New York: Guilford Press.

Lifter, K., & Bloom, L. (1989). Object knowledge and the emergence of language. *Infant Behavior and Development, 12,* 395–423.

Lindegren, M. L., Byers, R. H., Thomas, P., Davis, S. F., Caldwell, B., Rogers, M., et al. (1999). Trends in perinatal transmission of HIV/AIDS in the United States. *Journal of the American Medical Association, 282,* 531–538.

Linder, T. W. (1993a). *Transdisciplinary play-based assessment: A functional approach to working with young children* (Rev. ed.). Baltimore, MD: Paul H. Brookes.

Linder, T. W. (1993b). *Transdisciplinary play-based intervention: Guidelines for developing a meaningful curriculum for young children.* Baltimore, MD: Paul H. Brookes.

Luze, G. J., Linebarger, D. L., Greenwood, C. R., Carta, J. J., & Walker, D. Leitschuh, C., & Atwater, J. B. (2001). Developing a general outcome measure of growth in expressive communication of infants and toddlers. *School Psychology Review, 30,* 383–406.

Lynch, E. W., & Hanson, M. J. (1996). Ensuring cultural competence in assessment. In M. McLean, D. B. Bailey, & M. Wolery, *Assessing infants and preschoolers with special needs* (pp. 69–95). Columbus, OH: Merrill.

Lyons-Ruth, K., Zoll, D., Connell, D., & Grunebaum, H. (1986). The depressed mother and her one-year-old infant: Environment, interaction, attachment and infant development. *New Directions for Child Development, 34,* 61–82.

Madaus, G. F. (1988). The influence of testing on the curriculum. In L. N. Tanner (Ed.), *Critical issues in curriculum: 87th yearbook of the National Society for the Study of Education.* Chicago: University of Chicago Press.

Magrab, P. R. (1999). The meaning of community. In R. N. Roberts (Ed.), *Where children live: Solutions for serving young children and their families* (pp. 3–30). Stamford, CT: Ablex.

Mahoney, G., Spiker, D., & Boyce, G. (1996). Clinical assessments of parent-child interaction: Are professionals ready to implement this practice? *Topics in Early Childhood Special Education, 16,* 26–50.

Mailick, M. D., & Vigilante, F. W. (1997). The family assessment wheel: A social constructivist perspective. *Families in Society, 78,* 361–369.

Mardell-Czudnowski, C. & Goldenberg, D. S. (1998). *Developmental Indicators for the Assessment of Learning.* (3rd ed). Circle Pines, MN: American Guidance Service.

McCall, R. B. (1982). Issues in the early development of intelligence and its assessment. In M. Lewis & L. T. Taft (Eds.), *Developmental disabilities: Theory, assessment, and intervention.* New York: Spectrum Publications.

McCollum, J. A., & Stayton, V. D. (1985). Infant/parent interaction: Studies and intervention guidelines based on the SIAI model. *Journal of the Division for Early Childhood, 9,* 125–135.

McConnell, S. R., Priest, J. S., Davis, S. D., & McEvoy, M. A. (2002). Best practices in measuring growth and development for preschool children. In A. Thomas & J. Grimes (Eds.), *Best practices in school psychology* (4th ed., 1231–1246). Washington, DC: National Association of School Psychologists.

McCroskey, J., & Meezan, W. (1998). Family-centered services: Approaches and effectiveness. *The Future of Children, 8,* 54–71.

McCubbin, H. I., & Patterson, J. M. (1987). Family inventory of life events and changes. In H. M. McCubbin & A. I. Thompson (Eds.), *Family assessment inventories for research and practice* (pp. 79–98). Madison: University of Wisconsin-Madison.

McDevitt, S. C. (1988). Assessment of temperament in developmentally disabled infants and preschoolers. In T. D. Wachs & R. Sheehan (Eds.), *Assessment of young developmentally disabled children.* New York: Plenum.

McGonigel, M. J., Woodruff, G., & Roszmann-Millican, M. (1994). The transdisciplinary team: A model for family-centered early intervention. In L. J. Johnson, R. J. Gallagher, M. J. LaMontagne, J. B. Jordan, P. L. Hutinger, J. J. Gallagher, & M. B. Karnes (Eds.), *Meeting early intervention challenges: Issues from birth to three* (pp. 95–131). Baltimore, MD: Paul H. Brookes.

McGowan, R., & Johnson, D. (1984). The mother-child relationship and other antecedents of childhood intelligence: A causal analysis. *Child Development, 55,* 810–820.

McLean, M., Bailey, D. B., & Wolery, M. (1996). *Assessing infants and preschoolers with special needs.* Columbus, OH: Merrill.

Meier, J. H. (1976). Cognitive function normal development—mental retardation. In R. G. Johnston & P. R. Magrab (Eds.), *Developmental disorders: Assessment, treatment, education.* Baltimore, MD: University Park Press.

Meisels, S. J. (1989a). Can developmental screening tests identify children who are developmentally at risk? *Pediatrics, 83,* 578–585.

Meisels, S. J. (1989b). High stakes testing in kindergarten. *Educational Leadership, 46,* 16–22.

Meisels, S. J., Jablon, J., Marsden, D. B., Dichtelmiller, M. L., & Dorfman, A. B. (1994). *The work sampling system: An Overview* (3rd ed.). Ann Arbor, MI: Rebus Planning Associates.

Meisels, S. J., Liaw, F., Dorfman, A., & Nelson, R. F. (1995). The Work Sampling System: Reliability and validity of a performance assessment for young children. *Early Childhood Research Quarterly, 10,* 277–296.

Meyers, C. E., Mink, I. T., & Nihira, K. (1990). Home Quality Rating Scale (Rev.). Los Angeles: University of California, Los Angeles, Department of Psychiatry and Biobehavioral Sciences.

Minuchin, S. (1974). *Families and family therapy.* Cambridge, MA: Harvard University Press.

Moos, R. H., & Moos, B. M., (1986). *Family environment scale manual* (2nd ed). Palo Alto, CA: Consulting Psychologist Press.

Morgan, G. A., Maslin, C. A., Jennings, K. D., & Busch-Rossnagel, N. (1988). Assessing mothers' perceptions of mastery motivations: Development and utility of the Dimensions of Mastery Questionnaire. In P. M. Vietze & R. H. MacTurk (Eds.), *Perspectives on mastery motivation in infancy and childhood.* Norwood, NJ: Ablex.

Munson, L. J., & Odom, S. L. (1996). Review of rating scales that measure parent-infant interaction. *Topics in Early Childhood Special Education, 16,* 1–25.

National Education Goals Panel. (1999). *The national education goals report: Building a nation of learners, 1999.* Washington, DC: U.S. Government Printing Office.

Nehring, A. D., Nehring, E. F., Bruni, J. R., & Randolph, P. L. (1992). *Learning Accomplishment Profile-Diagnostic Standardized Assessment.* Lewisville, NC: Kaplan Press.

Neisworth, J. T., & Bagnato, S. J. (1996). Assessment for early intervention: Emerging themes and practices. In S. L. Odom & M. E. McLean (Eds.), *Early intervention/early childhood special education: Recommended practices* (pp. 23–57). Austin, TX: Pro-Ed.

Newborg, J., Stock, J., Wnek, L., Guildubaldi, J., & Svinicki, J. S. (1984). *Battelle Developmental Inventory (BDI).* Scarborough, Ontario, Canada: Nelson Thomson Learning.

Nihira, K., Weisner, T. S., & Bernheimer, L. P. (1994). Ecocultural assessment in families of children with developmental delays: Construct and concurrent validities. *American Journal on Mental Retardation, 98,* 551–566.

Nordquist, V. M., & Twardosz, S. (1990). Preventing behavior problems in early childhood special education classrooms through environmental organization. *Education and Treatment of Children, 13,* 274–287.

Odom, S. L., Horn, E. M., Marquart, J. M., Hanson, M. J., Wolfberg, P., Beckman, P., et al. (1999). On the forms of inclusion: Organizational context and individualized service models. *Journal of Early Intervention, 22,* 185–199.

Odom, S. L., Peterson, C., McConnell, S., & Ostrosky, M. (1990). Ecobehavioral Analysis of Early Education/ Specialized Classroom Settings and Peer Social Interaction. *Education and treatment of children, 13,* 316–330.

Olson, D. H., Portner, J., & Lavee, Y. (1985). *FACES III.* St Paul: University of Minnesota, Family Social Science.

O'Neill, R. E., Horner, R. H., Albin, R. W., Sprague, J. R., Storey, K., & Newton, J. S. (1997). *Functional assessment and program development for problem behavior: A practical handbook.* Pacific Grove, CA: Brooks/Cole.

Osofsky, J. D. (1999). The impact of violence on children. *The Future of Children, 9,* 33–49.

Osofsky, J. D., & Fenichel, E. (Eds.). (1996). Islands of safety: Assessing and treating young victims of violence. *Zero to Three, 16,* 1–48.

Osofsky, J. D., & Thompson, D. (2000). Adaptive and maladaptive parents: Perspectives on risk and protective factors. In J. P. Shonkoff & S. J. Meisels (Eds.), *Handbook of early intervention* (2nd ed.), Cambridge, NY: Cambridge University Press.

Owens, R. E. (1989). *Language development: An introduction.* Columbus, OH: Merrill.

Parke, R. D., & Tinsley, B. J. (1987). Family interaction in infancy. In J. D. Osofsky (Ed.), *Handbook of infant development.* New York: John Wiley & Sons.

Parks, S. (1996). HELP Strands: Curriculum-based Developmental Assessment Birth to Three Years. Palo Alto: VORT Corporation.

Parten, M. (1932). Social participation among preschool children. *Journal of Abnormal and Social Psychology, 27,* 243–269.

Petersen, N. S., Kolen, M. J., & Hoover, H. D. (1989). Scaling, norming and equating. In Robert L. Linn (Ed.), *Educational measurement* (3rd ed.; pp. 221–262). New York: Macmillan.

Phillips, D. K., Henderson, G. I., & Schenker, S. (1989). Pathogenesis of fetal alcohol syndrome: Overview with emphasis on the possible role of nutrition. *Alcohol Health and Research World, 13,* 219–226.

Piaget, J. (1952). *The origins of intelligence in children.* New York: International Universities Press.

Pianta, R., & Egeland, B. (1994). Predictors of instability in children's mental test performance at 24, 48, and 96 months. *Intelligence, 18,* 145–163.

Pianta, R., Egeland, B., & Sroufe, L. A. (1990). Maternal stress and children's development: Prediction of school outcomes and identification of protective factors. In J. Rolf, A. Masten, D. Cicchett, K. Neuchterlein, & S. Weintraub (Eds.), *Risk and protective factors in the development of psychopathology.* New York: Cambridge University Press.

Priest, J. S., McConnell, S. R., Walker, D., Carta, J. J., Kaminski, R. A., McEvoy, M. A., et al. (2001). General growth outcomes for children between birth and age eight: Where do we want young children to go today and tomorrow? *Journal of Early Intervention, 24,* 163–180.

Provence, S., & Lipton, R. C. (1962). *Infants in institutions.* New York: International Universities Press.

Raab, M. M., Dunst, C. J., Whaley, K. T., LeGrand, C. D., & Taylor, M. (1994). Preschool Assessment of the Classroom Environment Scale-Revised. Unpublished scale. Pittsburgh, PA: Allegheny-Singer Research Institute.

Ragozin, A., Basham, R., Crnic, K., Greenberg, M., & Robinson, N. (1982). Effects of maternal age on parenting role. *Developmental Psychology, 18,* 627–634.

Ramey, C. T., Ramey, S. L., & Lanzi, R. G. (1998). Differentiating developmental risk levels for families in poverty: Creating a family typology. In M. Lewis & C. Feiring (Eds.), *Families, risk, and competence* (pp. 187–205). Mahwah, NJ: Lawrence Erlbaum Associates.

Ramey, C. T., Trohanis, P. L., & Hostler, S. L. (1982). An introduction. In C. T. Ramey & P. L. Trohanis (Eds.), *Finding and educating high-risk and handicapped infants.* Baltimore, MD: University Park Press.

Repp, A. C., & Munk, D. D. (1999). Threats to internal and external validity of three functional assessment procedures. In A. C. Repp & R. H. Horner (Eds.), *Functional analysis of problem behavior: From effective assessment to effective support* (pp. 147–167). Belmont, CA: Wadsworth.

Roberts, R. N. (1999). Supporting families with children in a community. In R. N. Roberts (Ed.), *Where children live: Solutions for serving young children and their families* (pp. 31–69). Stamford, CT: Ablex.

Rogers, S. J. (1982). Techniques of infant assessment. In G. Ulrey & S. J. Rogers (Eds.), *Psychological assessment of handicapped infants and young children.* New York: Thieme-Stratton.

Rosenblith, J. F. (1974). Relations between neonatal behaviors and those at eight months. *Developmental Psychology, 10,* 779–792.

Rosenblith, J. F. (1975). Prognostic value of neonatal behavioral tests. In B. Z. Friedlander, G. M. Sterritt, & G. E. Kirk (Eds.), *Exceptional infant: Assessment and intervention* (Vol. 3). New York: Brunner/Mazel.

Rosman, N. P., & Oppenheimer, E. Y. (1985). Maternal drinking and the fetal alcohol syndrome. In S. Harel &

N. J. Anastasiow (Eds.), *The at-risk infant: Psycho/socio/ medical aspects* (pp. 115–120). Baltimore, MD: Paul H. Brookes.

Rossetti, L. M. (1986). *High risk infants: Identification, assessment, and intervention.* Boston, MA: College-Hill Press.

Rossetti, L. M. (1990). *Infant-toddler assessment: An interdisciplinary approach.* Boston: Little, Brown.

Rossi, P. H. (1989). *Down and out in America: The origins of homelessness.* Chicago: University of Chicago Press.

Rotunno, M., & McGoldrick, M. (1982). Italian families. In M. McGoldrick, J. K. Pearce, & J. Giordant (Eds.), *Ethnicity in family therapy.* New York: Guildford Press.

Rubenstein, J., & Howes, C. (1976). The effects of peers on toddler interaction with mothers and toys. *Child Development, 47,* 597–605.

Ruff, H., & Lawson, K. (1990). Development of sustained, focused attention in young children free play. *Developmental Psychology, 26,* 85–93.

Sainato, D. M., Lyon, S. R. (1989). Promoting successful mainstreaming transitions for handicapped preschool children. *Journal of Early Intervention, 13,* 305–314.

Salvia, I., & Ysseldyke, J. E. (1995). *Assessment* (6th ed.). Boston: Houghton Mifflin.

Sameroff, A. J., & Chandler, M. J. (1975). Reproductive risk and the continuum of caretaking casualty. In F. D. (Ed.), *Review of child development research* (Vol. 4). Chicago: University of Chicago Press.

Sameroff, A. J., Seifer, R., Barocas, R., Zax, M., & Greenspan, S. (1987). Intelligence quotient scores of 4-year-old children: Social-environmental risk factors. *Pediatrics, 79,* 343–350.

Sander, L. (1969). The longitudinal course of early mother-child interaction—cross-case comparison in a sample of mother-child pairs. In B. M. Foss (Ed.), *Determinants of infant behavior* (Vol. 4). London: Methuen.

Satir, V. (1983). *Conjoint family therapy* (3rd ed.). Palo Alto, CA: Science and Behavior Books.

Satir, V. (1988). *The new peoplemaking.* Mountain View, CA: Science and Behavior Books.

Satir, V., & Baldwin, M. (1983). *Satir step by step.* Palo Alto, CA: Science and Behavior Books.

Sattler, J. M. (1992). *Assessment of children* (Rev. 3rd ed.). San Diego: Jerome M. Sattler.

Scherer, J. J. Matching Assistive Technology and Child (MATCH). Webster, NY: Institute for Matching Person & Technology, Inc.

Schlesinger, H., & Meadow, K. (1972). *Sound and sign: Childhood deafness and mental health.* Berkeley: University of California Press.

Schneider, J. W., Griffith, D. R., & Chasnoff, I. J. (1989). Infants exposed to cocaine in utero: Implications for developmental assessment and intervention. *Infants and Young Children, 2,* 25–36.

Searle, J. (1965). What is a speech act? In M. Black (Ed.), *The origins and growth of communication.* Norwood, NJ: Ablex.

Seligman, M., & Darling, B. R. (1989). *Ordinary families, special children: A systems approach to childhood disability.* New York: Guilford Press.

Shere, E., & Kastenbaum, R. (1966). Mother-child interaction in cerebral palsy: Environmental and psychosocial obstacles to cognitive development. *Genetic Psychology Monographs, 73,* 255–335.

Shinn, M., & Weitzman, B. (1996). J. Baumohl (Ed.) Homeless families are different. In *Homelessness in America.* Oryx Press. Available from National Coalition for the Homeless, 1012 14th Street NW, Suite 600, Washington, DC 20005.

Shores, E. F., & Grace, C. (1998). *The portfolio book: A step-by-step guide for teachers.* Beltsville, MD: Gryphon House.

Shuster, S. K., Fitzgerald, N., Shelton, G., Barber, P., & Desch, S. (1984). Goal attainment scaling wth moderately and severely handicapped preschool children. *Journal of the Division of Early Childhood, 8,* 26–37.

Sigel, I. E. (1982). The relationship between parental distancing strategies and the child's cognitive behavior. In L. M. Laosa & I. E. Sigel (Eds.), *Families as learning environments for children.* New York: Plenum.

Silber, S. (1989). Family influences on early development. *Topics in Early Childhood Special Education, 8,* 1–23.

Simeonsson, R. J. (1994). Toward an epidemiology of developmental, educational, and social problems in childhood. In R. J. Simeonsson (Ed.), *Risk resilience and prevention: Promoting the well-being of all children* (pp. 13–31). Baltimore, MD: Paul H. Brookes.

Simeonsson, R. J., Huntington, G. S., & Short, R. J. (1982). Individual differences and goals: An approach to the evaluation of child progress. *Topics in Early Childhood Special Education, 1,* 71–80.

Skeels, H. M., & Dye, H. B. (1939). A study of the effects of differential stimulation on mentally retarded children. *Proceedings and Addresses of the American Association on Mental Deficiency, 44,* 114–136.

Slentz, K. L., & Bricker, D. (1992). Family-guided assessment for IFSP development: Jumping off the family assessment bandwagon. *Journal of Early Intervention, 16,* 11–19.

Slobin, D. (1986). *The cross-linguistic study of language acquisition* (Vols. 1 & 2). Hillsdale, NJ: Erlbaum.

Smilansky, S. (1968). *The effects of sociodramatic play on disadvantaged children: Preschool children.* New York: John Wiley & Sons.

Smith, A. (1994). Introduction and overview. In T. J. Kiresuk, A. Smith, & J. E. Cardillo (Eds.), *Goal attainment scaling: Applications, theory, and measurement,* (pp. 1–14). Hillsdale, NJ: Lawrence Erlbaum Associates.

Smith, C. (1993). Cultural sensitivity in working with children and families. In J. L. Paul & R. J. Simeonsson (Eds.), *Children with special needs: Family, culture, and society* (2nd ed.; pp. 113–121), Fort Worth, TX: Harcourt Brace Jovanovich.

Solomon, R., Clougherty, S. L., Shaffer, D., Hofkosh, D., & Edwards, M. (1994). Community-based developmental assessment sites: A new model for pediatric "child-find" activities. *Infants and Young Children, 7,* 67–71.

Sostek, A. M., Quinn, P. O., & Davitt, M. K. (1979). Behavior, development, and the neurologic status of premature and full-term infants with varying medical complications. In T. M. Field, A. M. Sosteck, S. Goldberg, & H. H. Shuman (Eds.), *Infants born at risk: Behavior and development.* New York: Spectrum.

Sparrow, S. S., Balla, D. A., & Cicchetti, D. V. (1998). *Vineland Social-Emotional Early Childhood Scales Manual.* Circle Pines, MN: American Guidance Service.

Spitz, R. (1947). Hospitalism: A follow-up report. *Psychoanalytic study of the child* (Vol. 2). New York: International Universities Press.

Sprague, J. R., & Horner, R. H. (1999). Low-frequency high-intensity problem behavior: Toward an applied technology of functional assessment and intervention. In A. C. Repp & R. H. Horner (Eds.), *Functional analysis of problem behavior: From effective assessment to effective support* (pp. 98–116). Belmont, CA: Wadsworth.

Spring, J. (1988). *Conflict of interests: The politics of American education.* New York: Longman.

Squires, J. (1996). Parent-completed developmental questionnaires: A low-cost strategy for Child-Find and screening. *Infants and Young Children, 9,* 16–28.

Sroufe, L. A. (1979). Socioemotional development. In J. D. Osofsky (Ed.), *Handbooks of infant development.* New York: John Wiley & Sons.

Stacey, K. (1994). Contextual assessment of young children: Moving from the strange to the familiar and from theory to praxis. *Child Language Teaching and Therapy, 10,* 179–198.

Stedman, D. J., & Eichorn, D. A. (1964). Comparison of the growth and development of institutionalized and home-reared mongoloids during infancy and early childhood. *American Journal on Mental Deficiency, 69,* 391–401.

Stevenson, J., & Richman, N. (1978). Behavior, language, and development in three-year-old children. *Journal of Autism and Childhood Schizophrenia, 8,* 299–313.

Summers, J. A., Dell-Oliver, C., Turnbull, A. P., Benson, H. A. Santelli, E., Campbell, M., et al. (1990). Examining the Individualized Family Service Plan process: What are family and practitioner perspectives? *Topics in Early Childhood Special Education, 10,* 78–99.

Super, C., & Harkness, S. (1986). The developmental niche: A conceptualization at the interface of child and culture. *International Journal of Behavioral Development, 9,* 545–569.

Thoman, E. B., Becker, P. T., & Freese, M. P. (1978). Individual patterns in mother-infant interactions. In G. P. Sackett (Ed.), *Observing behavior: Theory and applications in mental retardation* (Vol. 1). Baltimore, MD: University Park Press.

Thomas, A., & Chess, S. (1977). *Temperament and development.* New York: Brunner/Mazel.

Thomas, A., Chess, S., & Birch, H. G., (1968). *Temperament and behavior disorders in children.* New York: New York University Press.

Tjossem, T. D. (1976). Early intervention: Issues and approaches. In T. D. Tjossem (Ed.), *Intervention strategies for high risk infants and young children.* Baltimore, MD: University Park Press.

Tourse, P., & Gundersen, L. (1988). Adopting and fostering children with AIDS: Policies in progress. *Children Today, 17,* 9–14.

Turnbull, A. P., & Turnbull, H. R. (1986). *Families, professionals, and exceptionality.* Columbus, OH: Merrill.

Tzuriel, D., & Klein, P. S. (1987). Assessing the young child: Children's analogical thinking modifiability. In C. S. Lidz (Ed.), *Dynamic assessment: An interactional approach to evaluating learning potential* (pp. 268–287). New York: Guilford Press.

Tzuriel, D., & Klein, P. S. (1988). *Children's Analogical Thinking Modifiability (CATM) Test manual.* Ramat-Gan, Israel: Bar Ilan University.

U.S. Conference of Mayors. (1998). *A status report on hunger and homelessness in America's cities: 1998.* Washington, DC: U.S. Conference of Mayors.

U.S. Department of Health and Human Services, National Center on Child Abuse and Neglect. (1996). *Child maltreatment 1994: Reports from the states to the National Center on Child Abuse and Neglect.* Washington, DC: U.S. Government Printing Office.

Uzgiris, I., & Hunt, J. M. (1975). Assessment in Infancy: Ordinal Scales of Psychological Development. Urbana: University of Illinois Press.

Vernon, P. E. (1950). *The structure of human abilities.* New York: John Wiley & Sons.

Vissing, Y. (1996). *Out of sight, out of mind: Homeless children and families in small town America.* Lexington, KY: The University Press of Kentucky.

Voress, J. K., & Maddox, T. (1998). Developmental Assessment of Young Children. Austin, TX: Pro-Ed.

VORT Corporation. (1995). HELP for Preschoolers: Assessment Strands: Ages 3–6 Years. Palo Alto: VORT Corporation.

VORT Corporation. (1997). HELP for Preschoolers: Assessment and Curriculum Guide. Palo Alto: VORT Corporation.

Vygotsky, L. S. (1978). *Mind in society: The development of higher psychological processes.* Cambridge, MA: Harvard University Press.

Vygotsky, L. S. (1993). *The collected works of L. S. Vygotsky: The fundamentals of defectology* (Vol. 2). R. W. Rieber & A. S. Carton (Eds.), J. E. Knox & C. B. Stevens, Trans. New York: Plenum.

Wachs, T. D. (1979). Proximal experience and early cognitive-intellectual development: The physical environment. *Merrill-Palmer Quarterly, 25*(1), 3–41.

Wachs, T. D. (1988). Environmental assessment of developmentally disabled infants and preschoolers. In T. D. Wachs & R. Sheehan (Eds.), *Assessment of young developmentally disabled children.* New York: Plenum.

Wachs, T. D. (1998). Family environmental influences and development: Illustrations from the study of undernourished children. In M. Lewis & C. Feiring (Eds.), *Families, risk, and competence* (pp. 245–268). Mahwah, NJ: Lawrence Erlbaum Associates.

Wachs, T. D., Francis, J., & McQuiston, S. (1978). *Psychological dimensions of the infant's physical environment.* Paper presented to the Midwestern Psychological Association, Chicago.

Walker, H. M., Severson, H. H., & Feil, E. G. (1995). *Early screening project: A proven Child Find process.* Longmont, CA: Sopris West.

Washington, V. (1985). Social and personal ecology influencing public policy for young children: An American dilemma. In C. S. McLoughlin & D. F. Gullo (Eds.), *Young children in context: Impact of self, family, and society on development.* Springfield, IL: Charles C. Thomas.

Watson, J. B. (1913). Psychology as the behaviorist views it. *Psychological Review, 20,* 158–177.

Watson, J. B. (1919). *Psychology from the standpoint of a behaviorist.* Philadelphia: Lippincott.

Watson, J. S. (1976). Early learning and intelligence. In M. Lewis (Ed.), *Origins of intelligence: Infancy and early childhood.* New York: Plenum.

Watson, M. W., & Fischer, K. W. (1977). A developmental sequence of agent use in late infancy. *Child Development, 48,* 826–836.

Wechsler, D. (1989). The Measurement and Appraisal of Adult Intelligence (4th ed.). Baltimore, MD: Williams and Wilkins.

Wechsler, D. (1989). Wechsler Preschool and Primary Scale of Intelligence-Revised. San Antonio, TX: The Psychological Corporation.

Wechsler, D. (1991). *Wechsler Intelligence Scale for Children—Third Edition.* San Antonio, TX: Psychological Corporation.

Wehman, P. (1977). *Helping the mentally retarded acquire play skills.* Springfield, IL: Charles C. Thomas.

Werner, E. E. (1990). Protective factors and individual resilience. In S. J. Meisels & J. P. Shonkoff (Eds.), *Handbook of early childhood intervention.* New York: Cambridge University Press.

Whiting, B. B. (1980). Culture and social behavior: A model for the development of social behavior. *Ethos, 8,* 95–116.

Whiting, B. B., & Edwards, C. (1988). *Children of different worlds: The formation of social behavior.* Cambridge, MA: Harvard University Press.

Wicker, A. W. (1979). *An introduction to ecological psychology.* Monterey, CA: Brooks-Cole.

Winton, P. J. (1988). The family-focused interview: An assessment measure and goal-setting mechanism. In D. B. Bailey & R. J. Simeonsson (Eds.), *Family assessment in early intervention.* Columbus, OH: Merrill.

Winton P. J., & Bailey, D. B. (1988). The family-focused interview: A collaborative mechanism for family assessment and goal-setting, *Journal of the Division for Early Childhood, 12,* 195–207.

Wolery, M., & Bredekamp, S. (1994). Developmentally appropriate practices and young children with disabilities: Contextual issues in the discussion. *Journal of Early Intervention, 18,* 331–341.

Wolff, P. H. (1982). Theoretical issues in the development of motor skills. In M. Lewis & L. T. Taft (Eds.), *Developmental disabilities: Theory, assessment, and intervention.* New York: Spectrum.

Woodcock, R. W., & Johnson, M. B. (1989). Woodcock-Johnson Psychoeducational Battery-Revised. Allen, TX: Developmental Learning Materials.

Yarrow, L. J., Rubenstein, J. L., & Pedersen, F. A. (1975). *Infant and environment: Early cognitive and motivational development.* Washington, DC: Hemisphere Publishing Corp.

Yoder, P. J. (1987). Relationship between degree of infant handicap and clarity of infant cues. *American Journal of Mental Deficiency, 91,* 639–641.

Zeanah, C. Z., & Scheeringa, M. (1996). Evaluation of post-traumatic symptomatology in infants and young children exposed to violence. *Zero to Three, 16,* 9–14.

Zeitlin, S., Williamson, G. G., & Szczepanski, M. (1988). Early Coping Inventory. Bensenville, IL: Scholastic Testing Service.

Zelazo, P. R. (1979). Reactivity to perceptual-cognitive events: Application for infant assessment. In R. Kearsley & I. Sigel (Eds.), *Infants at risk: Assessment of cognitive functioning.* Hillsdale, NJ: Lawrence Erlbaum Associates.

Zelazo, P. R. (1982a). An information processing approach to infant cognitive assessment. In M. Lewis & L. T. Taft (Eds.), *Developmental disabilities: Theory, assessment, and intervention.* New York: Spectrum.

Zelazo, P. R. (1982b). Alternative assessment procedures for handicapped infants and toddlers: Theoretical and practical issues. In D. D. Bricker (Ed.), *Intervention with at-risk and handicapped infants: From research to application.* Baltimore, MD: University Park Press.

Zelazo, P. R., & Weiss, M. J. (1990). Infant information processing: An alternative approach. In E. D. Gibbs & D. M. Teti (Eds.), *Interdisciplinary assessment of infants: A guide for early intervention professionals.* Baltimore, MD: Paul H. Brookes.

Zelle, R. S. (1983). Meeting developmental and habilitative needs of infants and toddlers. In R. S. Zelle & A. B. Coyner, *Developmentally disabled infants and toddlers: Assessment and intervention*. Philadelphia: F. A. Davis Co.

Zelle, R. S., & Coyner, A. B. (1983). *Developmentally disabled infants and toddlers: Assessment and intervention*. Philadelphia: F. A. Davis Co.

Zero to Three/National Center for Clinical Infant Programs. (1994). *Diagnostic classification of mental health and developmental disorders of infancy and early childhood*. Arlington, VA: Zero to Three/National Center for Clinical Infant Programs.

Zimmerman, I. L., Steiner, V. G., & Pond, R. E. (1992). Preschool Language Scale-3. San Antonio, TX: The Psychological Corporation.

Subject Index

Name Index